The Mendoza Family
in the
Spanish Renaissance
1350 to 1550

Helen Nader

Rutgers University Press
New Brunswick, New Jersey

LIBRARY OF CONGRESS CATALOGING IN PUBLICATION DATA

Nader, Helen, 1936–
    The Mendoza family in the Spanish Renaissance,
1350 to 1550.

    Bibliography: p.
    Includes index.
    1. Mendoza family. 2. Spain—Civilization—
711-1516. 3. Renaissance—Spain. I. Title.
DP60.M4N3   946′.02′0922   79-9945
ISBN 0–8135–0876–2

To my mother
HELENEH
AND TO THE MEMORY OF MY FATHER
WADE

Contents

Preface

The Mendoza and their admiring biographers have left us a wealth of archival and secondary materials for the study of intellectual and social history. The Mendoza's poetic works, which have long been considered classics (they have been included in Castilian anthologies ever since the early fifteenth century), are available in modern editions. Their prose works—the histories, letters, essays, and translations on which modern Renaissance scholars depend—have not fared as well. There are recent critical editions of Pedro López de Ayala's translation of the *Moralia in Job* by St. Gregory[1] and of Fernán Pérez de Guzmán's *Generaciones y semblanzas*.[2] But the other published histories, translations, and essays by the Mendoza appear in editions whose critical apparatus and editorial policies are less than satisfactory. For most of the Mendoza family, only a small sample of correspondence survives, mostly communications with the crown on diplomatic or administrative matters. For the family's Tendilla branch, which moved to Granada in 1492, we are fortunate to have the speeches and letters of the second count of Tendilla. The speeches, which are recorded in the *Actas del Cabildo* (city council minutes) of Granada during the years 1495 through 1506 and 1512 through 1513, are a fascinating record of Tendilla's political rhetoric.[3] The letters, which survive in his secretary's dictation books, are housed in two different locations in Madrid: one volume from the years 1508 through 1512, which has long been known to scholars, is deposited in the manuscripts section of the Biblioteca Nacional.[4] In 1967, I identified and transcribed two more volumes—from the years 1504 through 1506 and 1513 through 1515—in the Sección Osuna of the Archivo Histórico Nacional.[5] There are over one thousand folios in these three volumes, and the total number of letters is probably over six thousand—by far the largest collection of letters written by a Spaniard before the seventeenth century. The attitudes toward the monarchy, religion, history, and the classics that Tendilla expresses in these letters are markedly different from the attitudes hispanists attribute to Castilians of his aristocratic and old Christian background. Tendilla was not part of the innovative generation in the Mendoza family—that of the early fifteenth century—nor is he the central figure of this book; but because he was loyal to the values of that earlier generation, his letters serve as a check upon my interpretation of Mendoza attitudes in the earlier period.

For the social and economic history of the Mendoza, there is copious material in the family papers, purchased by the Spanish state in the nineteenth century and housed in the Sección Osuna of the Archivo Histórico Nacional in Madrid. Cataloging of this monumental collection is still going on, and already there are over a thousand *legajos* (bundles) in the catalog, the earliest dated in 1315. The collection includes wills, dowry contracts, litigation, depositions, sales contracts, leasehold contracts, rent rolls, political alliances, letters, inventories, genealogies, and a wealth of other materials not available in archives of official state papers. A handful of scholars have utilized isolated documents from Osuna, but the documents have never been subjected to a systematic study. Another important group of documents, now lost, was copied in a history of the Mendoza family written by Gaspar Ibáñez de Segovia (d. 1709), married to the last of the Tendilla branch of the Mendoza family, who was one of Spain's most prolific historians. His "Historia de la Casa de Mondéjar"[6] utilizes hundreds of documents still extant in the family archives during his lifetime, though he laments that much had already been lost. Since he had a surprisingly modern taste for economic data, the documents he copied are especially valuable for the history of the Tendilla estate. Portions of about fifty more documents pertaining to the Mendoza family were copied by Ibáñez's friend, Luis de Salazar y Castro, royal secretary to Carlos II. These seventeenth-century copies are still available in the Salazar y Castro Collection of the Real Academia de Historia in Madrid.[7] A modern history of the Mendoza family, the *Historia de Guadalajara y sus Mendozas* by the provincial archivist of Guadalajara, utilizes and publishes the sixteenth-century notarial documents in the Guadalajara archives pertaining to the Mendoza family.[8]

On several points, the documentary evidence from the family archives does not agree with the standard interpretations of Spanish social history—largely because of the very nature of the archival documents. During most of the period under discussion, the customer's copy of a notarial document constituted the legal, original document. It was not until 1502 that Castilian notaries were required to maintain protocols— bound volumes of their copies, which were thenceforth legally the original documents. Consequently the principle source for the rich supporting and correcting evidence from notarial documents for fourteenth- and fifteenth-century Castile is the notarial documents preserved in family archives—the Sección Osuna in the case of the Mendoza and several other families. Often the Osuna documents present a picture of Castilian society contradictory to that presented in histories based on the documents issued by the royal secretariat and chancery that are found in the state archives. Wherever there is enough documentary evidence from Osuna to support a variant interpretation, I have chosen to present the conclusion supported by the family papers. This is especially true in my interpretations of the relationship between crown and aristocracy, of inheritance practices, of the function of noble titles, and of the political motives and methods of the Mendoza during succession crises.

In transcribing the documents, I have been faithful to the original spelling and spacing, following the norms of the Escuela de Estudios Medievales of the Consejo Superior de Investigaciones Científicas.[9] For the sake of clarity in difficult passages, I add punctuation and capitalization, spell out abbreviations, and substitute modern b, u, and v for V, and modern c, s, and z for ç. Doubts and interpolations are bracketed.

In the bibliography, I have followed modern Spanish usage for all Spanish names in order to conform to modern cataloging and publishing practice. For example, Diego Hurtado de Mendoza will be listed as "Hurtado de Mendoza, Diego," and Fernán Pérez de Guzmán as "Pérez de Guzmán, Fernán." But in both the text and the index I have followed the usage of the fourteenth, fifteenth, and sixteenth centuries. Typical of several other aspects of social and intellectual Spanish life, the Castilian name system in these three centuries was chaotic. The medieval practice had been for a man to be known by his first name and a patronymic—his father's name with the suffix ez to signify "son of." When a man left his village or solar he added its name to his own with the preposition de. The founder of the Mendoza family fortune, for example, was Pedro González de Mendoza (d. 1385)—Pedro, son of Gonzalo, from Mendoza. In the fourteenth century, however, this system broke down among the aristocracy, and the Trastámara revolution put an end to it completely. The use of the place name was inflexible among aristocratic families, even after they had been away from their *solares* for many generations, and thus the place name became firmly fixed as the family name.[10] The combination of first name and patronymic was discarded almost entirely in order to perpetuate the names of heroic ancestors.

Women's names followed this same system, and women neither changed their names upon marriage nor added their husbands' names in the modern Spanish usage. It was common for one or more children of a marriage to carry the mother's family name instead of the father's. For example, the most famous member of the Mendoza family, Iñigo López de Mendoza (1398–1458), marquis of Santillana, and his wife, Catalina Suárez de Figueroa, named their children Diego Hurtado de Mendoza, Iñigo López de Mendoza, Pedro Hurtado de Mendoza, Pedro González de Mendoza, Juan Hurtado de Mendoza, Mencía de Mendoza, María de Mendoza, Pedro Laso de la Vega, Leonor de la Vega, and Lorenzo Suárez de Figueroa. Seven of them carried the father's family name of Mendoza; two carried the paternal grandmother's family name of la Vega; and one carried the mother's family name of Figueroa. It is some consolation to know that fifteenth-century Castilians were also confused by this jumble of names. In 1475, a royal scrivener referred to a brother of the duke of Infantado as "Lorenzo Suárez de Mendoza." In his will, the duke calls the same brother "Lorenzo Suárez de Figueroa."[11]

This chaos, however, existed within certain limits during the fifteenth century. Within the family, certain first names were combined only with certain second names, e.g., always Iñigo López, never Iñigo González or Iñigo Hurtado; Pedro González or Pedro Hurtado, but never Pedro López de Mendoza; Garcilaso de la Vega, but never Garcilaso de Mendoza. By 1550, this small number of traditional names had been borne by more than four hundred members of the family, to the despair of the historian, who finds that for five generations without interruption the señor de Fresno de Torote was named Juan Hurtado de Mendoza.[12] In 1515, there were so many men named Iñigo López de Mendoza that they must be distinguished as Iñigo López de Mendoza[a], Iñigo López de Mendoza[b], and so on through Iñigo López de Mendoza[g]. In an attempt to break away from this system, the generation of Santillana's grandsons named their sons after French and Italian saints, but they all chose the same four names—Luis, Bernardino, Antonio, and Francisco— so that in the sixteenth century the problem becomes to distinguish from among four bishops named Francisco de Mendoza, or two military commanders and one ambassador named Bernardino de Mendoza.

It was the practice in the fifteenth century to sign letters and notarial records with the first two names only. Until 1492, one can be certain that any aristocrat who signs with a traditional Mendoza name combination—such as Iñigo López or Garcilaso—is a member of this extended Mendoza family. After 1492, the problem was complicated by the practice of giving the names of baptismal sponsors to adult converts, so that in the sixteenth century a member of the Mendoza family was usually surrounded by numerous namesakes who were his secretary, his physician, his rent collector, and so on .

Thus, Tendilla—Iñigo López de Mendoza (1442–1515)—was the son of Iñigo López de Mendoza, count of Tendilla (d. 1479); the grandson of Iñigo López de Mendoza, marquis of Santillana (1398–1458); and the baptismal sponsor of his mayordomo, Iñigo López, and of his physician, Iñigo López. In an effort to keep confusion to a minimum in the text, I have used the full name, title, and dates in the first reference and the title alone or family name alone in subsequent references, although in many cases the titles are anachronisms. Thus I refer to Iñigo López de Mendoza (1398–1458) as Santillana throughout and to Iñigo López de Mendoza (1442–1515) as Tendilla throughout, although Santillana did not receive his title until 1445 and Tendilla did not inherit his title until 1479 and was elevated to the title marquis of Mondéjar in 1512. I hope that this scheme will help the reader keep the cast of characters straight. It may help to keep in mind that not every Mendoza was a member of this particular family, nor were all the members of the family named Mendoza. Membership in "la casa de los Mendoza" was determined by a subtle blend of common ancestry, property, action, and values.

This book would not have been possible without the expertise and encouragement of many others. The University of California at Berkeley and Stanford University provided faculty research grants at critical moments. A research fellowship from the American Council of Learned Societies made it possible for me to spend a fruitful year exploring the documents in the Spanish archives. To all of these institutions I am grateful for their faith and generosity.

Archival research can be successful only when the archives themselves provide the researcher with access to their resources, and in this aspect of my investigation I have been particularly fortunate. Spanish archivists have given unstintingly of their expertise and time. I am indebted to the staffs of the Archivo Histórico Nacional and the Archivo Histórico de Protocolos in Madrid; the Archivo General de Simancas; the Archivo de la Real Chancillería de Granada; the Sección de Manuscritos of the Biblioteca Nacional, Madrid; and the Biblioteca de la Real Academia de Historia. I am most appreciative of the efforts in my behalf by Consuelo Gutiérrez del Arroyo and Ana Pardo, whose intimate knowledge of the Sección Osuna at the Archivo Histórico Nacional was invaluable in tracing the estate documents of the Mendoza family.

Through the years that the book has been developing, I have benefited from the good advice of Arthur Askins, Anne Lee Gearhart, Herbert Kaplan, Robert Littman, M. Jeanne Peterson, Randolph Starn, Gerald Strauss, Andrew Villalon, William D. Phillips, Jr., and Donald Weinstein. Above all, I must express my appreciation to my teachers, William J. Bouwsma and Gene Brucker, whose wisdom and generosity of spirit have been a constant source of inspiration.

Genealogical Table of the Mendoza Family

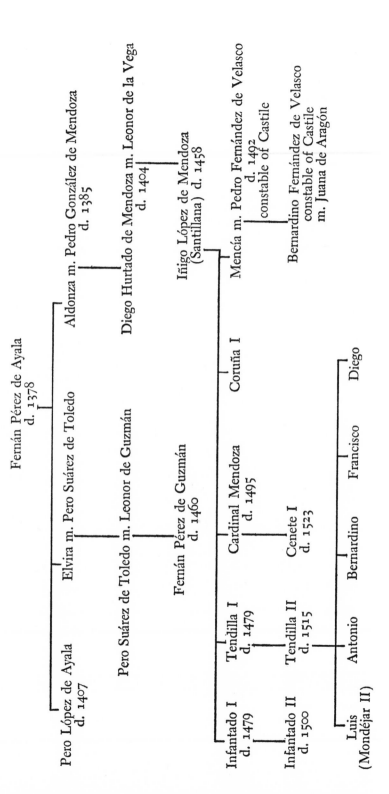

Introduction

I do not have to do anything which might prejudice my loyalty
or that to which I am committed, nor anything different from
what my ancestors did.[1]

These proud and defiant words were written by the second count of
Tendilla, Iñigo López de Mendoza (1442–1515)—governor of the newly
conquered kingdom of Granada; a Castilian nobleman intensely loyal
to king Fernando the Catholic; a seigneurial lord with life and death
jurisdiction over hundreds of tenants; a landlord dependent upon agricultural rents for his income; a man whose intellect and world-view were
formed in the Mendoza family household in the provincial capital of
Guadalajara, far from universities, urban society, and the royal court.
Although we should expect Tendilla's attitudes to be provincial and
medieval, humanist contemporaries considered him to be one of the
lights of Castilian intellectual life. In an inscription sculpted in marble
in imitation of the ancient Romans, he described himself as "GENERALIS
GRANATENSIS REGNI. CAPITANEUS AC ILLIBERITANORUM ARCIUM PRIMUS
PRAEFECTIS."[2] Tendilla thus saw himself not as a medieval knight com-
manding the Castilian fortress of the Alhambra but as the military governor of the ancient Roman acropolis of Illíberis—a self-perception we
would expect to find in one of his urban, republican contemporaries in
Renaissance Florence.

In 1917, Elías Tormo realized the significance of this inscription and
investigated all the inscriptions composed by Tendilla, as well as each of
the buildings he commissioned. Tormo found that Tendilla and his
uncle, cardinal Mendoza, first introduced the architectural and monumental styles of the Italian Renaissance into Spain and, with great
excitement, he concluded that "to the Mendozas of the fifteenth century

1

and, more specifically, to the Tendillas, so unjustly obscured and forgotten, we are indebted for the beginning of the Renaissance in Spanish monuments."[3] This conclusion fitted neatly into the traditional interpretation that humanism was brought into Castile by Italian humanists during the reign of the Catholic Monarchs (1474–1504), in particular by Pietro Martire d'Anghiera (1457–1526)—a Milanese humanist whom Tendilla brought from Italy in 1487 on his return from an embassy to the papacy.[4] On the basis of this evidence, Tendilla has borne for more than fifty years the distinction of being the "importer of the Renaissance" into Castile.

More recently, José Cepeda Adán has noted a more conservative side of Tendilla's character, characterizing him as a transitional figure who bridged the medieval world of fifteenth-century Castile and the Renaissance world of the sixteenth-century "new monarchies."[5] Politically, Cepeda sees in Tendilla a continual vacillation between "a yesterday which he makes resound with chivalrous deeds and a today which makes him think in the political rigidity of a state construed along new Renaissance lines." According to Cepeda, this vacillation stemmed from Tendilla's conflicting loyalties—to his own rebellious noble class, on the one hand, and to king Fernando (the archetypal Machiavellian Renaissance monarch), on the other. Tendilla's rhetoric and personality therefore demonstrate ambivalence, even vacillation, between the medieval and the Renaissance—between "this proud and vigorous Mendoza who dismisses an opponent with a peremptory and unequivocal phrase and the astute Renaissance politician who calculates and waits, and who knows the 'virtù' of manipulating men." These Renaissance contradictions in a medieval man Cepeda attributes to "the transcendental voyage to Italy." To Cepeda, Tendilla is the symbol of a Spain torn between the values of a native, medieval, and agrarian tradition and those of foreign, modern, and urban origin—a view of Spanish intellectual history first expressed in the fifteenth century and still universally accepted by Spanish historians.

Were we to accept the assumption that there was no Renaissance in Castile before the reign of the Catholic Monarchs, Tendilla would indeed deserve his reputation as the introducer of the Renaissance into Spain. To make such a sharp break with the past, however, would have been a revolutionary move, and (as Cepeda has indicated) Tendilla was most conservative. Nevertheless, he did not feel torn between a medieval past and a Renaissance future. Tendilla's loyalty lay only to one part of the past: what his ancestors had done and, specifically, what his grandfather and great-grandfathers had accomplished at the beginning of the fifteenth century in raising the Mendoza family to the social, political, and intellectual leadership of Castile. These accomplishments were recorded in the histories and poetry written by the Mendoza themselves as early as 1395 and over the generations formed a family tradition. Between this tradition and the demands of the Catholic Monarchs, Tendilla did face conflicting loyalties: during the reign of Fernando and Isabel, the royal government increasingly rejected the Renaissance values Tendilla proudly and with good reason identified with his own family. To accept the new values of the royal court, the Mendoza of the sixteenth century would have had to reject the Renaissance political, religious, and esthetic values they found in their ancestors' prose and poetry. Tendilla's refusal to deviate "from what [his] ancestors did" actually represented his commitment to the Mendoza family's Renaissance past.

Tendilla and the other Mendoza of the Trastámara period (1369–1516) both revered the ancestors who had created the family's power and fortune and immortalized the ancestral memory by repeating the family's glorious names for generation after generation. But the family had few illusions about its true origins or the nature of its power. When Tendilla spoke of his ancestors, he spoke of the five outstanding figures of the previous four generations: his father, Iñigo López de Mendoza, first count of Tendilla (d. 1479); his uncle, Pedro González de Mendoza, cardinal of Santa Croce (d. 1495); his grandfather, Iñigo López de Mendoza, marquis of Santillana (d. 1458); his great-grandfather, Diego Hurtado de Mendoza, admiral of Castile (d. 1404); and his great-great-grandfather, Pedro González de Mendoza (d. 1385), mayordomo mayor (high steward) to king Juan I (1379–1390). The Mendoza viewed the family in a historical perspective typical of the Renaissance: they did not push the family's Castilian and aristocratic origins back to a time before the founder of the family's fortunes—Pedro González de Mendoza (d. 1385)—became active in Castilian military and administrative affairs. Nor did they attribute the family's spectacular rise in Castilian society to loyalty to the crown or to some other lofty principle. The Mendoza recognized that their aristocratic status was no older than the Trastámara dynasty itself and that it was the product of their ancestors' political agility in serving—with both sword and pen—that revolutionary and illegitimate dynasty. At the same time, they admired the ancient Romans' ability to combine worldly careers with artistic sensibilities, and they consciously cast themselves and their ancestors as the spiritual heirs of the ancient Romans in Spain—men of arms and letters.

That the Mendoza developed an important intellectual tradition is not an entirely new idea in Hispanic studies. For more than a century, the coincidence that many of Castile's greatest poets and historians in the fifteenth and sixteenth centuries—including Garcilaso de la Vega, Gómez and Jorge Manrique, Diego Hurtado de Mendoza, Fernán Pérez de Guzmán, and the marquis of Santillana—were members of the extended family descended from Pedro López de Ayala's father has intrigued scholars.[6] But this melding of family and literary tradition has inspired neither studies of the Mendoza's role in a Castilian Renaissance nor investigations of family history in Castile. Scholars have concentrated instead on more glamorous or more sensational figures—Isabel the Catholic or the conversos—as mobilizers of an Italianate Renaissance in Castile. The intellectual distance between Italian culture and the Castilian mind seemed so great that only the power of enlightened kings or the desperation of a persecuted minority appeared capable of bridging the gap. Thus the chronological inconsistencies, self-contradictions, and insularity of these traditional analyses have not prevented them from becoming the established interpretation, even among serious scholars—largely because there seemed to be no other alternative.

Traditional histories repeat the generally accepted position that the Renaissance came to Spain from Italy in the wake of the political reforms of the Catholic Monarchs, who brought peace, enlightened government, and justice to Castile and so ended Hispanic isolation from Europe and an endemic civil warfare which had prevented indigenous cultural development. According to this theory, Isabel's father, Juan II, did encourage literature but failed to control the rebellious nobility; and her half-brother, Enrique IV (1454–1474), allowed the political situation to degenerate further so that Castilian civilization fell to the level of a corrupt, rebellious, and anti-intellectual aristocracy. Once the Catholic Monarchs had established civil peace in the kingdom in 1492, however, they were able to introduce the Italian Renaissance into Spain. Isabel, especially eager to raise the intellectual level of her kingdom, and cardinal Cisneros inspired a new age of cultural activity and provided a foundation for it by introducing educational reforms: Isabel established a school at the royal court and hired Italian humanists to teach not only her own children, who were tutored by the Geraldini brothers, but the sons of the nobility as well; Cisneros founded the University of Alcalá where his Polyglot Bible, edited by Italian-trained humanists, set the model for the development of Renaissance scholarship. The theory has further claimed that although the fruits of this endeavor did not—and could not—fully ripen until well into the sixteenth century, when Castilian fanaticism gave way to a more European openness, the political and educational reforms of the Catholic Monarchs laid the foundations for the Golden

4

Age of Spanish literature and culture—the true intellectual Renaissance of the reign of Charles V (1518–1555).

Perhaps the most eloquent statement of this historical tradition appeared as recently as 1961:

> The age of Ferdinand and Isabella was Spain's springtime, a spacious time of heroic deeds, of creative ardor, of cascading national energies. Under these talented and energetic monarchs Spain emerged from her medieval isolation to assume the first place among the powers of Europe. The turbulent Castilian nobility was tamed, the Moors were expelled, the Spanish kingdoms united in the pursuit of common goals. Industry and trade were encouraged, and Spanish literature and art were launched on a glorious course.[7]

Historians of all nationalities accept this view—one of the few things about Spain on which all agree. Not long ago, J. H. Elliott presented a new synthesis of the traditional theory. He described Castile under the Catholic Monarchs as "an open society, eager for, and receptive to, contemporary foreign ideas"; and he further proposed that during the reign of Charles V the "open Spain" became the policy of a political faction led by the Mendoza, while the duke of Alba led a more xenophobic group whose position Elliott called the "closed Spain" policy. Elliott's association of the sixteenth-century Renaissance with a political party is innovative, although in other respects he has retained the traditional interpretation of Spanish intellectual history in which the triumph of the Counter Reformation in the reign of Philip II (1555–1598) marked the triumph of Castilian conservatism over the new, liberal, and dynamic attitudes of Renaissance and Reformation Europe and insured all those disastrous results known collectively as "the decline of Spain."[8]

Unfortunately, this traditional interpretation has never worked. It is based largely on the self-serving claims of the Italians themselves—Pietro Martire d'Anghiera, Lucio Marineo Sículo, and Francesco Guicciardini—and on the assumption that the Italian Renaissance flourished late in the fifteenth century. Not only did the Italian Renaissance originate much earlier, but it is difficult (if not impossible) to discover any society or group of scholars active in late-fifteenth-century Europe who could have provided the inspiration for a renaissance in the Spain of the Catholic Monarchs. Certainly it would be difficult to find a more pedantic—or more pompous—scholar than Pietro Martire, the Catholic Monarchs' Italian humanist-in-residence; and scholars have not been able to discover any sixteenth-century writer—humanist or otherwise—whom he educated or substantially influenced.[9] Lucio Marineo had the talent to inspire a renaissance, but his views on rhetoric were so opposed to those of Spanish humanists trained at Bologna and his connections with Castilian society so slight that he had little effect on the intellectual life of Castile. Indeed, his famous "humanist" history may have been plagiarized from a Spanish vernacular chronicle.[10] Nor do Guicciardini's superficial knowledge of Castile and anti-Spanish prejudices commend him as a source of information on Castile.[11] The Geraldini brothers came to Spain as children and received their education in Castile; they could not have imported humanism from Italy.[12]

Spanish literature provides even less evidence for the impact of the Italian Renaissance during the reign of the Catholic Monarchs, for this period is one of the most conservative in the history of Spanish literature. Only two works stand out from the general mediocrity of the time—Manrique's *Coplas por la muerte de su padre* (1476) and Rojas's *La Celestina* (c. 1499)—as brilliant syntheses of themes and attitudes that were commonplaces of fifteenth-century Castile. Nothing produced at the court of the Catholic Monarchs fits any modern definition of Renaissance poetry or prose. Thus maintaining the traditional theory in the face of such uncooperative evidence necessitates some curious chronological juggling: humanist works written in the first half of the fifteenth century are labeled "proto-Renaissance"; or being recognized as humanist, they are pronounced to belong to the last years of the century so they can, by chronological association, be attributed to the influence of the Catholic Monarchs.[13] Even the advent of printing came inconveniently for the traditional interpretation: because the first book printed in Castile appeared during the reign of the despised Enrique IV, the 1472 Segovian edition has to be "considered as a most exemplary anticipation" of the cultural and religious activity of the Catholic Monarchy.[14]

The evidence for a Renaissance in Castile in the early sixteenth century is slightly better. Garcilaso de la Vega (1501–1536) wrote the first successful Petrarchan sonnets in Castilian.[15] Although no one would deny the genius and lyric beauty of Garcilaso's poetry, forty sonnets make a rather puny Renaissance. Moreover, scholars now dispute whether his model was the work of the Catalan poet Ausías March or the Italian sonnet tradition he encountered while fighting in Italy. Thus, the importation of Italian humanists into Castile during the reign of the Catholic Monarchs does not explain any Italianate Castilian Renaissance of the fifteenth century; it does not even demonstrate the existence of such an intellectual movement. In short, the Renaissance of the Catholic Monarchs has been constructed by so labeling any respectable work of literature written during their reign (regardless of whether or not the work is in fact Renaissance in character) and by taking materials from other periods and attributing them to the period of the Catholic Monarchs through "anticipation" or "delayed inspiration."[16]

When historians of the Italian Renaissance want to comment about the Spanish Renaissance and depend for their information upon Hispanists devoted to the proposition that there could not have been a Renaissance in Castile before the reign of Fernando and Isabel, and when these same scholars examine the literary works of the reign of Fernando and Isabel and find nothing during or after the period that could be defined as Renaissance, it is no wonder that they conclude that there was no Renaissance in Castile or that it arrived late or that it had only a superficial importance.[17] Thus the traditional interpretation of the Renaissance in Castile, by focusing attention on the reign of the Catholic Monarchs and perpetuating a series of gratuitous assumptions about the early fifteenth century, has become one of the greatest obstacles to the study of the Castilian Renaissance by scholars trained in the modern discipline of Renaissance studies. The result has been belief in an ever-widening gap between the brilliant accomplishments of the Italian Renaissance and the purported backwardness of fifteenth-century Castile—a gap which reflects the present state of scholarship rather than the true differences between Spain and northern Italy. While the present analysis may detract from the tradition that considers Fernando and Isabel the transcendental figures of Spanish intellectual history, it has the advantage of offering an approach and a perspective that make sense of otherwise contradictory and dissonant materials. This is particularly true of the problem which has most seriously plagued studies of fifteenth-century Castilian intellectual history: the need to explain the creation of Renaissance humanist literature by a society that did not fit any modern stereotype of a Renaissance society. Previous attempts to explain away this contradiction by attributing the Castilian Renaissance to Italianate influences have foundered on the problem of chronology, for the proven borrowings from Renaissance Italy occurred after the appearance of Renaissance literature in Castile. The present study, by focusing on the Mendoza family in its most innovative and prolific periods, presents both a new chronology of the Spanish Renaissance and a new interpretation of not only its social and intellectual origins but also its development in relation to the wider European Renaissance.

Throughout this book, Spanish culture will be compared with the Italian Renaissance—a Renaissance, however, that Jacob Burckhardt would hardly recognize. It is a Renaissance fervently religious, anti-scholastic, and voluntarist. It is a Renaissance in which the republican city-states, rather than Burckhardt's despotisms, look to classical antiquity for legitimacy. And it is a Renaissance of the fourteenth and early fifteenth centuries rather than Burckhardt's sprawling fifteenth and six-teenth centuries. In this Renaissance, the old heroes of the Burckhardtian interpretation—Machiavelli, Leonardo, Michelangelo, Raphael, Castig-lione—are replaced by a much earlier group—Petrarch, Salutati, Bruni, Donatello, Brunelleschi, and Masaccio—a group in many ways more interesting because it comprises the innovators, the instigators, the cre-ators of the historiographical, artistic, and rhetorical tradition upon which the more famous geniuses of the High Renaissance capitalized.

This more recent view of the Italian Renaissance, developed largely by historians in the United States under the influence of Hans Baron's *Crisis of the Early Italian Renaissance*,[18] has been the product of many of the same methods used by the Renaissance humanists themselves. Historians have focused their attention on the prose writings (especially religious and historical) of the humanist tradition. Modern scholars have examined the content, structure, style, and rhetorical effect of each work in its entirety and placed each in its own cultural and social ambience. This "American school" of Renaissance historiography has hardly pene-trated the scholarship of other countries; and this book, as far as I know, is the first attempt to apply its definitions and methods to Spanish intel-lectual history.

The values on which the Renaissance was built were laid out in the fourteenth century by intellectuals who regarded the problems then besetting Christians as manifestations of a widespread moral malaise. To Francesco Petrarch (1304–1374), "the first Renaissance man," the most pressing needs were to bring men to a lively personal awareness of Christian truth and to find practical moral guidelines for daily Christian life. He believed that by the cultivation of the will—by appealing more to man's emotional and arational nature than to reason—this malaise could be healed. In the beauty of the Latin classics, Petrarch and his fellow humanists found a sensual experience that filled them with the joy of God. They hoped to give the same joyous experience to others by presenting the familiar classics in their purest and thus most beautiful form, by finding new texts, and by writing imitations of the classics. These intellectuals assumed that the person who could be led to the love of God through such an esthetic experience would naturally be inspired to conduct his life in an ethical fashion; and to this end, they set out to present guidelines taken from the Latin classics: Seneca's letters with their homey, practical morality; the histories of Livy and Valerius Maximus with their edifying examples from the lives of the ancient Romans; and pagan poetry, such as the "Labors of Hercules," with its vivid exposition of ethical dilemmas. The humanists' passionate approach to Christian living through the rhetoric of the classics brought them simultaneously to reject many of the highest intellectual values of the medieval universities and adopt a historical perspective in which the Middle Ages appeared as a break with rather than a continuation of the ancient world. To Petrarch, the university professors with their scholastic methods not only were unfit to solve the practical moral and religious problems of the day but also were unaware of them. The very premises of scholasticism—ordering knowledge into rational and hierarchical categories and building arguments from premise through logical steps to rationally incontrovertible conclusion—were irrelevant to everyday living. Even if the scholastics did arrive at a correct substantive point, Petrarch believed, they could never inspire that feeling of awe and admiration for the truth necessary to generate an act of will because they presented their arguments in inelegant and corrupt Latin. Petrarch therefore dismissed the greatest intellectual achievements of the Middle Ages as inappropriate and ugly. The only portions of the university's curriculum the humanists considered useful to their objectives were moral philosophy and the esthetic disciplines of grammar and rhetoric. For Petrarch and others, the best examples of even these disciplines were to be found not in the works of the medieval scholastics but in the Latin works of antiquity. Petrarch did not need to discover lost or previously unknown classics to arrive at this conclusion: his models of persuasion and beauty were well known in the Middle Ages. By seeking moral and esthetic examples in these familiar works, however, Petrarch shed new light on the classics and gave them new life. Whereas the scholastics had mined the classics for rational definitions and logical methods, Petrarch and his fellow humanists looked to them for historical examples in the lives of illustrious men and for a rhetoric that would appeal to the irrational or arational elements in man's character. Thus the favorite classical authors of the early Renaissance were not the philosophical giants—Plato and Aristotle—but the rhetorical geniuses—Livy, Cicero, and St. Augustine. Although Petrarch owed more to medieval scholasticism than he was willing to admit, he inspired generations of humanists who accepted his radical shift in values from the rational to the emotional, from logic to rhetoric.

Petrarch wrote as a private citizen driven to seek new answers to questions raised by the institutional and religious collapse of the fourteenth-century church. His most innovative disciples, however, were employees of a public body—the Florentine Republic. Faced with the need to find solutions to serious political problems—a collapsing war against Milan, weakening political connections with Naples, the stress of relations with a non-Roman and divided papacy, and the collapse of the republican form of government—and to make these solutions palatable to the public, Petrarch's followers also turned to the classics. In his younger years, Coluccio Salutati (1331–1406) received religious inspiration from Ovid's imagery, just as Petrarch was inspired by Cicero's eloquence. During the most desperate hours of the Florentine war against Milan, Coluccio, as chancellor, was responsible for drafting the city's official propaganda. He realized that Cicero's speeches against monarchy contained arguments that could inspire the Florentines, in the name of republicanism, to endure the sacrifices necessary to carry on the struggle against a despotic adversary. By drawing a parallel between republican Rome and republican Florence, Coluccio himself inspired his disciple and successor, Leonardo Bruni Aretino (c. 1370–1444), to carry the parallel even further. In his *History of Florence*, Bruni described Florence as the heir of the ancient Roman Republic and suggested that other forms of government were derivative of a medieval—and therefore corrupt—tradition.

In thus responding to a variety of immediate practical problems, the humanists came to write history from a new perspective. In their efforts to emulate classical antiquity—the living faith of early Christianity, the ethical conduct of the ancient Romans, the persuasive eloquence of classical Latin—they studied classical works intensely and in their entirety and recognized each work as the product of a single person, in a particular society, at a specific time. This relativistic and particularistic approach shaped the humanists' views of both history and society. Rather than seeing the past as a record of God's judgment on men, or as a cycle, or as a decline from an ideal state, they regarded each historical period as unique and of interest for precisely this reason. Instead of defining a single political and social order as ideal and measuring the world against this standard, the humanists judged each society according to how well it suited its own time, place, and circumstances.

In changing content and perspective, the humanists also changed the form in which they presented their ideas. In the Middle Ages, the greatest minds generally wrote philosophical treatises, each of which might require several volumes to explicate a single, unified yet complex argument. The Renaissance humanists preferred the types of writing they found in classical Latin—history, speeches, letters, poetry, biography, and autobiography. That these were the forms in which the Bible was written only served to enhance their attractiveness to the humanists from the early fourteenth century onward.

Behind this chronology and these definitions of the Renaissance in Italy lie assumptions about fourteenth- and fifteenth-century cultural history that would have been unthinkable to Burckhardt and his contemporaries and are still foreign to students of Spanish history. Hispanists continue to work along the lines laid out by the great interpreters of Spanish intellectual history—Marcelino Menéndez Pelayo, Ramón Menéndez Pidal, Marcel Bataillon, and Américo Castro—without questioning their premises. These interpreters consistently assume that fifteenth-century Spanish Christianity was monolithic and that any diversity of belief, even into the sixteenth century, was the product of borrowing from or reacting to other cultures—themselves monolithic. Spanish scholars have defined this unified fifteenth-century Catholicism in terms of the late nineteenth century as the narrow, Thomistic, and almost puritanical Catholicism in which they themselves were raised. Instead of regarding the "heterodoxies" of the fifteenth century as a new norm common to all of Europe, these Hispanic scholars see such diversities as departures from an objective "Catholic" norm fixed in the thirteenth century and attribute them to the influence of Judaism, Islam, Erasmianism, or Lutheranism. Such an anachronistic approach to Catholicism is not new—one need only read a few paragraphs of Ludwig von Pastor's *History of the Popes* to see how the mentality of Vatican I pervaded nineteenth-century historical interpretations of the church. But Renaissance and Reformation scholars, both Protestant and Catholic, for both Italy and transalpine Europe have long abandoned such anachronism.[19]

It is time to do the same for Spain, to look anew at the Iberian experience without the cloudy cataracts of time-honored interpretation, and to employ the assumptions of modern Renaissance scholarship: that there is—and was—no objective definition of Catholicism, that the diversity of the fifteenth century was a new norm rather than a falling away from a pure state, and that this diversity was common not only to all of Western Europe but also to the two "oriental" cultures resident in Spain at the time. Neither Judaism nor Islam was ever monolithic, certainly not in the fourteenth and fifteenth centuries; yet Hispanists still treat them as coherent, even immutable, bodies of thought in which the Castilians encountered ideas foreign to Western civilization. But cultural exchange usually operates in a different way, and Arabic scholars now believe that the West either reborrowed what the Islamic world originally derived or adapted from the West anyway or took over what was compatible with Western culture, particularly in the "neutral sphere" of technological advance.[20]

Linked to these general assumptions about Spain's participation in Europe-wide phenomena in the fourteenth and fifteenth centuries are a separate series of assumptions about Castilian intellectuals and intellectual life that also merit reconsideration. Were fourteenth- and fifteenth-century Castilian authors the passive recipients of literary devices and attitudes they used without self-consciousness or discretion? Literary style is generally purposive: the Castilian humanists were as aware of what they were doing as the Italians and chose and shaped their structures, whether traditional or innovative, to achieve specific effects.[21] Thus the prose authors of early Trastámara Castile were aware of the literary and political implications of imitating the classics; and their Renaissance works need to be labeled as such.

The debate over arms versus letters in fifteenth-century Castile, moreover, does not necessarily reflect a conflict between military and literary values. The conclusion of modern Hispanists[22]—that Castilians rejected Renaissance intellectual values because these had been rejected by the hidalgos, the leaders of Castilian society, who felt a conflict between their profession of arms and the Renaissance value of letters—ignores the participation of two quite different professional groups, the caballeros and the letrados, in the controversy. Both of these groups were hidalgos, but close study reveals that the caballeros defended the compatibility of arms and letters, while the letrados argued that letters were not appropriate to the military profession and should be left to those most fluent in Latin—that is, to them. The caballeros supported their position by their actions: the overwhelming majority of poets, historians, bibliophiles, and translators of the classics in fifteenth-century Castile were caballeros. This conjunction of the military profession with literary productivity, furthermore, had been characteristic of Castilian society for several centuries, yet arms versus letters was not one of the traditional debates (such as water versus wine or age versus youth) of medieval Castilian literature.[23] Nor does the controversy appear until the 1420s, after don Alfonso de Cartagena had made the first translations of Cicero into Castilian. Don Alfonso was in fact the most frequent participant in the debate and the principal spokesman for incompatibility of arms and letters. And both the timing and the person suggest that in Castile the topic was regarded as a classical *topos*, not only a manifestation of the bitter professional rivalry between caballeros and letrados but also a rather naive attempt to show that both groups knew their Cicero.

If we approach Spanish intellectual history with these assumptions of modern Renaissance scholarship, it is possible to place the Mendoza in their own historical context. By focusing on a single extended family, moreover, we can sufficiently limit the study to provide a depth of analysis and richness of texture while still permitting breadth of perspective and examination of the fundamental problems the Renaissance historian must somehow place in their social milieu. To use family history as an approach to the Renaissance in Spain—to propose that a single extended family neither royal nor converso could produce a Renaissance—is a radical departure from the traditional approach to Spanish intellectual history. But the abundant material for the Mendoza permits the historian to study them and, through them, the sociocultural history of Renaissance Castile.

It will be obvious that this study, while it may answer some questions about Spain, raises many questions about the Italian Renaissance. The fact that the Castilian Renaissance can be described in terms of a family tradition and that this tradition can clearly be attributed to the social and political circumstances of agrarian and monarchical Castile in the late fourteenth century—without reference to Italy—should, I think, raise some serious questions about what we have recently regarded as the necessary relationship between urban republicanism and the Renaissance in Italy. The history of the Mendoza family suggests that a Renaissance may develop under conditions different from those found in Italy and that the appearance of Renaissance attitudes in the rest of Europe may not necessarily result from a diffusion of the Italian Renaissance. The Castilian chancellor Ayala, for example, was writing history of a Renaissance form and substance in 1395. Both this early date and Ayala's ignorance of things Florentine suggest that the origins of the Renaissance in Castile were contemporaneous with and independent of the Italian Renaissance.

The subsequent history of the Castilian Renaissance offers suggestive parallels with that of Florence. From 1395 until about 1460, a small group of the most politically active and intellectually prestigious men in Castile wrote innovative Renaissance works under the influence of their ancestor, Ayala. After 1460, a group of writers more dependent upon the state than its partners became the intellectual leaders of the kingdom; and their work marks an important shift to a type of professional humanism. During the sixteenth century, several of Ayala's descendants revived his attitudes; but their political careers were failures and they were unable to exercise intellectual leadership. Chronologically, the Castilian Renaissance seems to have followed much the same course as the Florentine, at about the same time.

To those who believe that the Florentine Renaissance was the product of a particular political situation, it has seemed that the Florentines wrote in the heat of the political crises that inspired them. In contrast, Ayala wrote thirty years after the events that inspired him; but Ayala's political milieu seems to meet one of Burckhardt's requirements for the development of the Renaissance in the Italian city-states: he served an illegitimate government. Ayala wrote to justify his adherence to a monarchy, but none of the arguments developed by the medieval scholastics could be used to support Ayala's king, for Enrique II was illegitimate in every sense of the word. Barred by this fact from using the traditional moral, theological, and theoretical arguments, Ayala had to make a complete break with traditional Castilian historiography. Instead of taking his model from the medieval historians and theorists, he turned to the ancient Romans and to rhetoric. Thus Ayala, writing in defense of a monarchy, arrived at the same political and rhetorical models as Salutati, writing in defense of a republic.

For historians of the Florentine Renaissance, the fifteenth-century histories written as political propaganda have been among the most fruitful sources for the study of changing styles and attitudes. The fifteenth century had no parallel in Spain in the production of propagandistic chronicles, for it was an age of so much innovation, intellectual as well as political, that it was difficult for the participants in political affairs to depend on traditional theoretical or moral explanations of their behavior. In this situation, political events spawned political propaganda, each side trying to justify its behavior to both contemporaries and future generations. The sheer number of Castilian chronicles from the fifteenth century is impressive, but equally impressive is their variety—the styles and contents range from confused patchworks of earlier political chronicles mixed with rudimentary moralizing, through imitations of Froissart's courtly idealizations of war, to histories designed as political propaganda utilizing subtle rhetorical and classical devices to manipulate the reader's feelings. The chronicles of this latter type, with their full-fledged sense of historical perspective, their secularism and relativism, were written in an emotional atmosphere for a Castilian audience constantly bombarded with competing tracts and chronicles. By embedding speeches and letters into these histories, the fifteenth-century chroniclers left us a record of their most valued intellectual accomplishment—their rhetorical abilities—just as the Florentine city council minutes have provided us with a record of changing rhetorical values in the shifting political climate of that city.

Another aspect of Renaissance politics that has seemed to distinguish the Italian city-republics from monarchies was the opportunity for their citizens to participate in government directly and thus develop rhetorical skills. It is nevertheless possible that the differences between the Florentine and Castilian forms of government did not produce different attitudes toward rhetoric. The Trastámara monarchy was neither a monolithic nor a hierarchical organization that could make decisions quickly or without considering different points of view. Enrique II was able to take and keep the throne because he had the support of the most powerful military lords of Castile during the civil war and because he afterwards shared political, financial, and judicial power with his supporters. The Trastámara monarchy began as a revolutionary government with a regicidal king who ruled with the consent of powerful interest groups, many of whom were as powerful as he. Because conflicting groups had equally valid claims on the favors of the throne, decisions were reached only after extensive discussion; and in this situation, rhetorical skills were as highly valued by the citizens of the Castilian monarchy as they were by the citizens of the Italian republics.

The give-and-take of debates in the assemblies of the city-republics apparently provided the forum where rhetorical skills were developed. In Castile, this forum was the king's council: to be an active citizen in the Trastámara monarchy, one had to be a counsellor to the king—"del consejo del rey"—and this right to speak directly to the king distinguished the ricoshombres or aristocracy from other wealthy citizens in the early Trastámara period. During the reign of Fernando and Isabel, when the king's council was filled by letrados, intellectual leadership shifted to these new counsellors. Throughout the Castilian Renaissance, the intellectual leadership of the kingdom was held by men privileged to debate before the king, who attempted to influence royal policy through their rhetorical skills.

One of the greatest differences between the Renaissance in Castile and that in Florence lies in the contrast between the social backgrounds of the authors of the two movements. Although the Renaissance attitudes we associate with men of "middle class" background in Florence were developed in Castile by aristocrats, in some ways the aristocratic authors of early Trastámara Castile did not fit our usual notions of the nobility. They were newly arrived in a society of great social mobility and wanted to enhance their status through marriage, titles, and political positions; they were obsessed with acquiring and increasing wealth; they organized themselves around the extended family for social, political, and educational purposes; and they were proud of being as adept in letters as they were in arms. Their values, aspirations, and preoccupations were not as different from those of the Florentine humanists as we might expect.

Perhaps the most interesting aspect of the Castilian Renaissance is its clear link with the papal court in Avignon. Although Ayala and his descendants were responding to political conflicts within Castile and addressing a Castilian audience, they drew heavily and skillfully upon the resources collected at Avignon during the fourteenth century. And the fact that both Petrarch and Ayala were educated at the papal court in Avignon may open some new avenues of speculation for those historians who believe that the classical erudition of the Florentine humanists may have had its roots in Avignon.

Renaissance Castile indicates how much historians of the Italian Renaissance have missed by ignoring the works of the Italian humanists' contemporaries. By leaving the analysis of these non-Italian works in the hands of scholars not trained in the Renaissance, we have allowed the many similarities between Italian and non-Italian intellectual history to go unnoticed. While Renaissance scholars continue to display ever more precisely the brilliant accomplishments of Italy, the Castilian accomplishment has been increasingly portrayed as obscurantist, anti-intellectual, and insular. Yet even this brief examination of the attitudes of the Mendoza family indicates that the Castilian Renaissance and the Florentine Renaissance are strikingly parallel in their chronology, values, and techniques, an observation which suggests that the two societies were more similar than historians have commonly assumed. The more we have been assured that agrarian, monarchical, rural Castile did not produce an indigenous Renaissance, the more we have been convinced that the mercantile, republican, urban milieu of the northern Italian city-states was a necessary condition for the development of the Renaissance. If, as I propose here, military aristocrats writing in defense of an illegitimate monarchy and drawing upon the intellectual resources of the papal court at Avignon formulated a Renaissance of their own, then the political, social, and cultural similarities between Castile and Florence assume much greater significance. It is not necessary to argue that the Castilian Renaissance achieved the greatness of the Florentine Renaissance to suggest that Castilian historical prose of the fifteenth century has been seriously underrated as Renaissance literature: fifteenth-century Castilian prose is worthy of study both as humanist literature in itself and because of its implications for our understanding of the Renaissance as a European-wide phenomenon.

Part One

Crisis and Creativity
1350-1460

I

Political Propaganda
and the Writing of History in
Fifteenth-Century Castile

Castilians of the fifteenth century wrote of and in a bewildering atmosphere of social and political upheaval. There was no well-defined medieval tradition to serve as a guide amid the confusion of the period. Instead, Castilians embarked upon a series of innovations in every aspect of life without discarding the old patterns in any systematic way, without reconciling the conflicts that inevitably developed between old and new, and without correlating new systems with one another.[1] Throughout the Trastámara period, Castilian intellectuals sought new solutions to the inevitable problems of a dynasty which had acquired the throne through civil war and fratricide: they tried to define the nature of the state, to interpret its transformations during their own lifetimes, and to define its proper relationships with the papacy and the empire. The major efforts in defining Castile's relationships with the papacy and empire were postponed until the reigns of the Catholic Monarchs and of Charles V, but the task of defining, interpreting, and regularizing Castilian politics and society began immediately upon the accession of the house of Trastámara. Loyal adherents of the new dynasty embarked upon a massive propaganda campaign—in the form of chronicles—to clothe their revolutionary triumph in credible respectability. Ironically, the result was not one but two contradictory and increasingly incompatible definitions of Castilian monarchy and society.

The most important innovations in society and politics were made by Enrique II himself, who—recognizing that the greatest threat to the monarchy past and future came from within the royal family itself—

created a counterbalance to the king's relatives by delegating political power to two other groups, the caballeros (military professionals) and the letrados (university graduates with advanced degrees in canon or civil law). Enrique II gave large portions of the royal patrimony, the only noble titles in Castile, and the two highest military offices of the kingdom to his relatives, but he made sure that they all reverted to the crown upon the death of the holders. No members of the royal family were given high political office. The two highest political offices of the kingdom and all of the territorial governorships were given to the caballeros, who received no titles but did receive a portion of the royal patrimony and other lands, which they were required to convert into mayorazgos (perpetual trusts).[2] Thus, the caballeros held the highest judicial (criminal law) and military powers on the territorial level. Their political influence was in turn checked by the all-pervading influence of the *Audiencia*, the king's own court of civil and administrative law with jurisdiction in cases involving the aristocracy, whose high offices were filled by letrados. During the fifteenth century, the caballeros and the letrados for the most part played the role Enrique II had intended for them: they provided the military and judicial resources with which the Castilian kings resisted repeated attacks from their own Trastámara relatives. Their political and social views, however, began to diverge markedly: the caballeros continued to see themselves and the monarchy as partners in a secular, aristocratic, and particularist government; the letrados developed a theory of monarchy that placed the king at the apex of a divinely ordained and immutable hierarchy of institutions administered by anonymous bureaucrats.

These two definitions of the Spanish monarchy were developed by intellectuals whose educational backgrounds and professions were so divergent that their most basic assumptions—about the relationship between the past and the present, the nature of historical sources, the validity of universal models derived from philosophy, and the worth of man's rational and irrational natures—were equally divergent. While the caballeros developed a set of assumptions that produced histories similar to the humanist histories of their Florentine contemporaries, the letrados developed a theoretical model based on medieval scholastic ideals. During most of the century, these two historical approaches coexisted in support of their mutual objective; but at the end of the century, changing political circumstances made the letrado approach more attractive to the Catholic Monarchs. This letrado interpretation of Spanish history swept the field so completely and for so long—it prevails to the present day—that the very existence of the Renaissance historical tradition in fifteenth-century Castile was almost forgotten. Understanding the process by which Spanish society rejected humanist historiography is one of the keys to understanding the nature and development of the Renaissance in Trastámara Castile.

Of all the varieties of history that abounded in fifteenth-century Castile, only the Latin chronicles written by letrados have attracted the attention of literary critics. They have been analyzed by Robert B. Tate, who has shown the degree to which the official chronicles of Fernando and Isabel were derived from the Latin chronicles, which in turn were dependent upon the seminal works of don Pablo de Santa María and of his son, don Alfonso de Cartagena.[3] Don Alfonso, his father, and his students introduced a political theory, a literary style, and a theological approach that were new to Castile, and they revived the interest in universal history and histories written in Latin which had been neglected since the thirteenth century. Except for theology, these innovations were developed to their fullest extent by don Alfonso's students—Rodrigo Sánchez de Arévalo, bishop of Palencia and Castile's representative to the papal court; and Alfonso de Palencia, Latin secretary and chronicler to Isabel and principal source for W. H. Prescott's still-influential *History of the Reign of Ferdinand and Isabel the Catholic.* Because these men exercised a profound influence on the literary and religious attitudes of the royal court and on the subsequent historiographical development of Castile, the importance of their innovations in the writing of Spanish history is incalculable.

The earliest formulator of the letrado theory was don Pablo de Santa María (1350–1435), bishop of Burgos and former head rabbi of Burgos. After his conversion to Christianity in 1390, don Pablo studied at the universities of Salamanca and Paris and achieved such facility in the method and substance of scholastic theory that he was privileged to argue before the popes of Avignon. In 1412, don Pablo wrote a summary of the medieval chronicles of Spain, and in 1418 he completed an extended and versified version of his summary. In this work, the "Edades del mundo," don Pablo adapted early Spanish history to Old Testament names and chronology. He retained the tradition that Hercules was the first Spanish king, but he changed the name of Geryon to Gideon, claimed that Gideon had ruled the Castilian nation rather than a province that later formed part of the Roman Empire, and treated the Carthaginian and Roman periods very briefly in order to devote more attention to the Goths and the Reconquest. This shift of emphases from classical myth to Old Testament history, from the Romans to the Goths, and from Roman province to Castilian nation became one of the distinguishing characteristics of the letrado treatment of Spanish history.

Don Pablo's son, don Alfonso de Cartagena (1384–1456), also studied at Salamanca, became bishop of Burgos, and revised Spanish history. He spent much of his adult life outside Spain as a representative of the Castilian king and acquired a circle of acquaintances among Italian humanists, who seem to have had considerable respect for him.[4] He had an enormous influence on Castilian historiography because he took into his household and educated a number of famous clerics who later became officials in the court of the Castilian Monarchs. His most famous work is a speech made in 1434 before the Council of Basle in which he argued that Castile's representatives should take precedence over those of England because of the greater antiquity of the Castilian monarchy (according to his father's revision of early Spanish history) and because the Castilian king's war against the infidel proved that he was second only to the emperor in obeying the divine will.[5] In this speech, which he entitled the *Anacephaleosis*, don Alfonso was interested in demonstrating the superiority of Castile to other nations by establishing both its antiquity and even more the relation of its chronology to those of various other kingdoms. He assumed that the natural political order was a divinely ordained hierarchy and that the order of command descended from God to pope to emperor, thence to the kings in chronological order of acquiescence to the divine will.

Although don Pablo and don Alfonso were concerned with developing historical evidence and theories for the precedence of the Castilian monarchy in international affairs, the revolt against Enrique IV in 1464 led two of don Alfonso's students to concentrate on developing theories of monarchical precedence within Castile itself. Rodrigo Sánchez de Arévalo (1404–1470) accompanied don Alfonso to Basle and spent most of the rest of his life in Rome employed in the papal administration.[6] He was the most extreme and the most voluble of the letrado theorists in expounding the majesty and supremacy of the Castilian monarchy. A collection of his writings, published in Rome in 1469 under the title *Historia Hispanica*, not only expounds don Pablo's views on the historical antiquity of Castile and don Alfonso's on the international superiority of the Castilian monarchy but also goes on to claim that Castile held the preponderance over Portugal, Navarre, Granada, and the rest of the peninsula in preclassical times. When Juan Pacheco's faction appealed to the pope to depose Enrique IV, Sánchez de Arévalo responded with two tracts, "De Monarchia," and "De Regno Dividendo," in which he described Castile, in Tate's words, as "a unified realm under a single monarch responsible to God alone, the protector of the common weal, and defender of the faith."[7] In order to meet the threat to the monarchy presented by the alliance between Pacheco and the papacy, he claimed that the papacy had no political jurisdiction over the Castilian monarchy. The neat pyramidal hierarchy with the papacy at the top, which had been the core of don Alfonso de Cartagena's theory, was converted into a pyramidal hierarchy with the king at the top, but it was still a divinely ordained and well-defined hierarchy. After 1464, this extreme monarchism became more attractive to letrado writers as Castilian political concerns shifted away from international affairs and toward internal conflicts.

The letrado theory of monarchy was ardently and eloquently espoused during the reign of Enrique IV by Alfonso de Palencia (1423–1490), who studied with don Alfonso de Cartagena and George of Trebizond and served as royal chronicler and Latin secretary to the Castilian monarchs from 1456 to 1474.[8] Palencia's chapters on ancient history have been lost, but the chapters of his *Decades* that chronicle the reign of Enrique IV are among the most influential works in Spanish historiography. In the *Decades*, Palencia measures Enrique IV against Sánchez de Arévalo's theoretical monarch and finds him wanting. Palencia launches a vicious attack on the king, charging that he had not retained the royal power God had given to him exclusively but parceled it out to favorites, that he had brought the nation to civil war instead of promoting its unity, that he had made treaties favorable to the Muslims and detrimental to the Christian knights instead of carrying on the Reconquest, that his immorality and weakness had brought scorn and disgrace to Castile instead of a predominance over the rest of the peninsula. Although Palencia recognized the contradiction between his theories and reality, he blamed Enrique IV for not conforming to the theory.

Palencia's *Decades* was the source for the first few chapters of the *Memorias del reinado de los Reyes Católicos* by Andrés Bernáldez (d. 1513?), who chronicled the period from 1490 to 1513.[9] Bernáldez adopted not only Palencia's judgments of Enrique IV but also his whole theory of monarchy and its role in a divinely ordained hierarchy. To Bernáldez, the monarch was God appointed, invested, in Tate's words, "not only with a right to exercise royal power but with a duty to every member of the community and set apart with his ancestors as the guardian of the common weal."[10] Castile was described as the heart of a unified peninsula, which it had dominated in antiquity and which it would again dominate by force of its moral and political superiority.

Thus the final object of the state to these writers became Hispania—the moral, political, and geographical recuperation of Spain under the leadership of the divinely inspired and appointed Castilian monarch.

The two most influential formulators of the letrado theories, don Alfonso de Cartagena and Rodrigo Sánchez de Arévalo, did not reside in Spain much of the time. They wrote in response to forces outside of Spain until 1464, and the theories they developed bear little relation to the realities of Spanish politics and society for three-quarters of the fifteenth century. Sánchez de Arévalo was aware of this discrepancy but tried to claim that Enrique IV really did fit the theory. Palencia also recognized the discrepancy between theory and reality and used it effectively as an accusation against Enrique. But the reign of the Catholic Monarchs seemed to eliminate the discrepancy itself. Even before the succession war ended in 1480, the Catholic Monarchs announced a program of reform and centralization which appeared to the letrado theorists as the first stage in the fulfillment of their hopes for a strong, moral monarchy and a unified Spain under the hegemony of Castile. Reality had evidently changed radically after 1480; and the extreme monarchism, which borders on messianism, in the royal chronicles written from 1480 to 1513 reflects the exuberance of theorists whose theories are suddenly made credible by contemporary events. It is especially significant that no new developments in the letrado theories of state were made during the reign of the Catholic Monarchs. With theory and reality apparently joined, there was no longer any need to adjust the theory.

The historiography of the letrados was distinguished by a concern for order and continuity. Their interest in history was spurred by a desire to discover those characteristic institutions that could be traced back to antiquity without interruption and therefore glorified as the essence of the Spanish political structure. They studied the Roman period, not as a society peculiar to its own time and circumstance but as one part of the continuum of Spanish history; and to emphasize the permanence of the Spanish characteristics, they concentrated on reconstructing the more obscure periods before and after the Roman period. In their eagerness to find these consistencies, the letrados were uncritical of the sources for the Visigothic period and took liberties with the sources for the pre-Roman period. Their search for patterns of universality and continuity and their concern with establishing those patterns as indigenous to Spain prior to the Roman period probably represent a response to their involvement in international affairs and the international organization of the church.

Even before the letrados developed their theory of the state, another group of writers, the caballeros, were writing chronicles and other prose works whose assumptions and objectives were completely different from those of the letrados. The caballero writers are more difficult to assess in terms of individual contributions to theory, partly because of the incomplete state of our own knowledge about the documents and partly because they themselves were not much concerned with theories.[11]

The first and greatest of these caballero historians was Pedro López de Ayala (1332–1407)—poet, soldier, diplomat, canciller mayor of Castile, translator of Boccaccio and Guido delle Colonne, and commentator on the book of Job. His Crónicas de los reyes de Castilla are full of details about events and personalities he knew from first-hand experience.[12] He appears to have been driven to record and give immortality to all he knew and to judge motives, persons, and events with an implacable sense of right and wrong, wisdom and foolishness. With clinical precision, he describes the frailties, vices, strengths, and virtues of those whose decisions shaped his era. Underlying this attention to detail is an assumption that the events and decisions of his lifetime would be of enduring importance to Spain and that future generations would look back to this period to find explanations, causes, and insights. By carefully arranging his material, he forces his readers to make moral and political judgments by which to guide their own careers. He assumes that the future of the Castilian state depends upon the moral character and political sagacity of his readers. What he does not assume is equally significant: he is interested neither in the early history of Spain nor even in the reigns preceding his own lifetime; he proposes neither a system of hierarchies nor a theory of Castilian sovereignty as a political objective; he concerns himself with relationships not as they should be but as they are and as they seem to work best. In writing history, Pedro López de Ayala assumed that the state is made up of mutually dependent and yet precariously balanced and competing political groups. If the monarch is the ultimate authority in the state, he is the first among equals, and his duty is to maintain a balance among all parties so that no one group can tyrannize over the others.

These concepts are similar to those of Fernán Pérez de Guzmán (c. 1377–1460), whose Generaciones y semblanzas was completed about 1450.[13] Guzmán was a nephew of Ayala, enjoyed a distinguished political and military career under Juan II, and retired from public life after losing favor with the king. During his retirement, he maintained a correspondence with his friend, don Alfonso de Cartagena, and with don Alfonso's brother, Alvar García de Santa María. Guzmán does not seek into Spanish origins prior to Roman times, and he emphatically rejects the extreme monarchism of the letrados. In his view, the monarch is the supreme ruler of Castile by virtue of his power over the military and the church, not because of any God-given authority, and the extent to which the king exercises his powers is determined by his own abilities and the degree of cooperation he receives from the great political powers within the country. Although Guzmán assumes that the family is the basis of loyalty and action, he insists that all citizens of Castile have a direct obligation to their country that requires them to reject personal obligations and loyalties when these threaten the country as a whole. No theoretical scheme of loyalties or hierarchies can adequately guide political actions in a world where each political crisis and each participant is unique.

The last caballero chronicler of the Trastámara period was Diego de Valera (1412–1488).[14] Valera was educated at the court of Juan II; he was knighted at the battle of Huelma by his patron, the marquis of Santillana; traveled throughout Europe as a representative of the king; and retired from the court of Enrique IV, whom he disliked. After 1482, he was appointed corregidor of Puerto de Santa María by the Catholic Monarchs; and although he was never official royal chronicler, he wrote three chronicles dedicated to Isabel. These histories utilize a variety of sources, including don Alfonso de Cartagena's *Anacephaleosis* and Palencia's *Decades*. Valera emphasizes the active role the king should take as military leader and proposes several financial measures to ease the strained treasury of the Catholic Monarchs. He describes the king as giver of justice and the nobility as military and political advisers to the king. Valera was himself fond of giving unsolicited advice to Fernando, either in letters or in speeches in the Cortes. Far from believing that the monarchs were divinely inspired, Valera thought that they were in constant need of his own worldly advice and even cautioned Fernando against overconfidence, pointing out that some of the king's military victories had been won by sheer luck and in spite of his poor judgment.[15]

Valera did not believe that the structure of the Castilian state was ordained by any divine plan. It had developed over a long period of time and in fact contained many features consciously borrowed from other governments, especially the French.[16] His judgments of historical personages were less harsh than those of Pedro López de Ayala and more perceptive than those of Fernán Pérez de Guzmán, but he used them in the same way—to provide moral and political examples for future generations. He assumed that men can shape their own actions and they must struggle against the larger forces of history to uphold and improve society.

This assumption on the part of Valera and the other caballero writers led them to emphasize biography. Ayala included brief biographical sketches in his histories and described individuals both effecting historical change and subject to historical change. Fernán Pérez de Guzmán wrote almost all his prose works in the form, to use the words of Montaigne, of "separate lives, being concerned rather with motives than with events, more with what arises from within than with what arrives from without."[17] Valera, his enthusiasm for recording every detail coupled with his failure to discriminate the important from the trivial, presents gossip as biography in discussing relatively unimportant persons but makes some effort to present serious biographical sketches of the most important persons.

The increasingly incompatible nature of the caballero and letrado concepts can be seen in the way the two groups regarded the two most famous accomplishments of the Catholic Monarchs—the Reconquest of Granada and the reforms. Some of the most extreme views on both sides were expressed by Valera and Bernáldez. Bernáldez's attitude toward the Reconquest of Granada is evident throughout the *Memorias,* but its most striking and succinct expression is contained in his description of the monarchs' entry into the conquered kingdom:

> And thus they brought this holy and laudable conquest to a glorious conclusion and saw before them what many kings and princes had wished to see: a kingdom of so many cities and towns and such a multitude of villages situated in such strong and fruitful lands, all won in the space of ten years. What could be the meaning of this but God's desire to provision it for them and put it in their hands?[18]

This idea that God intervened directly in the affairs of His chosen monarchs seemed to satisfy Bernáldez as an explanation of how the war was successfully fought. He also notes that throughout the campaign the Christians were aided by a series of droughts and other natural phenomena which "seemed to be made and provided by the divine Providence, and thus it was believed by all the Christians that God miraculously provided for them at those times."[19] Inasmuch as Bernáldez believed this was God's war, the Muslim enemies were necessarily "enemies of God, murderers who kill without piety, as they did before the kingdom of Granada was won, who impiously murdered Christians whenever they could."[20] God rewarded Fernando and Isabel's creditors in explicit (and material) terms:

Those who had given those taxes and donations, providing the means and resources for this very holy act of war, found that with their rewards they were richer than they had ever been before. This is understood by that which the angels said at the glorious nativity of Our Redeemer, when they sang the *gloria in excelsis Deo, et in terra pax,* etc. Finding themselves rich with what had been distributed to them, good Christians and of good will and fearful of God, they correctly discerned that all the good things the monarchs had done they owed to God: because God guides the heart of the good king and does not enable the king to make war by himself nor with his own, but with the help of his vassals and their goods.[21]

The monarch appears almost to be passive: God had predetermined that Fernando should triumph, had arranged the weather for this purpose, and had even determined that Fernando's own resources would be inadequate—so that he would have to call upon his subjects and thus increase the number of people doing God's will. Bernáldez considered all aspects of the Reconquest to be manifestations of divine Providence: Granada had been intended and provisioned for the Castilians; and although many kings and princes had tried to win it, Granada remained in the hands of the enemy until God enabled the chosen king, Fernando, to win it back and avenge His enemies.

Bernáldez's pious exultations stand in sharp contrast to Valera's caballero attitude toward the Reconquest. Valera is lavish in his praise not only of Fernando, "our most victorious king in this holy and great war [who exerted] superhuman efforts" and placed himself in grave dangers during the campaign, but also of the other great heroes. The highest praise he offers is couched in terms of chivalry: "They did that which the Catholic faith and nobility required them to do."[22] The only aspects of nature he considers noteworthy are topography as military terrain—which he describes in terse and yet evocative detail—and human nature, which leads men to make military blunders even in a crusade.[23] He accepts the nobility's financial support of the war as a matter of course and advises the king of many practical ways of raising money, even suggesting that when everything else fails "it would not be unseemly to eat out of clay vessels, and melt down the silver vessels, and sell the jewels, and take the silver from monasteries and churches, and even selling offices would be a holy work."[24] He advises Fernando to accept the queen's intervention in war councils, since "she was not fighting less with her donations and prayers than he was with his lance."[25] Valera thought that war was won not by God's will but by the most strenuous exertions of men who had to worry about money and natural cul-de-sacs and foolish commanders. Valera referred to the Muslims not only as enemies of the faith but also as believers in God and as admirable knights, noting that the Muslims were "willing to die in order to defend their honor and property and liberty" and exhorting the Christian soldiers to do the same.[26]

He describes Reconquest battles in the same tone he uses to describe battles of the civil wars, and his descriptions lack the apocalyptic overtones that suffuse Bernáldez's battle scenes. Valera moves calmly from the battlefield to the banquet hall. In one chapter, for example, he presents in gory detail the disastrous ambush at the Ajarquía and the survivors' return to the royal camp—where the seating arrangements, table service, and ladies' clothing are all discussed with the same seriousness.[27] To Valera, knighthood itself was a religious vocation; and anything the knight did for his own honor, according to chivalric standards and with success, was a glory to God and to the king. It is in this limited sense that Valera saw religious significance in the Reconquest. He referred to it as a holy war because the papacy had granted a bull of crusade for it,[28] but his description of the Reconquest was couched in secular terms—praising the king for his courage and vigor, criticizing him for poor military judgment, attributing success or failure to physical circumstances and human abilities, recognizing the Muslims as worthy enemies in battles, and suggesting specific methods of raising funds.

Bernáldez and Valera both wrote of the conquest of Granada, but they saw and described two different wars. Bernáldez saw God and His chosen agents, the Catholic Monarchs, defeating His enemies and entering into the Promised Land. Valera saw a secular war of territorial conquest fought in the pursuit of honor, property, and liberty by the king and his fellow knights.

Despite the caballeros' presentation of history as the judgment of posterity on the deeds and persons of the past and their clear desire to inspire virtuous men to wise action in the future, they never assume that because man can shape his own actions and judge those of the past he can therefore shape his fate; nor do they conclude that because man must make the effort to maintain and improve society he can therefore control history. They assume that a larger force—Fortuna, inexplicable and unpredictable—ultimately decides man's fate and the course of history, although "it is a virtue to struggle against fortune."[29] They do not confuse Fortuna with God, and they do not consider worldly success or failure to be God's judgment on individuals or causes. Bernáldez's statement that "Our Lord shows His justice in battles more than in any other thing, and thus He did here, so that the greatness of the victory showed the justice of the cause," would be completely foreign to the caballeros.[30] Their pessimism about the larger issues in history gives them the appearance of stoics and sets them distinctively apart from the letrados' messianic optimism about achieving Hispania through moral regeneration from the top.

This difference in perceptions is evident in the two groups' attitudes toward specific reforms. Bernáldez regards the changes made by the Catholic Monarchs as the fulfillment of a divine plan and accepts reports of their success without question. He reports with satisfaction the conversion of the natives of the Canary Islands, the assumption of the masterships of the military orders by Fernando, the increasing dependence of Isabel on the advice and services of clerics and letrados.[31] He reserves his greatest enthusiasm for the new Inquisition. He has no doubt that the Inquisition has been the salvation of the country, rejoices in the large number of heretics burned and imprisoned, and even hints that the Inquisition was succeeding in spite of the resistance of cardinal Mendoza.[32] There is no acknowledgment that the foundations for these reforms and great undertakings were well laid in previous reigns: they appear as the spontaneous creations of the Catholic Monarchs in fulfillment of the divine plan for Castile.

Valera displays many doubts and reservations about these same reforms and undertakings. He attributes their instigation to the monarchs' desire to control the government more effectively; and although he generally approves of this, he reminds the rulers that any institution, no matter how well conceived, is subject to the weaknesses and perversions of those who administer it. He is critical of the increasing use of Roman law instead of custom as a basis for court decisions and dredges up a citation from Aristotle to argue that "there are two types of law: one is natural, the other is legalistic."[33] He criticizes the excesses of the *hermandades* and the Inquisition, blaming them on the greed and vindictiveness of their administrators. He cautions the monarchs against selfish use of their increased military and judicial powers and warns Fernando against relying on the military advice of clerics and other men inexperienced in war.[34]

Valera regards even pious endeavors with a note of skepticism, noting for example that the Christianity of the Canary Islands was questionable because the natives had been converted under the threat of slavery.[35] He also traces the early stages of these same reforms in the reigns of Juan II and Enrique IV, when they were already regarded with some reservation by caballero writers,[36] and considers them to be specific responses to specific problems. Bernáldez and Valera view the reforms almost exactly as they view the Reconquest—Bernáldez saw them as the fulfillment of a larger plan, and Valera saw them as human reactions to particular problems.

These two concepts flourished and existed side by side throughout the fifteenth century, and each represents an "educated opinion" of the day. Bernáldez's attitudes are typical of the letrado writers whose education was oriented toward the universities, with their emphasis on scholastic argument and their models provided by Roman law. Valera's attitudes are typical of the caballero writers whose education was centered in noble courts, where argument was based on historical example and models were found in the lives and deeds of individual heroes. Their approaches to history and to the monarchy reflect two different world-views that influenced their perceptions of every aspect of life. The letrados and the caballeros—the two leaders of Castilian society, politics, and culture— held conflicting views even when they were acting on the same side in a political conflict. This tolerance appears to have changed abruptly during the reign of the Catholic Monarchs, whose political circumstances made it imperative that only one of these traditional perceptions of history and society should remain popular.

The political needs of Fernando and Isabel developed from the political and social upheavals of the fifteenth century. Enrique II's distribution of political power successfully joined the military and legal aristocracy to the king's cause but also excluded from power two groups whose ranks were constantly renewed in the fifteenth century—the king's relatives and upwardly mobile knights. Fernando de Antequera, brother of Enrique III of Castile and himself king by election of Aragon (1412–1416), set the pattern these two latter groups would follow in their efforts to acquire hereditary lands and offices—control of the highest positions in the military orders, with their financial resources; fame as military leaders in the Reconquest; and control over the king's decisions through personal influence at court. All the seditious and rebellious movements of the fifteenth century found their rallying points in the infantes—first the sons of Fernando de Antequera and then the younger children of Juan II of Castile—while several estateless but ambitious and talented men attached themselves to the king's cause and identified their own fortunes with those of the monarchy. Consequently, Castilian politics in this period could be characterized by the career of a talented and ambitious courtier who gains the king's confidence, successfully organizes the monarch's defense against the attacks of the infantes and his campaigns against the Muslims, and is rewarded with lands, income, high office in the military orders, and marriage into the aristocracy. He is then attacked by the aristocracy and bureaucracy because the concentration in one person of hereditary wealth, military power, and political influence over the king constitutes a threat not only to the balance of powers established by Enrique II but also to the monarch's independence. As a result, Castile offers the spectacle of civil wars fought by caballero and letrado advocates of a strong monarchy against a king whose campaign is led by his favorite courtier and manned by caballero and letrado advocates of a strong monarchy.

The widespread demand for a stronger monarchy is the best evidence of the lack of strong royal leadership during most of the century. Isabel's father, Juan II (1406–1454), neglected his political and judicial responsibilities, delegating his powers to his favorite, don Alvaro de Luna. Don Alvaro began to seem a greater threat to the monarchy than the infantes he successfully repulsed, and disaffected nobility raised enough threats of rebellion to force the king into arresting and executing don Alvaro. But the king died soon afterward; and his son, Enrique IV (1454–1474), delegated much of his power to a new favorite, Juan Pacheco. When Enrique IV replaced Juan Pacheco with a new favorite, Beltrán de la Cueva, Pacheco tried to recoup his losses by denouncing both Beltrán and the king. To this end, he and his party spread doubts about the king's daughter, the princess Juana, claiming that she was really Beltrán's daughter, that the queen was unfaithful, that the king was impotent, and that the true heir to the throne was Enrique's half-brother, Alfonso. Enrique IV vacillated between defense of his daughter's legal rights and attempts to prevent bloodshed by compromising with Pacheco, achieving neither and increasing the confusion of everyone.

Unfortunately for the rebels, Alfonso, their popular candidate for the throne, died prematurely in 1468 and they were

> in great fear, dreading the indignation of the king, whom they had basely insulted with letters and words during the division, and finding no other means of defending themselves except to continue the schism which they had begun in the kingdom, elevated the lady princess Isabel as queen of the kingdom in place of her brother [Alfonso].[37]

This arrangement was not very comfortable at first, since Juana's legitimacy was much more probable and popularly believed than the rebels' propaganda conceded, and Isabel could not be expected to assume the popular military role of Alfonso. Both of these problems were mitigated by the marriage of Isabel to Fernando, son and heir of the only surviving son of Fernando de Antequera, Juan II of Aragon (1458–1479). Since his father was still alive and actively managing his kingdom, Fernando was free to assume the military leadership of his wife's cause. The party that supported Isabel in the belief that she would depend upon them and be a nominal ruler whom they could control were so disillusioned with this turn of events that they switched their allegiance to Juana, while the former supporters of Juana became the Isabelline party.

Immediately upon the death of Enrique IV, Fernando and Isabel took possession of the royal government; but the division between the two factions reduced the administration to chaos, and all sections of the population took advantage of this opportunity to give vent to acts of violence. The ensuing civil war dragged on for eight years. When victory for Isabel was assured in 1480, the Catholic Monarchs found themselves rulers of a people both tired of civil war and eager to accept such energetic and attractive monarchs. They were still faced with the twofold problem of establishing the legitimacy of their claims to the throne and disarming the rebellious party, which was defeated but still potentially dangerous. In these circumstances, the royal chronicles became the royal propaganda.

Initially the royal historians undertook to encourage popular acceptance of Isabel's claims by impugning the memory of Enrique IV and the reputation of Juana. They incorporated into the royal chronicles the *Decades* of Palencia—the most vitriolic of Enrique's enemies. Hernando del Pulgar, appointed royal chronicler in 1482, began his *Crónica de los Reyes Católicos* with twenty chapters about Enrique IV translated directly from the *Decades*; and Bernáldez began his *Memorias* with a few paragraphs about Enrique IV selected from the first twenty chapters of Pulgar.[38] Antonio de Nebrija's account of the first part of Isabel's reign is a fairly direct translation of Pulgar, and the history published by Dr. Lorenzo Galíndez de Carvajal in 1517 is a composite of the royal chronicles since the reign of Juan II. Not all of the chronicles were available to Carvajal, so he filled in the gaps by writing a few chapters himself, using a translation of the *Decades* for his information about Enrique IV.[39] The received version of Enrique's reign and of the legitimacy of Isabel's claim to the throne was based on the works of this group of historians—Palencia, Pulgar, Bernáldez, Nebrija, and Carvajal.

It is significant that none of these historians based his history of the reign of Enrique IV either on his own experiences during the reign or on an examination of various sources. Pulgar, at least, was in a position to do both; but he explained that sometimes lies and false accusations "are necessary to clearly demonstrate the right which this princess doña Isabel had to the succession of this realm."[40] So they all took their material and their point of view from Palencia. This is not to say that after 1480 the popular or learned opinions of Enrique IV were all suddenly changed to the Isabelline point of view. Enríquez del Castillo had been a partisan of Enrique's and praised him in a chronicle that Palencia destroyed. Enríquez del Castillo later reconstructed it, still treating Enrique fairly but tempering the tone of the work to suit Isabel, from whom he expected a grant of money for the work. Valera, although he disliked Enrique and had left the royal court in disgust, never wrote anything to harm Enrique during or after his lifetime. Valera's chronicle of Enrique's reign, the *Memorial de diversas hazañas*, was based in part on the *Decades* and in part on Enríquez del Castillo's work, but he often corrected Palencia's information according to his own memory, reproached the rebels for their disloyalty to the king and their unchivalrous attack on the queen and princess, and made no attempt to hide the weaknesses of the king. Valera criticized Enrique for making conflicting statements under oath about the succession to the throne, thus hiding the truth and creating needless suspicions, and for acting in a manner unbecoming to a knight.[41] These "opposition" chronicles received neither financial support nor official recognition from the Catholic Monarchs.

The official revision of the history of the previous reign appears to have been successful in stilling the doubts of "those who still suspected that their assumption of the throne had been a virtual usurpation,"[42] but the accusations against Enrique themselves created a problem: in throwing slime at Enrique, they dirtied the throne itself. The personal prestige of the monarchs was very high after 1480, but the prestige of the Castilian monarchy as an institution had to be raised to a level that would forestall any attack by the rebels.

The theoretical arguments needed for this task had already been developed in the works of the letrado historians, and they acquired some credibility as a result of the proposed Reconquest of Granada and the reforms. After 1480, the letrado concept of the monarchy was not only credible but also desperately needed. Throughout the reign of the Catholic Monarchs, the letrado theory of state and society, irrevocably bound to Isabelline propaganda, became the theoretical bulwark of the Catholic Monarchs, of the bureaucracy, and—after the death of Isabel in 1504—of the enemies of Fernando.[43]

While the letrado concept of society enjoyed official encouragement, the caballero theories suffered a period of disuse: from the composition of Valera's *Memorial de diversas hazañas* in 1488 until the publication of don Diego Hurtado de Mendoza's *De la guerra de Granada* in the seventeenth century, no caballero histories or treatises were published in Castile. The political needs of the Catholic Monarchs dictated that of the two major theories of Castilian history that flourished in the fifteenth century only the letrado theory was appropriate for their purposes. The rejected caballero concept of politics and history—with all its Renaissance characteristics—remained neglected throughout the sixteenth century.

II

The Mendoza Rise to Power

The Mendoza came originally from the province of Alava and incorporated themselves into Castilian society during the reign of Alfonso XI (1312–1350).[1] Alava—a mountainous region bounded by Castile, Navarre, and Aragon—is one of the Basque provinces incorporated into the Castilian monarchy with *fueros* (royal charters) during the reign of Alfonso XI. Before the Mendoza moved to Castile, Alava had been a battleground for generations in the feuds of the local seigneurial families. By 1332, the Mendoza had been feuding with the Guevara clan for at least a century; and other Alavese clans that moved to Castile in the fourteenth century—including the Ayala, the Velasco, and the Orozco—had all shed blood in these feuds and suffered a high death toll in incidents ranging from night ambushes to pitched battles in full armor. Once the Alavese moved to Castile, they ended their feuds, incorporated themselves into the Castilian fighting force, and climbed the ladder of rewards available to those who gave military service to the king.

By virtue of being caballeros, the Alavese who moved to Castile in the fourteenth century were *hidalgos* (gentry). All members of the hidalgo class—caballero or letrado—shared a common responsibility for the res publica: they were the public administrators of Castile. The caballeros' first responsibility was to recruit, maintain, provision, and command an army that could be put at the disposal of the crown in wartime. The caballeros provided these armies to the crown not because of feudal obligation but as military entrepreneurs. The top ranks of the caballeros became *vasallos del rey* while the lower ranks served in the armies of the *vasallos* or in the king's guard. According to the thirteenth-century definition of Alfonso X el Sabio, *vasallos del rey* were those

36

who received horses, money, or lands in return for outstanding military service.[2] In practice, the king usually rewarded a vasallo del rey after each occasion on which he presented himself and his army to the king prepared for war. In addition to rewards presented in the form listed by Alfonso X, the crown assigned caballeros to posts in the royal administration, with their respective incomes and perquisites. The caballeros therefore held the overwhelming majority of royal administrative posts: they were the admirals of the fleets; adelantados (military governors)[3] and notarios mayores (chief notaries) of the provinces; corregidores (royal administrators) of the cities; and alcaides (military governors) of the royal fortresses, including both the walls, towers, and bridges of the cities and the royal castles and fortified towers of the countryside. Caballeros also received positions in three of the corporate jurisdictions—the municipalities, the Mesta, and the military orders. By right, hidalgos held one-half the regimientos (seats with full voting rights) in the city councils; and the two procuradores each city sent to the Cortes had to be hidalgos. Caballeros held the highest offices in the Mesta and exercised a monopoly on the encomiendas (commanderies) of the military orders. Caballeros also had the right to possess señorío (jurisdiction), which they acquired either by purchase or through royal merced (gift) and which usually coincided with the lands they owned. Each of these officials appointed his own client caballeros as tenientes (administrators) of the offices he held in absentia, as holders of the subordinate offices under his patronage, and as gobernadores of his seigneurial estates. Thus caballeros filled the royal, corporate, and seigneurial administrations from top to bottom, from the national to the local level, in city and countryside. In the fourteenth and fifteenth centuries, only the jurisdictions of the universities, the church, and the Audiencia remained outside the grasp of the caballeros.

In the offices they held, the caballeros exercised judicial, executive, legislative, and military functions; for the Spanish concept of the separation of powers tended to distribute power among various corporate groups and allow them to exercise all the functions of government rather than to distribute the functions themselves. Thus the caballeros were judges of the first instance in criminal cases within the jurisdictions of their public offices and judges of the first and second instance in criminal and civil cases within their own señoríos. Because Castilian practice judged criminal and civil cases according to custom through a process of deposition and arbitration, a university education in Roman law was not necessary for a caballero properly to fulfill the judicial functions of his office. Thus, when the Mendoza and other caballero families from Alava moved to Castile, they became participants in the public life of the kingdom through a range of activities impossible in a more feudalized or more centralized monarchy.

The first Mendoza to appear in the service of Castile was Gonzalo Yáñez de Mendoza. He fought against the Muslims at the battle of Algeciras—along with Chaucer's parfit gentil knyght—served as *montero mayor* (chief huntsman) to Alfonso XI, moved to the Castilian province of Guadalajara, and settled in the city of Guadalajara where he became a *regidor* (city councilman) after marrying a sister of Iñigo López de Orozco. An Alavese, Orozco had received the office of *alcalde entregador* (chief justice) of the Mesta in reward for his military services to the king. He was a regidor of the city of Guadalajara and one of the richest men of the province. Even in the career of this very early Mendoza some of the characteristic patterns of the family history can be seen: Gonzalo Yáñez was by profession a caballero, fought in battle against the Muslims, received royal office as a reward, became a regidor of the city in which he lived, and married into a propertied and influential family.

Gonzalo's son, Pedro González de Mendoza (d. 1385), was particularly adept at choosing the winning side at a propitious moment; and under his leadership, the Mendoza became established as one of the rich and powerful families in fourteenth-century Castile. Pedro González accomplished this by abandoning king Pedro in 1366 and supporting the illegitimate pretender to the throne, Enrique de Trastámara. The Trastámara revolt had its roots in the private life of Alfonso XI.[4] When Alfonso died of the plague which had devastated his army at the siege of Gibraltar (1350), he left only one legitimate son—the sixteen-year-old Pedro who became king of Castile. But Alfonso also left seven illegitimate children by his mistress, Leonor de Guzmán. With the cooperation of Pedro's principal counselor, Juan Alfonso de Alburquerque, the widowed queen María ordered the murder of her hated rival, Leonor de Guzmán; and this murder, in 1351, set the pattern for Pedro's reign. Leonor's sons and grandsons—known as the *epígonos*—began a career of vengeance for her murder. One of the oldest of the epígonos—Enrique, count of Trastámara—became the focal point of the dissatisfied parties in Castile, and Pedro counterattacked by summarily executing any vasallo del rey he suspected of allying with the epígonos. In his twenty years as king (1350–1369), Pedro murdered more than sixty vasallos del rey, some of them in such a cruel way that he has been given the epithet Pedro the Cruel. Although the epígonos enjoyed the support of a few great families—especially the Manrique, la Vega, Mexía, and Albornoz—they were unable to match Pedro's superior forces. Fearing for their own lives, they spent much of their time in exile in France or Aragon, especially after Pedro killed Enrique de Trastámara's twin, Fadrique, master of the Order of Santiago (1358).

During the first sixteen years of Pedro's violent reign, Pedro González de Mendoza and his uncle, Iñigo López de Orozco, supported Pedro, receiving privileges and income in return for military service.[5] This pattern was broken in 1366, when Enrique de Trastámara raised an army of Castilian, Aragonese, and French knights, invaded northern Castile, and marched on Burgos, site of Pedro's campaign headquarters. Although Pedro's vasallos del rey, including the Alavese, had mobilized for the campaign and wanted to make their stand there, Pedro abandoned Burgos to Enrique, who entered the city and proclaimed himself king. In the face of Pedro's desertion, Mendoza, Orozco, and the other Alavese caballeros—probably acting under the leadership of Fernán Pérez de Ayala—refused to follow Pedro. Ayala's son, Pedro López de Ayala, joined Enrique and became his alférez mayor de la banda—the same office he had held under Pedro. Mendoza and Orozco, speaking for the city of Guadalajara, proclaimed their allegiance to Enrique, promptly receiving extensive lands and privileges from him and incurring Pedro's undying hatred. Enrique also gave Mendoza two strategic towns north of Madrid, Hita and Buitrago. Because these fortified towns remained loyal to Pedro, Mendoza had to conquer them in order to gain his war prizes.[6] Mendoza became mayordomo mayor to Enrique's son, and Orozco became a regular member of Enrique's council.

While Enrique and his supporters triumphantly marched south through Toledo, Pedro took ship in Seville and fled to Bayonne, where he formed an alliance with the English crown prince—Edward, the Black Prince. The Trastámara civil war now became part of the Hundred Years' War, France taking the side of Enrique and England supporting Pedro.[7] The Black Prince regarded Pedro's cause as just—and probably profitable—and invaded Castile by way of Alava. Enrique, after achieving some success in small skirmishes against this much larger, more experienced, and more modern army, decided to engage in full-scale battle. Although the resulting battle of Nájera (3 April 1367) was a disaster for the Enriquistas, the events immediately following it precipitated the formation of the Mendoza family as a political party and became the inspiration for the Renaissance in Castile.

Enrique escaped to France, while Orozco, Mendoza, Pedro López de Ayala, Pedro Manrique, Pedro Fernández de Velasco, and most of the other Enriquista captains were taken prisoner. Pedro murdered Orozco in cold blood after he surrendered on the battlefield, and only the intervention of the Black Prince saved the other Enriquista captains from the same fate. Disgusted with their ally's behavior, the English returned to more pressing affairs in France, assured of a profit from their Spanish venture when they received the ransoms of the Trastámara captains. The prisoners soon paid up, Enrique returned to Castile with French and Aragonese reinforcements, and in the next two years the Enriquistas defeated Pedro's armies and isolated him from outside assistance. Enrique murdered Pedro in 1369 and consolidated his power in the peninsula through the help of the Mendoza and other caballeros, whom he rewarded for their services. Enrique's mercedes, or rewards, formed the core of the Mendoza patrimony; and in the fifteenth century, they were to become the basis for the greatest fortune in Trastámara Castile.[8] The Mendoza fortune was thus built upon their adherence to the Trastámara cause at a critical moment. As military entrepreneurs, they offered their services to the most profitable cause and in so doing acted as a political party. As their fortune and power grew during the next century, the mere fact of their choosing one side over another became enough to tip the balance in favor of the side they chose.

The events at Nájera, more than any other single event, shaped Trastámara society and Mendoza politics throughout the fifteenth century. Mendoza's shift from Pedro to Enrique in 1366 had been a shrewd and hard-headed move to the winning side. Modern historians of the Mendoza claim that Pedro González de Mendoza deserted Pedro because he was disgusted with the king's murderous disregard for justice, but this claim does not explain why Mendoza served Pedro loyally and profitably for fifteen years after the king committed his first murder —that of Garcilaso de la Vega—in 1351. Mendoza deserted Pedro only after the king's blundering resulted in the loss of Burgos and it appeared that he would not be able to win the war. A rather tenuous adherence to Enrique's cause was converted into fervent commitment at Nájera when Mendoza's uncle, Iñigo López de Orozco, was catapulted into the select company of Enriquista martyrs. From that time on, Mendoza actively supported the Trastámara dynasty and its politics and allied himself with other Enriquistas who had undergone the same sort of conversion at Nájera. Generations of Mendoza sons would bear the name Iñigo López.

Soon after the disaster at Nájera, the freed captives began to form a series of marriage alliances with one another and with the epígonos. The leaders of the Trastámara revolution thus sealed their political alliances through marriage ties. The extended family that grew out of the Nájera group, formed by a unique common historical experience, became a closed corporation within the Castilian aristocracy. During the fifteenth century, the Nájera prisoners and their descendants would marry into other Castilian families and ally themselves with a variety of political forces within and without the kingdom. But throughout the Trastámara period, the descendants of the Nájera prisoners remained set apart from other members of the aristocracy by their common ancestry, inextricably bound up with the experience at Nájera and a common interpretation of its political implications.

In supporting Enrique's rebellion, the captives at Nájera committed themselves to a king who acted as if the monarch had a contractual relationship with his subjects and as if services not included in the subject's contractual obligations had to be rewarded in material ways. In his first grant of lands to Pedro González de Mendoza,[9] Enrique argued that loyalty to one's lord must be maintained as zealously as one's eyesight, for loyalty was the cement which bound men together into society, without which no one could survive alone. But he also claimed that kings and lords are obligated by the loyalty of their subjects to reward them and increase their fortunes. The very origins of their dynasty bound the Trastámara kings to this contractual relationship with the Nájera prisoners and their descendants. The natural consequences of this fact for the Mendoza were enormous. From the time Pedro González de Mendoza committed himself to the Enriquista cause at Nájera, the Mendoza became the pillars of the Trastámara dynasty. They were also the prime beneficiaries of the Trastámara rewards.

Before Nájera, Pedro González de Mendoza had formed a marriage alliance with the Pechas, a Guadalarjara family prominent in the Castilian government. His wife died without issue; and after Nájera Mendoza married again, this time to a woman from Toledo, a daughter of Fernán Pérez de Ayala—a prisoner at Nájera and leader of the Alavese clans in Castile. The eldest son of this second marriage married an illegitimate daughter of Enrique II, and the youngest son married a close relative of Enrique's queen. Mendoza's eldest daughter, Juana, married Diego Gómez Manrique, a brother of Pedro Manrique, one of the first supporters of Enrique's revolt. Manrique was also a relative of the queen and a prisoner at Nájera. The other daughters married men less wealthy and powerful but equally Enriquista in their politics. Among his in-laws, Pedro González de Mendoza could count a niece and a nephew of the king and queen, the king's daughter, and five men who had died or been taken prisoner at Nájera. With these marriages,

Mendoza built a network of Enriquista connections that bound his descendants to the party that had triumphed in the civil war and to the prisoners at Nájera.

The most important alliance Pedro González de Mendoza formed after Nájera was his marriage to Elvira de Ayala. The Ayala had been among the first of the Alavese clans to immigrate to Castile; and by the time of the revolt, they had already achieved a high social status and a claim to leadership. The Mendoza's alliance with this aggressive and upwardly mobile Ayala clan, rather than their alliance with the royal family, proved decisive; for apart from the fact that a number of the Ayala were exceptionally shrewd and successful political figures, the Trastámara nobility became involved in a series of internecine feuds that led to their decline in influence in the generation after Nájera.[10] Most important of all, the Ayala—Fernán Pérez and his son, Pedro López—would provide the intellectual leadership of the Nájera group and of the Renaissance in Castile.

This extended family spawned by the events at Nájera became the most powerful political group in Castile and held the highest political and military offices of the kingdom. Pedro González de Mendoza himself was mayordomo mayor to Juan I (1379–1390); and his brother-in-law, Pedro López de Ayala, became canciller mayor of Castile. Both of them were del consejo del rey. One of Mendoza's sons-in-law, Diego Gómez Manrique, was adelantado mayor of Castile; another, Díaz Sánchez de Benavides, was caudillo mayor (military governor) of the diocese of Jaén. Pedro González de Mendoza and his in-laws thus held the two highest political offices of the kingdom and two of the territorial military commands.

This profitable policy of active military and political support of the new dynasty was continued by Mendoza's eldest son, Diego Hurtado de Mendoza, admiral of Castile. The admiral's public life was a glorious succession of victories, but his private blunders cost the Mendoza their alliance with the Ayala clan. As admiral of Castile, he rendered valuable military services in the wars against Portugal, defeating Portuguese fleets in three separate naval engagements. In the power struggle during the minority of Enrique III (1390–1406), he supported the winning side by allying himself with his uncles, Pedro López de Ayala and Juan Hurtado de Mendoza, thus becoming del consejo del rey at a time when his uncle, Pedro López de Ayala, was also del consejo del rey and canciller mayor. Sometime before 1395, the admiral received the patronage of the city offices of Guadalajara as a merced, and since he had earlier received the right for himself and his descendants to name the city's procuradores to Cortes, the Mendoza henceforth were able to dominate the principal city in the province of Guadalajara.[11] When his career was cut short by death in 1404, the admiral was reputed to be the richest man in Castile.[12] He had inherited a large fortune from his father and added large tracts of land to the Mendoza estates. He received estates as mercedes from both Juan I and Enrique III that increased his holdings in the provinces of Guadalajara and Madrid.[13] He also extended the family's interests into Asturias through his second marriage, to Leonor de la Vega, in 1387. As the sole heiress of the Vega fortune, Leonor de la Vega brought extensive seigneurial lands in Asturias into the Mendoza estate, including sheep-grazing lands, salt mines, and seaports, sources of an important part of the Mendoza income in a period of extensive wool trade between Castile and Flanders.[14]

Leonor de le Vega also brought to the Mendoza a proud and ancient lineage. In contrast to that of the newly arrived Mendoza, the Vega family's high social status was venerable by Castilian standards.[15] Since the Vega also had a talent for getting themselves killed in colorful circumstances while in the service of God and king, the Vega name brought with it a heavy accretion of fame and anecdote. Leonor's great grandfather, Garcilaso de la Vega (d. 1326), had been canciller mayor, adelantado mayor of Castile, and justicia mayor of the king's household under Alfonso XI. While organizing the king's defenses against the rebellion of don Juan Manuel, he was assassinated in Soria during mass. Her grandfather, Garcilaso de la Vega (d. 1351), also adelantado mayor of Castile and justicia mayor of the king's household under Alfonso XI, had been the first murder victim of Pedro the Cruel. Her father, Garcilaso de la Vega, died in the battle of Nájera fighting for Enrique.

This marriage was also a renewal of the alliance system which the Mendoza had formed with the Enriquista aristocracy, involving as it did the family which had suffered most at the hands of Pedro the Cruel and been among the first supporters of the Trastámara cause. These connections were further strengthened by the second marriage of the admiral's eldest sister, Juana, to Alfonso Enríquez, a nephew of Enrique II. Enríquez succeeded Mendoza in the office of admiral of Castile, and this office became hereditary in the Enríquez family—a powerful connection the Mendoza used to good advantage throughout the fifteenth century, long before their cousin, Fernando the Catholic, a great grandson of Juana and Alfonso, became king.

Admiral Diego Hurtado de Mendoza and his father transformed the Mendoza from a provincial military family into a wealthy, aristocratic dynasty that dominated an entire city and province, held the highest national offices, and enjoyed many family ties to a powerful network of prestigious families, including the royal family itself. All of this was accomplished through their active participation in national affairs, including military service, personal influence at court, or high national office.

The admiral had another, even greater claim to the reverence accorded him by his descendants: he was the father of the greatest cavalier of the fifteenth century, Iñigo López de Mendoza, first marquis of Santillana (1398–1458). Santillana's reputation in Spanish history rests on his great literary achievements. In the history of the Mendoza, his reputation also rests on his great political achievement—the recuperation and preservation of the Mendoza fortune during a period of internal and external attacks on the Enriquista political order.

Before the admiral died in 1404, he tried to assure the inheritance of his small children by naming two of his powerful relatives as their tutors: his uncles, Pedro López de Ayala, canciller mayor of Castile, and Juan Hurtado de Mendoza, prestamero mayor (military governor) of Vizcaya. This effort was doomed to fail because of the admiral's own pecadillos. Although his decision to marry Leonor de la Vega was his own—made after his father died in the battle of Aljubarrota (1385)—it appears that the couple were at odds from the beginning. The admiral was away when their first son was born, and Leonor had the child baptized Garcilaso in honor of her glorious ancestors. In an early will, the admiral stipulated that the boy's name should be changed to Juan Hurtado de Mendoza in honor of the Mendoza's glorious ancestors.[16]

Although the couple had several children, they maintained separate households. Leonor lived in Carrión with her mother, and the admiral in the Mendoza family residence in Guadalajara—with his cousin, Mencía de Ayala. We do not know what Mencía's father, the canciller mayor, thought about his daughter's living arrangement; but it is clear from the documents that the admiral and Mencía were sharing bed as well as board. The original twist to this otherwise ordinary story lies in the fact that the admiral named Mencía as one of the executors of his will. The widowed Leonor de la Vega was thus left at the mercy of a woman she must have despised, and the two bereaved ladies fought so bitterly over the terms of the will that predatory relatives—especially the Manrique—found it convenient to usurp the far-flung estates of the Mendoza inheritance.

After the old canciller mayor died in 1407, Leonor broke off all relations with the Ayala family; and the estrangement between the Mendoza and Ayala lasted until Santillana became an adult, to the disadvantage of both families. To compensate for the loss of Ayala support, Leonor sought another alliance to protect her children's estate: in 1408, she and Lorenzo Suárez de Figueroa, master of Santiago, signed a marriage contract for their children. Although Leonor was abandoning her ties with the Ayala, she continued the Mendoza's policy of marriage to the Nájera group, for Lorenzo Suárez de Figueroa's wife was a daughter of the martyred Iñigo López de Orozco. But the master of Santiago died in 1409, and the double marriage did not provide the security Leonor had sought. The one remaining tutor, Juan Hurtado de Mendoza, plunged into the political conflicts of the minority of Juan II, leaving the admiral's widow without help and with limited success in defending her children's inheritance against the claims of their Manrique relatives.[17] In the years before he was old enough to take an active part in politics, Santillana's estate was eroded so seriously that it took him a lifetime of strenuous political and legal activity to restore it.

Modern historians, influenced by Isabelline propaganda and rooted in the constitutional history of earlier centuries, consistently interpret the first hundred years of Trastámara rule—especially the years of Santillana's political activity—as a struggle between monarch and nobility.[18] Neither the chronicles nor the other documents of the period support this view, and the Mendoza and their allies certainly did not see the political choices of their day in such simplistic terms. Instead, they saw themselves bound to the illegitimate Trastámara dynasty by their own success in overthrowing the legitimate monarch. Although the Mendoza were loyal to the dynasty as an ideal, the day-to-day behavior and character of the royal family made it difficult for even the most devoted subjects to figure out what course of action would be loyal. To begin with, the Trastámara were a short-lived lot: the Trastámara monarchs before Fernando and Isabel died at an average age of thirty-eight; of all six Trastámara monarchs in Castile, only two were survived by more than one legitimate son. The early Trastámara were mostly minors ruled by squabbling regents or weak characters controlled by their favorites. Furthermore, the Trastámara dynasty was split in 1412 when Juan I's younger son, Fernando de Antequera, was elected king of Aragon. As regent for his nephew, Juan II, Fernando had provided each of his sons with a rich estate. The eldest, Alfonso, was to inherit his father's vast holdings in Castile. The second, Juan, received the lordship of some of the richest cities in Castile (including Medina del Campo), became duke of Peñafiel, and married the heiress to the crown of Navarre. The third son, Enrique, not only became master of Santiago in 1409 but also received a number of rich estates, including Alburquerque, Ledesma,

45

Salvatierra, and Miranda. The fourth son, Sancho, became master of Alcántara in 1409—at the age of eight. When Fernando was elected king of Aragon, it might have been expected that he and his sons—now the infantes of Aragon—would give up their Castilian possessions for lands in Aragon. Instead, they held on to them; and when Castile tried to retrieve some of this wealth after Fernando's death in 1416, the infantes used Aragon as a refuge and staging ground for attacks on Castile—the principal cause of political instability there during the first half of the fifteenth century.

The Mendoza thus did not enjoy the luxury of a straightforward choice between monarch and nobility. During most of the fifteenth century, they had to choose between a weak Trastámara king in Castile and a dynamic Trastámara king in Aragon—between the Castilian king's corrupt favorite and the Aragonese king's avaricious sons. This pattern of conflict within the royal family is of course one of the political constants of medieval Castilian history: Alfonso X el Sabio was attacked and deposed in all but name by his son, Sancho; Alfonso XI was attacked, betrayed, and deserted by his uncle, don Juan Manuel; Pedro was attacked, defeated, and killed by his half-brother, Enrique de Trastámara; Juan I had to imprison and exile both a cousin and a half-brother for sedition; Juan II spent the first forty years of his reign defending his kingdom from the attacks of his cousins, the infantes of Aragon; Enrique IV was deposed in absentia and burned in effigy by the supporters of his half-brother, Alfonso; and Isabel the Catholic usurped the Castilian throne from her niece, Juana de Castilla. The caballeros shifted their support from the king to his relatives and back whenever they could see an advantage in following one side or the other. Inasmuch as these struggles continued without a decisive victory for most of the century, about one-half of the caballeros must have supported the crown at all times, although the membership in each party was in constant flux. There was no "noble party" any more than there was a "royal party," and the picture we are usually given of a class conflict between monarchy and nobility is a cliché that persists despite all evidence to the contrary.

For Santillana, as head of the Mendoza family, the protracted conflict between Juan II and his cousins presented a painful moral dilemma: this was a conflict not only between a king and his relatives but between two equally legitimate branches of the Trastámara—to whose dynasty the Mendoza owed all their worldly success and were intensely loyal. Fernando de Antequera was a hero to his contemporaries because he did not follow the usual pattern of royal relatives: he did not try to usurp the throne from his ailing brother, Enrique III, or from his infant nephew,

already held, avoiding the larger issues (which seemed insoluble), and turning their attention to smaller, more manageable problems. Santillana continued the family policy of forming marriage alliances to strengthen political alliances, but he formed alliances with a greater variety of political groups than had his father and grandfather.[23]

In contrast to the small families of three previous generations, ten of Santillana's children lived to adulthood. Like the Israelites in the wilderness, the Mendoza multiplied extraordinarily during the fifteenth century. They married young (often more than once), bore many children, lived to ripe ages, and thus acquired personal influence to cover any political eventuality. Santillana seldom participated in the consejo del rey and never accepted a high political office, but he was related through marriage to most of the high officials of the kingdom; thus he was able to avoid the burdens of high office while retaining some influence over official decisions. This political caution is characteristic of Santillana's leadership of the Mendoza family: he exchanged the aggressive extension of political and economic interests on a national scale, which had characterized the admiral and Pedro González de Mendoza, for a slow and deliberate rebuilding, consolidation, and preservation of the family's military and seigneurial control over local affairs.

After Santillana's death in 1458, the titular leadership of the family passed to his eldest son, the second marquis of Santillana; but the effective leadership was carried by one of the younger sons, Pedro González de Mendoza, bishop of Calahorra. Three other sons, Pedro Hurtado de Mendoza, Lorenzo Suárez de Figueroa, and Iñigo López de Mendoza, took an active role in the wars Enrique IV carried on against the Muslims from 1454 to 1464.[24]

In 1464, the kingdom began a new chapter in the traditional struggle between the monarch and his relatives.[25] During the first ten years of his reign, the childless Enrique's heir was his half-brother Alfonso, the son of Juan II's second marriage. In expectation of Alfonso's accession to power, a political party formed around him, led by Enrique's favorite, Juan Pacheco, and other caballeros of Portuguese extraction. When Enrique divorced his first wife and married again and Juana was born to his new queen, Juan Pacheco and his party continued to support Alfonso as heir, claiming the superiority of male inheritance, while the king and Cortes recognized princess Juana as heiress. Most of the nobility, as usual, shifted support from one party to another and signed confederations in an effort to gain a political advantage if a crisis should arise. When Enrique IV replaced Juan Pacheco with a new favorite, Beltrán de la Cueva, Pacheco tried to recoup his losses by denouncing both

Beltrán and the king. Enrique IV was extremely mild-mannered, almost passive; and with the memory of don Alvaro de Luna's execution still vivid in Castile, he chose to follow a policy so narrowly directed at avoiding risk, without any apparent larger goal, that both enemies and supporters interpreted his behavior as weakness.

Early in 1465, Pacheco and his allies felt strong enough to declare open rebellion against the king. Enrique announced his intention of marrying Alfonso to Juana and declared Alfonso his heir. This maneuver successfully ended the immediate military crisis, but Enrique repudiated the agreement as soon as the crisis passed; and the rebels, being the most powerful party, dethroned him in absentia in Avila on 5 June 1465, burned him in effigy, and declared Alfonso king. Before this, the Mendoza held back from taking sides in the succession dispute; but they had long considered Juan Pacheco an enemy because of some property disputes, and the events at Avila enraged and alarmed them. The bishop of Calahorra published a speech denouncing the events at Avila, and he and his brothers rushed to the king's defense with an army of eight hundred cavalry. Enrique rewarded the Mendoza brothers generously: he gave the *tercias* (the royal share of the tithe) of Guadalajara to the bishop of Calahorra, the royal town of Santander (with its annual income of seven hundred thousand maravedís in taxes and pasture fees) to the marquis of Santillana, and royal incomes from sources near their own estates to the other brothers. In September, the opposing armies hurled insults at each other across a field outside Olmedo and actually engaged in combat. After this battle of Olmedo, which was considered a victory for the royal forces, the king turned Juana over to the Mendoza as a hostage for his pledges to them, and bishop Pedro González took up residence at the royal court to make sure the king would not again capitulate to his enemies. On 5 October 1465, in a field outside Arévalo, the marquis of Santillana (representing the king's party) and the count of Benavente (representing the rebel party) signed a confederation that ended hostilities in the kingdom until the end of February 1466. This breathing space gave everyone time to form more confederations; and by the summer of 1467, the rebel party had signed on so many allies that the king again started to make concessions to them. At this point, the Mendoza believed that the king was his own worst enemy and tried to protect him from himself by persuading him to sign a pledge that he would make no treaty or agreement with Alfonso or any of his partisans without the advice, agreement, and consent of the bishop of Calahorra. On 6 August 1467, the king renewed this pledge for a term of thirteen months. Faced with such uncharacteristic intransigence on the part of the king and believing themselves to be militarily superior, the rebels issued a challenge. The two armies actually engaged in battle at Alaejos on 20 August 1467. Although the fighting had barely started when it was stopped by a violent hailstorm, the Mendoza considered Alaejos a great victory for their side because they held the advantageous position when the fighting stopped. Unfortunately for the rebels, Alfonso died prematurely in 1468, and they put forward his sister Isabel as heiress to the throne.[26] Thus Isabel the Catholic, the last Trastámara monarch of Castile, entered the Castilian political scene in the tradition of her family—as a pretender to the throne leading a rebellion against her own half-brother.

The Mendoza were perhaps too impressed with their "victory" at Alaejos and insufficiently impressed by the determination and ability of Isabel, for they relaxed their vigil over Enrique. In September 1468, at a time when the bishop of Calahorra was not with the royal court, Enrique followed the advice of Juan Pacheco, met with Isabel, abjured the rights of Juana, and recognized Isabel as his legal heiress—on the condition that she should not marry without his consent. The Mendoza were angered and disgusted by this betrayal, and the bishop of Calahorra drew up a statement of protest on behalf of Juana. Copies of this document were nailed to church doors in several towns, including Ocaña where Isabel was staying.

In the next two years, the Mendoza withdrew from the succession question: Enrique named Pacheco as Juana's new tutor, and the Mendoza surrendered her to the king and her new guardian sometime in 1468; Isabel married Fernando in 1469, and his father, Juan II of Aragon, began to solicit Mendoza support for the Isabelline party.[27] In 1473, the Mendoza formally agreed to support Isabel as rightful heiress in exchange for clear title to Castilian lands claimed by both Juan II of Aragon and the Mendoza and a cardinalate for the bishop of Calahorra. The opportunism of this move should not blind us to the equally compelling motive of loyalty to the Trastámara dynasty.

The marriage of Fernando and Isabel eliminated the conflict which had torn the loyalties of the nobility in opposing directions and kept Castile in a state of turmoil for over fifty years. When Enrique died in 1474, Fernando and Isabel were supported by the Mendoza and their traditional allies, and Juana was supported by Pacheco and his allies. The Mendoza provided most of the leadership and manpower that enabled Fernando and Isabel to win the civil war (1474–1480), a fact Isabel gratefully acknowledged in 1475 when she conferred the title of duke of Infantado on the second marquis of Santillana, thanking him and seventeen of his relatives for their leadership of her cause, and saying that he had provided so many people and such force that no other grandee of the kingdom could equal him in the conservation of her estate.[28]

The Mendoza's participation in the later phases of the Isabelline war of succession was almost desultory, reflecting their lack of emotional commitment to her claims. The Mendoza participated in sieges but in no pitched battles during the war. The duke of Infantado received his title at Toro in 1475 as a reward for anticipated military services against the king of Portugal, but he appears to have been elsewhere when the battle actually took place almost a year later. As soon as the Portuguese withdrew from Castile, the Mendoza and Juan II of Aragon persuaded Isabel to make peace with Pacheco and his Castilian allies. Isabel later broke the peace, but the Mendoza—especially after the poet Jorge Manrique was killed leading a royalist attack on a Pacheco fortress—refused to serve, and the queen had to call off the attack.

When Isabel broke the agreement a second time and attacked Pacheco in 1479, Infantado, as one of the guarantors of the agreement, sent an army under the command of one of his sons to Pacheco's defense; and the prospect of war against the Mendoza finally persuaded Isabel to make and keep an agreement with Pacheco. Throughout this affair, which dragged on from 1476 to 1480,[29] the Mendoza maintained an even-handed detachment until it was no longer possible for them to avoid involvement; and then they committed themselves to a fellow nobleman rather than to the monarch.

The thoroughgoing lack of commitment to the monarchy as an institution and to the queen as a person was not typical of the Mendoza's attitude toward Fernando. They were attracted to Isabel's party specifically by her marriage to Fernando: the negotiations that brought the Mendoza into the Isabelline camp in 1473 were conducted by the bishop of Calahorra and Juan II of Aragon. Thus the Mendoza allegiance to Fernando was based on the most prosaic and the most romantic of reasons: he was their cousin;[30] he had proved himself a knight by the age of seventeen; he was the namesake of their hero, Fernando de Antequera, and son and heir of Fernando's only surviving son, Juan II of Aragon; and by his marriage to Isabel, he reunited the Trastámara dynasty. The very Mendoza who avoided large-scale commitments in Isabel's war of succession were those most enthusiastic and active in the conquest of Granada—under the leadership of Fernando. In his own character, Fernando personified the vigor of the early Trastámara; and by his marriage to Isabel, he had eliminated the single greatest source of dissension and rebellion in fifteenth-century Castile. The Mendoza had found a chivalric leader who commanded their respect and a Trastámara who would reunite the dynasty: to his enterprise they committed themselves and their armies.

In reward for their services, the Mendoza again received noble titles and clear legal title to disputed lands. The second Santillana was elevated to duke of Infantado in 1475, and Infantado's eldest son was made count of Saldaña. Santillana's second son, Iñigo López de Mendoza, was made count of Tendilla in 1467 (?); and the third son, Lorenzo Suárez de Figueroa, was made count of Coruña in 1468 (?). The youngest of Santillana's sons, the former bishop of Calahorra, became cardinal of Santa Croce—popularly known as the cardinal of Spain since there was never more than one Spanish cardinal at a time—bishop of Sigüenza, archbishop of Seville, and administrator of the bishopric of Osma. In 1485, cardinal Mendoza gave up the archbishopric of Seville in favor of a nephew—brother of the second count of Tendilla—and was named archbishop of Toledo. He received royal and papal legitimation of his sons, the privilege of establishing two mayorazgos for them, and two titles of nobility for the eldest: count of Cid and marquis of Cenete. As primate of Spain, cardinal Mendoza became a permanent resident of the royal court, where he was popularly believed to exercise so much influence over Fernando and Isabel that he was called the third king of Spain.[31]

Their switch from champions of the rights of princess Juana to leaders of the Isabelline party was the climactic moment of the Mendoza's political history. At Nájera in 1367, Pedro González de Mendoza had been just one of a number of Trastámara party captains—a minor one at that. Mendoza support of Isabel in 1474 made her queen of Castile. The Mendoza had become kingmakers—the largest, wealthiest, and most powerful political force in Castile.

The Mendoza's actions in the Isabelline war of succession followed the pattern established in the Trastámara war: they remained loyal to the legitimate ruler until it became profitable to shift allegiance to the illegitimate party. In this case, the illegitimate party represented the survival of a unified Trastámara dynasty; and Mendoza loyalty to this dynasty had become more compelling than any considerations of loyalty to the legitimate heir or duty to the monarchy as a legitimate institution. After the marriage of Fernando and Isabel in 1469, to have supported Juana would have been to destroy the Trastámara dynasty. The Mendoza fortune had been built entirely on a policy of support of this dynasty; and so long as the Trastámara ruled in Spain, the Mendoza would be loyal to them.

III

Pedro López de Ayala and the Formation of Mendoza Attitudes

The Mendoza's political behavior during the Trastámara revolution and immediately afterwards was an improvised response to a series of exceptional situations. Later generations of the family, by adapting to changing conditions, matched the success of their ancestors; but they began to see their own actions as part of a consistent pattern of behavior and values, a family tradition that could be traced back to the foundations of the Trastámara dynasty. The fifteenth-century Mendoza imbibed this family tradition principally from the historical works of their ancestor, Pedro López de Ayala (d. 1407), canciller mayor of Castile and the pivotal intellectual figure of early Trastámara Castile. Ayala utilized the literary and rhetorical skills he learned as a boy in Avignon to write the political propaganda of the triumphant Trastámara revolution; and in the process, he wrote the first Renaissance history in Castile, the *Crónica del rey don Pedro*. Ayala's lifelong contacts with Avignon; his political involvement in the illegitimate Trastámara monarchy; his study, translation, and imitation of classical and modern models, all prepared him for the writing of Renaissance historical propaganda. Like his Italian contemporaries, Petrarch and Salutati, Ayala, through his genius shaped the esthetics and opinions of generations of his descendants in the fifteenth and sixteenth centuries.

Pedro López de Ayala was educated under the influence of two men: his father, Fernán Pérez de Ayala (d. 1385), and his great-uncle, cardinal Pedro Gómez Barroso (d. 1348). Pedro López was exceptionally close to his father—Fernán Pérez says that his son's attentions and obedience to his parents far exceeded the ordinary bonds of filial duty—who was a man of exceptional political and intellectual abilities.[1] Fernán Pérez's grandfather and his oldest brother were both killed in ambushes in Alava; and his father (d. c. 1330) moved to Castile and became the adelantado mayor of Murcia, first for don Juan Manuel and then for Alfonso XI. As a young man, Fernán Pérez served in the household of Leonor de Castilla; and in 1346, Alfonso XI sent him to Aragon to negotiate a marriage settlement between Leonor and the Aragonese king. After successfully arranging the marriage terms, Fernán Pérez went on to Avignon to negotiate the necessary papal dispensation. There he visited his uncle, cardinal Pedro Gómez, and his son, who was being educated in the cardinal's household.

In 1349, at the siege of Gibraltar, Fernán Pérez bought from the king's mistress, Leonor de Guzmán, most of the lands, fortresses, and seigneurial jurisdiction in several valleys of Alava, thus becoming the largest landlord and most powerful señor of the area.[2] Soon afterward, king Pedro named him *alguacil mayor* (chief constable) of the city of Toledo; and Fernán Pérez began to form marriage alliances between his numerous children and those of Fernán Gómez de Toledo, one of the most influential (and prolific) members of the city government. Although Fernán Pérez's political interests were focused on Toledo, he tried to maintain some kind of rational authority over his Alavese territories by drawing up a fuero defining the judicial structure of the lands of Ayala. This *Fuero de Ayala*—a valuable example of seigneurial legislative activity—and a genealogical history of his family that he probably wrote in imitation of don Juan Manuel's history of his own royal lineage are the only known writings of Fernán Pérez de Ayala. Both the *Fuero* and the genealogy were read, copied, added to, and commented upon by generations of Fernán Pérez's descendants, even those who had no seigneurial jurisdiction in Alava.[3] In addition to his political role in forming the biological and political Mendoza family in the wake of the Trastámara wars, Fernán Pérez through his writings exercised an intellectual influence in forming the family's sense of itself as an ancestral reference group associated with the province of Alava.

Fernán Pérez intended Pedro López de Ayala for a career in the church, and to this end he sent his son to Avignon to be educated and advanced in his career by cardinal Pedro Gómez Barroso. Fernán Pérez was the legal heir and favorite nephew of the cardinal; and the boy immediately benefited from the patronage of his great-uncle by receiving a benefice in the cathedral of Toledo. Pedro López's tutelage under the cardinal did not last long, for the cardinal died in the plague of 1348, when Pedro López was sixteen years old; but the youth was deeply influenced both by his education in the cardinal's household and by the cultural and intellectual ambience of Avignon at midcentury.

In the fourteenth century, Avignon was a focal point of the European world. When Clement V (1305–1314) fled Rome and settled in Avignon with his curia and chancery, Avignon replaced Rome as the center of an international bureaucracy. Almost overnight the city attracted some of the best minds in Europe—and their libraries. In the next twenty years, it became one of those massive concentrations of population, activity, and resources so conducive to intellectual and artistic ferment. Francesco Petrarch was the most brilliant product of this milieu, but he was not alone. If we read between the lines of Petrarch's correspondence, it seems as if the whole city had filled up with enthusiastic lovers of the Roman classics. By 1348, Seneca's tragedies had all been presented on stage there; Petrarch and his fellow university students read not only law but also Cicero, Vergil, and Ovid. The most eagerly read Fathers were Jerome and Augustine, who would become the favorites of the Florentine Renaissance because of their reputation as rhetoricians; and the many manuscripts of Livy that Urban V (1362–1370) added to the papal library show that even the jurists in the papal court were enthusiastic students of classics other than the law.

Petrarch and his friends in Avignon set out to imitate and translate the classics; and two of these friends, Pierre de Berçuire and Giovanni Colonna, were to provide the models for Spanish translations and imitations of the classics. Prior of the Benedictine house of St. Hilarion in Paris, Berçuire lived in Avignon from 1320 to 1340; and his French translation of Livy inspired and guided Ayala's later translation of Livy into Castilian. Colonna (d. 1348) devoted himself to imitating the classics with a *Liber de Viris Illustribus* and a *Mare Historiarum*, both of which served as literary models for Ayala's nephew, Fernán Pérez de Guzmán.[4]

Modern historians tend to assume that the Pyrenees were a serious barrier to travel between Spain and the rest of Europe; but fourteenth-century Spaniards evidently did not find them particularly difficult to cross. Throughout the Avignon papacy, there was a steady flow of Castilians to the papal court, seeking patronage, political refuge, and education. In 1394, when Ayala made his embassy to Avignon, there were about two hundred Spaniards, including sixty-one Castilians, studying law there. For educated Spaniards, Avignon became more than a place of study and a papal court, it was a preoccupation.

The ecclesiological problems posed by the papacy's transfer from

Rome to Avignon and the even more difficult problem of the Great Schism after 1378 occupied an important place in the writing and policymaking of both Castilians and Aragonese.[5] Spaniards traveled to Avignon to form alliances or negotiate settlements, and many remained to make their careers in Avignon. But the traffic went both ways. Most Spaniards returned to Spain after completing their studies or diplomatic missions, and each might bring back with him a new treatise on rhetoric, a translation of Livy, a new appreciation of Seneca's tragedies, or a determination to match the Roman historians with a history of Castile or Aragon. By the end of the fourteenth century, Spaniards were among the most important figures at the papal court; and Castilians who had resided in Avignon were the political leaders of Castile, including Enrique de Trastámara himself, who had sought refuge and assistance in Avignon during the most desperate moments of his career.

The Castilians at the papal court were greatly outnumbered by the French and Italians. Positions at the court depended upon patronage by the college of cardinals, and there were only five Castilian cardinals throughout the entire fourteenth century. The Spaniards at Avignon nevertheless played an administrative and intellectual role far greater than their insignificant numbers would lead us to expect. Most of what we know about the Avignon papacy we owe to French historians who regarded the Spanish as intruders, so the effectiveness of Spanish administrators and their influence on papal policy have not been appreciated by modern historians.

While Ayala was studying in Avignon, Barroso's household was both the focus of the Spanish community there and one of the political and cultural centers of the entire court. Pedro Gómez Barroso had been a favorite of Sancho IV and was named bishop of Cartagena by Alfonso XI. In Cartagena, Pedro Gómez and his brother-in-law, Pedro López de Ayala (d. c. 1330), adelantado of the kingdom of Murcia, tried to settle the differences between don Juan Manuel and his nephew the king. If the two brothers-in-law did not achieve the impossible in this task, they did accomplish something almost as difficult—their own political survival in a situation that required a delicate balance between serving the king and serving the rebellious don Juan Manuel without incurring the enmity of either. In 1327, Pedro Gómez was named cardinal by John XXII, and he immediately established a household in Avignon. Barroso played an important role in the papal curia from the very beginning. To the astonishment of French historians, the French pope, Benedict XII (1334–1342), appointed this "étranger" to negotiate a truce between France and England in 1337. Barroso was also one of the inner circle of six cardinals who effectively conducted the affairs of the papacy under another French pope, Clement VI (1342–1352).

As far as we know, Barroso was the only cardinal to maintain a painter in his household along with the usual complement of chaplains, chamberlain, physician, servants, legal aides, and relatives. One of the religious currents at Avignon was a pietism that emphasized the joys of good works, and Barroso appears to have been an enthusiastic participant. His good works included founding the Dominican convent at Sainte-Praxède. Barroso also acted as patron to Alvaro Pelayo, a Franciscan from Galicia who had studied with Duns Scotus in Paris. In 1327, Pelayo dedicated his major work, *Super Statu et Planctu Ecclesiae*, to Barroso.[6] The most respected if not the only Castilian theologian of any note during the fourteenth century, Pelayo was a pioneer in grappling with the most pressing ecclesiological problem of the day, the legitimacy of a papacy not resident in Rome. The work dedicated to Barroso was the first treatise to deal with this topic in depth, and it became the cornerstone of the Avignon papacy's claims to legitimacy.

Ayala reacted to the theologians' disputes the way Petrarch did: he condemned them as irrelevant to the problems of Christian life.[7] He was more favorably impressed by another Spaniard active in Avignon, Gil Alvarez de Albornoz, archbishop of Toledo, with whom he and his father later formed political alliances.[8] Albornoz succeeded Pedro Gómez as the Spanish cardinal (1350–1367) and was in turn succeeded by Ayala's cousin, Pedro Gómez Barroso (1371–1374), who had also been educated by his great-uncle and namesake, the first cardinal Barroso. Through these intellectual and political connections, Avignon exercised a significant influence over the culture of early Trastámara Castile.

After cardinal Pedro Gómez died, Pedro López, finding himself without a patron at the age of sixteen, returned to Castile where he abandoned his clerical status and began a career as a caballero. Ayala served a military and political apprenticeship in his father's household, and in 1359 he outfitted a galley which he commanded in king Pedro's naval expedition against Valencia and Catalonia. As a reward for this service, Pedro appointed him alguacil mayor of the city of Toledo to replace his father, who had been elevated to the highest office of the city, alcalde mayor.

Among the difficulties of his new office, Pedro López encountered the task of executing the often unjust orders of king Pedro against his vassals in Toledo, many of them Ayala's relatives. In 1360, Pedro ordered Ayala to evict his own brother-in-law, Vasco the archbishop of Toledo, and send him into exile. In the next few years, Pedro summarily executed several of Ayala's Toledo relatives, but he remained loyal to the king until his desertion of Burgos in 1366. Ayala was taken prisoner fighting against Pedro at Nájera and taken captive fighting against the Portuguese at Aljubarrota in 1385. He quickly rose to prominence under the Trastámara kings, for whom he led several embassies to France, Aragon, and Avignon, and became canciller mayor of Castile in 1398.[9]

During his long and active career and after his retirement to a Jeronimite monastery, Ayala was a prolific author and translator. During his year-long captivity in Lisbon after the battle of Aljubarrota, he wrote a manual of falconry, the Arte Cetreria, and most of the four hundred verses of his most famous work, the Rimado del Palacio. He later translated Livy, Boccaccio's De Casibus Virorum Illustrium, Guido delle Colonne's Historia Troiana, and St. Gregory's Moralia in Job. He also added some sections to his father's genealogy of the Ayala family; and after his last visit to Avignon in 1396, he wrote chronicles of the reigns of the four kings he had served—Pedro, Enrique II, Juan I, and Enrique III.

His translation of Moralia in Job is particularly interesting as an example of his humanist approach to the classics, for Ayala not only translated the work but also went back and made a second translation in order to correct some unintelligible passages.[10] Instead of trying to rationalize these passages by discovering some obscure meaning in the apparently nonsensical or contradictory words, Ayala assumed that the Latin of the texts he was using was corrupt. By comparing different copies and guessing at how a copyist might have mistaken one word for another, he was able to produce a purified, elegant text. In this endeavor, he seems to have gone beyond his translation of Livy, in which he says he tried to clarify some obscure and difficult words. In his second translation of Moralia, Ayala worked on the humanist assumptions that the original Latin had been clear and elegant and that obscurities must be attributable to errors in the medieval texts.[11]

Ayala's humanist skills and Renaissance attitudes reached their fullest expression in Crónicas de los reyes de Castilla, especially in the first of these, Crónica del rey don Pedro. As a work of art and as political propaganda, Crónica del rey don Pedro became both the rhetorical model and the political Bible of the Castilian Renaissance; but for the past four centuries it has been one of the most controversial works of Castilian literature. During the century after it was written, especially during the reign of Juan II, Ayala's history was accepted as an accurate account of the reign of Pedro the Cruel.[12] Its popularity among the reading public is attested by the fourteen manuscripts surviving from the fifteenth century and the early and frequent printings in Castile.[13]

In 1570, don Diego de Castilla, dean of the cathedral of Toledo and a descendant of Pedro the Cruel by way of an illegitimate son, claimed that Pedro had been a just and benevolent monarch and charged that Ayala had distorted the truth in order to excuse his own disloyalty to the king. Diego de Castilla had just met Gerónimo Zurita (1512–1580), royal chronicler of the crown of Aragon, while Zurita was traveling through Castile looking for manuscripts. When the dean tried to persuade Zurita to discredit and discard Ayala's version of events, Zurita thoroughly investigated the charges against Ayala. After examining a wealth of archival and manuscript evidence, he informed the dean—in polite but firm language—that Ayala's account was substantially correct. Zurita collated several manuscripts of Ayala's account and edited the chronicle for publication. In his critical notes, he amplified and clarified many details and pointed out several passages Ayala had redrafted to soften his vivid account of Pedro's cruelties—probably, Zurita thought, after Pedro's granddaughter, Catherine of Lancaster, married Enrique III and it became politic to smooth over old antagonisms.[14]

Despite Zurita's careful analysis, Ayala's *Crónica del rey don Pedro* continues to be praised as impartial and vilified as self-serving. In the nineteenth century, Prosper Mérimée romanticized Pedro and claimed that Ayala's chronicle was a tissue of lies.[15] In the twentieth century, Ayala's most enthusiastic admirers consider him to be totally impartial,[16] whereas his severest critics accuse him of "sinuosity."[17] More moderate critics consider Ayala biased but generally reliable, attempting to "justify his own career while violating the historical truth as little as possible."[18]

Modern historians cannot check Ayala's account against external sources: there is no other Castilian chronicle of the reign of Pedro, and most of the archival documents available to Zurita in the sixteenth century have since disappeared. We also have little internal evidence to use in examining the charge of bias—Ayala scrupulously avoids making any explicit statement condemning Pedro or his actions. Anyone who reads the chronicle must nevertheless come away from the work with a vague feeling of uneasiness—of being manipulated into a critical judgment of Pedro without any evidence to support this condemnation.

To explain how Ayala achieves his effect without distorting the material, modern scholars have focused on the content of the chronicle. The dispute has centered on the extent to which Ayala omitted material damning to his own purposes while including material damning to

Pedro's reputation.[19] Ayala's success as a propagandist, however, does not lie in anything so superficial. His genius lies rather in his rhetorical control over the material, which enables him to play upon the emotions of the reader so subtly that he is not aware of how he is being manipulated.

Historians have long recognized that Ayala imitated the ancient Roman historians—especially Livy and Tacitus—in his descriptions of military affairs, in his chapter organization, in his use of speeches, and in his brief character sketches.[20] Ayala's use of classical models is, however, much more extensive and sophisticated than scholars have recognized. In his chronicles—as in Italian Renaissance historiography—classical forms serve political purposes. This intimate association of classical models with Enriquista propaganda shaped the humanist and Renaissance attitudes of Ayala's descendants. Throughout the fifteenth century, they read the *Crónica del rey don Pedro* and absorbed Ayala's attitudes toward the classics, religion, and politics, along with his apologia for the family ancestors.

Ayala's chronicle begins with the death of Pedro's father, Alfonso XI, and ends with the death of Pedro himself. This is the only chronicle Ayala begins with the death of the previous king, and the device of beginning and ending with the two superficially similar scenes frames the chronicle and gives it dramatic symmetry. The contrasts between the two death scenes serve a political purpose—suggesting a subtle and effective argument in defense of Ayala's desertion of Pedro. The death and funeral of Alfonso XI occupy five long chapters, describing the majesty of Alfonso's accomplishments and the nobility of his companions, the grief of both the Castilian knights and the Muslim enemy, and the respect and honor Alfonso commanded even in death. These chapters provide a great contrast to the last, which describes Pedro's death in a furtive escape attempt, betrayed by those he trusted, stabbed on the ground by his own half-brother while none of the spectators came to his aid, and dismissed by the chronicler unmourned and without mention of a funeral.

The death and funeral of Alfonso XI are also used to introduce the major personages and factions of Pedro's reign—the new king; his mother, María; his illegitimate half-brothers and their mother, Leonor de Guzmán; and the principal military and political figures of the kingdom. In his description of the funeral cortege accompanying Alfonso's body from Gibraltar to Seville, Ayala displays the factions surrounding Leonor de Guzmán and her sons. The near-fatal illness of Pedro in Seville serves to introduce the factions surrounding Pedro's cousins and favorite. In describing the first year, which appears superficially to be a slow-moving account of an irrelevant royal funeral, Ayala thus establishes a standard of kingship against which Pedro is to be judged, introduces the major characters, delineates the conflicts that will make up the tragedy of Pedro, and provides the dramatic framework in which the tragedy will be played.

In the next year of the chronicle, Ayala uses three historical digressions to present the historical, political, and religious background against which the king and his enemies will operate. The first is a short treatise on the calendars of Christians, Romans, Jews, and Muslims; a history of their usage in Spain; and instructions on how to compute the year in each calendar. The second is a capsule history of the lands under the system of jurisdiction known as *behetrías*, in which Ayala traces their origins, speculates on the etymology of the word, and describes changes in their tenure. The third is a history of the judicial, military, fiscal, and religious institutions of the city of Toledo.[21] Ayala makes the point that many factors outside the chronological scope of his chronicle had a decisive effect on the events he is about to describe. He preserves the dramatic structure of the chronicle by compressing these chronological digressions into one year at the beginning of the work and by introducing each digression as the background for an event occurring in that year.

This digressive and slow-moving year at the beginning of the chronicle is balanced by the equally slow-moving and digressive eighteenth year near its end.[22] In this year, the rapid flow of the narrative shifts to a slow-paced series of chapters filled with speeches, dialogues, and an exchange of letters between Pedro and a wise Muslim. Here Ayala makes his fullest exposition of the political grievances, rationale, and ambitions of both the king and his enemies. Since this is the year of the battle of Nájera, this change of pace builds suspense by prolonging Pedro's greatest moment of military triumph. It also creates a strong parallel between Alfonso XI, struck down by the plague in his moment of military glory at Gibraltar, and Pedro, soon to be struck down by his bastard brother after the military victory of Nájera. By reintroducing themes from the first year—the vanity of worldly glory, Muslim respect for a just king—Ayala prepares the way for regicide in the twentieth year and reinforces the symmetry of the chronicle's overall structure.

The rest of the chronicle consists of a roughly chronological history of internal conflicts, diplomatic relations, and wars against the Muslims, with accounts of fiscal policy and events in foreign countries added to the ends of most years. Throughout the chronicle, Ayala uses literary and rhetorical devices to argue his thesis that Pedro's political fate was the consequence of unjust actions. Dialogue, speeches, and letters—interspersed with narrative and placed in the mouths of the principal actors—develop logically out of the action in a manner that enhances the impression of cause and effect. In only two instances does Ayala use extraneous material without integrating it into the action: in years eleven and twelve he inserts stories about a Dominican and a shepherd who prophesy disaster for Pedro if he does not change his ways.[23] These prophecies are a repetition of Ayala's thesis, but they do not arise out of the action: the prophets appear to inject a note of doom and foreboding, only to disappear into the oblivion from which they came.

The most memorable parts of the chronicle, and those which still arouse the most antagonism, are a half-dozen murder scenes in which suspense and pathos are skilfully combined for emotional effect. The classic example of this is the murder of Pedro's half-brother, Fadrique, master of Santiago.[24]

Ayala builds the suspense by moving the action forward only to delay it, alternating the swift pace of the king's actions with the slow reactions of the other actors. The king's headlong rush into fratricide is interrupted by a maneuver intended to calm Fadrique's suspicions and isolate him from his companions; by a barred door; by the confusion of the chief guardsman over which master is to be arrested; by the hesitation of the other guardsmen in obeying the king's orders; by Fadrique's flight; and finally by his stubborn clinging to life even after he has been beaten. There is a strong similarity between the construction of this scene and that of the last scene, in which Pedro is murdered by Enrique, Fadrique's twin.[25]

In both scenes, there is conflict between brother and brother; the victim is put off guard and separated from his companions; he becomes suspicious because of the behavior of those around him; there is confusion about his identity; and death is administered on the ground, by dagger, after a struggle. Through these parallels, Ayala links Pedro's death to that of Fadrique, minimizing the regicidal character of the final scene and emphasizing fratricidal revenge.

All these devices attest to Ayala's artistry and to the soundness of the classical education he received in Avignon. The speeches and letters he uses liberally in this chronicle are probably the fruit of his observations while translating the many speeches in Livy and in Guido delle Colonne's *Historia Troiana*. The rhetorical device that gives form to the entire work—its overall structure as dramatic tragedy—as well as the careful balancing of parallel scenes, the use of dialogue to heighten suspense, the prophecies of the ghostlike monk and shepherd, the suspense of the murder scenes, and the careful attention to detail in these scenes, bear a strong resemblance to the Senecan tragedy he had seen on stage. There is also a classically humorous flavor to the chapters in which the noble ladies of Toledo, indignant over the king's treatment of the queen, mobilize their husbands in her defense.[26]

Even more significant than his use of classical models is Ayala's skilful use of rhetorical and literary devices to arouse emotional reaction in the reader. This appeal to the will, typical of the humanist writers of Renaissance Italy, is most prominent in the *Crónica del rey don Pedro*. In the later *Crónica del rey don Juan*, Ayala characterizes the reign of Pedro the Cruel as beginning with expectations of peace and stability but degenerating into a series of civil disorders.[27] In contrast, the *Crónica del rey don Pedro* gives the impression that all the political disasters of the latter part of Pedro's reign were the inevitable consequence of the unjust acts committed at the beginning of the reign. Ayala states this thesis twice, once at the beginning of the chronicle and once at the end, but these are simply clarifications or summations, rather than attempts to convince.[28] The emotional truth of the thesis, the implacability for which Ayala is so famous, the impression that the final tragedy is the logical and inevitable result of the first chapters, is achieved through Ayala's use of irony and emphasis on emotion rather than reason.

In the scenes describing the murder of Gutier Ferrández de Toledo, Ayala uses his usual method of changing pace to build suspense, and then he adds an ironic twist to the event by inserting a flashback that repeats an important element of the murder scene:

When they arrived at the lodging of Gutier Ferrández they dismounted there and entered with him into a room, and arrested him, and took him prisoner to the lodging of the master of Santiago. And when they arrived there, Martín López de Córdoba told him that the king had ordered his death: and Gutier Ferrández said: "I have never done anything to deserve death." Then Martín López told him that the king had sent to command that he surrender the alcazar of Molina and the castles which he held in tenancy and that he was to send letters to those who held the said castles so that they would surrender them to whomever the king would send with the letters, which they would bring and present there. And Gutier Ferrández said that it would please him to surrender all the castles which he held from the king: and he then ordered a secretary to write letters for the commanders of the alcazar and castles of Molina. . . . And this done, they made the said Gutier Ferrández enter a chamber, and there they cut off his head. . . . This day, the said Gutier Ferrández being prisoner in the lodging of the master of Santiago, he told the masters of Santiago and Alcántara and Martín López de Córdoba that if it please them he would like to send a letter to the king. And they told him to go ahead, and then he dictated a letter to a secretary which said this, "Lord, I, Gutier Ferrández de Toledo, kiss your hands and take leave of your grace, and go to another Lord even greater than you. And lord, surely your grace knows that my mother and my brothers and I have always been in your service since the day you were born, and we incurred many evils and suffered great fear for the sake of your service in the days when doña Leonor de Guzmán had power in the kingdom. Lord, I have always served you; however, I believe that because of telling you some things which complied with your service you are ordering me killed, which, lord, I believe that you do to satisfy your will: for which God pardon you; for I never deserved it from you. And now, lord, I say to you so close to the point of my death (for this will be my last counsel) that if you do not put up your knife, and if you do not stop doing such killings as this one, you will lose your kingdom, and place your person in danger. And I ask you as a favor to guard yourself, for I speak loyally with you, for in such an hour as this I must say nothing but the truth." And this letter was given to the king, and he was very angry that they had let him write it. . . . And after this the king left Seville and went towards Almazán, and arriving at a village of Atienza which is called Rebollosa, he heard that Gutier Ferrández was dead, and they brought his head to him there, and he was very pleased by it.[29]

In this example, Ayala varies the pace of the action by dwelling on the letters, also using them to develop an ironic contrast between Pedro's performance as king and Gutier Ferrández's as vassal. Pedro condemns Gutier to death and orders him to cooperate in his own destruction by writing to his subordinates. Gutier obeys with alacrity, writing first the demanded letters and then a letter of advice to the king. Aside from its content, this letter by giving advice to the king fulfills Gutier's duty as a vassal; and Pedro's angry reaction is the opposite of what a king's should be.

Irony pervades the chronicle. In the slow-paced year eighteen, for example, Ayala contrasts Pedro's speeches with his behavior and his boasting with the wise Muslim's criticism. The irony stems not only from Pedro's exultation in military victory just when he is on the verge of political disaster but also from the contrast between Muslim respect for Alfonso XI in the first year of the chronicle and the wise Muslim's criticism of Pedro in this last year of his success. As a general rule, Ayala uses parallel construction to draw ironic comparisons; and only through these ironic contrasts does he criticize Pedro. He does not argue political theory, he does not moralize, he does not condemn: he simply draws ironic contrasts. Ayala uses irony to reinforce the theme of the fall of great men—a topos that allowed him to draw on biblical overtones, on the popular *Libro de Alexandre*—with its story of Alexander the Great's fall through *soberbia* (pride) and *cobdicia* (lack of restraint) —and on his own experience in translating Boccaccio's *De Casibus Virorum Illustrium*.[30]

Ayala's use of these classical rhetorical devices for political purposes is unprecedented in Castilian historiography. His predecessor, the anonymous author of the chronicle of Alfonso XI, has no concept of history as a work of art. His chronicle has no dramatic structure: it recounts a series of events strung together by chronological proximity. There are no speeches or letters to focus issues or dramatize conflict—no irony, no innuendo, no change of pace to highlight critical moments. The artistic differences between the two works are startling when we compare the murders of Garcilaso de la Vega father (d. 1326) and son (d. 1351). The murder of Garcilaso the elder has all the makings of a great dramatic scene, since the victim was killed while attending mass. But the anonymous chronicler dispenses with it in two sentences:

> And Garcilaso was hearing mass in the monastery of San Francisco, with the caballeros and escuderos who had come with him from the king's household and many eminent people of the town; and they entered the monastery and there inside the church they killed Garcilaso, and Arias Pérez de Quiñones, and one of Garcilaso's sons, and most of the caballeros and escuderos who had come there with him, so that twenty-two infanzones and hidalgos died there with him. And the few who remained alive escaped disguised in monks' habits so that they could not be recognized. And now the history leaves this subject.[31]

In comparison with this colorless catalog of events, Ayala's description of the murder of Garcilaso the younger is a dramatic scene worthy of Seneca himself. The victim makes a stage entrance, engages in dialogue with Pedro, and states his defense to the court in a speech charged with piety, loyalty, and tenderness. Garcilaso asks for a priest to hear his confession, and the priest later reports that he searched Garcilaso and found no weapon. Garcilaso's brutal murder before the very eyes of the court is then described in bloody detail. His body is thrown into the street for the festival bulls to trample and then left in a field outside the city wall.[32] Ayala uses such rhetorical devices as pacing, dialogue, and innuendo to build suspense and empathy, arousing pity and fear in his audience. His anonymous predecessor, working with inherently more dramatic material but lacking rhetorical skill and political motive, was satisfied with a bland recitation of facts.

Literary critics have long recognized Ayala's skill in character assassination through the accumulation of details. His ability to make Pedro look bad without ever explicitly stating this judgment is the basis of his reputation for "sinuosity." More important are the rhetorical devices Ayala uses to make this accumulation of details seem convincing and those he uses to excuse his own behavior. His objective as a propagandist, after all, was principally to excuse his own desertion of Pedro rather than to condemn Pedro himself. Ayala's principal achievement is his success in placing his narrative in a political context that makes his own actions look normal and Pedro's actions abnormal. Ayala had to deal with four major problems in writing his apology: he had to explain why he deserted the legitimate king Pedro; he had to explain why he loyally served the same king for sixteen years; he had to explain why he gave the oath of loyalty to the illegitimate pretender, Enrique de Trastámara; and he had to convince his intended audience that it was in their interest to accept his interpretation of the Trastámara revolution.

The context Ayala presents is one of deudo—the bond of family, friendship, and vassalage that binds men together and obligates them to one another. For Ayala, deudo was the cement that bound society into a cohesive and peaceful state. Without it, there would be a state of predatory violence, and each man would be left to fend for himself. Although deudo within a nuclear family was legally imposed, the deudo that bound friend to friend and king to vassal had to be initiated by the persons involved and required a persistent mending of the relationship. Deudo was built upon love, loyalty, and gratitude—fragile motives easily destroyed by a single act of cruelty, insult, or aggression. Without the assurance of deudo, a man would feel isolated, vulnerable, alone in the world.

For Ayala, the most pressing problem in writing his history of the reign of Pedro was explaining what drove him to break the oath of fealty to Pedro—to rupture the bond of deudo that gave him his status as a vasallo del rey. The enormity of Ayala's act was such that he could offer only one excuse—that in breaking with Pedro he was honoring a higher obligation to familial deudo. Ayala does not pretend that his desertion was not serious. Instead he argues that the alternative was even more serious—to fail in his deudo to his family. Throughout the chronicle, Ayala shapes the material to show that his choice was not between right and wrong but between the lesser of two evils.

A second problem Ayala faced was explaining why he waited sixteen years—from Pedro's accession in 1350 to his desertion of Burgos in 1366—to break his oath. Ayala had to explain his loyalty as well as his disloyalty. If Pedro was a tyrant, or had no right to the throne, or did not fulfill the obligations of kingship, Ayala should not have waited sixteen years to do his duty as a citizen and oppose him. Throughout the chronicle, Ayala avoids attacking Pedro's right to the throne or his fulfillment of the office. He shows Pedro as an excellent military leader, an astute policymaker in foreign affairs, and a frugal manager of the kingdom's fiscal affairs. Ayala, in fact, so insists upon Pedro's abilities in most aspects of government that he has provided his detractors with the evidence used to accuse him of defaming the king's character. Writers who call Pedro a good king insist upon referring to him as Pedro the Just, using material from Ayala's chronicle to support their position.

Ayala's third major problem was accounting for his oath of loyalty to Enrique de Trastámara, a man who could never legally have inherited the throne. Enrique was illegitimate and not even the eldest brother. Ayala could neither espouse Enrique as a superior claimant by right of inheritance nor argue that Enrique was morally superior or politically or militarily more competent. On the basis of the evidence presented in his chronicle, Ayala did not think Enrique was much better than Pedro, if he was any better at all. Again, Ayala's solution was to show that the choice between Enrique and Pedro was a choice between the lesser of two evils, not between right and wrong.

Ayala had to take into account one final consideration in excusing his own behavior—the audience to whom he addressed his apology. They were, in fact, his own descendants, the people who benefited most from Enrique de Trastámara's usurpation of the throne and Ayala's desertion of Pedro. In a sense, Ayala designed his tract to solidify his family's loyalties to the Trastámara dynasty. In order to do this, he tried to show that the very survival of the family had been at stake in the conflict between Pedro and Enrique. In the most horrifying and dramatic moments in the narrative, Pedro's murder victims are Ayala's relatives. Although this aspect of the chronicle is largely lost on modern readers who do not have a grasp of the family's genealogy, it must have been obvious to Ayala's descendants. Just in case they missed the point, Ayala spelled it out for them. At the end of the scene in which Pedro kills Fadrique, Ayala adds the following information:

> After this was done, the king sat down to eat there near where the master lay dead. This master don Fadrique left the following children:

70

count Pedro, whose son is count Fadrique, son-in-law of the admiral Diego Hurtado [de Mendoza]; and Alfonso Enríquez, the one who died; and Alfonso Enríquez, admiral of Castile, son-in-law of Pedro González de Mendoza; and Leonor, wife of Diego Gómez, mother of Constanza wife of Carlos de Arellano, and of Diego Pérez son-in-law of Diego López de Stúñiga, and of Fernán Sánchez Sarmiento Dean, and of the wife of Pero Pérez de Ayala.[33]

In no case does Ayala explicitly state these political theses. They are presented by innuendo through rhetorical devices repeated and amplified throughout the chronicle. On a political level, as a history of conflict between the king and his subjects, Ayala's chronicle offers no answers. Ayala makes no rational or theoretical case against Pedro to justify the desertion after Burgos or the regicide. There is no political theory of monarchy, no Christian theology, no universal standard of morality to guide the reader in judging the king and his vassals. It is on another level, that of moral conflict within each vassal who struggled to choose between equally compelling values—loyalty and survival—that the chronicler offers his apology. In 1366, Ayala himself chose survival rather than loyalty, but the decision involved years of doubt and questioning. When he wrote the chronicle thirty years later, he was most interested in the events of the reign of Pedro that led the king's vassals to this decision. It is the loyal vassals, rather than the king himself, who become deserters and regicides and undergo historical change. Pedro's behavior and attitudes remain the same, only becoming more extreme throughout the chronicle; but the behavior and attitudes of his subjects gradually reverse themselves until those most loyal in the first chapters finally support the ultimate act of disloyalty—regicide—in the last.

Ayala is at his best when he traces the excruciatingly slow development of this reversal. Throughout the chronicle, and with increasing frequency as events pile up near the end, he describes the fear and doubts that assailed the knights as the king's choice of murder victims became more unpredictable. Ayala does this with a few short sentences at the ends of murder scenes: "And some other knights of Toledo did not want to be in the plot, and remained loyal to the king. And the plot was very dangerous, as it later became clear."[34] The king "ordered that his aunt, queen Leonor of Aragon, be killed . . . and it was done . . . and all those who loved the service of the king were very grieved by this."[35] Pedro murdered his two teenage half-brothers, "and it saddened many of those who loved the king's service that they should die this way, for they were innocent and never harmed the king."[36] Pedro captured don Pero Núñez de Guzmán and "had him killed very cruelly in Seville, and the manner of his death was too ugly and cruel to describe, and those who truly loved the king's service were very grieved by it and they were not pleased by such acts."[37] After Pedro exiled the archbishop of Toledo, "all those who were there in Toledo held this to be a very great insult, although they did not dare to say a single thing, so great was the fear that they had of the king."[38] Finally, when Pedro abandoned the city of Burgos in 1366, Ayala explains that "very few of the knights and squires of Castile went with him, while all the others remained in Burgos, for they did not like him, rather they were pleased by all of this for there were some whose relatives he had killed and they were always afraid of him."[39]

If Ayala had wanted to defend his desertion of Pedro by showing that Pedro was a bad king, Pedro's desertion of Burgos was the perfect incident on which to build such a case. But Ayala does not attempt to justify his actions on a political or moral basis; he makes them understandable as acts of passion: the desertion was motivated by fear and the regicide by vengeance. The king killed the relatives of some of his vassals, and they were afraid of him. This action based on fear is convincing because the entire chronicle has been constructed to support it. Ayala dwells on the murders and shapes them into dramatic scenes because they were crucial incidents in alienating the vassals from the king by increasing their fear of him.

The regicide presented a different rhetorical problem, since Ayala did not participate in it and since it was committed after he had given his loyalty to Enrique. By constructing the regicide to echo the death of Fadrique, Ayala points out the personal nature of the conflict between Pedro and Enrique and implies that Enrique's vassals had nothing to fear from him. As revenge for Pedro's murder of his twin, Enrique's murder of Pedro seems understandable. But Ayala does not justify its regicidal aspect in any way; he detaches himself from the scene by depersonalizing his account of its climactic moments. In all the other murder scenes, Ayala introduces dialogue with the words, "he said"; but in the final moments of the regicide he uses the more distant "they say that he said." By placing a third person between himself and the action, Ayala dissociates himself from the event and minimizes the reader's involvement.

Using all these devices—dramatic structure, ironic comparison, appeal to the emotions—Ayala wrote a tightly constructed literary masterpiece which also serves as an apology for his own actions. Strong as their emotional impact is upon the modern reader, these devices must have affected Ayala's fifteenth-century descendants even more strongly because Ayala used still another device to impress his ideas upon them. He always speaks of himself in the third person, and he speaks of his relatives without mentioning their relationship to him. He never mentions that Gutier Ferrández was his brother-in-law twice over, but this must have been as obvious to his descendants as the fact that except for Fadrique and Pedro the victims in the murder scenes Ayala described in detail were his own relatives. We can imagine Fernán Pérez de Guzmán or the marquis of Santillana reacting to the king's murder of Díaz Gutiérrez, Ayala's uncle;[40] or of Gutier Ferrández, Guzmán's uncle; or of Garcilaso de la Vega, Santillana's great-grandfather.[41] Ayala relies heavily on the reader's knowledge of family relationships to increase the force of his thesis. Only with some awareness of these relationships can we understand the direct connection between Gutier Ferrández's warning to Pedro that "if you do not stop doing such killings as this one, you will lose your kingdom, and place your person in danger," and Ayala's laconic statement that "there were some whose relatives he had killed and they were always afraid of him."

Ayala's use of the forms of dramatic tragedy was peculiar to his *Crónica del rey don Pedro*. His chronicles of kings Enrique II, Juan I, and Enrique III are written in the more usual narrative form, with little manipulation of the material into dramatic climaxes and without the irony that pervades the chronicle of Pedro. In all four of the chronicles, however, Ayala's critical approach to the sources of historical information and his concern with historical change remain consistent. For his few excursions into history before his own lifetime, Ayala relied on "what the ancient Chronicle tells us, and what is found in other ancient books which are authentic, and even what has survived by memory from generation to generation until today."[42] In writing the history of his own lifetime, he depended on his own observation and on reliable eyewitness accounts, which he claims to use with the greatest caution.[43] His skepticism toward even the most venerable historical works and his belief in the superiority of eyewitness accounts seem to have been taken directly from Guido delle Colonne's prologue to *Historia Troiana*.[44] Citation of sources is a common feature of Castilian chronicles since the thirteenth century, but Ayala's critical approach to the sources for ancient history and his insistence on reliable eyewitness accounts for contemporary history are important innovations.

Ayala's attitudes toward the Castilian past and toward historical change were also innovations; they seem to have been shaped as much by his methods as by the political circumstances in which he wrote. His attitude toward the Visigothic period, for example, stands in sharp contrast to the attitudes of earlier chroniclers, who filled page after page with fabricated genealogies of Visigothic rulers and incredible stories of their reigns. Ayala dismisses the Visigothic period, apparently because he could not find reliable sources for it,[45] and he ridicules what was known of the Visigoths in an ironic summary of their history: "And you must know that from the first Gothic king in Spain who was a Christian, who was called Atanarico, until the king don Rodrigo, who was the last king of the Goths, there were thirty-five kings."[46] The chroniclers working under Alfonso X lamented the lack of written accounts for the pre-Roman period but accepted mythologies like Ovid's as reliable historical accounts.[47] Instead of relying on these, Ayala used Roman historians as sources for the Roman period and declined to write about pre-Roman Spain or the Visigoths. He did not attribute the origins of any Spanish institutions to the Visigothic period: he traced words, taxes, and calendars to the Roman period and political, military, and legal institutions to the Reconquest.[48] For Ayala, Spanish history began with the Romans; the Visigothic period, with its lack of written records, was a dark age; and the period of the Reconquest was the formative period for most Castilian institutions—institutions shaped by the frontier society that still existed in Ayala's lifetime.

Ayala was not familiar with the historical writing of the Italian Renaissance, but he developed a historical perspective parallel to that of the Italian humanists. The centuries separating the Roman Empire from the fourteenth century did not link the present with the ancient past; they were a gulf separating Spain from its classical past.

Ayala also departed from the norm of earlier Castilian chronicles by urging institutional changes as a response to changing religious, political, and military conditions. In the *Crónica del rey don Juan I*, he urges the king to change the method of dealing with treasonable members of the royal family, describing how French kings called legists from the university to hear both sides of such a case and suggesting that Juan also call together a panel of letrados to hear the case of his half-brother, count Alfonso.[49] Ayala seems to be suggesting that Castilian justice was primitive compared to French justice and his speech concerning the incident of count Alfonso is typical of many urging kings to measure the benefits of an outmoded traditional institution against those possible under a new institution established through the king's initiative. It is significant that Ayala is not responding to abuses: he suggests that the need for change arises not because of a falling-away from an ideal state but because old solutions become anachronistic in a society continually changing, and even improving.

This Renaissance assumption that institutions must be judged in their historical context is particularly striking in the three digressions in year two of the *Crónica del rey don Pedro*. In all three, Ayala is writing institutional history; and he describes the historical education of these institutions. In the treatise on calendars, he describes the origins of each dating system used in Castile; and although he is obviously proud that the Castilians have continued to use the era of Caesar in dating their official documents, he approves of the king's decision to discard this usage because it was meaningful only in the context of the Roman Empire.

This treatment is consistent with his handling of political history— devoid of attempts to explain political action in terms of theory or of any other system of rational explanation. In the *Crónica del rey don Pedro*, Ayala frequently presents whole letters and speeches arguing political theory; but these are presented in pairs, so that an argument that Pedro has become a tyrant, for example, is inevitably followed by a parallel argument that Pedro is king by all legal standards.[50] Since every logical argument is nullified by an equally logical counterargument, all theories of political behavior are implicitly discredited as useful explanations of the course of events. Although Ayala offers an explanation of political behavior and historical causation, it appears only in his assumption that actions can best be judged by their consequences. Gutier Ferrández's letter to Pedro—the only letter Ayala allows to stand unchallenged by a counterargument—specifically argues that Pedro should change his behavior because it will lead to disaster. In the *Crónica del rey don Juan*, he warns the king against unjust executions by citing the evil consequences they have produced in the past.[51]

Much of the implacability of Ayala's chronicles arises from his assumption that the consequences of political actions are predictable because human behavior is predictable. In Ayala's view, all people, whether kings or vassals, want to behave in a loyal and dignified manner but consistently misinterpret other people's behavior and miscalculate the effects of their own words and actions, thus beginning to act out of fear and a desire for vengeance. Vengeance and fear are the only motives he suggests for Pedro's behavior, the only explanations he offers for the regicide and desertion. Ayala does not condemn action based on such emotional motives. In fact, the whole purpose of the *Crónica del rey don Pedro* is to show that the Enriquista party's fear and Enrique's desire for ven-

geance were based on a realistic and correct assessment of Pedro's behavior. Ordinary emotions, indeed, appear to be virtues in Ayala's work.
The most damning indictments of Pedro, for example, are scenes in
which he fails to display any emotion at all—calmly eating a meal in
the presence of his brother's body—or his response is perverted—receiving Gutier Ferrández's letter with anger and his head with pleasure.
In this, as in every aspect of his work, Ayala's approach to the writing of
history is that of a Renaissance humanist: he uses a classical rhetorical
device, *amplificatio*,[52] to present his case; he avoids explanations based on
logic, theory, or morality, in favor of explanations based on historical
context and emotional motivation. In Florence, only Francesco Guicciardini—that most Renaissance of all Italian historians—matched Ayala's
freedom from the traditional schematizations of history and his pene-
trating psychological analyses. In Castile, Ayala's achievement was
unique: none of his successors achieved his psychological insight or his
rhetorical genius. Yet Ayala's descendants absorbed his most important
innovations—his historical perspective, his love of the classics, his distrust of theoretical systems of thought and his apologia for the family's
political past. His intellectual inheritance shaped the caballero renaissance in the fifteenth century.

IV

The Mendoza in the
Fifteenth-Century Renaissance

Ayala's chronicles became a book of martyrs for the descendants of the Enriquista captains who fought at Nájera. In his history, they found the story of their ancestors' sacrifices for the Trastámara dynasty; and bound together by the past, as well as their own success, they formed the powerful, self-conscious new nobility of the fifteenth century. Their glorious past became inextricably bound up with Ayala's Renaissance attitudes and humanist rhetoric. As a result, the Castilian nobles—military aristocrats in a monarchical, agrarian society—became the principal spokesmen of the Renaissance in Castile. The most innovative features of the Italian Renaissance—the historical approach, the admiration for the ancient Romans, the optimism about human will with its concomitant reliance upon rhetoric, the pessimism about the capabilities of the human intellect with its concomitant rejection of scholasticism—also came to be identified most closely with the caballeros. The Mendoza family in Guadalajara became the focal point of this Renaissance. First associated with the Mendoza in Ayala's chronicles, it was refined and handed on from generation to generation through a system of education centered on the family household. The Renaissance reached its fullest development in the mid-fifteenth century when the Mendoza as patrons and artists dominated Castilian cultural life to the same degree they dominated its political life.

Several sequences occur so consistently in the lives of the Mendoza that they may be considered the formative factors in their intellectual and religious attitudes. There appears to have been a single curriculum of primary education common to all educated caballeros. From the age

77

of about five until puberty, children were taught reading, writing, arithmetic, geometry, and Latin. The texts for these subjects included versions of Aesop's *Fables*, Papias's Latin vocabulary, and Latin grammars by Juan de Pastrana and Alejandro de Villadedios. These texts would hardly meet the approval of a modern classics teacher, and they were bitterly attacked by professional humanists like Antonio de Nebrija and Luis Vives, for they were minor works chosen for their religious and moral lessons rather than their style.[1] Although Latin was valued highly, it was the last subject introduced into a student's primary curriculum; and since this phase of a caballero's education ended at the age of twelve or fourteen, Latin instruction on the primary level probably did not last more than three or four years, even under optimal conditions. For most educated caballeros, these few years of rather mediocre primary education were their last formal instruction in writing and in Latin.

After a primary education in his parents' household, a boy was sent to the household of a close relative whose position in a center of power offered the boy the greatest exposure to the practice of statecraft and diplomacy and the most effective patronage for his intended career. Education in a noble patron's household concentrated on the martial arts and public administration taught through informal methods rather than lectures or reading. In the household of his patron, a young man accustomed his body to armor and physical hardships and learned to handle arms, to hunt, to speak persuasively, to arbitrate disputes, to supervise the building of fortifications, to serve at table, and to sing. He learned these skills by practicing and by following the example of his patron. He acquired the theoretical knowledge necessary for his profession, but he probably saw it as the wisdom of the patron rather than as part of a systematic body of theory.

At first sight, the noble household as a system of humanist education looks like all weakness and no strengths. Students were chosen for their relationship to the patron rather than any intellectual ability; they did no systematic reading or writing and forgot what Latin they had learned; and the patron himself might be completely uninterested in matters intellectual but still considered a master of the profession.

But the students in the aristocratic household did learn to compose an important type of literature—lyric poetry—and they were trained in rhetoric—the skill most highly prized by the Italian humanists. Poetry, in the form of song, was one of the martial arts—a favorite form of relaxation in military encampments. Along with jousting, it was the principal entertainment of the noble court. When the young marquis of

Santillana left the household of the Aragonese crown prince, Alfonso the Magnanimous, at the age of eighteen, he received the tools of the caballero profession as a parting gift: a German crossbow, a shield covered in silk, an ax, a double-edged sword, and a harp.[2]

The highest attainment of Castilian political life was to achieve a position in the consejo del rey, which entitled a man to speak directly to the king without intermediaries, either through letters or through attendance at the consejo real, and so to participate in the debates through which royal policy was formulated. To be an effective counselor to the king, the caballero needed oratorical and persuasive eloquence; and careful attention was paid to the development of rhetorical skills, from the basic elements of volume and quality of the voice, clarity of pronunciation, pace, and gestures to the more difficult problems of content and ordering of the material. Some of the rhetorical works of Quintillian and Cicero were available in fifteenth-century Castile; and a sophisticated treatise on rhetorical theory emphasizing the need to shape the style to the audience was written by a Spaniard, Martin of Córdoba, probably in Avignon about 1374.[3] Although this work was known in Castile by the end of the fourteenth century, the texts used to teach rhetoric continued to be the Gramática of Pedro Elías and the Graecismus of Evrard de Béthune. In an important innovation, noble patrons began to order translations of speeches from the Latin classics that could serve as models for the young caballeros being trained in their households. Here, too, students learned more from example than from theory.

Gómez Manrique's education was probably typical for a caballero of a distinguished family. He spent his teenage years in the household of his much older brother, Rodrigo Manrique, master of Santiago. Rodrigo was one of the great military figures of the day—his son, Jorge Manrique, immortalized his father's military fame in the Coplas por la muerte de su padre—and Gómez gives full credit to his brother for the best military training possible. The fact that Rodrigo educated both Gómez and Jorge—two of the great warrior-poets of the century—casts credit on his household as an institution of military education. In his later years, Gómez like many caballeros turned to grave moral and political questions that required forms other than lyric poetry; and he apologizes that his education did not prepare him for a career in letters. He is too modest, of course: his many references to Livy reflect an intimate and profound knowledge of the first three books, which had been translated by Ayala.[4] As adults, both Gómez Manrique and Santillana felt apologetic about their lack of expertise in Latin, yet both were able not only to read the classics in translation (or in Latin with the help of a translation) but also to imitate and build upon the classics in their own creative works.

In this respect, the Mendoza were luckier than most nobles because they were educated in households with intellectual resources, where the patrons were bibliophiles and sponsors of translations, as well as del consejo del rey. Ayala was educated in the household of his great-uncle, Pedro Gómez Barroso; Guzmán in the household of his uncle, Ayala; Santillana in the households of his great-uncle, Gutierre de Toledo, archdeacon of Guadalajara, and of Alfonso the Magnanimous; and Santillana's sons and grandsons in his own household in Guadalajara.

After a young man spent several years in his patron's household, he obtained public office through the efforts of his patron. A caballero's life after his assumption of civic responsibility alternated between the extremes of intense activity as a warrior, politician, and administrator and detachment from public life while in prison, captivity, banishment, or retirement. During the periods of public activity, a caballero was repeatedly faced with conflicts that forced him to choose between loyalty to family and loyalty to monarch or between rival claimants to the throne. During the periods of respite, he often reflected upon the strains and conflicts he endured in his career and sought to explain his actions. Such periods of respite often mark a shift in the caballero's literary interests from poetry largely concerned with sentiment and piety to prose characterized by introspection, polemics, and didactics. Among men who lived to be very old, the shift to polemical prose is marked, particularly in cases where a writer's retirement was involuntary.

The two most important factors in the formation of the Mendoza were their education as caballeros in a vernacular and secular tradition and their involvement in public affairs. The caballero education prepared them to take advantage of both Castilian intellectual traditions and Renaissance humanism, for the distinguishing characteristics of Castilian intellectual life in the Middle Ages were the early use of the vernacular and the absence of scholasticism. Throughout the peninsula—in Aragon, Portugal, and Castile—the vernaculars became the official languages of administration and judiciary in the thirteenth century.[5] In Castile, Fernando III (1230–1252) declared Castilian the official language of the royal chancery and decreed that all public documents and laws be redacted in Castilian. His son, Alfonso X el Sabio, ordered that in judicial decisions the usage of Toledo was to prevail in cases of dubious or disputed meanings. The importance of this shift lay in its effect on later generations of public administrators, who would not need Latin in order to administer justice. Deliberations in the royal council, legal proceedings in courts of first and last instance, communications between the crown and its subjects were all in the vernacular. Latin was limited to the church, the universities, and the crown's correspondence with foreign countries. Most educated Castilians, especially those engaged in the administration of the res publica, continued to have at least a passive knowledge of Latin, but Latin was not necessary for the conduct of the secular affairs of the kingdom.

The official action adopting Castilian in place of Latin did not mark a great transformation from Latin to vernacular culture: Castile had not produced an indigenous tradition of Latin scholarship since the Arab invasion in the eighth century. The great Latin works of Castile in the twelfth and thirteenth centuries were written by Castilians educated outside Spain, and their example did not inspire any flourishing of Latin letters in the later Middle Ages. Caballeros, as well as clergy and letrados, placed a high value on Latin as a sign of erudition and means of knowing the classics firsthand. For all practical purposes, however, Latin was not part of Castilian secular culture; and the general ignorance of Latin did not cut Castilians off from an indigenous intellectual tradition. Although this Castilian insistence upon the vernacular probably had much to do with the vigor and elegance of the vernacular in the fourteenth and fifteenth centuries—a language modern readers still read with relative ease—it also created obstacles to Castilian absorption of medieval Latin literature written in other countries.

The caballeros participated in some of the most bewildering political events of Castilian history, and it is no coincidence that the greatest burst of literary activity among them occurred during the period of the early Trastámara. Caballero attitudes were the product of and response to the political and religious conflicts of the early fifteenth century. The prose works of the caballeros provide a record of the anxieties and doubts, the hope and pessimism they felt as they tried to balance and reconcile their commitments to family and monarch, to king and pretender, to pope and antipope.

In trying to find a way through the thicket of moral dilemmas surrounding them, the caballeros did not resort to the solutions offered by medieval scholasticism. Cut off from scholastic arguments in favor of monarchy by their own commitment to a dynasty illegitimate by any standard of medieval political theory, ignorant of scholastic methodology, and generally prejudiced against it because of its failures during their own lifetimes, they welcomed the alternative offered by the ethical and religious lessons the humanists were drawing from the classics. But the very caballeros most receptive to humanist attitudes and assumptions because they lacked the scholastic discipline also lacked fluency in Latin. This defect in their education—as well as their patriotic preference for Seneca—cut them off from the Ciceronian style popular among Italian humanists. The caballeros' skill in composing poetry and their rhetorical experience in the consejo real nevertheless gave them an unequalled mastery of imagery and eloquence in Castilian. They thus acquired orally and in the vernacular the rhetorical skills that characterized Italian humanists writing in Latin. One consequence of this paradox is that in fifteenth-century Castile humanist ideas were expressed almost exclusively in the vernacular by a military aristocracy responding to the problems of public life.

Although their inspiration and audience were Castilian, the Mendoza freely borrowed literary and rhetorical devices from their French and Italian contemporaries. Castilians came into contact with the literature of other countries almost exclusively at the international papal court, first in Avignon and then at the councils. As the means whereby the Mendoza discovered the classics, the papal court had its deepest intellectual influence upon Castile. We have seen that Pedro López de Ayala was educated in Avignon while Petrarch and his fellow humanists were active there. During Ayala's career in Castile, he maintained close contact with Avignon through his cousin, the second cardinal Pedro Gómez Barroso, and through the Aragonese cardinal and future antipope, Pedro de Luna. An early and important ally of Enrique de Trastámara, Luna had persuaded Juan I of Castile to support the Avignon papacy.[6]

During Ayala's embassy to Avignon (1394–1395), he worked with Juan Fernández de Heredia (c. 1310–1396), grand master of Rhodes in the Order of St. John, who negotiated Aragonese support for Enrique de Trastámara.[7] After the Catalan companies conquered and occupied the duchy of Athens early in the fourteenth century, the Aragonese monarchs began collecting Greek manuscripts, especially histories of the eastern Mediterranean since classical times. While leading an expedition against the Morea, Heredia became interested in the history of the area and began buying manuscripts and commissioning their translation from Greek into Latin. When he returned to Avignon, he maintained a team of scholars in his household to edit, transcribe, and translate his collection of Greek, Latin, and vernacular histories. Heredia used these sources to write his own histories of Aragon and its possessions in the eastern Mediterranean. His library was an important source of books and translations for the entire peninsula in the early part of the century. The Aragonese kings exchanged manuscripts—and hunting dogs—with him;[8] and king Martin, by special agreement with the Order of St. John, inherited several historical works from his estate that were eventually acquired by the marquis of Santillana. Even Renaissance Florence benefited from Heredia's book collecting: the first copy of Plutarch's *Lives* there was copied from the translation Heredia commissioned while in the eastern Mediterranean—perhaps the copy that the Florentine chancellor, Coluccio Salutati, requested from him in a series of flattering letters.[9]

The Mendoza enthusiastically embraced the attitudes of the humanists at Avignon and followed the Italians' lead in rediscovering the glory of ancient Rome; but as Castilians, they thought of it as the product of all the Roman Empire, not just of Italy. For the Mendoza, the rediscovery of Rome meant the rediscovery of their own Roman past; and they proceeded to become amateur etymologists—reading inscriptions, tracing Castilian placenames to their Latin origins, and convincing themselves that Castilian was the language most purely descended from Latin. They were proud of the "Spanish" Romans, and the works of Seneca, Lucan, and Quintillian were among the first classics translated into Castilian. They modeled their prose on that of Seneca, actively cultivated stoic philosophy, and without exception wrote exclusively in Castilian.

In their eagerness to exalt the Spanish contribution to the classics, the Mendoza disregarded the two most common features of the Renaissance in Italy—the Ciceronian model and the use of Latin. But far from indicating a rejection of the Renaissance, their use of the vernacular is evidence of their total absorption of one of the crucial assumptions of the Renaissance—that they were the legitimate heirs of the ancient Romans by virtue of both Spain's historical membership in the Roman Empire and their own artistic and intellectual tastes. Gómez Manrique argued that it was appropriate for caballeros to devote themselves to moderate study of Roman histories in order to benefit from the theory behind their practice of war and government—citing the examples of Alexander the Great, Julius Caesar, Quintus Fabius, and the marquis of Santillana—for it would be just as shameful for a caballero to ask a letrado how he ought to respond to or make a request or how to organize a campaign or invest a fortress as for one silversmith to ask another how to burnish a plate.[10] Using the Romans as a model placed their own intellectual and stylistic achievements in a historical perspective that considered the Middle Ages irrelevant and looked to the ancient world for guidance.

All these characteristics of the Spanish Renaissance are evident in the historical works of the two most innovative prose authors of the period, Fernán Pérez de Guzmán (1377?–1460?) and the marquis of Santillana (1398–1458). Much of their work combines esthetics with politics and private pleasure with public propaganda. Writing during periods of either harsh captivity or retirement, Pedro López de Ayala claimed that reading and writing were as necessary to the well-being of the soul as physical exercise to that of the body.[11] Guzmán, in exile on his estate at Batres, complained that he was cut off from all enlightened and excellent works and forced to live among rustics and laborers; but he continued to read, write, and translate and consoled himself as best he could by corresponding with other writers and translators.[12] Santillana claimed that the classics offered a singularly effective antidote to the vexations and travail of Castilian political life.[13]

These explicit statements, as well as the sheer volume of these men's work, indicate the importance of literary activity to them as a source of consolation and pleasure. It is even more significant that they used those same literary talents to explain and justify their political careers to the public and to future generations. In defending their political actions and attacking those of their opponents, Guzmán and Santillana echoed their uncle, Ayala, in using the classical and rhetorical devices of Renaissance humanism.

Guzmán traveled to Avignon with Ayala in 1394–1395; and he first appears in the chronicles as a participant in the incident at Tordesillas in 1420 when he joined the alliance of his cousins, Santillana, Alba, Velasco, and Gutierre de Toledo. He acted as a negotiator between the infante Enrique and Juan II of Castile, and the chronicles depict him performing heroic deeds in the wars against the Muslims. Guzmán never succeeded in adding to his inherited estate, acquiring public office, or building a private army. As a result of his opposition to don Alvaro de Luna, he was imprisoned on charges of treason in 1431 along with his allies, Alba, Velasco, and Gutierre de Toledo. After their release, the rest of the allies returned to their positions of power; but Guzmán retired to his estate at Batres—whether voluntarily or not we do not know—where he collected a library, wrote poetry, exchanged books and letters with other erudites, commissioned the first Castilian translations of some of Seneca's epistles, translated Giovanni Colonna's *Mare Historiarum*, and wrote his prose masterpiece, *Generaciones y semblanzas*.[14]

In *Generaciones y semblanzas*, Guzmán displays many of Ayala's historical methods and attitudes, but he made important innovations by casting his history in the form of biographical sketches and including a prologue, considered to be the first Castilian treatise on the nature of history and duties of the historian. Generaciones consists of thirty-four biographies of kings, knights, prelates, and courtiers active during the reigns of Enrique III and Juan II and personally known to Guzmán. The material anticipates the pattern used a generation later by the Florentine biographer, Vespasiano da Bisticci: each sketch includes the subject's genealogy; his appearance, manners, and habits; his deeds and fortune; his virtues and vices; and his age at death.[15] Guzmán often departs from this pattern to puzzle over contradictions in character, trace the origins of a war with Portugal, castigate weak rulers and praise strong ones, urge the writing of histories, describe (with a touch of envy) the good fortune of an otherwise undistinguished man, defend the faith and nobility of conversos, lament the condition of Castile, and narrate the history of the conflicts in which he had been involved—the struggle to limit the power of don Alvaro de Luna and the wars between Juan II and the infantes of Aragon.

These digressions are not the work of an absent-minded or undisciplined amateur. Guzmán inserts them knowing that they depart from his stated form but justifies them on the grounds that they are "necessary and the material requires them." He often makes the transition from a long digression back to the biography with the words, "returning to the subject."[16] Extracted from the framework of the biographies, these digressions comprise a collection of essays revealing Guzmán's doubts, questions, and opinions on some of the most controversial subjects of his day. On political matters, for example, he reveals his loyalty to his relatives, especially the Ayala–Mendoza–Stúñiga alliance that triumphed in the regency struggles of Enrique III's minority; his partiality for Fernando de Antequera and the infante Enrique; and his hostility toward Juan II and don Alvaro de Luna. These opinions, and the political activity stemming from them, were the "treason" for which Guzmán was imprisoned. He acknowledges that writing a history of the reign of Juan II from this point of view was dangerous, but he was determined that posterity should know the truth and that the events of his lifetime should be preserved in a "simple and truthful manner."[17] In order to write and circulate his apology safely while his enemies were still powerful, Guzmán wrote each biographical sketch only after its subject died. By using the biographical form unprecedented in Castilian historiography, he was able to bury his arguments in the surrounding narrative.

Biography as a literary form was of course nothing new to the fifteenth century, and Guzmán's models are fairly obvious. He may have seen Heredia's copy of Plutarch in Avignon, but his direct model for organizing the material is clearly *De Viris Illustribus* by Petrarch's friend Giovanni Colonna (d. 1343). Another of Guzmán's works, *Mar de Istorias*, is largely a paraphrase of Colonna's *Mare Historiarum*; and there are strong similarities between Colonna and Guzmán in their organization of biographical material into origins, physical and moral characteristics, public career, and written works. Both men used the biographical sketches of Sallust, Tacitus, Valerius Maximus, and the derivative saints' lives of the Middle Ages as models.

There are interesting and significant differences between Guzmán's *Generaciones* and its model. Giovanni Colonna's biographies were impressive works of scholarship—employing careful research to pull together many bits of information scattered through ancient literature. His biography of Seneca, for example, is a superb synthesis of data culled from disparate sources. Despite their fidelity to the facts and to classical forms, Colonna's sketches remain works of scholarship based on second-hand information. Guzmán, with less scholarship but with a personal knowledge of his subjects, transforms the biographical sketch into a work of art by adding impressionistic details that could have come only from first-hand knowledge.

Guzmán's precision is most notable in his description of the rhetorical abilities of his subjects. Colonna's comments on this topic are conscientious but vague: he tells us, for example, that Julius Caesar was eloquent.[18] Guzmán occasionally uses such general terms to describe the speaking manner of a prelate—don Pedro Tenorio, archbishop of Toledo, had a powerful voice that well reflected the courage and strength of his spirit—but rhetoric was too important to be dismissed so lightly when speaking of the caballeros; for to Guzmán and his colleagues rhetoric was second only to arms in the manly arts.

In describing the people he knew most intimately—the royal family and his own relatives in the party formed after Nájera—Guzmán provides vivid details: Fernando de Antequera's speech was wandering and weak; the conversation of Enrique III was harsh; admiral Diego Hurtado de Mendoza argued well and humorously, but he was so bold and outspoken that Enrique III complained of his taking liberties and of his temerity; admiral Alfonso Enríquez was brief and succinct in his arguments but discreet and prudent, and spoke with humor; and Guzmán's ally, Diego López de Stúñiga, was distant in his conversation and a man of few words, but according to those who used to engage in discussion with him, he was a man of good sense who drew profound conclusions in a few words. In describing his formidable enemy, don Alvaro de Luna, Guzmán had to admit that "in the discussions and debates of the palace, which are another, second type of valor, he showed himself to be quite a man."[19]

Guzmán's most notable innovation lies in his use of biography as a vehicle for contemporary history. The inspiration for this innovation was probably Guzmán's complex blending of traditional Castilian attitudes toward the Bible as history with his perception of the Gospels as both history and biography. The Old Testament, which was traditionally regarded as a group of chronicles, is repeatedly cited in the thirteenth and fourteenth centuries as a model in preserving the memory of notable men and events.[20] Guzmán has the same attitude toward the Gospels, which he perceives as biographies. In the prologue to *Generaciones*, he justifies the use of reliable second-hand accounts by citing the Gospels:

> For there never was and never will be events of such magnificence and sanctity as the birth, life, passion and resurrection of Our Lord Saviour Jesus Christ; but of its four historians, two were not present at it but wrote from the accounts of others.[21]

The idea that two of the Gospels were secondhand derives ultimately from a comment by St. Augustine that new Christians must be embraced and supported in the faith by old Christians, just as the two second-hand accounts of the Gospel—Mark and Luke—are embraced and supported by the first-hand accounts—Matthew and John.[22] Guzmán transformed this comment into a dictum by shifting his perspective from the Gospels as standards of religious behavior to the Gospels as historiographical standards. This approach typifies Guzmán's handling of most literary and religious works, no matter how venerable or sacred they might be.

Another innovation Guzmán includes in his prologue is a set of rules for writing good history.[23] He believes that three conditions must be met: first, a historian must be "discreet and wise and have a good rhetoric in order to put the history in a high and beautiful style, for good form honors and enhances the material"; second, the historian should be present at the "principal and notable acts of war and peace and since it would be impossible for him to be at all the events, he should at least be discreet in accepting information only from persons who were present at the events"; and third, "the history should not be published in the lifetime of the king or prince in whose reign or jurisdiction it was ordered, so that the historian may be free to write the truth without fear."

Guzmán claims that he took this prologue from Guido delle Colonne's *Historia Troiana*, and he does seem to have taken his idea about the superiority of eyewitness accounts from Guido's statement that Dares and Dictys were more reliable than Homer because they were eyewitnesses to the events they described.[24] The rest of the prologue is mostly made up of traditions familiar in the classics and in the Castilian chronicles. The final injunction, to delay publication until after the king's death, is the logical extension of his contempt for Pedro del Corral, a contemporary chronicler whom Guzmán accuses of lying to flatter the powerful. It may also reflect his anger at don Alvaro de Luna for taking the official chronicle out of the hands of Alvar García de Santa María and placing it in the hands of a less capable and less honest writer. The prologue, like the biographical sketches themselves, combines Castilian tradition, classical themes, and Guzmán's response to his political situation.

In spite of the severe limitations imposed by his literary form, Guzmán's account of political events is cohesive and clear, in contrast to the other chronicles of the reign of Juan II—confusing jumbles of detail without unifying points of view and without literary distinction. It is the measure of Guzmán's talent that *Generaciones*, justly famous as a work of art, is also the most coherent history of the period. Thirty-four biographical sketches, all overlapping chronologically, are not conducive to a cohesive, sequential presentation of historical events, but Guzmán keeps confusion to a minimum by exercising considerable control over the material.

The major political events of the reign are described and presented in chronological order, and no event appears twice, although each one could logically have appeared in several biographies.

Guzmán also controls the material so as to place his own party in the best possible light. His descriptions of Juan II and of don Alvaro de Luna are superbly executed character assassinations. In his account of Fernando de Antequera, he goes to great lengths to explain away Fernando's cupidity, while he harshly condemns the cupidity of don Alvaro de Luna.[25]

Guzmán's great admiration for Fernando de Antequera is implicit in his observation that although regencies are usually marked by chaos and injustice, during Fernando's Castile enjoyed a government of justice, integrity, and gallantry that gave way to chaos and injustice when the king himself ruled. The only explanation of this paradox could be found in the contrasting characters of Fernando de Antequera and Juan II. Guzmán could never explain to his own satisfaction why the king was so weak or why, after years of meekly submitting to the will of don Alvaro, he suddenly, uncharacteristically, and unjustly turned on the favorite and had him executed.[26] On the other hand, Guzmán did not doubt that Fernando de Antequera had been the ideal ruler because of his fine character: Fernando's integrity led him to treat the infant king with respect and love; his wisdom enabled him to handle the affairs of government with justice; and most important of all, his courage and gallantry as a knight led him to campaign against the Muslims and besiege the city of Antequera. The regent abandoned this war simply because his high sense of duty—in contrast to his inclinations as a Christian knight—forced him to exchange the war against the Muslims for the burdens of the kingdom of Aragon.

Guzmán even tries to justify the one egregious fault in Fernando's character he could not ignore—his greed. Guzmán admits that Fernando's sons, the infantes of Aragon, were able to keep Castile in a state of constant disruption and civil war because their father had given much of the Castilian royal patrimony and income to them while he was regent. Guzmán nevertheless absolves Fernando of the charge of greed by explaining that he acted according to the example set by every other grandee: as his power and privilege mounted, he took for himself as much as he could of honors, offices, and vassals. This weak argument may have seemed convincing to Guzmán because he and his allies regarded society as a free enterprise system in which wealth and power were the material evidence of ability and sagacity. Guzmán also believed that Fernando's ambition was directed toward a worthy goal—the unification of the peninsula under the leadership of the Trastámara dynasty—and that such a worthy end justified the means.[27] Guzmán considered Fernando de Antequera the ideal Christian knight. His acquisition of the crown of Aragon was clear proof of his great character and high ideals, and Guzmán looked back upon the period of the regency as the golden age of the Trastámara dynasty.

In contrast to his idealistic view of the past, his judgments upon the political leaders of the reign of Juan II were harsh and disillusioned:

> These lord princes and the great cavaliers who followed or counseled them I would certainly absolve of disloyalty or tyranny towards the king's person and his crown, believing that they never held him in disrespect. But I would not dare to excuse the mistaken manner and incorrect intent by which I believe they failed in all ways, not only not completing their undertakings, but even losing and suffering in them, [as did] innocent and blameless people because of them. Nor will I ignore nor consent to the opinion which some hold in ignorance

and simplicity, and some preach and publicize in their own favor, saying that they followed the king solely out of their zeal for loyalty and love. I am not saying, nor would it please God for me to say it in injury to such noble and great men, that they were not loyal and very respectful towards the king, but I do say that this loyalty was alternated and mixed with great interests . . . and so I conclude that in regard to the truth, although some were more plausibly and attractively right than others, still the principal intention of each was to profit, to such a degree that one could say that in regard to the pure truth, in this case none of the parties was correct.[28]

These open prejudices have been the most criticized aspect of Guzmán's work. Less obvious—and more effective—is Guzmán's arrangement of the material for his own purposes: political events are distributed among the various biographies to show his allies at their best moments and his enemies at their worst. This device brings order to the material by organizing confusing events around a single point of view. It also shifts *Generaciones* from the level of history to that of apology.

Like his uncle, Ayala, Guzmán rested his apology on the irrational and the personal. He does not argue political principles, structures, or theories. In his view, Castilian society was so particularistic that even *deudo* hardly served to bind men together, and every man acted for his own profit. Guzmán believed that it was natural for a caballero to accumulate property, vassals, and income and that the degree to which he succeeded in self-enrichment indicated the degree to which he would attract more clients and allies and therefore exercise greater influence in national affairs—which in turn increased the chances of accumulating wealth. Although Guzmán saw nothing inherently wrong with such a society, he did believe that an accumulation of wealth and power in the hands of an unscrupulous man could have evil consequences because such a man would use his influence in the royal government for unwise purposes. Rather than criticizing the system, Guzmán criticized individuals like don Alvaro de Luna, who abused it.

Guzmán assumes that the object of political action is to maintain an equilibrium among the various groups who already share sovereignty—each must exercise it responsibly and act as the guarantor of the sovereignty of others. He ascribes failure in fulfilling this political duty to faulty character and faulty relationships. The gist of his attack on Juan II is that the king, because of his indolent nature, failed to assume the responsibilities of his office. Don Alvaro de Luna, to satisfy his cupidity, exceeded the proper bounds of his office and infringed upon the sovereignty of the king. Conversely, the gist of Guzmán's defense of his allies is that they were men of good character who therefore fulfilled their responsibilities and respected the rights of others.

Although both Ayala and Guzmán place great emphasis on personality, they explain the relationship between personality and political behavior in different ways. For Ayala, political behavior seems to be an accumulation of responses between individuals—a never-ending sequence of action, reaction, and counteraction. These responses are usually motivated by emotion—fear, jealousy, or revenge—and always determined by personality. For Guzmán, personality shapes political behavior, but individuals respond not to one another directly but to the way each fulfills his role, which is in turn determined by personality. Guzmán uses this standard as his basis for judging political success, first describing a subject's personality, then recounting his performance, and finally presenting an assessment of the two. Because Guzmán never defines his standards and because he obviously has a different standard for each office, he is usually considered to be lacking all standards except his own advancement.[29] In fact, Guzmán's standards are very high: they are based on a total acceptance of the status quo—an acceptance precluding any attempt to systematize, question, or explain the historical development of political offices. Guzmán's rigid adherence to this nonsystem of standards and his constant juxtaposition of irrational human nature with rational moral expectations makes Generaciones appear both extremely chaotic and completely static.

To a great degree, Generaciones reflects Guzmán's political life. Both Guzmán and Ayala struggled through periods of serious political and moral conflict; but whereas Ayala wrote to defend the resolution of his conflicts, Guzmán was never able to resolve his to his own satisfaction. He and his cousin, Santillana, spent their adult lives torn between the Castilian and Aragonese branches of the Trastámara dynasty. These forty years of unresolved conflict color every aspect of Guzmán's work. His interest in personalities, his alternations between claims and counterclaims, his puzzlement at the inexplicable turns of fortune, his failure to judge the efficacy of any political policies—all seem to arise from the irresolution of his own dilemma. He was never able to give his loyalty wholly to a single political leader; he suffered the disadvantages of a political career without any of the rewards; and he died before the conflicts that consumed most of his energy as a statesman and writer for forty years had been resolved. Achieving no success in his lifetime, Guzmán sought consolation in stoicism and in the hope for favorable judgment from posterity, a judgment he attempted to influence through the *Generaciones.*

As an apologist, Guzmán uses methods and attitudes similar to Ayala's: first-hand or reliable second-hand accounts; a literary form unprecedented as a vehicle for history; a talent for displaying his own party to the best advantage by controlling the form, sequence, and juxtaposition of events; and reliance upon irrational factors, such as character, emotions, and Fortuna, to explain political behavior.

Guzmán's approach to the distant past, however, is strikingly different from Ayala's. When Ayala could not find reliable documents for such periods, he said so and declined to write about them. Guzmán writes about them but states his doubts about the reliability of the sources.[30] He is both more outspoken in his criticism of the sources and more uncritical in his use of them.

Guzmán's attitude toward the distant past reflects his attitude toward contemporary history. He was enamored of the Romans, admiring both their devotion to duty and their integrity; and the one institutional reform he proposes was modeled on a Roman institution. He suggests that the Castilians should detect and punish false historians by creating an office of censor modeled on the Roman censorship.[31] Guzmán never doubts that contemporary Castilians were equal to the ancient Romans as warriors, but he thinks the Romans far superior as historians. His preference for Roman historians was proverbial, and his imitator during the reign of the Catholic Monarchs, Hernando del Pulgar, said: "The noble caballero Fernán Pérez de Guzmán was right when he said that in order for writing to be good and true, the knights should be Castilians and those who describe their deeds should be Romans."[32] He regarded his own age as a period of decline from the Roman past just as he regarded the reign of Juan II as a decline from the golden age of Fernando de Antequera. He has little sense of anachronism and makes no attempt to place Roman institutions in their historical context.

In his approach to literature and to the past, he presents two apparently contradictory attitudes: he uses literature historiographically, and he uses the distant past ahistorically. This paradox is just one source of the many tensions in *Generaciones.* Guzmán's tolerance of paradox and ability to sustain unresolved tension are his most interesting characteristics as a political figure; and his apology, with all its contradictions and ambiguities in form, style, and content, is a uniquely apt reflection of his political career.

In politics and literature, Guzmán was overshadowed by his younger cousin, the marquis of Santillana (1398–1458).[33] Santillana absorbed many of the interests and attitudes of Ayala and Guzmán, but his contact with the literature of other countries came through Florence as well as Avignon. His education, in his grandmother's household in Carrión de los Condes (Burgos), appears to have been unusually provincial. Much of his reading seems to have been in the Galician-Portuguese cancioneros and in even more parochial traditions, such as the Proverbs of Sem Tob de Carrión and popular poetry.

His interest in the classics and in Florentine letters was awakened in 1414 when, at the age of sixteen, he participated in the poetry readings at the coronation of Fernando de Antequera as king of Aragon. There he came to admire the erudition of Enrique de Villena, and soon afterward he asked Villena to translate Dante's *Divine Comedy* into Castilian. Villena obliged, also writing a treatise on the art of poetry; and these two works had a lifelong influence on Santillana's literary production.[34]

Santillana's literary interests were further encouraged by his close political associations with Guzmán and with don Alfonso de Cartagena, bishop of Burgos, who gained a great reputation for erudition both as a participant at the Council of Basle and as a correspondent of Leonardo Bruni.[35] Santillana surrounded himself with men trained in Italy, employing them in his household as translators, researchers, secretaries, and chaplains. He proudly commissioned the first Castilian translations of Vergil's *Aeneid*, Ovid's *Metamorphoses*, and Seneca's tragedies. He admired Giotto and Bruni, read and annotated Dante throughout his life, and wrote the first Castilian sonnets in imitation of Petrarch. His cousin, Gómez Manrique, in fact, compared him to the Florentines:

> Por cierto no fué Boecio
> ni Leonardo de Arecio
> en prosa mas elegante;
> pues en los metros el Dante
> ant'él se mostrara necio.[36]

Santillana's understanding of political and historical causation was almost identical with Guzmán's. He was as pessimistic about the condition of Spain and even more hostile toward don Alvaro de Luna, whom he criticized harshly in verse. Santillana described his confusion and despair in a lamentation modeled on Old Testament prophecies of doom. Whereas this form is more conventional than any of Guzmán's, the essence of Santillana's complaint is the same: it has become impossible to discern a proper course of action.

Like Guzmán, Santillana reacted to the political chaos of his own time by idealizing the past—especially the period of the regency and the earliest Trastámara. Urging a return to the integrity and good customs of the past, he became preoccupied with his family's past glories and tried to perpetuate their memory in many small but significant ways. He named all his children after heroic ancestors; and his military actions exhibited an anachronistic and quixotic gallantry, as though he were deliberately imitating the heroes of Nájera, Aljubarrota, and Antequera.

Santillana was more optimistic about human potential than Guzmán and placed greater emphasis on the direct responses between individuals. These attitudes can probably be attributed to the fact that Santillana's political career was successful. The conflicts he experienced were resolved to his material advantage if not to his intellectual or ethical satisfaction.

Whereas Guzmán's innovation lay in adapting literary forms to history, Santillana's lay in applying history to literary forms. Shortly before 1449 at the request of the constable of Portugal, Santillana collected the poetry he had written throughout his life in one volume.[37] The letter that serves as a preface to this collection is the first major example of Spanish literary history and criticism. In it Santillana describes not only the various forms of poetry but also the dissemination of poetry from one language to another and its historical development over a long period of time. He suggests that the *tercio rimo*, for example, was spread from Italy to southern France thence into the Iberian peninsula during the fourteenth century. In tracing the development of Latin poetry, he jumps from the ancient Romans to Petrarch, explaining only: "Let us leave behind ancient histories and come closer to our own times." He is at a loss to describe the poetry of the early Middle Ages, ascribing to that period the transferral of poetic development from Latin to the Romance languages but claiming that it would be too difficult to trace the stages by which this transformation took place.

He knows of the poetry of Alfonso el Sabio only by hearsay but knows at first hand a number of poems from the fourteenth century and distinguishes between the forms popular then and those most commonly used in his own day. Santillana was proud of his family's role in developing contemporary poetic forms. He describes the work of about fifteen Castilian poets, of whom five are his relatives: Pedro González de Mendoza, "my grandfather"; Pero Vélez de Guevara, "my uncle"; Fernán Pérez de Guzmán "my uncle"; and the duke of Arjona, don Fadrique, "my lord and my brother." Santillana's admiration for the classical authors was as great as Guzmán's, but he had a more profound sense of the historical distance between the ancient and modern worlds. He attempted imitations of foreign contemporaries rather than of the ancients, but he saw himself and his family as part of a Castilian achievement that in its sophistication and beauty could be compared to classical poetry.

Santillana's innovation lies in his historical perspective. His letter for the edification of a young prince is of special significance because he assumed that an art form is best understood through a study of its historical development. He also believed that in pursuing the historical approach he was following the example of the ancient Stoics.[38] In this approach, in his attempt to model his methods on those of the ancients, and in his sense of the distance separating the ancient and modern worlds, Santillana resembles both his contemporaries in Renaissance Italy and his predecessors in the Castilian Renaissance: his great-uncle, Ayala, and his cousin, Guzmán.

Ayala, Guzmán, and Santillana took the same historical and rhetorical approaches both to describe their secular careers as politicians and poets and to accommodate religion. Ayala and Guzmán were directly, if unsuccessfully, involved in Castilian efforts to resolve the Schism. Guzmán and Santillana were intimately bound to the career of the converso bishop Alfonso de Cartagena, Castile's principal spokesman at the Council of Basle. One of their relatives, Nuño de Guzmán, was present at the Council of Florence. All three men were deeply involved in and troubled by the ecclesiological problems of the Schism and the councils. They were also drawn by inclination and family ties to the Jeronimite Order and its emphasis on the Devotio Moderna.

The religious attitudes of the Mendoza family show marked similarities and contrasts to those of the Florentine humanists. The art commissioned by the Mendoza does not reflect that emotional involvement with the Nativity and the Passion characteristic of early Italian Renaissance painting. The famous retablo painted by Jorge el Inglés for Santillana and his wife depicts the donors at prayer within their own household with a group of angels singing above. Instead of the popular saints or scenes from the life of Christ, the base of the retablo contains the portraits of four fathers of the church.[39]

The libraries of Guzmán and Santillana also indicate an admiration for patristic erudition and pious devotion. Guzmán's library contained a copy of Sallust (dedicated to him by the translator, his cousin Vasco de Guzmán) as well as the usual Castilian range of selections from the classics—Lucan, Valerius Maximus, Pliny, Seneca, Livy, the "Phaedo of

Plato," and Vegetius's *De Re Veterinaria*—and Castilian chronicles and customary law.[40] The only religious work in Guzmán's library was a devotional treatise on the Ten Commandments attributed to his ancestor, cardinal Pedro Gómez Barroso.

Santillana's library was much richer than Guzmán's not only in quantity but also in works by contemporary authors, both Castilian and Italian.[41] For a few years, Santillana had a young relative in Florence, Nuño de Guzmán, who had run afoul of his father and fled Castile to make his fortune in Italy.[42] On Santilliana's orders, Nuño bought books, commissioned copies and translations, and kept Santillana informed of Florentine intellectual affairs. He was in a particularly good position to do all of these, being on friendly terms with Gianozzo Manetti, Pier Candido Decembri, and Leonardo Bruni. Santillana wanted specific classical and contemporary works, and his taste in contemporary Italian authors was impeccably Renaissance: Petrarch, Salutati, and Bruni were his favorites.

Perhaps Santillana's greatest departure from Castilian tradition lay in his collection of church fathers, a new enthusiasm in Florence after the council there. He had copies of Augustine, Eusebius, John Chrysostom, Basil, Ambrose, Gregory, and Jerome, in translations by George of Trebizond, cardinal Bessarion, and Ambrogio Traversari. There is no evidence that Ayala, Guzmán, or Santillana read the apocryphal stories of Christ's childhood that were popular elsewhere; and neither Guzmán nor Santillana possessed a single work of medieval theology.

There is, as we would expect, a great contrast between these libraries and those of the letrados, for both were shaped to some extent by the professions of their owners. Apart from the usual pious works and selections from the classics common to fifteenth-century libraries, letrado collections were made up of canon and civil law and occasionally of works on theology. The libraries of the military aristocracy contain redactions of customary law and manuals of hunting, agriculture, horse breeding, chess, war, and other caballero concerns.[43] The libraries of Guzmán and Santillana also reveal the great gulf in taste that separated them from other aristocratic families personally affected neither by the events at Nájera nor by Ayala's *Crónica del Rey don Pedro*.

One of the most famous libraries of the century, that of the counts of Benavente, was inventoried about 1455.[44] Perhaps the Benavente should not be considered typical of the Castilian nobility. They were a Portuguese family, the Pimentel, who supported Castilian claims to the Portuguese throne during the reign of Juan I and immigrated to Castile where they were granted their noble title by Enrique III. The counts of Benavente, however, quickly adapted to Castilian culture and became famous in fifteenth-century Castile as poets and men of letters. Part of their reputation rested on their library, which reflects the taste of both the counts of Benavente and their Castilian admirers, educated but not particularly aware of the Renaissance. The collection, some 120 titles, is made up of the usual pious works, manuals, chronicles, and excerpts from the classics. The most elaborately bound item—and obviously the pride of the collection—was a copy of Seneca that the count commissioned from a manuscript lent him by the king. The several medieval encyclopedias and most of the Latin classics could have originated in Spain or Avignon. There are two works by Boccaccio but none by Petrarch. Only one book can reasonably be attributed to fifteenth-century Florence: a "book by Leonardo" was probably Leonardo Bruni's treatise on nobility. The Benavente taste in religious books reflected popular taste in northern Europe rather than the religious enthusiasms of Florence. There are no selections from the church fathers, but two copies of the *Vita Christi*. The greatest number of works by a single author are those of the thirteenth-century religious philosopher, Ramón Llull.

Perhaps the greatest contrast between Benavente's taste and Santillana's can be seen in their selections from medieval encyclopedic works. The counts of Benavente had a copy of the massive medieval encyclopedia, *Proprietatibus Rerum*, compiled by Bartholomeus Anglicus. Santillana had the moralization of this work by Berçuire, *Reductorium Moralis*, and of this only the volume devoted to Ovid. Although the two libraries were collected during the same period, Santillana's makes Benavente's look provincial and medieval. Santillana did not order books from Italy or Avignon by the pound: he did not passsively receive books that happened to be renaissance because of the taste of Florentine booksellers and merchants. Santillana was predisposed to Florentine humanism by his family's tradition, and his collection reflects a deliberate and well-informed selection.

Most of the Mendoza's writing about religious subjects consists of poetry on the lives of saints or the miracles of the Virgin. There are long moralizing poems on such themes as the seven mortal sins and short lyric poems dedicated to the Virgin. They do not write about the Nativity or the life of Christ, and they do not engage in theological speculation. Ayala, in fact, was noted for his active opposition to theological speculation. Sometime before 1404, the poet, Ferrán Sánchez Calavera, posed the question of Free Will as the subject of a poetic debate to Ayala and several other "very learned scholars of this kingdom."[45] Of the seven poets who responded, four accepted its validity entirely and arrived at conclusions by citing authorities or presenting theological arguments. The Muslim physician to Santillana's father replied that although the question had a reasonable and just solution it was beyond the comprehension of man. Gonzalo Martínez de Medina, a supporter of the Jeronimite Order and the Devotio Moderna, expressed a distrust of speculation in confronting the mystery of predestination, appealing to the authority of the Bible but not to the decretals or theologians. Ayala rejected the validity of the inquiry entirely on the grounds that man is incapable of understanding the mysteries of revelation and must humbly surrender to God's will without daring to speculate upon it. He cites no authorities except his own earlier poetry, and he offers no arguments. Like Petrarch, his fellow student in Avignon, Ayala had developed a sense "of the immensity and inscrutable power and mercy of God" and a concomitant skepticism about man's ability to understand God and His works through manmade systems such as theology or natural philosophy.[46]

Ayala's extreme distrust of rationality in religion was complemented by the devotionalism of Guzmán's religious essays. As usual, Guzmán's standards are nonsystematic but very high. His essay on the ideal bishop favors the exemplary life over theological knowledge. He expects the bishop to

> illustrate and elucidate the office and, like a star, enlighten his region and province, and thus, as it is written in the law, wherever he may go, purify and cleanse with the purity and integrity of his life . . . and have more authority with the virtue of his heart than with the power of the staff.[47]

In his essay on the devout life, Guzmán rejects the efficacy of all good works except prayer:

> Almsgiving is very meritorious, as your grace knows, but some use it and practice it because they are of a naturally free and liberal condition; others fasting, because they are naturally abstemious; some chastity, because they are by nature cold; many silence, either because they do not know how to speak well, or because they are silenced from speaking; others pilgrimages, out of a desire to see foreign lands and nations; and some even listening to sermons, more for the sweetness of the eloquence than for the devotion or edification contained in them. Likewise for other good works, which your grace will understand and

perceive better. But to very attentive prayer, I believe that there is no motive or inclination except faith and devotion.[48]

All works except prayer are corrupted by the nonpious motives that arise out of personal inclination, in the same way that politics are corrupted by evil motives arising out of character defects.

Santillana is noted for his abundant use of classical allusion to express his faith. His references to the classics seem self-conscious and strained, but he seems unaware of his own assumption that poetic allegory serves to bridge the gap between mythology and revelation. He often unselfconsciously identifies classical erudition with poetic inspiration and both of these with Christian faith.[49]

Ayala's rejection of a theological approach to religious questions, Guzmán's extreme devotionalism, and Santillana's eclecticism are all used in the same way the Florentine humanists used them—to encourage a willful surrender to the divine mysteries. They do this by emphasizing the will rather than the intellect, devotional practices rather than rational understanding, and esthetic impact rather than theological purity.

Since we do not know what the religious attitudes of Castile had been in previous centuries, it is impossible to determine the degree to which the Mendoza's attitudes in the fifteenth century were a departure from earlier norms. As we shall see, don Alfonso de Cartagena and his students were becoming interested in theology in the fifteenth century, but the Mendoza remained either oblivious or hostile to it. Like their Florentine contemporaries, they looked to the ancient church rather than to medieval theologians for religious erudition.

Their attitudes towards Jews, Muslims, and conversos were shaped by a common assumption that standards of behavior, knowledge, and esthetics are universal and independent of religion. Throughout his four chronicles, Ayala uses the Jewish and Muslim calendars as consistently and comfortably as the Christian. He often places his own views in the mouths of Muslims, to whom he attributes a high degree of political and moral wisdom. He also presents an extensive account of a Jewish financier, who successfully reformed the tax collection system of king Pedro and increased the royal treasury, but was accused of abuses arising from cupidity and executed. Ayala uses this incident to draw a parallel with king Pedro, whom he also accuses of cupidity and whose fortune he describes in terms parallel to that of the Jew. Ayala here applies a single standard to the two men despite their different religions. Santillana displays this same attitude, though more self-consciously, when he praises and quotes the poetic proverbs of Sem Tob de Carrión: "Proverbs are not less good because they are said by a Jew."[50]

Despite popular attacks on conversos that became increasingly frequent during their lifetimes, Guzmán and Santillana remained completely accepting toward them. Both considered themselves close friends, political allies, and intellectual colleagues of don Alfonso de Cartagena. In a lengthy digression from his laudatory sketch of don Alfonso's father, don Pablo de Santa María, Guzmán passionately defends the good faith and nobility of conversos, using historical and contemporary examples to support his cause and criticizing the rigidity and lack of discrimination of those who attacked the good faith of all conversos on racial grounds.[51]

In their approach to religious matters, these three authors neglect or reject the efficacy of the intellectual or authoritative approaches. They are concerned with piety and faith rather than theology or works, attempting to stimulate both through an appeal to the will and arousing emotions through esthetic and rhetorical devices; and they emphasize the achievement of the desired results rather than the correctness of the means or source.

In both intellectual and religious matters, Ayala, Guzmán, and Santillana used a historical, eclectic, and rhetorical method distinctive to their extended family and to the period from 1390 to 1450. The coincidence of their active involvement in political and religious affairs in a period of civil war, regicide, prolonged dynastic conflict, schism, and conciliarism was probably of the greatest significance in the formation of their attitudes. The number of poets and historians in this extended family, the consistency of their career patterns, the high level of their political and literary activity, and the reappearance of Enriquista names among them over generation after generation all suggest that their intellectual and religious attitudes were formed in the military and political conflicts of the Trastámara civil war and owed their subsequent development to the successful maintenance of the family as both a cultural and social unit.

Part Two

Success and Stagnation
1460-1550

V

The Mendoza Abandon
the Field

The Catholic Monarchs rejected the caballero concept of the state largely because it was inadequate for their political needs. The failure of the politically powerful nobility to impose their views on a relatively weak monarchy, however, was caused not by the weaknesses of the caballero theories but by the peculiarities of the nobility's position at the end of the fifteenth century. By organizing around the family as a stable political and social force in an otherwise chaotic society, the Castilian nobility successfully survived the chaos of the early fifteenth century, first taking advantage of the chaos to increase their own political and economic power and later withdrawing from national affairs to consolidate their control over local affairs. As a result of this shift, by 1500 the nobility dominated local politics and society but had generally abdicated their earlier role as formulators and executors of national policy.

This shift from national to local concerns, with a corresponding shift from public to private interests, can be clearly seen in the career of cardinal Mendoza, the most powerful prelate of fifteenth-century Castile and leader of the noble family most closely identified with the caballero writers. In the course of accumulating power, wealth, and status during the reign of the Catholic Monarchs, the Mendoza displayed all the strengths and weaknesses that would first sustain and then defeat the caballero Renaissance in the intellectual conflicts of the sixteenth century.

The genealogical and political foundations of the family were laid in the disastrous days after the battle of Nájera. Their opportunity for a greatly accelerated rise began with the decimation of the old nobility and ricoshombres at the end of the fourteenth century and continued with the need for new political and military leaders in the internecine warfare of the royal family during the early fifteenth century. The form in which the Mendoza banded themselves together—the family—was not inevitable, but its legal features made it as effective a social and economic force as such corporate groups as gilds and municipalities. The family's political and economic effectiveness was encouraged by the legal structure of the nuclear family, by bonds of loyalty within the extended family (which encouraged political unity), and by the accumulation of noble titles and mayorazgos, which made the *primogenitus* estate the economic center of gravity in the family.[1]

The unity of the nuclear family was shaped by the legal status of adult sons. Before the reforms of the Cortes of Toro in 1505, a son did not achieve legal majority until his father died: an adult son could not establish an independent household, sign contracts, pledge an oath of homage, raise or command an army, or perform any other public act without the consent of his father.[2] With these disabilities, it was inconceivable—and obviously not expected—that a son should make his fortune or political career outside the family circle.

In the extended family, ties were not so legally compelling, but emotionally they were almost equally compelling. Members of an extended family—which was self-defining, of course—were obliged to act together against enemies of the family and in support of allies. Both the obligations and the relatives bound by it were called deudos. This same deudo bound the vasallos del rey to the king—where there were no fixed legal obligations between parties there nevertheless was a deudo— a bond of mutual obligation and benefit.

In December 1443, Santillana drew up an alliance with his cousin, Luis de la Cerda, count of Medinaceli. Both were great-nephews of Ayala, and they were consuegros (co-fathers-in-law) since Santillana's daughter, Leonor, married Medinaceli's son and heir, Gastón. The bond between consuegros was close, and the two men had long been close friends. Their statement of purpose explaining their alliance is worth quoting at length because it reveals the remarkable mixture of politics, affection, and self-interest that made up the bond of deudo.

> Inasmuch as in this kingdom there have been great disturbances, wars, scandals, and deaths and it is to be expected that there will be more in the future because of the reason which is known to everyone and this has taken place because it has been nourished so much by anger and hatred among the grandees of the kingdom in opposition to each other so that they are very divided in opinion and cannot easily agree

and in order to remedy this it will be first and foremost very appropriate and even necessary to achieve unity and friendship among the said grandees of the kingdom and, although they are not all easily brought into one accord, one should not leave off doing among a few of them that which is good and, rather, since they must look for and procure friendship together with those with whom they have the greatest deudo and with whom they are closest, since discord among these is most dangerous, therefore we don Luys de la Cerda count of Medina and señor of the Port of Santa María and Yñigo Lopez de Mendoza señor of la Vega wish and make known to all who may see this present document that for the service of God and the king our lord, in order to give a good start to the aforesaid accord, our full and free will is that among ourselves and our houses, being in such great deudo by consanguinity and the marriages of our children and grandchildren as we are, there may not nor can there reasonably arise any discord nor division at all. Further, that . . . we shall be together in one will and opinion through love, confederation, alliance, and good accord as the aforesaid deudos wish and mandate in the following manner: that we will guard and treat each other well and honestly each to the other and we will attempt to achieve each for the other that the said lord king should give mercedes to both of us and to each of us.[3]

During the fifteenth century, the Enriquista aristocracy intermarried so frequently that the entire nobility in effect constituted an extended family. In 1502, María de Mendoza, daughter of the count of Tendilla, was betrothed to a distant cousin, Antonio de Mendoza, eldest son of the count of Monteagudo. In their successful efforts to gain a dispensation for marrying within the bonds of consanguinity, the parents solicited depositions from "decent people," who testified that the young couple were even more closely related to a long list of other nobles so it was best for them to marry each other.[4]

In this situation, civil warfare was impractical, for one's enemies were also one's relatives, and it was almost unthinkable to break deudo by killing one's relatives. Because sons were not emancipated, the father of a numerous brood such as Santillana's had at his command a corps of political, administrative, and military lieutenants whose loyalty was more certain than that of the usual crew of subordinates. To lose one of these lieutenants in war was much more than a military loss; and after suffering disastrous losses at the battle of Aljubarrota in 1385, the Castilian aristocracy avoided pitched battles whenever possible—only two occurred between Castilian knights in the first half of the fifteenth century.

Death in battle was the exception rather than the rule during the early

Trastámara period, and it was not unusual for a caballero to demand remuneration from the king for such loss of a son, brother, or uncle. Spain's leading historian of the period, Luis Suárez Fernández, has pointed out that our only documentary evidence of civil strife before the reign of the Catholic Monarchs is the large number of confederations signed among the nobility.[5] Most of these confederations—which look so ominous and belligerent to Suárez—are really statements of impotence. Usually two parties agree to unite in warfare against their mutual enemies, but each reserves the right not to fight against his deudos, who are listed in careful detail. If one of the deudos of either party joined the enemy, there could be no battle.[6] Deudo did not always work as a means of preventing strife, but it was believed to work; and when relatives acted together or agreed not to fight one another, they used deudo to explain their actions. Family loyalties were considered reasonable and admirable motives for political activity.

The Mendoza displayed the unity arising out of their sense of deudo on various public and military occasions when the head of the family called upon his relatives to make a show of force in support of the family honor. Santillana's eldest son, later to be the first duke of Infantado, became embroiled in a feud with the count of Benavente over the possession of Carrión. Although the count had a royal decree ceding the town to him, Infantado regarded it as a usurpation of his family's ancestral rights. In expectation of a battle against the count in 1473, he drew up a list of the forces he would call up: fourteen hundred cavalry— seven hundred twenty-five from his own forces and six hundred seventy-five from his cousins, the counts of Treviño and Castañeda.[7] Of the seven hundred twenty-five cavalry under his own command, forty were his *continos* (regular members of his household cavalry), one hundred sixty were to be hired on salary, and the remaining five hundred fifty were the troops of twenty commanders loyal to him. Of these twenty commanders, all but five were brothers, nephews, sons, and in-laws.

The armies of Infantado and Benavente actually faced each other on a field outside Carrión, but Fernando the Catholic stepped between the two ranks and mediated a settlement before any blows were struck. A typical battle of early Trastámara Castile. Equally typical—and significant—is the duke of Infantado's ability to raise an army of fourteen hundred cavalry from within his own family. Despite the bitter antagonism over property between himself and his cousins, Pedro Manrique, count of Treviño, and Garci Fernández Manrique, count of Castañeda, their sense of deudo became paramount in the face of a military threat from outside the family.

In 1475, the Mendoza again rallied as a single military force, this time at Toro in defense of Fernando and Isabel against the king of Portugal. In anticipation of the battle, Isabel gave the second Santillana the title of duke of Infantado and expressed her thanks to him and his family for being the principal support of her cause. In the document granting this title, Fernando and Isabel name each of these captains of the Mendoza family and their relationship to Infantado:

> And mindful of the great men and caballeros—your brothers, sons-in-law, and sons, nephews, and relatives—who came to stand with me and with you in the said battle, whom it is proper to name here because of their great dignities and estates, and because of the great deudo which they have with you, especially the Most Reverend don Pedro González de Mendoza, cardinal of Spain, archbishop of Seville and bishop of Sigüenza, our uncle, your brother; and don Pedro de Velasco, count of Haro, condestable de Castilla, your brother-in-law; and don Beltrán de la Cueva, duke of Alburquerque, your son-in-law; and don Lorenzo Suárez de Mendoza, count of Coruña, viscount of Torija, your brother; and don Gabriel Manrique, count of Osorno, your cousin; and don Pedro de Mendoza, count of Monteagudo, your nephew; and don Diego Hurtado de Mendoza, bishop of Palencia, your nephew; and Alonso de Arellano, your son-in-law; and don Juan and don Hurtado de Mendoza, your brothers; and don Bernardino de Velasco, your nephew, son of the said condestable; and don Pedro de Mendoza and don Juan de Mendoza your sons; and don Bernardino de Mendoza, your nephew, son of the said count of Coruña; and don García Manrique, comendador mayor de Castilla, your nephew, son of the said count of Osorno; and many other caballeros of your lineage and estate.[8]

The crown recognized the Mendoza family as a distinct and significant social and political unit, with the duke of Infantado as the publicly recognized leader and membership in the unit defined by the individual's relationship to Infantado.

The bonds within a family were so strong that political allies or close friends could find no more appropriate terms in which to express their feelings of deudo than the vocabulary of family relationships. It was customary to refer to a colleague many years one's senior as "uncle"—as Isabel referred to cardinal Mendoza; to an ally of one's own age as "cousin"—as Fernando most frequently addressed the Castilian nobles; and to a much younger man as "nephew"—as the second Tendilla addressed his distant cousin, Pedro Laso de la Vega, elder brother of the great poet. In an age of revolution, royal minorities, institutional confusion, and innovation, the family formed a point of stability whose moral and emotional bonds could be as compelling as legal constraints and whose customs and vocabulary could lend an aura of stability to less permanent relationships.

This all-pervasive sense of the family as an agglutinative force—which, thanks to the chronicles of Pedro López de Ayala, the Mendoza seem to have felt more strongly than most—facilitated the Mendoza's rise during the social confusion that followed the Trastámara revolution. The Mendoza did not begin to receive titles until the mid-fifteenth century, but their rise to noble status was a direct result of the Trastámara revolution. Along with other Alavese clans—the Ayala, Guevara, Orozco, and Velasco—the Mendoza appear with increasing frequency as public administrators, war heroes, and ambassadors during the first two-thirds of the fourteenth century. Their social mobility was nevertheless limited by their nonnoble condition.

In fourteenth-century Castile, noble titles were part of the royal patrimony and therefore not heritable. Traditionally, only members of the royal family received them, and they reverted to the crown, along with their incomes, upon the death of their holders. In the fourteenth century, the great political strength of the nobles derived from their personal influence over the king, for normally only nobles were del consejo del rey—the epitome of Castilian political life. The royal military resources were organized under territorial governors appointed by the king, recruited from outstanding nonnoble members of the military and serving under a variety of titles according to the usage prevailing when each governorship was established—prestamero mayor, merino mayor, adelantado, caudillo mayor. The territorial governors could not match the nobles in political or social influence, although the king granted the status of ricohombre to a few nonnobles considered essential to the good governance of the kingdom—a royal treasurer, a frontier commander, a territorial governor—and admitted them to the consejo del rey. Although the Alavese were too recently arrived to achieve the status of ricoshombres, by the time the Trastámara revolt began they had achieved enough status to form family ties with them.

All of this changed in the last third of the fourteenth century, after the Trastámara civil war launched one of the most radical social revolutions of Castilian history.[9] Slowly but steadily the old noble and ricohombre families died, were suppressed, or went into exile; and the caballero families who had made up the bulk of the Trastámara fighting force became del consejo del rey, ricoshombres, and nobility. The Alavese clans who had immigrated in the early part of the century were exceptionally successful in this regard; and they came to play a political, economic, and cultural role far out of proportion to their numbers: by the 1470s, four of the sixteen titled families of Castile were of Alavese origin. The Mendoza benefited more than most, and Mendoza prestige was intimately bound up with the fortunes of the Trastámara dynasty.

Through natural attrition, war, political exile, and the short life spans of most of the early Trastámara, the number of the king's relatives declined steadily in the twenty years after Enrique II assumed the throne. By 1390, there were only six titled noblemen in Castile—two dukes, three counts, and one marquis—all of them Enrique's nephews and cousins and all holding personal titles which were created specifically for them and would die out or revert to the crown along with their estates when they died.

During the minority of Enrique III, this small group of bitterly feuding and ambitious royal relatives lost control of the regent government; and by the beginning of the reign of Juan II, all but two of the personal titles had died out. The nobility's places in the royal council were taken by caballeros who had supported Enrique de Trastámara in his revolt against Pedro and by Portuguese nobles who had supported Castile in Juan I's attempt to claim the Portuguese throne and taken refuge in Castile after the Portuguese victory at Aljubarrota (1385). Thus the caballeros Enrique elevated to the highest political offices to counterbalance the titled nobility replaced the nobles in the consejo del rey by the beginning of the fifteenth century without being noble themselves. They achieved the epitome of political office in Castile without achieving the highest social status.

It was a commonplace of monarchical societies that a king needs a nobility; and at the turn of the century, Castile had a scarcity of nobles. Juan I and Enrique III made an attempt to correct the situation by giving personal titles to a few favorites outside the royal family. These titles ordinarily would have been held by members of the royal family; and in some cases, the king actually deprived a seditious relative of his title or refused it to the heir of a mistrusted relative, giving it instead to a caballero powerful enough to defend it from the claims of royal relatives. But this stopgap measure merely changed personnel without changing the institution.

During the reign of Juan II, however, the chaos created by the infantes of Aragon showed that the early Trastámara measures to curb royal relatives had not succeeded. Don Alvaro de Luna tipped the balance of power away from the infantes by changing the institution of nobility itself: first he and then Enrique IV created a new type of nobility—one of the most successful innovations of the Trastámara period, outlasting every other creation of the dynasty, including the mayorazgo, the Inquisition, the Audiencia, and the new royal offices. Don Alvaro began his innovation in 1438 when he made Fernán Alvarez de Toledo count of Alba. This title was different from previous Castilian titles, first because it was hereditary, and second because the estate of Alba was not part of the royal patrimony—as a private estate, a señorío, it was outside the royal jurisdiction.

Hereditary titles of nobility proliferated during the next forty years, though the crown also continued to grant personal titles; and the caballero families who gained economic and political power during the Trastámara period now achieved the highest social status. This new nobility—recruited from Enriquista caballero families and refugee Portuguese aristocracy and receiving hereditary titles for estates they already owned—became the nobility of the late fifteenth century.

Since the new nobility did not receive royal estates with their titles— or any other estates they did not own before—their titles could be considered empty display. Buried in the litigation records of family archives, however, there is evidence that these titles were an effective tool for stabilizing the economy and society of the fifteenth century. Far from being mere labels, the new titles changed the legal status of the estates for which they were named. The Mendoza family received several titles during the fifteenth century; and in each case, they simultaneously gained clear hereditary rights to an estate that had been in litigation for years.

Title to the villages around the town of Santillana, for example, had been disputed between the Manrique and Mendoza families since the death of the admiral in 1404. Not only did the wheels of justice grind exceeding slow; but as soon as one party won a decision from the Audiencia, the rival party would appeal, and the estate would be in litigation all over again. When Juan II made Iñigo López de Mendoza marquis of Santillana in 1445, he not only created the first hereditary title of marquis in Castile but also cut through the judicial process by removing the dispute from the jurisdiction of the courts. By royal fiat, he granted legal title to the estate once and for all to whomever should hold the title of marquis of Santillana—Iñigo López de Mendoza and his heirs. The noble titles granted to the Mendoza by Juan II, Enrique IV, and the Catholic Monarchs—count of Real de Manzanares and marquis of Santillana (1445), count of Saldaña (1462), count of Tendilla (c. 1467), count of Coruña (c. 1469), marquis of Cid and of Cenete (1491), marquis of Mondéjar (1512)—were all of this type. The most significant clause in each new title was not that creating the title but that granting it "to you and your descendants for evermore."

These noble titles stabilized the family estate by removing much of it from litigation. When Santillana finally received his title in 1445, the litigation over his villages had been straining his resources for thirty years. He paid court, attorney, notarial, and scrivener fees; he used his military and political leverage with the crown to influence court decisions; and he sent armies to enforce—or defy—the Audiencia's decisions. As long as the estate was in litigation, Santillana could not enjoy its income, for the crown usually placed such estates under its own administration—to the crown's advantage. Afterwards, however, the marquisate of Santillana passed from generation to generation without dispute until 1580—when it was inherited by a woman. The right of female inheritance was then disputed in a lawsuit that lasted twenty-nine years.

In a cadet branch of the Mendoza family, the second count of Tendilla, as the universal heir of his first wife, Marina de Mendoza (d. 1477), claimed her estate of Mondéjar and carried his fight against Marina's sister through the law courts for over twenty-five years until Fernando the Catholic made him marquis of Mondéjar in 1512. Title to the town of Mondéjar was not disputed again until 1604, when the fourth marquis died without direct successors. Every noble title granted to the Mendoza family during the last half of the fifteenth century represented a major bloc of property immunized against the type of property litigation that had nearly destroyed their prosperity at the beginning of the century.

The social stability achieved by the creation of hereditary nobility outside the royal family and patrimony can be measured in centuries. Almost one-half of the titles died out after one or two generations, but new titles were frequently created for upwardly mobile families; and the nobility in the fifteenth and sixteenth centuries were a constantly changing, socially fluid group. A handful of new nobles nevertheless came to dominate Castilian political and social life in the Trastámara period just as the royal relatives had dominated it in the thirteenth and fourteenth centuries. Charles V regularized and ranked the noble titles in 1525, drawing up a list of twenty-five titles distinguished by wealth, power, and social status.

Although the number of titles increased in the sixteenth century and especially in the seventeenth and the families inheriting them changed several times in the next centuries, the titles retained their status, their landed estates, their seigneurial jurisdictions, and to a lesser extent, their wealth into the nineteenth century. The Mendoza's titular estates provided the material focal point of Mendoza loyalties for centuries.

Hereditary titles were intimately associated with the mayorazgo, another old institution the Trastámara reshaped and revitalized. The mayorazgo also endured for centuries—until a reforming government abolished it in 1836. Without the mayorazgo, nobles' estates would have been subject to the laws of partible inheritance and thus repeatedly reduced in size in the fecund fifteenth and sixteenth centuries. In placing a large portion of his property in a mayorazgo for his eldest son, Pedro González de Mendoza (d. 1385), founder of the family's fortune, believed that it would serve as the social and economic focal point of the Mendoza family and so perpetuate the family name forever.[10] He did not anticipate that the mayorazgo would outlive the family itself.

Spanish law required that all the children of a marriage should receive fair, though not equal, shares of their parents' heritable property (the *bienes partibles* or *bienes libres*). Before these were divided, the law permitted up to one-third of them to be set aside for the eldest son (who also received one-fifth of the rest) to *mejorar* or enlarge the principal estate of the family. The remaining eight-fifteenths were divided among the other children, sons in clerical orders receiving less than the others. This system was so closely followed in the Mendoza family that by the late sixteenth century a Mendoza daughter could describe her brother as the first born, "having inherited the third and the fifth of our father's bienes libres."[11]

In 1462, Enrique IV granted the title of count of Saldaña to the eldest son of the second marquis of Santillana. This was a significant innovation in Castilian inheritance practice—a title of primogeniture that allowed the eldest son to enjoy a portion of his father's estate until he inherited the principal mayorazgo himself. The two mayorazgos remained autonomous but not independent of each other. Saldaña was near the Mendoza properties most seriously threatened by the Manrique, and it became the task of the count to defend the family's claims there. With the duke of Infantado thus freed from these most difficult to manage of all the Mendoza properties, he could devote himself to the enjoyment of his economic and ceremonial perquisites as head of the Mendoza and one of the richest men in the kingdom. Economically emancipated, the counts of Saldaña remained subject to the legal jurisdiction of their fathers. Not until the Comunero revolt of 1520— fifteen years after all married adults were emancipated by the Laws of Toro—did a young count of Saldaña defy his father in political matters. The splitting up of the mayorazgo nevertheless indicates that the estate had grown too unwieldy for a single management as early as 1462.

In the last half of the fifteenth century, both the pace and the pattern of Mendoza development changed. The principal mayorazgo, which had changed and grown dramatically in the first half of the century, reached its ultimate growth and final form in the last quarter of the century. Just as by 1500 one title of nobility proliferated into a half-dozen, each held by a self-appointed leader, the thrust of the entire family's energies into the growth of a single unified mayorazgo—typical of the early Trastámara period—was diffused into more than twenty mayorazgos held by eldest sons of cadet branches scattered throughout Castile. These changes in the structure, size, and distribution of the Mendoza estates produced so many atomized and self-generating households, each with its own aspirations, that it is difficult to find coherent patterns of development. At least it can be said with assurance that the Mendoza were rich and getting richer.

It is difficult to measure the wealth of the Mendoza. Estate records are sparse before 1502, when notaries were first required to keep protocols. Rent rolls have survived in a haphazard fashion and in small quantities, usually transcribed into dowry litigation. Even if we could estimate the income from a given property, however, it would be difficult to know which properties the estate comprised at any given time. The Mendoza properties developed in an extremely fluid manner in this period: those received from the king for life reverted to the crown; others remained in the family permanently. The Mendoza bought properties, exchanged them, mortgaged them to raise capital, leased them for a safe annual return, sold them, bought them over again, divided them, and gave their incomes as dowries, religious donations, private gifts, payments for service, and acts of charity.[12] Even the supposedly inalienable property in the mayorazgo was as leaky as a sieve: throughout the Trastámara period, the Mendoza carried on a balancing act, moving property in and out of the mayorazgo to even up the inheritances of various sons and give them geographically compact properties and selling parts of the mayorazgo to raise the capital for adding new sections to it.[13]

A rough way to measure the growth and subsequent stabilization of the estate is to count the number of separate holdings mentioned in Mendoza legacies—a process English historians call "manor counting." In his will of 1383, Pedro González de Mendoza left thirty separate properties to his heirs—including three towns and twenty villages. His son, the admiral, left another twenty properties not mentioned in his father's will, including five and one-third towns and ten villages. In 1458, the marquis of Santillana left another twenty-six properties not mentioned in the admiral's will, including eight and two-thirds towns and fourteen villages. The duke of Infantado (d. 1479), did not individually list the estates willed to his heirs, but we know from other sources that in 1470 he acquired the four towns of the estate of Infantado that straddled the border between Guadalajara and Cuenca provinces, which he added to his mayorazgo, as well as another four villages. This was the last major addition to the principal mayorazgo of the Mendoza family for seventy years.[14]

These estates were the source of the Mendoza wealth, for their income was derived mainly from agricultural sources, although they also had recourse to some more varied and less consistent types of income. The bulk of their income consisted of seigneurial taxes and rents from agricultural leases, which appear to have been stable or even growing despite crop failures after 1480.[15] The wool producers of Castile prospered in the last years of the century, and since the Mendoza held lands in the Tajo Basin and north of the Guadarrama Mountains that straddled two of the four major sheepwalks of Castile, they received pasturage fees as well as profits from the sale of their own wool and of the honey and beeswax cultivated in their pasturelands.

Wool and honey were their major export products for the North Atlantic trade, but they also exported lumber to Valencia. In addition, they maintained a near monopoly on processing the fruits of the land for local markets—wine and olive presses, hemp mills, bakeries, forges, tanneries and tallow works, grain mills, salt mines, quarries, wine cellars—even the collection and marketing of herbs used as medicine, spices, and dyes. Santillana and Infantado received royal concessions for market fairs in their towns along the sheepwalks and major routes into the Tajo Basin. The sales taxes they collected from these fairs—usually set at a little over 3 percent—were an important source of income, zealously watched over by the dukes and their stewards.[16]

There were no demesne farms in the land tenure system of Castile, so the Mendoza did not directly manage grain production on their estates. They did receive and market the grain their tenants paid as a portion of their lease rents and as the tercias—which the crown frequently conceded to the señores as a merced. The bishopric of Sigüenza became almost hereditary in the Mendoza family; and as the Mendoza continued to produce large families until late in the sixteenth century, they continued to send younger sons into this and other lucrative positions in the church. By 1492, the Mendoza were by far the wealthiest noble house in Castile.[17]

The feature of the Mendoza that has most caught the attention of historians is their domination of the city of Guadalajara. The city's archivist, fray Francisco Layna Serrano, entitled his loving four-volume work on this subject *Guadalajara and its Mendoza.* It would be more aptly called *The Mendoza and their Guadalajara.* From the beginning of their residence in Guadalajara, the Mendoza bought up houses and commercial property in the city, as well as nearby farms, olive presses, grain and fulling mills, and pasture lands. The admiral bought a wine cellar with its *tinajas* (storage jars) and a tavern in the center of the city, known thereafter as "La Bodega del Almirante." The plaza in front of this bodega was known into modern times as the "Plaza del Almirante." Pedro González de Mendoza (d. 1385) began building some large houses in the city for the family's residence; and his son, the admiral, continued and expanded this project. Fernán Pérez de Guzmán associated the admiral's building projects with his sense of family:

> [The admiral] was very proud of his lineage and allied himself with his relatives with great love, more than any other grandee of his time, and he greatly enjoyed constructing buildings and built very good houses.[18]

By the last quarter of the fifteenth century, these houses were no longer capable of containing the hundreds of people in the Mendoza household; and the first duke of Infantado, his brothers and sisters, sons, nieces, and nephews began construction projects that would convert Guadalajara into a city of Mendoza palaces. The second duke of Infantado tore down the old family houses and replaced them with a single large palace in international gothic style—still the principal monument of the city. His uncle, cardinal Mendoza, built the first Renaissance palace in Guadalajara, as well as a Renaissance cloister for the parish church of Santa María de la Fuente. Infantado's brothers and sisters, especially Antonio de Mendoza and Brianda de Mendoza, built palaces, schools, orphanages, and chapels in the city. In the sixteenth century, several titled members of the family maintained palaces in Guadalajara as their principal residences—the duke of Infantado and his eldest son, the count of Saldaña; the count of Coruña; and the marquises of Priego and Montesclaros—as well as smaller residences throughout the city.[19]

The size of the Mendoza households and the extent of their building projects must have had an important impact on the economy of Guadalajara, especially on the construction and crafts industries. At the height of their building activity, the family hired foreign-trained architects to supervise their construction projects; but the work was carried out by craftsmen from the city and province of Guadalajara under direct contract between patron and craftsman. Layna has published a number of these contracts, and the entire construction process resembles the procedures used in the building of the Strozzi Palace in Florence.[20]

The city of Guadalajara had an abundant supply of water, and those who could afford the necessary plumbing enjoyed running water in their houses. One of the first steps in each Mendoza construction project was a petition to the city council for a greater flow of water. In one instance, the Mendoza gave the city an artesian well outside the city in exchange for a greater volume of water within it. Then came contracts for the manufacture and installation of the piping—followed by contracts for foundation works, bricks, tiles, stone columns, and carved ceilings. All were manufactured to the patron's specifications, often described simply as "like the sample the duke has shown him."

Once the construction was completed, the palace furnishings also provided some contracts, but Spanish houses—even those of the nobility—tended to be sparsely furnished. What furnishings the Mendoza did buy were not easily supplied by local artisans. The furnishings most frequently left as legacies were beds with their linens and hangings, armor, tapestries, gold, silver, and precious stones. Not much of this was of local craftsmanship. The fifteenth-century Mendoza commissioned gold and silver pieces from craftsmen in Barcelona; the marquis of Santillana and the first and second dukes of Infantado commissioned paintings from foreigners, such as Jorge el Inglés. The second Infantado bought much of his silver, gold, and tapestries at the sale of Philip I's household effects in 1506.

By the sheer weight of their physical presence, the Mendoza shaped the appearance and economy of Guadalajara; and their impact on the society and politics of the city was overwhelming. Inasmuch as the Mendoza were the only noble family in the city, Guadalajara was spared the rivalries and feuds that tore apart other Castilian cities such as Toledo, Burgos, and Córdoba. Technically, Guadalajara was a royal villa, and traditionally its government and seigneurial income had belonged to the queen. Enrique II, Juan I, Enrique III, and Juan II, however, had given the city's income and government over to the Mendoza. Pedro González de Mendoza (d. 1385) was alcaide of the city's alcázar and had the right to collect the *portazgo* (transit tax). In addition to these privileges, his son, the admiral, received the right to name the alcalde, regidores, and alguaciles (mayor, city councilmen, and constables).

Layna reports that until the end of the eighteenth century the city carried out an annual ceremony of petitioning the duke of Infantado to assume the city's government "to save it from discord" and celebrating his gracious acceptance with a show of trumpets and banners. Thus the fiction of an independent city and the reality of Mendoza control were maintained. As far as we know, there were no uprisings, violent feuds, or overt attacks on the Mendoza by the people of Guadalajara, though the city was always touchy about its status as an independent city.

Royal advisers were likewise unhappy about a royal villa remaining in private hands and occasionally tried to wrest control from the Mendoza in the name of the crown. In 1441, don Alvaro de Luna prevailed upon Juan II to give the government of Guadalajara to crown prince Enrique. In 1459, Juan Pacheco occupied the city in the name of Enrique IV—with or without the king's command is not clear. In both cases, the Mendoza simply packed up and moved their households to their fortified castles in Hita and Buitrago, returning to Guadalajara after winning back the crown's favor.

In fact, the Mendoza's weight in Guadalajara seems to have amounted to more than the sum of its parts. Although physical presence, military and political power, and economic activity all played a role, all had weaknesses. The Mendoza could not control Guadalajara either militarily or politically. In any instance when the crown failed to support the Mendoza, the family fled, trapped between the city and royal forces. They had no close military strongpoints to use against Guadalajara: their closest sure fortresses were Hita and Buitrago. The Infantado wealth came not from Guadalajara or her province but from lands in Alava, Asturias, and the Duero Basin. The family could control the city's government through appointments to city offices; and it is common to find Mendoza younger sons, in-laws, secretaries, and clients serving as members of the city council. Even so, there were times when the crown intervened and made its own appointments in the city. The city council also occasionally asserted its theoretical independence, complaining, for example, that the Mendoza were enlarging their own households at the expense of the city: the new residents increased the burdens on city services, but their tax-free status as hidalgos reduced the proportional tax base of the city's population.[21]

The Mendoza lived in Guadalajara largely because they preferred urban life to rural, like most Castilian aristocrats. Fernán Pérez de Guzmán wrote to his cousin Santillana complaining—in a tone reminiscent of Machiavelli's complaints while he was exiled from Florence—that living in his village of Batres he was surrounded by rustics and cut off from all cultural life.[22] And Tendilla, Santillana's grandson, wrote to a friend: "Although everyone claims that you are staying in [the village of] Las Arenas, I don't believe them because, as the wise man said, the country is a nice place to visit but not to live in."[23]

In addition to preferring the stimulation of urban life, the Mendoza developed a specific affection for Guadalajara, where they were surrounded by family, friends, and clients. After Tendilla moved to Granada, he thrived on the conflicts and variety of one of Spain's largest and most cosmopolitan cities. But when he felt defeated and isolated, he regretted leaving Guadalajara where "I left behind all that was mine and dismantled my household there full of the servants of my grandparents, and of my father and children."[24] Even this most independent of the Mendoza continued to regard Guadalajara as the focus of stability, earthly comfort, and family pride.

Secure in their wealth, their social status, their control over local administration, the Mendoza continued to be one of the major powers in the kingdom; but they did not regard politics in the same way their ancestors had. In contrast to the all consuming passions and moral conflicts with which Pedro López de Ayala and Fernán Pérez de Guzmán engaged the political issues of their day, the Mendoza of the reign of the Catholic Monarchs regarded politics with a serenity that approaches aloofness. Lacking emotional engagement, no political policy, no political figure became identified with the Mendoza family: there was no compelling cause around which the whole family could rally as a single political or military force. Just as the family's landed estate had begun to subdivide and the noble titles to proliferate, the political leadership of the family splintered among several talented figures, who—while not competing with each other—did not act as a unified party.

If it were necessary to single out one Mendoza as the most famous political figure of a family that produced so many, it would surely be cardinal Mendoza.[25] His active and successful role in strengthening the fortunes of the family can hardly be disputed—although the political results, as we shall see, were not felicitous. His popular image as the "third king of Spain," the *eminence grise* shaping the policies of the Catholic Monarchs, is more difficult to justify on the basis of scholarly

research. A careful examination of the chronicles and the archival documents, in fact, indicates that cardinal Mendoza was outstanding principally in the degree to which he remained true to his generation's very
limited ideals and focused on material and social advancement.

Pedro González de Mendoza was the youngest of Santillana's ten
children. His parents intended him for a church career; and when he
was about twelve years old, they sent him to live with their cousin,
Gutierre Gómez de Toledo, bishop of Palencia. Gutierre Gómez was a
nephew of Pedro López de Ayala; and in the tradition of that family,
he resided and made his career in the city of Toledo, of which he became
archbishop in 1442. Through the patronage of this powerful relative,
Pedro González received the benefice of the archdeaconate of Guadalajara. He also received a thorough grounding in Latin in the archbishop's household. When Gutierre Gómez died in 1445, Pedro González had not yet received a bishopric; and the young cleric spent several
years at the University of Salamanca, living on his comfortable income
as archdeacon of Guadalajara and reading canon law. There is no record
of his having matriculated, and he never took a degree. During this
residence in Salamanca, however, his father wrote the famous letter
asking Pedro González to translate the *Iliad* from Latin into Castilian.
In the prologue to his elegant and intelligent translations of the *Aeneid*
and some books of Ovid's *Metamorphoses*, Pedro González states that
he made these translations during his vacations.[26]

After seven years at the university, Pedro González still had not
moved up in his ecclesiastical career; and in 1452, he departed for the
royal court, where he won the attention and favor of don Alonso de
Fonseca, archbishop of Seville, whose patronage launched Pedro González on his great career. In 1454, he became bishop of Calahorra; and
after residing a year in his diocese, he returned to the royal court and
began to win the favor of the new king, Enrique IV. His first move
into politics occurred in 1460, when he negotiated an agreement between the king and the Mendoza. The king agreed to return control
over the city of Guadalajara to Pedro González's brother, the second
Santillana, in exchange for some fortresses and Santillana's son, Juan
Hurtado de Mendoza, as security for the agreement. From this time
until 1468, Pedro González remained with the royal court almost continuously, protecting Mendoza interests from the manipulations of the
king's favorite, Juan Pacheco, and urging the king to take firmer action
against his enemies. His role as spokesman for both the Mendoza and
Enrique IV was apparent not only in the numerous alliances he arranged

in this period but also in his public speeches supporting the king and his daughter, Juana, after the rebels deposed him in absentia in Avila (1465) and after Enrique met with Isabel at Toros de Guisando (1468).[27]

Although Pedro González and the Mendoza remained loyal to Enrique throughout his reign, their active support changed to a passive abstention from politics after 1469, when two events changed both the situation in Castile and Pedro González's own priorities: the marriage of Fernando and Isabel reunited the two branches of the Trastámara dynasty; and the first of Pedro González's illegitimate sons, Rodrigo, was born.[28] From this time on, the Mendoza brothers, led by Pedro González, consolidated their forces and offered them to Fernando and Isabel in return for lavish promises of income and territory. Pedro González also used his position as leader of the family to extract from the royal couple and from the papal legate, Rodrigo Borgia, mercedes, a cardinalate, and the archbishopric of Seville.

As an immediate consequence of these events, the Mendoza adopted their policy of watchful abstention from politics until the death of Enrique IV. Pedro González embarked upon a twenty-year career of financial and political manipulation that acquired a private fortune for his illegitimate sons and increased the income and offices of the whole Mendoza family. In exchange for Mendoza support of Isabel, Pedro González was made archbishop of Seville and cardinal of Santa Croce; and Juan II of Aragon guaranteed Mendoza possession of the Infantado estates in Castile that Juan II of Castile had given them in an effort to dispossess the Aragonese king of his power in Castile.[29]

The cardinal's first concern was to build a landed estate for his son, Rodrigo. Through royal merced, purchase, and trade he acquired six major estates in Castile, Valencia, and Granada and placed most of this property in mayorazgo. He then obtained assurance that no one could interfere with Rodrigo's inheritance by acquiring legitmation of his sons from both pope and crown and two titles of nobility for Rodrigo—marquis of Cenete and count of Cid—from the crown. The magnitude of the cardinal's accomplishments as a financial manager can be seen by comparing the income of his ecclesiastical offices with that of the estate he built for his son: in 1485, after he became archbishop of Toledo, his annual income reached 65,000 florins (45,500 ducats); in 1501, Rodrigo was estimated to have an income of 16,000 florins (11,000 ducats).[30] In the twenty-one years from 1469 to 1490, the cardinal built a private fortune with an income one-quarter the size of that of the archbishopric of Toledo, the richest see in Spain.

For the rest of his life, cardinal Mendoza used his position as head of the family to provide the crown with a powerful and consistent military force. At the same time, he used his influence over the young monarchs to enrich himself and his family, placing his relatives in positions of power throughout the kingdom and securing their legal hold on their estates with titles of nobility.[31] At the height of Pedro González's influence over Enrique IV, about 1467, two of his brothers received titles of nobility: Iñigo López de Mendoza became count of Tendilla and Lorenzo Suárez de Figueroa became count of Coruña. Pedro Fernández de Velasco, who was married to their eldest sister, Mencía de Mendoza, became constable of Castile in 1472, and the office became hereditary in their family. Through the cardinal's influence with Fernando and Isabel, the eldest brother, Diego Hurtado de Mendoza, marquis of Santillana, also became duke of Infantado in 1475, confirming his possession of the Infantado estates.

When the cardinal became archbishop of Toledo in 1485, he appointed another of his brothers, Pedro Hurtado de Mendoza, as adelantado of Cazorla, the important archdiocesan military command on the frontier with Granada. A sister, María de Mendoza, was married to the adelantado of Andalucía, Pero Afán de Rivera. In 1476, they were given the hereditary title of count of los Molares; and in 1492, the office of adelantado was made hereditary in their family. The cardinal's third sister, Leonor de la Vega, had married their cousin, the count of Medinaceli; and in 1479, their title was elevated to duke of Medinaceli. In 1491, when the duke asked the cardinal, as head of the family, to arrange a suitably honorable marriage for his only daughter, Leonor, the cardinal acquired both the position of alcaide of Guadix (Granada) and two noble titles for his own son Rodrigo, who then married Leonor.

Two of the cardinal's nephews, Iñigo López de Mendoza and Diego Hurtado de Mendoza, sons of the count of Tendilla, were appointed captain general of Granada (1492) and bishop of Palencia (1473) respectively. At the specific request of the cardinal, Diego Hurtado succeeded his uncle as archbishop of Seville in 1485. Looking back on these golden days, Tendilla in 1514 would recall the royal nomination of his brother as archbishop of Seville in these words: "The cardinal my uncle said to the marquise of Moya, 'I told the queen that if she gives the archbishopric of Seville to a favorite she gives me nothing, but if she gives it to anyone but my nephew I will never again live at her court.'"[32] Through this policy, the cardinal added to the family's wealth and gave them new power over local areas of royal administration, most notably in Andalucía, but he also began a physical dispersion of the most talented members of the younger generation that would change the tightly knit party of his own generation into individually powerful but disunited branches of the Mendoza family.

From the sixteenth through the twentieth centuries, loyal sons of Guadalajara and descendants of the Mendoza family have written biographies of cardinal Mendoza; and since the seventeenth century, they have referred to him as "the Great Cardinal." Despite all these laudatory biographies—or perhaps because of them—the cardinal remains a shadowy figure in the reign of the Catholic Monarchs. In the chronicles of the period and in the documents emanating from the royal chancery, his name appears in almost every incident of historical significance: Isabel accepting the oaths of homage in Segovia in 1474, the triumphal entry into the city of Granada in 1492, the royal audience with Christopher Columbus. While all must agree that he was in constant residence at the royal court and controlled many royal as well as ecclesiastical appointments, we cannot be sure of what advice he gave at any given juncture. The royal chronicler, Hernando del Pulgar, who was a client of the cardinal and never missed a chance to give credit to the Mendoza, simply mentions the cardinal's presence without attributing royal decisions to his influence, whereas he credits other counsellors, such as the queen's confessor, fray Hernando de Talavera, with persuading the monarchs to take such important actions as the mercedes reform of 1480.[33]

Even on such an important question as the Inquisition, for example, the evidence is slight and contradictory. It is hard to understand why the cardinal, a bishop himself, would want to remove inquisitorial powers from the bishops, where they had traditionally resided, and give them to the crown. Instead of using his episcopal inquisitorial powers to investigate reports of judaizing in his own archdiocese of Seville, the cardinal had drawn up and published a set of guidelines to instruct new Christians in the daily conduct of Christian life. When the new Inquisition was established, it opened its operations in the archdiocese of Seville, as if to emphasize the contrast between the cardinal's methods of dealing with judaizers and its own. Nevertheless, the chronicler, Bernáldez, an eyewitness to the events in Seville, seems to accuse the cardinal of creating obstacles to the Inquisition's operation. Furthermore, we should assume that the papacy would not have approved the establishment of the royal Inquisition unless it had been supported by the cardinal. Yet the negotiations leading to papal approval of the new Inquisition were conducted directly between the papacy and the monarchs, without reference to the cardinal; and the papal correspondence suggests that the negotiations were carried out with something less than candor.[34]

Thus, the superabundance of archival evidence shedding light on the cardinal's activities in building the Mendoza wealth and creating fortunes for his illegitimate sons presents a stark contrast to the paucity of materials relating to his political activities at court. At the time of this writing, there is no calendar of the cardinal's papers; and only a small portion of his correspondence has been uncovered and edited, whereas his private estate papers constitute the largest and most complete collection of estate documents in the vast Sección Osuna of the Archivo Histórico Nacional. This disparity between the documentation for his public and private lives adds to the impression that once he had succeeded in mobilizing the Mendoza family behind the Isabelline party and securing the throne for Isabel and Fernando, the cardinal concentrated his creative energies on his private affairs.

The most that can reasonably be concluded with the material now available is that his principal accomplishment lay in leading the Mendoza family in a united policy, to the benefit of both the crown and the Mendoza, while his reputation as a formulator and director of royal policy rests more on the tendency of some traditional historians to explain historical change by the deeds of Great Men than on any evidence from the archives or chronicles of the period.

The Mendoza of the early Trastámara period had been aggressive, upwardly mobile military entrepreneurs, constantly balancing profits against risks and deeply troubled by the political and moral expediencies their careers seemed to demand. In many respects, the social instability and moral conflicts of these early Mendoza are similar to those of their Florentine contemporaries. In the course of the fifteenth century, however, the Mendoza were transformed from an upstart clan into the epitome of a noble dynasty. Through marriage, manipulation of inheritance laws, service to the crown, purchase, and even shady dealings, the heads of the family increased their heritable lands, the number of towns and cities they controlled, and the number of residents under their jurisdiction. They became noblemen and began to multiply the number of their titles until they became the most titled family in the kingdom. For most Mendoza in the late fifteenth century, the social manifestations of their position—the family itself, the estates, the households, the noble titles—were sufficient cause for satisfaction, and the old need to refer actions and ideas to the glorious past became less pressing. The earlier generations, which had risked everything to found the family's fortune and power and developed a Renaissance humanism to justify their actions, gave way during the reign of the Catholic Monarchs to a generation rich, comfortable, and uncurious. In the process of transforming the family into a noble dynasty, most of the Mendoza developed a way of life and a social milieu hostile to the sustenance of Renaissance humanism.

The family loyalty of Santillana's sons does not seem to have extended to the next generation. After the cardinal's death, the leadership of the family passed to the constable of Castile, Bernardino Fernández de Velasco, the son of Santillana's eldest daughter, Mencía de Mendoza. That it should have been the constable, based in Burgos, rather than the duke of Infantado, based in Guadalajara, who led the Mendoza during the critical years when the royal succession passed from the Trastámara to the Hapsburg dynasties is something of an anomaly for historians. Traditionally, historians of the Mendoza have treated the dukes of Infantado as the effective, as well as symbolic, head of the family throughout the centuries. But contemporary observers, both foreign and domestic, and members of the family in other parts of the kingdom recognized the constable as the spokesman for the Mendoza in matters of national policy.[35]

Part of this can be explained by the Infantado's exaggerated focus on private matters—sometimes of a spectacularly scandalous nature—and on their sedentary lives caused by a tendency to gout throughout the sixteenth century. It is also evident that the constable was one of the most incisive and vigorous men of his generation, whose influence was certainly not diminished by his second marriage, to Fernando's illegitimate daughter, Juana de Aragón, and by his command of the royal military forces. The constable, however, presided over a Mendoza family less amenable to a single leader. The very positions of power the cardinal had acquired for this younger generation enabled them to follow careers independent of the constable. The palace of the duke of Infantado in the city of Guadalajara continued to be the physical center of the family, and the Mendoza who remained in New Castile and maintained households in Guadalajara accepted the leadership of the constable. Nevertheless, even among these Mendoza, disputes and rivalries—especially between Infantado and the count of Coruña—served to weaken loyalties to the family as a single political and military unit. More serious threats to family unity were posed by two of Santillana's grandsons in the kingdom of Granada—the cardinal's eldest son, Rodrigo, marquis of Cenete, and the second count of Tendilla.

Cenete acted independently of the Mendoza in every way, apparently out of his own independent and arrogant nature, which had led the cardinal to specify in his will that his properties in Guadalajara—including his newly built palace—be sold in order to prevent conflict between Cenete and the duke of Infantado.[36] From his base in the kingdom of Granada—where, thanks to his father, he owned vast estates, held the post of alcaide of the city of Guadix, and became a member of the city council of Granada—Cenete pursued a career marked by brashness, opportunism, and scandal. His political actions were bewilderingly unpredictable. In 1502, he secretly married, and in 1506 kidnapped, the woman Isabel the Catholic had forbidden him to marry. In 1514, the crown brought charges against him for entering the city of Valencia fully armed without royal permission. In 1523, he impulsively joined his younger brother, the count of Mélito, viceroy of Valencia, in crushing the Germanía revolt.[37] In 1535, Cenete's second daughter, heiress to his title and fortune, married the heir of the duke of Infantado. Thus these two branches of the Mendoza were reunited and have since formed a single house. The Cenete branch of the Mendoza family in Granada played a spectacular but erratic role in political and artistic life during the reign of the Catholic Monarchs. Since Cenete left no male heirs and his successors were incorporated into the estates and titles of the dukes of Infantado, this branch of the family did not play an independent role during the rest of the sixteenth century.

The career of Cenete's younger brother, Diego Hurtado de Mendoza (d. 1536), count of Mélito, showed exactly the opposite pattern. Mélito himself played a moderately important role as viceroy of Valencia in the early years of the reign of Charles V. His only grandchild, Ana de Mendoza (1540–1591), was betrothed to Philip II's favorite, Ruy Gómez da Silva, in 1553; and this couple, named princes of Eboli in 1559, became the focal point of a political party at the royal court. J. H. Elliott has described this Mendoza party as advocating an "open Spain" policy in contrast to the "closed Spain" advocated by the party of the duke of Alba.[38]

The period of Eboli ascendancy in Castilian politics—roughly from 1555 until Ruy Gómez' death in 1573—falls outside the scope of this book, but it should be noted that the Eboli's "open Spain" policy was typical not of the Mendoza family as a whole but of the branches of the family cardinal Mendoza created as separate power bases in the kingdoms of Granada and Valencia.

The most capable and famous of Santillana's grandsons was the second count of Tendilla. Through the influence of his uncle, the cardinal, Tendilla was named captain general of the kingdom of Granada and alcaide of the Alhambra. Immediately after the conquest, he moved his entire household to Granada, where the family resided in one of the Muslim palaces of the Alhambra. Tendilla was as capable of the flamboyant gesture as his cousin Cenete, but he was intensely loyal to Fernando the Catholic; and during the succession disputes after 1504, he was one of a handful of Castilian nobles who remained loyal to Fernando and opposed the efforts of Philip of Burgundy to take over the kingdom. Caught up in the tumultuous affairs of the kingdom of Granada, Tendilla became increasingly isolated from the rest of the family. The most important result of this isolation was to increase the Tendilla conservatism and with it the Tendilla conviction that they were the only members of the Mendoza true to the family's traditions.

During most of the reign of the Catholic Monarchs, there were no serious conflicts within the nobility and no national crises that might have put family loyalties to the test. Tendilla and his cousins—separated by the generational sprawl of an unusually fecund family and by the geographical dispersion of their careers—pursued successful policies independently of any considerations of the family as a whole. When succession disputes again generated serious conflicts within Castile, the Mendoza were unable or unwilling to act as a single group; and Tendilla in particular followed a course in opposition to that of the rest of the family. In the atmosphere of crisis, suspicion, and rebellion that gripped Castile after the death of Isabel in 1504, the Mendoza were forced to choose between the traditional policies, which had brought the family success in the past, and new policies, which would bring success in the future. The third duke of Infantado, nominal head of the Mendoza, and the constable, the effective leader of the family, flexibly chose new policies to maintain the family's strength as a political unit. Tendilla, the most vigorous and talented Mendoza of this generation, chose to maintain the tradition. So long as Castile was ruled by the Trastámara, his policies were successful. When it became clear that the Trastámara dynasty in Castile would end with Fernando, however, Tendilla's policies undermined both his political influence and his prosperity, thus precluding the possibility of united family action and thereby weakening the political effectiveness of the whole Mendoza family. By playing the "spoiler," the conservative Tendilla exercised a greater influence on the political fortunes of the Mendoza family than either of his much richer and more powerful cousins—the constable and the duke of Infantado. Because of its influential political role in the reign of the Catholic

Monarchs, because of its singular devotion to the Mendoza traditions, and because Tendilla's correspondence is the largest extant body of prose by a Castilian nobleman, this branch of the family provides the most interesting and significant focus for an investigation of the Mendoza in the last half of the reign of the Catholic Monarchs.

VI

The Letrados:
Counterpoise to the
Caballero Renaissance

When the nobles abandoned their earlier roles as national political leaders, their places were quickly filled by equally ambitious and newly prestigious professionals—the letrados. As the letrados increasingly gained control over the Castilian monarchy's political policies, they also assumed the intellectual leadership of Castilian society, substituting their own theories and values for those of the caballeros. The change in political leadership became apparent at the Cortes of Toledo in 1480 when Fernando and Isabel made one of their most famous reforms of Castilian political institutions: they changed the size and composition of the consejo real, which previously had a majority of caballeros, so that henceforth seven of its twelve members were to be letrados. The consejo real, which had traditionally been dominated by the military aristocracy, would now be dominated by the legal profession. Furthermore, the Catholic Monarchs expanded the duties and prerogatives of the consejo real so that many important matters previously handled personally by the monarchs now came under the jurisdiction of the consejo.

Historians have long believed that this change from government by the aristocracy to government by a meritocracy is a watershed in the political and intellectual history of Castile.[1] Politically, the new consejo's centralization of the administration is supposed to mark the end of the corrupt caballero society of the Middle Ages and the beginning of the modern state. This new monarchy, in turn, is supposed to have created the social world necessary for introducing the Renaissance into Spain. The traditional assessment of Isabelline Spain as a period of political revival and vigorous pursuit of Renaissance ideals depends largely on our assessment of the changes brought about by the reforms of 1480.

For historians of early modern Spain, the question of the reforms of 1480 is part of one of the most compelling problems in Spanish history, both in its own right and as an example of the increasing dissonance between our traditional views and the conclusions arising out of modern research in archival materials. Such research shows that the greatest increase in the number of letrados in royal service occurred during the reigns of Juan II and Enrique IV, and that Fernando and Isabel simply formalized this new composition of the royal administration.[2] This research also shows that the fiscal reforms of 1480 regularized and confirmed the nobility's right to portions of the royal income, rather than depriving them of it as had previously been believed.[3] Furthermore, the documentary evidence does not corroborate the tradition that the caballero administration before 1480 was corrupt; and there is an outright contradiction between the stereotype of the reformed consejo real and the well-known evidence of corruption in the consejo during the sixteenth century. Preliminary conclusions drawn from this research rather than from tradition indicate that the reforms of 1480 confirmed the patterns of pre-Isabelline Castile: a political life remarkably free of civil war and bloodshed; expansion of the ruling dynasty into Aragon and Naples; the shifting of appellate legal jurisdiction from the personal justice of the king in council to the professional Audiencia and other royal judges; and, most important, the institutionalization of the bonds of loyalty and cooperation between the monarch and the aristocracy.

As a result of studies based upon archival evidence, the Castile formed by the caballero administration before 1480 appears more and more as a vigorous and stable society. Whatever the moral character of the caballeros may have been—and this is still a matter of prejudice and speculation—the evidence does not support the belief that the caballero administration before 1480 was degenerate, corrupt, or chaotic.

This new evidence about pre-Isabelline Castile in itself casts doubt upon the traditional assessment of the letrado administration. Historians have believed that the significance of the reforms of 1480 lies in the shift in personnel—that by transferring power from the aristocracy to a meritocracy the Catholic Monarchs ended corruption in government. The assumption behind this tradition—that the legal profession is less susceptible to the temptations of corruption and avarice than the military profession—was one that even letrados themselves could not accept. Dr. Lorenzo Galíndez de Carvajal (1472–1532), the most eminent jurist on the new consejo real, warned Charles V against trusting certain mem-

bers of the consejo who were both letrados and corrupt.[4] The warning
appears to have been in vain. Although we do not yet know the details
of the operation of the consejo during most of the fifteenth century, we
do know that during the reign of the Catholic Monarchs and throughout
the sixteenth century, bribery, extortion, and nepotism were typical of
the consejo's operations.[5] In "reforming" the consejo real, the Catholic
Monarchs had created a majority of letrados—not of incorruptibles.

Although the reform of 1480 did not achieve a change in practices, it
did achieve a significant change in ideals. This revolution in expectations,
more than any other single factor, shaped sixteenth-century attitudes
toward the Castilian past. It still shapes popular ideas about the Renaissance in Spain.

The letrados in the royal council of Fernando and Isabel brought to
their positions a coherent and rational concept of the goals of the government and of their role in it, the concept developed by don Alfonso
de Cartagena and his students long before the reign of the Catholic
Monarchs. This letrado concept of the history and nature of the Spanish
monarchy, based on medieval scholastic political theory and Roman law,
formed a sharp contrast to the assumptions of previous royal councils.
The consequences of this change in the consejo's ideals were all-encom-
passing for, as we have seen, the letrados started from the assumption of
a rational universal order. Their ideas about history and politics were
part of a total system whose values extended into every aspect of daily
living. Their sense of right and wrong would be applied to every field of
endeavor. Even those who, like the Mendoza, were not engaged politically would feel the pressure of their growing influence.

The letrados took their assumptions about the nature of historical
change from the medieval chronicles of Spain.[6] In the medieval chronicles, history is regarded as the working-out of God's will—the verification
in the affairs of man of God's revelation. For the letrados, military and
political disasters must have been the products of man's sins and God's
judgment. In order to make the numerous disasters of Spain's history fit
in with this point of view, the letrados became preoccupied with fixing
blame. Since the same sins are repeated century after century in the
medieval chronicles—kings fail to fight the Muslims, nobles rebel, clerics
become lax—the letrados presented a view of Spanish history as a
steady decline or, at best, stasis. Even when these historians get caught
up in their millenarian fantasies about the Catholic Monarchs, the personalities and individual actions of the monarchs are subordinated to this
pattern, and the letrados' history of this reign becomes an undifferen-
tiated series of royal good works rewarded by divinely mobilized good

fortune. Whereas the caballeros regarded historical change as the result of adaptations to changing conditions, the letrados regarded change as providential punishment or reward.

On the subject of religion, don Alfonso de Cartagena and his father, don Pablo de Santa María, were exceptionally rigid. Scholars have recently become interested in the substance of the arguments these two conversos turned against their former coreligionists, but the tracts they wrote against the Jews are as significant for their method of argument as they are for their content. Both don Pablo's "Scrutinium Scripturarum" (1432) and don Alfonso's *Defensorium Unitatis Christianae* (1449) are among the first attacks on the Jews, they are the only ones written in Latin, and don Alfonso's work is perhaps the first thorough theological treatment of the subject in Castile.[7]

This concern for theology, far from being typical, is one of the most significant innovations in Castilian intellectual life in the fifteenth century. It appears in Castile for the first time in don Pablo's work; and until 1500, it was peculiar to the Cartagena household and a handful of Castilians who had studied theology at Paris. Don Alfonso's work was not adequate to provide the foundation for Castile's theological needs in the reign of the Catholic Monarchs, but it does indicate the degree to which don Alfonso and his students were inclined to break with the Castilian tradition of a pietist, eclectic, and nonintellectual approach to religion. Don Alfonso and his students, in sharp contrast to the caballeros, became preoccupied in their written works with the problems of right-thinking and sought to answer these problems through theology.

Don Alfonso's approach to the problem of the Jews is similar to his approach to the question of proper religious practices, laid out in a response to Guzmán's inquiry on the subject.[8] Guzmán had judged the piety of religious practices by the purity of the Christian's motives; don Alfonso judged them by their Biblical authenticity or their theological correctness. These ideas were not just speculation on don Alfonso's part: he tried to put them into practice both in his private life—which, in contrast to the private lives of the Mendoza prelates, was irreproachable— and by sponsoring reforms in the religious houses of his diocese. The reforms to which he lent his authority were of such an extreme, eremitical nature that they aroused the antagonism of the people of Burgos, who resorted to violence to break up the reformed cells.[9] But by the end of the fifteenth century, concern for correct religious practices had become one of the most popular aspects of the monarchy, with tragic consequences for the conversos.

The same concern for universal standards of correctness which had infused the letrados' attitudes toward history and religion also shaped their esthetic standards. Almost all of their prose works were written in Latin; and their style, whether in Latin or Spanish, was modeled on the elegant periods of Cicero. Don Alfonso made the first Spanish translations of the "Rhetorica ad Herennium" and of Cicero's "De Inventione," "De Officiis," and "De Senectute."

Because of their enthusiasm for Cicero and because the letrados broke with the historiographical traditions of the thirteenth and fourteenth centuries by writing their histories in Latin, just when the Italian humanists were also writing histories in Latin, don Alfonso and his students are often hailed as humanists or precursors of the Renaissance.[10] It should be noted, however, that the letrados' esthetic standards were imitative of those of the Italian humanists. They developed neither an esthetic standard of their own nor one that could be considered peculiarly Spanish. Just as they minimized the Roman period of Spanish history, they rejected the style of the "Spanish" Romans and tried to meet the Italians on their own terms. Because the letrados were addressing an international audience, rather than the Castilian audience of the caballeros, they adopted the language and the style most widely appreciated outside of Castile.

Although they adopted the decorative elements of Italian humanism, the letrados rejected the substance of the Italian humanists' rhetorical approach toward the classics. Don Alfonso, for example, attacked Bruni's translation of Aristotle on the grounds that by aiming for elegance Bruni had violated the rational character of Aristotle's thought. Specifically, don Alfonso objected to Bruni's substitution of a Ciceronian vocabulary for the vocabulary of the medieval translation. Don Alfonso's attack was based not on a superior knowledge of Greek, which he did not know at all, but on his assumptions that the medieval and ancient worlds were so closely linked that tampering with one would violate the other and that a theology based on the rationalism of Aristotle was central to the Christian faith.[11] This was the only issue on which don Alfonso openly attacked the humanists; but in all their written works, the letrados rejected the most basic religious and historiographical assumptions of the humanists.

Don Alfonso and his school were clerics deeply involved in the problems of the fifteenth-century papacy, and it was to the papal court that they directed their works. In order to impress that audience, they wrote not only in Latin but in the Ciceronian style that became popular among Italian humanists after the discovery of Cicero's rhetorical works. Don Alfonso and his students were probably the most adept Ciceronians of fifteenth-century Spain, and scholars have been misled by this fact into believing that their ideas were also humanist. For this reason, and because the caballero writers have never received their due as Renaissance humanists, don Alfonso and his students have been regarded as the focus of Renaissance humanism in fifteenth-century Castile.

In a sense, however, don Alfonso was the head of an anti-Renaissance movement. He and his disciples were introducing into Castilian intellectual life a sophisticated theory of divine-right monarchy that had never been either practice or theory, not even in theoretical works as imperialistic as those of Alfonso el Sabio. Although Spain was the scene of much of the translation that provided the basis for the great scholastic works and the juristic treatises of both the Christian and Muslim worlds, the Castilians never incorporated the scholastic discipline into their intellectual life. When they borrowed from the Arabs, they chose to imitate or translate encyclopedic works of practical knowledge or collections of fabulae that provided moral precepts. It was these that interested them rather than the logical or juridical proofs that are the great accomplishments of Muslim scholasticism.

The scholastic works of thirteenth-century Castile, the *Chronicon Mundi* (c. 1236) by el Tudense (Lucas, bishop of Tuy); the *De Rebus Hispaniae* (1243) of El Toledano (Rodrigo, archbishop of Toledo); and the *Planeta* by el Toledano's disciple, Diego de Campos, canciller mayor of Castile, are notable works that draw heavily upon scholastic methods—but all three authors were educated outside Spain.

As far as we know now, none of the scholastics writing in Castile from the twelfth through the fourteenth centuries was educated in Castile. The scholasticism and theology that aroused Petrarch's ire in France and Italy were almost nonexistent in Castile. Ayala's famous outburst of scorn for scholastics was not directed against Spanish theology, but against the scholastics at Avignon whose casuistry and petty wrangles exacerbated rather than solved the pressing ecclesiological problems of the century. When don Alfonso and his disciples returned from the Council of Basle and began to write Latin works in defense of the Castilian monarchy based on scholastic argument and bolstered with theology, they were introducing a new type of argument and a new political theory. The fact that don Alfonso and his students were both letrados and converso clerics suggests that their educational and religious background made them more receptive to the method and substance of scholastic argument than to the Renaissance humanism they encountered at Basle.

The early education of these letrados followed the same pattern as that of the caballeros: young boys were taught reading, writing, and grammar while living at home; they were then sent to live in the household of a prelate, where they mastered Latin; read the classics, theology, and law; and served in the prelate's household and chapel. At about the age of eighteen—long after the age when a caballero ended his formal academic training—a young cleric, supported by a benefice acquired through the efforts of his patron, went to a university where he followed the course of study for the licenciate in civil or canon law.[12]

Once the student matured and an appropriate post became vacant, the patron secured an appointment for his student, and that ended the student's university career. Those students who had powerful patrons did not take the degrees for which they had supposedly been studying: many of them did not even matriculate in the university; and a few of them pursued their studies in Italy or France while they were waiting for their patrons to find posts for them. Technically, they were not letrados because they did not take higher degrees in law, but they regarded themselves as letrados.

Don Alfonso and his students were an ecclesiastical elite—fluent in Latin, trained to argue in the categories and logic of the scholastics, filled with admiration for Roman law. Little of this higher education was relevant to secular life in Castile, but it did give don Alfonso and his students a facility with the language and methods of the theology developed in France and with the few Latin works that had been produced in medieval Castile. Don Alfonso, his family, and his students—as clerics and converts—may also have felt a special affinity with the religious attitudes of medieval works. The medieval Latin chronicles—from Isidore to el Toledano—were written by clergy combatting the heresies of their own days and determined to enlist the monarchy as an ally in their crusade. Whether the religious enemy was Arian, Adoptionist, Muslim, or Jewish, the medieval clerical historians and the letrados assumed that correct religious beliefs were efficacious in reforming society.

The Mendoza's failure to produce histories that would counterbalance the letrados' tendency to mix history and religion opened the way for the letrados to become the uncontested formulators of Castilian religious policy. The Mendoza had been eclectic, pietistic, and tolerant in their religious beliefs in the early fifteenth century; and as we shall see, they continued to hold these attitudes throughout the Trastámara period. But while the Mendoza held to this moderate position, both popular sentiment and official government policy shifted to a more intolerant attitude. The pace of popular uprisings against Jews and conversos quickened in the politically turbulent years after mid-century; and in the riots of

1449, 1467, and 1474, the crown had to use all its military and persuasive powers to defend Jews and conversos from popular persecution.

As the riots became more violent, however, the government's actions became less successful; and in 1478, the crown instituted a new policy designed both to protect the innocent and to allay the suspicions of the zealous. In its efforts to protect conversos from popular race prejudice, the government established the Inquisition—a judicial institution that would assess a converso's Christianity on the basis of his beliefs and practices rather than his race. It is no coincidence that this judicial solution to a religious problem occurred just when the letrados, with their views of an all-powerful state, their legal training, and their concern for correct religious beliefs and practices replaced the aristocracy as the principal advisers of the crown.

The first efforts at establishing an Inquisition were made by Enrique IV, without success. But the Catholic Monarchs, with the cooperation of the pope, placed the Inquisition in the hands of the Dominicans and Franciscans, directly responsible to the monarchs and claiming jurisdiction in all parts of the kingdom, whether on royal, episcopal, or seigneurial lands. The establishment of the Inquisition is the first issue on which letrados and caballeros displayed overt opposition. Clearly there was a conflict of interest, since seigneurial lands would now be subject to a judiciary responsible to the crown instead of the señor and to a written law instead of the customary justice typical of the seigneurial jurisdictions. It was not the nobles but the letrados—especially the graduates of the Colegio de San Bartolomé at the University of Salamanca—who would profit from the Inquisition.[13]

On a more subtle level, the establishment of the Inquisition posed a serious challenge to the Mendoza's Renaissance religious attitudes; for the Inquisition was operating in response to and in accordance with a growing emphasis on works in Spanish religious life. This enthusiasm for works, typical of the rest of Europe in the same period, has been imperfectly studied in Spain; but it seems to have had its earliest expression in attempts at monastic reform, expanded in episcopal efforts to reform the secular clergy, and reached its most popular expression in the Inquisition, which extended the new standards of correct works to the laity.

There had been attempts to reform the monastic orders in the fourteenth and fifteenth centuries, which often went to extremes of austerity and devotionalism. Pedro de Villacreces (d. 1422), initiator of the Observant reform among the Franciscans around Valladolid and Burgos, advocated an introspective and nonspeculative piety similar to the *Imitatio Christi*:

I received the master's degree at Salamanca, which I didn't deserve, for I learned more weeping in the darkness in my cell than studying by candle in Salamanca or in Toulouse or in Paris. . . . How foolish we are studying our sciences and being curious about the sins and defects of others and forgetting our own. . . . I would rather be a simple old man with the charity of the love of God and my neighbor than to know the theology of Saint Augustine and of Scotus the subtle doctor.[14]

Some modern scholars of the movement have described this attitude as "positive theology," but it contained an element of anti-intellectualism that became popular among some Franciscans in the late fifteenth century and profoundly affected the order's curriculum in the universities. Villacreces urged his followers not to put study before humility, obedience, prayer, and devotion. The reading he prescribed for the reform avoided the liberal arts and civil and canon law and placed great emphasis on the Bible and its commentators, such as Nicholas of Lira; but he advised against readings such as the Sumas de Casos or Bartolus. Furthermore, he cautioned the observants against a critical reading of the Bible itself: "And let them read it with interest and not worry much about those passages where intricate questions occur, for you must know that all heresies arise from misunderstood and presumptuously interpreted Gospels."[15]

Villacreces, like his contemporary, Pedro López de Ayala, rejected theology as an approach to the religious life; but in contrast to Ayala's humanist assumption that biblical passages "where intricate questions occur" had been corrupted through centuries of miscopying and could be clarified by comparison of texts and the application of critical linguistic standards, it did not occur to Villacreces that there might be error in the texts. He assumed that error arose from misinterpretation, and he regarded this with such horror that he enjoined his followers from engaging in any theological interpretation at all.

This emphasis on austerity as a form of good works and the refusal to cultivate theology are typical of the reforms of the Augustinian and Benedictine orders at the same period and are closely related to the adoption of the Devotio Moderna by the newly founded Jeronimites. Austerity combined with an aversion to theology seem also to have been important elements in the reform efforts of the fifteenth-century Dominicans around Burgos who had been supported by don Alfonso de Cartagena.[16]

All of the reform efforts in the orders in the fourteenth and fifteenth centuries are characterized by their devotional spirit, their adoption of an extremely austere life, often of an eremitical nature, their rejection of theology, and their lack of coordination with one another, even within a single order. They remained scattered both geographically and chronologically throughout the fifteenth century, despite the efforts of powerful and dedicated men like don Alfonso de Cartagena and cardinal Juan de Torquemada to unify and standardize them. Even cardinal Cisneros's famous reform of the Franciscans did not long survive him.[17]

During the reign of the Catholic Monarchs, many prelates, influenced by the reform movements in the orders, attempted to reform the regular clergy and settle the jurisdictional disputes that persisted between cathedral chapters and their bishops. The archbishops of Toledo and Seville repeatedly tried to reform the administration and judiciary of their dioceses and to improve the education of their clergy by improving cathedral schools. The government also tried to reform the secular clergy. In every succession crisis and every regential conflict after 1367, the Trastámara kings naturally attempted to mobilize the church's resources in support of their dynastic interests. Enrique IV in 1473, Isabel in 1480, and Fernando in 1512, all convened synods at a moment of crisis in an attempt to use the church's influence as political leverage. All of these synods were called under the pretext of clerical reform, and all of them issued reform edicts, but none of these synods was successful either in reforming the clergy or in substantially aiding the monarchy.[18]

By the end of the reign of the Catholic Monarchs, neither the regular clergy nor the secular had been successfully reformed, but the reform of lay religious practices came to be regarded as a valid and desirable function of the letrados, operating through legal structures—the government, the church hierarchy, and the Inquisition. Throughout western Europe in the late fifteenth century, reformers were trying to meet the rising religious expectations of lay and clergy, while popular religious enthusiasms and anxiety encouraged the proliferation of good works—pilgrimages, relics, cults, indulgences. In Spain, much of the leadership of both the reform effort and the emphasis on works was assumed by the letrados, who through the Inquisition focused the attention of their informants and their judicial officials on examining the religious practices—the works—of the accused. The old attitude of the Mendoza—that good works and correct religious practices were not efficacious if they were not prompted by sincere piety—was now suspect.

The Mendoza religious tradition and their position as the intellectual and cultural leaders of society were also weakened by new developments in education during the reign of the Catholic Monarchs. All through the Trastámara period, the universities fulfilled their function of training lawyers for the royal courts and administration, while the royal and noble households were the intellectual centers of society. In the reign of the Catholic Monarchs, the universities experienced a quantitative and qualitative expansion: the number of colleges and students multiplied, and the curriculum expanded to include the humanist disciplines. Then, as the Inquisition moved from the earliest, most visible cases of suspected judaizing and began to take up the more complex problems of the Alumbrados and Erasmians, the universities responded by adding theology to their curriculum. By the early sixteenth century, the universities had become the centers of both humanist and religious studies for the first time. To a great degree, the universities were filling a vacuum left by the decline of the noble and royal households as educational institutions.

Education in noble households had shaped two of the most significant humanist developments of the early fifteenth century—the translation of the classics and the development of the vernacular as an effective rhetorical tool. In their search for classical models of political thought and persuasion, the caballeros were active readers, collectors, and imitators of the classics. At this point, however, the defects in their education became a handicap and led to innovation. Without a good grasp of Latin, the caballeros found it difficult to understand the very works they were trying to imitate, much less to appreciate their syntax. To solve this problem, they commissioned translations they could use as supplements—cribs—in reading the Latin originals.

The translator, in order best to assist the reader with the Latin original, made a literal translation without aiming for poetry or elegance. As a result of this practice, some of the earliest—and worst—translations of the classics were made for fifteenth-century caballeros. To the caballeros, it did not matter that these translations were depressingly awful as vernacular literature. They used them as aids to reading the Latin classics; and although they were sensitive to the form and structure of the classics and imitated them with remarkable success, they were not linguistically equipped to appreciate the niceties of philology or linguistic criticism. The marquis of Santillana did not feel confident in Latin; so he maintained Dr. Pedro Díaz de Toledo in his household as secretary and translator and commissioned translations of the Aeneid, Ovid, and Homer from both Enrique de Villena and his own son, the cardinal. Yet it was Santillana, not the translators, who wrote excellent vernacular imitations of the Odes of Horace.[19]

The caballeros' defective education also had a profound—but more positive—effect on their own vernacular prose. In contrast to the letrados, the caballeros wrote exclusively in the vernacular; and they modeled their prose on that of Seneca, partly out of national pride because he was a Spaniard and partly in the belief that Seneca's sentences were short and pithy. After the days of Alfonso X, el Sabio, brevity became the rhetorical ideal of the aristocracy; and one of the highest praises a caballero could make of another was that he could express profound ideas in a few words. Guzmán, for example, criticized Vergil for covering a minimum of wisdom in a maximum of verbiage.[20] Guzmán and his fellow caballero authors were not prepared to write in Ciceronian periods, even in the vernacular. Nevertheless, their mastery of imagery, pace, and structure in the writing of poetry enabled talented men such as Ayala or Guzmán to create masterpieces of rhetorical persuasion without a complex syntax whenever the political situation demanded it. Through their system of education, a family such as the Mendoza could hand down its family traditions—the deeds of ancestors, rhetorical ideals, and aesthetic preferences. By the end of the century, this tradition had lost its innovative quality and no longer served to produce literary geniuses.

The most famous educational institution of the fifteenth century was the "poetic court" of Juan II of Castile. It is a tradition of Spanish intellectual history that the sons of the nobility were educated at the royal court and that the poetic court of Juan II encouraged letters during the first half of the fifteenth century. When we examine the historical evidence for the royal court as a center of literary activity and as an educational center for the nobility, the theory turns out to have little substance. Juan II's reputation as a patron of the arts rests upon the fact that Guzmán said he was fluent in Latin and the Italian humanist Leonardo Bruni wrote to him praising his love of study and the protection he gave to erudites. But Juan II did not produce any work of literature, nor did he maintain any humanists at his court, nor did he commission the works dedicated to him by Italian humanists. They seem to have been beguiled into dedicating works to him by Juan's representatives at the Council of Basle, especially by don Alfonso de Cartagena, who has never received full credit for being one of the world's great public relations men.[21]

Since the received version of fifteenth-century Spanish history was developed by don Alfonso and his students, their view of Juan II as a patron of letters became embedded in the traditional historiography of Spain. In the late nineteenth century, a French nobleman wrote a literary history concentrating on three poets of the reign of Juan II—Enrique de Villena, Fernán Pérez de Guzmán, and the marquis of Santillana—

and called his book *La Cour littéraire de Don Juan II*.[22] This title seems to have influenced later scholarship on the period: it seems never to have occurred to later scholars to ask what connection these three poets had with the court of Juan II. In point of fact, they had very little to do with it. Enrique de Villena, when he lived at court, lived in the royal court of Aragon. Guzmán produced his written works when he was living in his village of Batres, exiled from the royal court by the disfavor of don Alvaro de Luna. The marquis of Santillana spent a total of three or four months at the court of Juan II—to make sure that the king kept his political promises.

Dazzled by the supposed poetic court of the king, historians have simply assumed that the royal court was an important educational institution for the development of fifteenth-century humanism. But this too turns out to be without substance. No sons of the nobility that I have been able to trace were educated at the royal court. I have found only those who went as hostages for their families' good behavior in moments of political tension; and this hardly seems like a favorable condition for humanist education at a court which did not have any humanists.[23] The only aristocrat educated at court that I have been able to find is don Alvaro de Luna, Juan II's favorite. As the son of an illegitimate branch of the Aragonese family of Pedro de Luna, the antipope Benedict XIII, he was sent to the Castilian royal court at the age of eighteen to be a companion to the young Juan II.

Don Alvaro produced a respectable body of lyric poetry, received a torrent of favors from his king, became constable of Castile, and received a noble title. The traditional theory holds that the sons of the nobility were educated at the royal court to tie their families to the crown; but the only case we have shows just the opposite: a child from the petty aristocracy—and an illegitimate one at that—became a nobleman because of the crown's ties to him.[24] In some cases, orphans of aristocratic lineage went to the court for patronage: the future poet, Garcilaso de la Vega, and the future Great Captain, Gonzalo Fernández de Córdoba, for example, went to the court of the Catholic Monarchs at about the age of eighteen to win military posts because they had no family connections to work through.

Two humanists are traditionally considered to have been educated at the court of Juan II. The first was the chronicler, Diego de Valera, the son of a converso physician, who went to the court about the age of fifteen and served as a page for several years. As we have seen, however, Valera moved from the royal court to the household and army of Santillana before he was twenty-one. For the next forty years, he served in private households and in foreign countries as representative of the king. His writing was done within the context of these noble households rather than within the royal court.

The second humanist was Hernando del Pulgar, who was probably educated in the royal secretarial school in circumstances much less glamorous than those of a poetic court. The secretarial schools exercised a greater influence on fifteenth-century political theory and had a greater impact on modern Castilian historiography than anyone has suspected. By far the most important royal secretary of the fifteenth century was Dr. Fernán Díaz de Toledo (d. 1457), a converso who took his degree in law. By the end of his life, he held the offices of royal refrendary, secretary, *oidor*, *notario mayor de los privilegios rodados*, and *relator*. In his own day, he was one of the most highly respected and active members of the royal household—much favored by Juan II and frequently mentioned in the chronicles as an administrator and member of the *consejo del rey*. He has recently and justly become famous for his arguments against the Statutes of Toledo, which excluded conversos from public office. In his own household within Juan II's ambulatory court, the relator maintained a school for training secretaries. This is probably where Pulgar received his training, for Pulgar tells us that he began serving in the king's court at an early age and that he remembers the way the boys were educated in the relator's household.[25]

Typically, the secretarial education consisted of learning to write legibly, spell correctly, and properly compose the royal documents. The training in the relator's household must have been exceptional in its Latin education, for the secretaries educated in his household included some of the Latin erudites of fifteenth-century Castile. These included Dr. Alonso de Montalvo; the relator's sons, Dr. Pedro Díaz de Toledo, Luis Díaz de Toledo, and Fernando Díaz de Toledo; and Hernando del Pulgar. Pulgar, in turn, claimed that he himself had educated more than forty boys in his own household.

These secretarial schools deserve a full-scale study, for Fernán Díaz and his successors formed one of the most influential intellectual schools of Spain. The relator drew up or composed the royal documents. Most of these, naturally, followed a set form, and any well-trained secretary could dictate them to a scrivener. But the reign of Juan II was one of legal and political innovation, and the secretarial staff were called upon to draw up royal orders for which there were no formularies. In this circumstance, it was the relator who provided arguments and rhetoric for unprecedented actions—which then became the formulae followed every time the crown resorted to this same action. The relator's formulation of royal documents became the official line of argument. Since Fernán Díaz educated two of the most influential interpreters of royal policy during the reign of the Catholic Monarchs, it is not surprising that there is a consistency of political theory and rhetoric among the documents dictated by Fernán Díaz, the chronicles of Pulgar, and the legal redactions drawn up by Montalvo. The high level of erudition and Latinity in the relator's household was exceptional, and the educational level of secretaries trained after his death seems to have been much inferior. Francisco de los Cobos, who became not only secretary to Charles V but also one of his most powerful administrators, never learned Latin though he was educated in the court of the Catholic Monarchs in the household of an uncle who was a minor royal secretary.[26]

As the private households and royal court failed to take the lead in education in the last years of the century, the universities took on a new role.[27] At no time during the early Trastámara period were the universities the centers or promoters of Castilian intellectual life. This was true partly because of the university's weakness as a financial and corporate entity and partly because of the limitations of its curriculum. From the time of their foundation in the thirteenth century until late in the fifteenth century, Spanish universities suffered financial, staffing, and enrollment difficulties almost continuously. Alfonso X el Sabio endowed the University of Salamanca in 1252, but his son, Sancho IV (1284–1295), discontinued the endowment; and the faculty went on strike so the university hardly functioned during his reign. Fernando IV (1295–1312), reendowed the university, persuading the papacy to allow tithes to be used for this endowment, but later the papacy retracted this permission, the endowment lapsed, and the faculty struck again. In the mid-fourteenth century, the papacy itself endowed the university, established direct control over the curriculum, and licensed a new university in Valladolid. The universities continued to falter, and the reform initiative passed to the episcopate.

The one reform to have important impact on Spanish university life was the establishment of scholarship colleges within the university. The first of these was the Colegio de San Clemente, established in the University of Bologna by cardinal Gil Alvarez de Albornoz. Albornoz was zealous in his efforts to promote the better education of the clergy. As archbishop of Toledo, he had issued an order in 1329 giving each church in the archdiocese six months to send one out of every ten of its clerics away for higher studies, to conform with the decree of the provincial council of Valladolid in 1322. In his will, drawn up in 1364, he endowed the Colegio de San Clemente as a scholarship college for thirty Spanish students to "obviate, by the setting up of this house, the ignorance of the Spaniards among whom the knowledge of letters and the number of trained men have been much reduced because of the crises of wars and innumerable disasters which befell this province in his own time."[28]

This scholarship college, the model for university innovations, was itself modeled on colleges in southern France, which in sheer numbers and in proximity to the patronage of the Avignonese popes had probably been the most important centers of education for Spaniards in the fourteenth century. Albornoz himself had done his law studies at the University of Toulouse; and in the last decade of the fourteenth century, there were about three hundred thirty Spaniards studying in Avignon, Toulouse, and Perpignan.[29]

Inspired by the success of these scholarship colleges abroad, Diego de Anaya, bishop of Salamanca, established a similar scholarship college for fifteen students at Salamanca in 1401. This Colegio de San Bartolomé became the most powerful and most prestigious educational institution in the peninsula; and by the sixteenth century, membership there was the surest route to a position in certain key government posts. During most of the fifteenth century, Spanish higher education remained as it had been at the time of Anaya's foundation—two scholarship colleges of high prestige (one of them outside of Spain), a limited faculty, and a small number of graduates taking higher degrees. A new phase of university reform came in the last quarter of the century. In 1479, cardinal Mendoza received papal license for the Colegio de Santa Cruz in the University of Valladolid. This college provided twenty-seven scholarships and began functioning definitively in 1491. Cardinal Mendoza's college was the first of eight scholarship colleges founded in a burst of episcopal reforming zeal from 1479 to 1525. Of all these, only the Colegio de Cuenca, established in Salamanca in 1500 by Diego Ramírez de Villaescusa while he was bishop of Cuenca, came close to matching the Colegio de San Bartolomé in prestige; but the greatly expanded number of university graduates in Castile and their ability to gain access to the major governmental posts of the Hapsburg government made the universities, for the first time, important centers of education for public administrators in Castile.

While financial and organizational difficulties militated against the university's playing an important role in Castilian intellectual life during most of the fifteenth century, the university curriculum itself worked against the possibility of producing humanists. From the very beginning, the Castilian university was intended to promote the legal profession;

and through one reform after another, this is precisely what it did. Even though custom was the basis of most legal proceedings, the precepts of Roman law were regarded as the model of legal argument. The reading of Roman law, in its medieval redactions as canon and civil law, formed the core of the university curriculum. In order to equip the student for this reading, undergraduates were given a thorough training in Latin, lectures were given in Latin, and students were forbidden to use the vernacular in the classroom or during school hours. This, at least, was the ideal. In fact, papal and episcopal reformers repeatedly found that the students were using the vernacular, and sometimes even the lectures were being given in the vernacular. Still, since the vernacular had officially been the language of government and judiciary throughout the peninsula since the thirteenth century, the university was the only institution in Castile where Latin was spoken on a daily basis; and a university degree was associated, in fact and in the popular mind, with fluency in Latin.

Despite this proficiency in Latin, the universities did not provide an opportunity to study the language as a humanistic discipline. Nor did the Spanish faculty follow the philological methods the University of Bologna was applying to the study of the law in the fourteenth and fifteenth centuries. There was a Trilingual chair at the University of Salamanca, but throughout the fifteenth century its lectures were given by faculty proficient only in Hebrew. Even this instruction seems to have been of poor quality, since the lecturers were not able to make the appropriate analogies with Latin grammar and rhetoric. Perhaps because of its mediocrity, there were never more than seven or eight students enrolled in the course. In 1511, the rector tried to give the Trilingual chair to Hernán Nuñez, who was fluent in Greek, Hebrew, and Latin; but the faculty refused to accept this appointment on the grounds that the converso Alonso de Zamora, who had been giving the Hebrew lectures, would be thrown into unemployment after years of service. Given a choice between improving the quality of humanist education and protecting faculty tenure rights, the faculty chose to protect tenure.[30] As a result of these deficiencies, the universities had not produced humanists. The letrados were rightly regarded as Castile's masters of Latinity, but Castile's humanists had been caballeros, not letrados.

All of this changed during the reign of the Catholic Monarchs. The presence of a large number of students selected solely on the basis of scholarship, the prestige of the colleges' patrons, the universities' publishing facilities, and the very good salaries they offered, attracted Spain's greatest humanists back from Italy to the Spanish universities as lecturers in Greek, grammar, and rhetoric. This shift of patronage to the universities and away from the households of the nobility and prelates had a striking effect on the type of scholarship published in Castile. The old pattern of scholars spending their lives in the households of noblemen or prelates, shaping their research and literary production to suit the taste of their patrons, and adding the luster of their erudition to an intellectual tradition peculiar to each household was now exchanged for a pattern centered upon the international tastes and standards of the universities.

During the reign of the Catholic Monarchs, the "stars" of the new faculties were Antonio de Nebrija and Hernán Núñez, and their careers are indicative of the most important shifts in the intellectual focus of the period. Nebrija (1441?–1522) studied briefly at Salamanca and then spent ten years as a student in the Spanish College at Bologna.[31] He returned to Spain about 1470 and entered the household of his patron, Alonso de Fonseca, archbishop of Seville. After Fonseca's death, Nebrija may have lectured at Salamanca for a few years. He then entered the household of don Juan de Zúñiga, where he remained until about 1493. In 1502, cardinal Cisneros appointed him to the team revising the Greek and Latin texts of the Polyglot Bible; but Nebrija quickly antagonized Diego López de Zúñiga, the head of the team, and then Diego de Deza, the inquisitor general. Deza seized Nebrija's papers, Nebrija left the Polyglot project and Alcalá; and in 1504, received the chair of grammar at Salamanca. He returned to Alcalá as lecturer in rhetoric in 1514 and remained in that university until his death in 1522. Nebrija was a contentious character with many pet peeves, and he was involved in so many academic conflicts during his career that he is described as "the Unamuno of his day."[32]

Hernán Núñez (1470?–1553) studied at Valladolid and then at Bologna.[33] He probably spent eight years at Bologna, returning to Spain in 1498 to serve in a ducal household in Seville. He later took his father's seat in the city council of Granada, where he enjoyed the hospitality and patronage of Tendilla. In 1512, he went to Alcalá as an assistant to a Greek professor where he became a member of the Greek and Latin team of the Polyglot Bible. The next year, he received the Trilingual chair at Alcalá; but he fell into disfavor because of his participation in the Communero revolt in 1520. In 1523, he received the chair of Greek at Salamanca and in 1527 the chair of rhetoric, which he filled until his retirement.

The move of Nebrija and Núñez from private patronage to the faculties of the universities was matched by a shift in their linguistic interests. While in Tendilla's household, Núñez published a commentary on the *Laberintho* of Juan de Mena (1499 and 1505) and a translation of Aeneas Sylvius's *Historia de Bohemia* (1509). Both of these are Spanish works, and their publication reflects the literary taste of Tendilla. After Núñez moved to the university faculties, he published critical Latin editions of Seneca, Pliny, and Pomponius Mela. Nebrija made the same shift: while he was still in the household of don Juan de Zúñiga, he published his most famous work, the *Gramática de la lengua española* (1492); after he moved to the universities, all of his publications were in Latin—critical editions of the early Christian poets, Prudentius and Sedulius, a history of Fernando's conquest of Navarre, and a translation of Pulgar's history of the early years of the reign of the Catholic Monarchs.[34] Both Nebrija and Núñez were influenced by their noble patrons' preference for the "Spanish" Romans, but by making critical editions of the Latin, rather than translations into the vernacular, they addressed their works to an international community of scholars instead of a Castilian audience. The noble patrons, with their imperfect knowledge of Latin and their ignorance of the philological methods developed at Bologna, could not even appreciate the accomplishments of these humanists, much less participate in or give leadership to their efforts.

Private patrons were also excluded from an active role in intellectual life by changes in the university curriculum. Most of the colleges founded during the reign of the Catholic Monarchs simply expanded programs that were already strongly established in Castilian universities. The one significant innovation was cardinal Cisneros's insistence that at Alcalá the emphasis would be upon religion rather than law.

From the first university foundations in the thirteenth century until the first decade of the sixteenth century, theology had been neglected. In his theoretical work, the *Siete partidas*, Alfonso X el Sabio defined the university as a corporation of masters and students established in a specific place with the intention of pursuing knowledge in the arts—including grammar, logic, rhetoric, arithmetic, geometry, and astrology—and the law. Alfonso believed that "the science of law is the fount of justice and the world benefits more from it than from any other science." This theoretical regard for the law above all other disciplines was reflected in hard cash. Alfonso's endowment of chairs in the University of Salamanca gave the highest salaries by far to the law professors. And no chair was provided in theology.

When the papacy assumed control of the curriculum a century later, an effort was made to introduce theology; and in 1355, a doctor of theology is mentioned as a member of the faculty for the first time. As little as this may seem, more attention was being paid to theology in Salamanca than in the rest of the peninsula. Theology was not studied in the Portuguese university until the mid-fifteenth century.[35] The Aragonese University of Lérida, founded in 1300, had no faculty in theology or Scriptures until 1430. And the papacy, in its license granted in 1346, expressly forbade the teaching of theology at the University of Valladolid.

The first serious effort to establish theology as a regular discipline in the peninsula came in 1381 when the papal legate from Avignon, cardinal Pedro de Luna, instituted three chairs of theology in Salamanca. Either competent personnel were lacking to fill these chairs or there was not enough interest to keep them going, for in 1381 only one chair in theology was filled, and by 1393 they were all vacant.

Cardinal Luna's attempt to establish theology at Valladolid at the same time seems to have produced no result at all. As antipope Benedict XIII, Luna made a more successful reform in 1416, establishing two chairs of theology within the University of Salamanca and one each in the Franciscan and Dominican monasteries attached to the university. Despite these papal efforts, theology did not prosper in the Spanish universities. The great names among Salamanca's alumni were graduates in law, such as Alonso de Madrigal, el Tostado; and the only Spanish theologians of note during the fifteenth century, don Pablo de Santa María and cardinal Juan de Torquemada, received their theological education at Paris. The new scholarship colleges reinforced this emphasis on law. Cardinal Albornoz's Colegio de San Clemente at Bologna provided eight scholarships in theology and twenty-four in canon law. Cardinal Mendoza's Colegio de Santa Cruz had scholarships for six students of theology, thirteen in canon law, three in civil law, two in medicine, and three chaplains.

The first attempt to deviate from this traditional emphasis occurred in the reign of Fernando and Isabel when fray Alonso de Burgos, by the terms of his will, founded a college of theology—San Gregorio—at the University of Valladolid; but work on the building does not seem to have begun until after 1488; and the college suffered many difficulties before it finally began lectures some years later. The first successful shift from the law was made by cardinal Cisneros, who established the Colegio de San Ildefonso as the first of several colleges which opened between 1508 and 1528 and made up a new university, the University of Alcalá de Henares. Cisneros specifically wanted to avoid the emphasis on law that seemed to overwhelm the curriculum of the established universities because he wanted to educate the Spanish clergy in their religious role as pastors and missionaries. Typically Castilian and Observant, however,

Cisneros did not consider theology essential to religious education, and the theology college was one of the last to be added to the university.

The curriculum at San Ildefonso was distinguished from that of other universities in Spain principally by the absence of law courses and by an emphasis on biblical and patristic studies. Since these studies ideally required a knowledge of several ancient languages, Greek and Hebrew were emphasized in the arts curriculum, and the University of Alcalá reached its full development along these lines in 1528 with the opening of the Trilingual college. This college was dedicated to St. Jerome, the patron of biblical studies, and provided thirty scholarships: twelve in latinity and rhetoric, twelve in Greek, and six in Hebrew.

Cisneros's attempt to combine humanist philological methods with biblical studies, however, caused serious problems. These began during Cisneros' lifetime in the work on the Polyglot Bible and continued to plague the university throughout the sixteenth century. Nebrija, as soon as he began work on the Polyglot, aroused the suspicions of the Inquisition by his strictly linguistic translation without regard to theology. Nebrija believed that his purpose on the Polyglot should be to find the true meaning and intentions of the Scriptures—an attitude he never abandoned. In the dedication of his *Prudentii Opera* (1512), he defended this approach to the Scriptures, arguing that Christian doctrine should be made available in the most reliable editions and that all the Christian sources should be subjected to the same linguistic criticism applied to the pagan classics: their grammatical errors should be noted and their word usage should be analyzed in terms of its own time and place. The inquisitor general, Diego de Deza, saw this textual correction as an abuse that compromised the authority of the theologians and the tranquility of the church's theology. As we have seen, Nebrija was removed from the Polyglot project because of these attitudes, and the remaining team members complied with Deza's views.[36] The resolution of this dispute significantly hindered the development of a new humanist curriculum at Alcalá, without freeing theological studies from philological criteria. This confusion, combined with the typical Franciscan proclivity for rejecting intellectual pursuits in favor of the Observant life, produced alternating periods of caution and confidence in both humanist and theological studies at Alcalá throughout the sixteenth century.[37]

Cisneros's fears of the power of legal studies to overwhelm any effort to emphasize religion in the university curriculum was justified in retrospect by the fate of the most serious attempt to make theology an important part of Spanish university life. This attempt was made by the prior of the Dominican house at the University of Salamanca, Juan Hurtado de

Mendoza (d. 1525).[38] Before he came to San Esteban, Mendoza had formed an Observant circle in the Dominican house in La Piedrahita (Salamanca), where he was one of the most enthusiastic supporters of a local *beata*, sor María. But he became so extreme in his austerity and spiritualism that the provincial, García de Loaisa, dissolved the group and disciplined Mendoza.

Mendoza himself turned against the *beata*; and to combat the dangers of extreme pietism, began to emphasize the ministerial functions of the order. As prior of San Esteban after 1519, he made it into one of the most austere houses of the order, but he also actively sought out and brought into the order a growing number of bright young men whom he trained as scholars. Since the level of theological training in Castile was still elementary, he sent the most promising of his students to Paris for advanced theological degrees. The result was that the best of his students—Francisco de Vitoria, Domingo de Soto, and Francisco Suárez—returned from Paris brilliantly equipped to teach theology.

The tradition of legal studies was so strong in the Spanish universities, however, that theology became the servant of law, and the Dominican theologians began to apply the assumptions and methods of theology to the pressing legal and moral problems of the new Spanish Empire. This new infusion of the theology of Paris into the traditional legal curriculum was the glory of the University of Salamanca in the sixteenth century. By mid-century, the influence and skill of these Paris-educated Spaniards was so great that they were able to dominate the Council of Trent's deliberations on the crucial issue of justification.[39]

These developments in the universities in the reign of the Catholic Monarchs had the greatest impact on the intellectual and religious life of Castile. The noble houses could not compete with the universities in offering lucrative salaries to the Italian-trained humanists who had educated the children of the aristocracy and added luster to the literary reputations of their patrons during the previous century. When the humanists moved to the universities, they left behind the literary interests and language of the private patrons and took up those of the professional scholars. The noble households were losing intellectual prestige while the universities acquired new stature as the training ground of government administrators and the most active publishing centers of Castile. The letrado theories would be embodied in the decrees of the consejo real, shaping the religious life of Castile through the Inquisition and becoming the most prestigious intellectual attitudes of the reign of the Catholic Monarchs.

VII

Open Conflict:
Tendilla versus the Letrados

One Mendoza was not willing to abdicate the role of leader. While the family in Guadalajara accepted the inevitability of this changing intellectual leadership with a graciousness verging on indifference, the count of Tendilla in Granada fought against the trend. Conservative by nature and alienated from his Guadalajara cousins by property disputes, Tendilla's family loyalties were directed toward the ancestral reference group rather than to the extended family of his own day. From Tendilla's point of view, the family's political power, its place in society, its heroes all were associated with the Trastámara revolution and with the view of Castilian politics and history laid out by Pedro López de Ayala. Tendilla's adherence to the family's tradition, even at the expense of family unity, was reinforced by his two journeys to Renaissance Italy and by his isolation from the new intellectual centers of Castile. When Tendilla tried to persuade the consejo real to adopt his policies, however, it was not just an academic dispute over intellectual issues. For Tendilla, as royal governor of Spain's largest convert population in a period of political and religious upheaval, every royal decree held life and death implications. Tendilla did not realize until too late that in a society that had come to regard tolerance and moderation as deviance, it was no longer profitable to maintain the Mendoza family tradition.

Iñigo López de Mendoza, second count of Tendilla, was the eldest son and namesake of the first count of Tendilla (d. 1479).[1] He was educated in the household of his paternal grandfather and namesake, the first marquis of Santillana. He received his political and military apprenticeship in the households of his father and his uncle, cardinal Mendoza. His father inherited one of the mayorazgos created by Santillana; but with three sons and two daughters to provide for, he tried to increase his estate by service to the king. He was one of the staunchest supporters of Enrique IV and served as the king's ambassador to Nicholas V in 1454 and to Pius II in 1458. Tendilla, then sixteen years old, and his younger brother, Diego Hurtado de Mendoza, accompanied their father to Florence and Mantua on this second embassy. In 1467, the father was rewarded for his services with the title of count of Tendilla, and he was appointed tutor of the king's daughter, Juana, who was taken to live in the Mendoza family residence in Buitrago.

After Enrique disavowed Juana's rights to the throne in 1468, the first Tendilla and his brother, the future cardinal, appealed to the papacy for a restitution of her rights and publicized this appeal by nailing copies of it to the doors of the churches in several important towns. When the appeal failed, the elder Tendilla handed Juana over to her new tutor, Juan Pacheco, and seems to have retired from active public life. Young Tendilla and his brother, Diego Hurtado, then entered the household of their uncle, the cardinal, and formed part of his entourage during the summer of 1472 when he entertained the papal legate, Rodrigo Borgia, and arranged Mendoza support for Isabel as heiress of Enrique. Tendilla and his father stayed out of the early stages of the ensuing succession war, and they are the only Mendoza not mentioned in Isabel's statement of gratitude for the family's support in 1475. Apparently the elder Tendilla remained loyal to Juana, but he also refused to support Juana against his own family and stayed out of the conflict in order to preserve the family's unity.

The second Tendilla inherited his father's title and estates in 1479; and in the next twenty-five years, he more than compensated for the disadvantages of having withheld early support from the winning side. He did this through the Mendoza's traditional route to power and wealth—outstanding military service in the wars against the Muslims, heavy investment of his private fortune in the diplomatic and administrative service of the crown, and a politically and financially profitable second marriage. In addition, he and Diego Hurtado were favorites of their uncle the cardinal; and through the cardinal's patronage, Diego Hurtado became bishop of Palencia (1473), president of the consejo real (1483–1486), and archbishop of Seville (1485). Diego Hurtado followed in the footsteps of his uncle in more ways than one: he too fathered illegitimate sons, became cardinal of Santa Sabina, and resided at the royal court as protector of the family interests. With such alliances, Tendilla's career was bound to be favored by the Catholic Monarchs; but Tendilla himself was a man of exceptional political and military talents and had all the personal characteristics that modern historians consider typical of the Mendoza at their best—charm, courage, boundless pride, lively intelligence, sparkling wit, shrewdness, and prudence. Above all, Tendilla displayed a flair for cutting the Gordian knot with a wit and ingenuity that made him a legend even in his own lifetime.

In 1480, Tendilla married Francisca Pacheco, a daughter of Juan Pacheco, his father's rival as tutor to the princess Juana. This marriage culminated a series of moves taken by the Mendoza in 1478–1480 to prevent the destruction of the Pacheco by Isabel in the succession war. By this marriage, the Mendoza allied themselves with their traditional rivals in order to preserve that balance of powers within the kingdom typical of the Enriquista political structure; and Tendilla allied himself with a family already powerful in Andalucía and active proponents of war against Granada.

Tendilla took an active leadership in all phases of the conquest of Granada; and the chronicles of the conquest, especially Pulgar's, are peppered with references to his military feats.[2] In 1484–1485, Fernando appointed Tendilla alcaide of the city of Alhama, newly conquered from the Muslims, and because of its exposed position deep in Muslim territory, dependent upon an extended supply line and extremely vulnerable to siege. Tendilla's defense of Alhama is the first of his legendary deeds, recorded in detail by Pulgar, who received his information directly from Tendilla.[3] The winter of 1484–1485 was exceptionally wet; and after several weeks of rain, an old section of the city wall collapsed. Tendilla kept this secret from the Muslim patrols by having lengths of cloth painted to resemble the fallen portion of the wall and draping them over the opening while the section was rebuilt from within. A few weeks later, the garrison began to threaten desertion because the supply train with their wages was months overdue and the merchants of the city were refusing to extend further credit. Tendilla improvised a form of currency consisting of slips of leather with a specific amount of money and Tendilla's signature written on them, decreed that they were to be accepted at face value by the merchants, and promised to redeem them at full value when the siege was over. His ingenious use of the painted cloth and the leather currency were both modeled on the example of Frederick II at the siege of Faenza in 1240.[4]

In 1485, Fernando relieved Tendilla as alcaide of Alhama in order to appoint him ambassador to Innocent VIII.[5] Tendilla's instructions were to achieve several formidable goals: a treaty of peace between the pope and the king of Naples; renewal of the favorable bull of crusade of 1482 on a permanent basis; a papal license granting the patronage of all ecclesiastical offices in the cathedrals of the kingdom of Granada to the Castilian crown; and confirmation of a Bull of 1474 prohibiting the appointment of foreigners to Spanish benefices. Pulgar, always favorable to the Mendoza, claims that Tendilla was chosen for this important embassy because he was fluent in Latin and a prudent negotiator.[6] It is also likely that he was chosen because he already knew the powerful papal chancellor, Rodrigo Borgia; because the Mendoza and Borgia had already proved that they could work together against a hostile pope to the benefit of Fernando and Isabel; and because Tendilla's uncle, the cardinal, wanted a member of his family invested with adequate powers to approach the pope successfully with a request for the legitimation of the cardinal's sons.

In order to avoid prejudicing the Neapolitan issue, Tendilla was instructed to remain in a neutral city—Florence—until the peace treaty was achieved, and then to report to Rome. He left Spain in March 1486; arrived in Florence in June; struck up a friendship with Lorenzo d'Medici, for whom he arranged a marriage between Lorenzo's daughter and the pope's nephew;[7] made a secret trip to Rome to speed the negotiations; achieved a satisfactory treaty between Innocent VIII and Ferrante of Naples on 12 August 1486; and entered Rome officially in September 1486. In Rome, he "defended the honor of the Castilian crown" by insisting on his precedence over all other ambassadors, even using force to displace the French ambassador from the seat of honor at a papal mass, and he added to his own legend by performing two feats of ostentatious consumption. The pope was offended by Tendilla's sumptuous and frequent banquets, so he prohibited the Romans from selling charcoal or firewood to the Spanish ambassador in order to prevent him from cooking. Tendilla solved this problem by buying a few houses, dismantling them, and using their timbers for firewood. In another display of ostentation and ingenuity, Tendilla treated the entire papal curia to an elaborate banquet on the banks of the Tiber, serving each course on a different set of silver and throwing the soiled service into the river after every course. His biographers report that this made a tremendous impression on the guests; but after they left, Tendilla ordered his servants to raise the nets concealed beneath the surface of the river, and they successfully retrieved all the service except one spoon and two forks. The incident, with its overtones from Petronius, was later repeated by the Sienese Agostino Chigi.[8] In these incidents in Rome, as well as in his defense of Alhama, Tendilla displayed a talent highly prized by Fernando—an ingenuity in cutting through knotty problems without too much regard for legal or moral niceties. Fernando had adopted as his motto the words "Tanto monta" (so much for that) in admiration of Alexander the Great's cutting of the Gordian knot, and Tendilla's unorthodox but effective deeds could only have increased the king's appreciation of his abilities.

Furthermore, Tendilla achieved at least a limited success in most of his objectives during his embassy to Rome; he arranged a peace between the king of Naples and the papacy (12 August 1486); the Castilian crown received the patronage of the ecclesiastical offices of the cathedrals of Granada (13 July 1486 and 18 December 1486); the bull of crusade of 1482 (disliked by the papacy for financial reasons) was renewed for one year (1 September 1487), largely through the efforts of Rodrigo Borgia; the Castilian monarchs received pontifical indulgences for royal hospitals in Santiago and Granada, and a cathedral in Granada (28 August 1487); cardinal Mendoza received papal legitimation of his sons; and Tendilla and other members of his family received many indulgences for the building of monasteries and hospitals on their seigneurial lands. The only instruction he failed to achieve was renewal of the bull of 1474 restricting Spanish benefices to Spanish nationals.

Fernando renewed the campaign against Granada in 1489, and Tendilla played a principal role in both the campaigns and the negotiations that led to the capitulation of 1492. As a reward for these services, and through the influence of cardinal Mendoza, Tendilla was appointed captain general of the kingdom of Granada and alcaide of the Alhambra. A polychrome retablo in the cathedral of Granada commemorating the entry into the city of Granada on 2 January 1492 has aptly captured the political subtleties of this appointment—though not the literal truth of the event itself—by picturing the king and queen entering the city side by side, flanked by cardinal Mendoza on their right and Tendilla on their left.[9]

This appointment was the high point of Tendilla's career. All of his activities to this point—military, administrative, and diplomatic—had been successful, and his appointment as a territorial governor indicates the great confidence the Catholic Monarchs had in his abilities and loyalty. In later years, Tendilla looked back on the monarchs' confidence in his discretion with pride:

> On Tuesday, 2 January 1492, this city came into the power of the king don Fernando and the queen doña Isabel after they had besieged it

for a long time. The same day, their highnesses appointed as alcaide and captain of the said city and of the fortress of the Alhambra Iñigo López de Mendoza count of Tendilla and lord of Mondéjar, to whose discretion they entrusted all their guard and presidio with a considerable number of horses and infantes, and a few days later their majesties departed for Catalonia, leaving to the abovesaid count the alcazar and city, residing in it more than twenty thousand Muslims.[10]

When he accepted the appointment in Granada, he had every reason to expect that his affairs would continue to prosper. He had spent large sums in the royal service, especially during the defense of Alhama and the embassy to Rome, and by 1492 he had not been adequately rewarded. His vassals in Tendilla had cancelled the debt of 150,000 maravedís which he owed them, as their contribution to the defense of Alhama; and the Catholic Monarchs paid him the 1,300,000 maravedís he had spent on his embassy. But these were small recompense for what he had invested, and he expected that his governorship of Granada would bring him a profit. All the other territorial governorships with their incomes had been made hereditary by the Catholic Monarchs just before the entry into Granada as a means of repaying the military aristocracy without alienating portions of the kingdom of Granada from the royal patrimony. Naturally, Tendilla assumed that his governorship would also be hereditary in his family, and he moved his household from Guadalajara to Granada:

> [The Catholic Monarchs] set me here as in a new birthplace, and I left what was mine and I disbanded my household there of servants of my grandfathers and of my father and my own children . . . it seemed to me that the king our lord had decided to make these offices permanent in me and my successors forever.[11]

For a few years, his affairs continued to prosper. Almost all of the property Tendilla bought between 1492 and 1511 was in the kingdom of Granada, and it seems that by shifting his financial interests to Granada Tendilla expected to develop an economic and political preeminence there that would match the Mendoza's position in Guadalajara. Just as his ancestors had successfully shifted their interests from Alava to Guadalajara in the fourteenth century, Tendilla would have a "new birth" in the kingdom of Granada. But, as Tendilla himself recognized, this move cut him off from the rest of the Mendoza family and from his faithful servants. From this time on, his fortunes would no longer be dependent upon those of the Mendoza family but upon his own political and financial success in Granada.

Tendilla's chances of success were worse than he imagined. In addition to the usual problems of an administrator in the field who must prevail over powerful policymakers in the central government, he was to have difficulty communicating with the consejo real. By nature he analyzed problems in terms of how things really were, while the letrados in the consejo thought in terms of how things ought to be. And Granada was not what it ought to have been: the newly conquered kingdom would unexpectedly suffer crop failure, famine, epidemic, invasion, religious revolt and repression, economic dislocation, and political confusion. The consejo's disappointment in Granada would increasingly be expressed as dissatisfaction with Tendilla and all he stood for.

As captain general, Tendilla was directly responsible to the crown for the defense and public order of the kingdom. All of the military forces were under his command: a company of one hundred lances usually stationed in Vélez Málaga where they could guard the coast from the frequent Muslim invasions from Africa; one thousand infantry stationed in strategic fortresses around the kingdom under the supervision of alcaides nominated by Tendilla and appointed by the crown; and twenty-five *halaberderos* as Tendilla's personal guard. As governor, Tendilla held final criminal jurisdiction over all the military personnel in the kingdom; and as the leading citizen of Granada, he frequently acted as arbitrator in civil suits. When the monarchs were absent from Castile, Tendilla was invested with the powers of viceroy for all of Andalucía; but ordinarily there was no central administrative power in the kingdom of Granada. The spiritual needs of the kingdom were in the hands of Fernando de Talavera, archbishop of Granada; and the senior royal secretary, Hernando de Zafra, was entrusted with the task of surveying the resources of the kingdom for tax purposes and assessing the pace at which the crown should move in the transition from a Muslim to a Christian fiscal administration. Each city had made its own arrangements for self-government as it capitulated to the Christians; and in the final capitulation of 1492, the Muslims of the city of Granada were free to retain their language, religion, customs, and local forms of government. Technically, Tendilla's powers were limited to military and police matters; but because he was the only administrator with command over personnel throughout an otherwise heterogeneous society, he wielded an inordinate amount of political power in the kingdom.[12]

Almost nothing is known about the history of Granada from 1492 to 1499, but this period has survived in the "folk memory" as a golden age of peace and prosperity.[13] Disputes over the interpretation of the terms of the capitulation were settled by Zafra to the satisfaction of both Muslims and Christians;[14] Talavera made every effort to convert the Muslims through education and example, established a seminary to train priests in Arabic and in the missionary traditions of the church, and accommodated the new converts' Muslim dress, customs, and language. This period of peace was possible because both sides were willing to live in mutual toleration of one another, an attitude rooted in tradition and in the personalities of Tendilla and Talavera.[15]

But much of this mutual trust and cooperation was destroyed in December 1499, when Cisneros, archbishop of Toledo, visiting the city for the first time, engaged in a campaign of forcible conversion of the Muslims. Outraged by this violation of their treaty rights, the Muslims rebelled in the quarter of the city where Cisneros was lodged, the Albaicín, and a constable was killed. At first, Tendilla refrained from interfering in the jurisdiction of the municipal authorities, but finally he and Talavera went into the Albaicín to negotiate with the Muslim leaders. They agreed to submit when Tendilla, doffing his cap to the crowd, pledged that there would be no more forcible conversions and that no one except the murderers of the constable would be punished if the insurrection was ended. As a security for his pledge, Tendilla brought his wife and small children from the Alhambra and lodged them in a house in the heart of the Albaicín, next to a mosque. The story of Tendilla taking off his bonnet to the crowd and entrusting his wife and children to the Muslims became a legend "repeated in Granada from father to son." The violence had been controlled without further bloodshed and the reputations of Tendilla and Talavera were higher than ever with the Muslims. But the king was irritated with Tendilla for having allowed the situation to get out of control in the first place, and he wrote to Tendilla: "I am not surprised by the archbishop of Toledo who never saw a Muslim or knew them, but by you and the corregidor who have known them for so long."[16]

No sooner was the rebellion in the city ended than the Muslims in the Alpujarras heard of the forced conversions and rose up in revolt, attacking the Christian garrisons in Guéjar and Mondújar. This inspired another uprising in Ronda and its surrounding territory. The greatest captains of Spain—Tendilla, Alonso de Aguilar, Pedro Navarro, Gonzalo Fernández de Córdoba, and Fernando himself—succeeded in defeating the rebels, but only after some disastrous losses. When Fernando had written to Tendilla immediately after the uprising in the Albaicín, he had ordered him to proceed "with sense rather than rigor"; but after the uprising in the Alpujarras, the monarchs reversed the policy completely and issued a decree requiring all Muslims to be baptized or expelled from the kingdom by 11 February 1502. The Inquisition of Córdoba was ordered to begin inquiries in the kingdom of Granada, with jurisdiction over the newly converted Moriscos, despite the strenuous objections of the corregidor and Tendilla. Finally, the Catholic Monarchs reformed the city government of Granada, abolishing the Muslim council and establishing a single city government similar to those in most cities of Castile but with some concessions to the peculiarly Arabic character of the population. The most important feature of this new government was a city council presided over by the royal corregidor—the chief judicial and police officer of the city, appointed annually by the crown, directly responsible to the monarchs, and holding full executive and veto power in the administration of the council's decrees.

The political effects of these decrees and reforms was felt immediately. Some Muslims left Spain or took refuge in the wilderness of the Alpujarras rather than conform; most submitted to baptism. The religious unification of the country had been achieved almost overnight, to the relief of both the monarchs and their zealous advisers. But among the Moriscos—the new converts—there remained a memory, passed on from generation to generation, of two clear, incontrovertible facts: the conversions had been forced, and the Catholic Monarchs had violated the terms of the capitulation by extending the Inquisition's jurisdiction to the new converts.

The Muslims who had been a peaceful, cooperative citizenry, were overnight transformed into the Moriscos, a sullen, suspicious population. The unconverted outlaws in the Alpujarras began guerrilla operations against the Christian garrisons and extorted food and shelter from the Moriscos; while the unconverted Muslims who had emigrated to Africa inspired and led an almost continuous series of raids on the coast of Granada—stealing stock, pillaging towns, and kidnaping Christians and Moriscos alike. Thus the immediate and permanent effect of the decrees was to place an ever-increasing strain on the military and political resources of the kingdom.

At the same time, the decrees severely restricted the discretionary powers and jurisdictions of Tendilla and Talavera. The old Christian city council was a small group—probably there were twelve regidores—easily dominated by Tendilla and Talavera. As a result of the reorganization of 1501, the city council acquired its own meeting hall (the cabildo) in the city next to the silk exchange; the number of regidores was increased to twenty-four; and the new regidores were chosen from a population over which Tendilla had not previously exercized direct jurisdiction. The first corregidor of the city, Andrés Calderón, had served from the conquest until 1500 and worked closely with Tendilla. After 1500, the corregidores served only one-year terms; and although Tendilla boasted that he got along very well with each one of them until 1514,[17] there was no chance to work out a permanent political understanding between them and Tendilla, a situation reflected in the minutes of the city council. Before 1501, Tendilla's name appears at the head of the list of regidores present; but after 1501, his name takes second place to that of the royal corregidor.

By placing the new converts under the judisdiction of the Inquisition, the crown also took the greatest step toward reducing the influence of the archbishop of Granada over his own diocese, and given Talavera's own tendency toward toleration and moderation, placed him in the intolerable position of having to negotiate with the crown on behalf of the new Christians and in opposition to the advice of the archbishop of Toledo. The Inquisition's powers also intruded upon the jurisdiction of the city council and the corregidor. Among the first citizens investigated by the Inquisition were two of the city's constables; and when the corregidor, Diego López de Avalos, refused to hand them over to the Inquisition, claiming that he not the Inquisition had jurisdiction in the city, the Catholic Monarchs replied with a cédula ordering the corregidor to hand over the constables for penitence and forbidding him to submit a brief arguing that the Inquisition was another jurisdiction, "because everything is ours."[18]

Tendilla's jurisdiction was not affected directly by any of the decrees, but his credibility and his status as the principal representative of the crown were both diminished. The decrees directly contradicted the promises Tendilla had made to the Muslim leaders in the insurrection of the Albaicín and mark a serious erosion of Tendilla's freedom to act at his own discretion with the assurance that his actions would be approved by the crown. Furthermore, one of the decrees of 1500 had ordered the removal of the chancillería (supreme court) of Ciudad Real to Granada. The decree did not alter the legal jurisdiction of either the chancillería or Tendilla, and the chancillería did not move to Granada until 1505; but it seems clear that the crown was intent upon establishing in Granada another representative of the monarchy with powers and influence equal to those of Tendilla.

On a local scale in the kingdom of Granada, the Catholic Monarchs were making that same shift from a government by the military aristocracy to a government by letrados, which had long been accomplished in the central government. From this time on, Tendilla and his successors fought a losing battle against the jurisdictional expansion of the Inquisition and the chancillería of Granada.

In addition to all the increased problems of policing and defending the kingdom and the city of Granada with diminished power, Tendilla suffered some personal losses that further weakened his influence at court and cast a gloomy shadow over the rest of his life. Years later, Tendilla still remembered the tragic events of 1502 with a sense of loss: "We lost two sons in one week and three daughters and another son a few days later and then the two lord cardinals and my brother Pedro and the brothers of the countess and we consoled ourselves, each one [consoling] the other, for there is no other consolation."[19] With the death of Tendilla's brother, Diego Hurtado de Mendoza, archbishop of Seville and cardinal of Spain, Tendilla lost his most loyal and powerful support in the royal court.

This was the first of a series of epidemics and natural disasters that plagued Granada for the next few years, destroying the prosperity of the kingdom and further weakening Tendilla's military position. By 1515, the kingdom the Catholic Monarchs and Tendilla had expected to be a paradise that would yield new riches had begun an irreversible trend of economic and demographic depression. The Catholic Monarchs never returned to Granada after 1502: there was not enough food in the kingdom to support a royal visit, but Tendilla remained at his post through famine and plague, drought and flood, depression and depopulation. From his command post in the Alhambra, he policed the highways, built fortresses and watchtowers along the coast and the major commercial routes, filled posts left vacant by the plague, established a school for orphans, collected taxes, supervised the sale and distribution of food to the poor, and organized and supplied expeditions against the coast of Africa.

Tendilla's attention to duty during this series of local crises is exemplary in itself. But his efforts to maintain the peace and prosperity of the kingdom of Granada take on a heroic quality when they are viewed in the perspective of his involvement in the national political crises of the same period. It was typical of the Trastámara dynasty that the great political crisis of the reign of the Catholic Monarchs revolved about the succession to the throne; and it was typical of Tendilla that his own actions during the conflict were shaped by a single overriding consideration—his personal loyalty to Fernando and to the Trastámara dynasty—with little concern for the policies followed by the constable as head of the Mendoza family.

It is a universally accepted custom in the writing of Spanish history to turn from domestic to foreign affairs after the great triumphs of 1492, on the assumption that the monarchs' reforms had brought peace and order to the kingdom and that their preoccupation with foreign policy after 1492 reflects a lack of distractions from internal disorder.[20] In fact, a period of internal peace did follow the conquest of Granada; but it was largely due to the coincidence that a number of the principal political figures of the kingdom died immediately after the conquest, from January through October 1492; and there was a period of readjustment while new leadership developed.[21] Nor did it last long; for beginning with the death of the crown prince Juan in 1497, the royal family suffered a series of untimely deaths which threw the royal succession into doubt.

By the time Isabel died in 1504, it was clear that Juana, the Catholic Monarchs' eldest surviving child, would inherit Castile and Aragon, and her eldest son, Charles, would succeed her. But Charles was only four years old, and Juana was widely regarded—even by her parents—as too emotionally unstable to be capable of ruling alone. Philip of Burgundy, Juana's husband, was the logical regent; but both Fernando and Isabel were convinced that Philip would sacrifice the well-being of both Juana and Spain in the interests of his own Hapsburg dynastic ambitions in northern Europe. Faced with nothing but unpalatable alternatives in disposing of the governance of her kingdom, Isabel wavered and wrote a codicil to her will, contradicting the will itself. In the end, it was not clear whether Fernando, Philip, and archbishop Cisneros, together and in that order, should be regents, or Philip alone. Philip, with a show of German arms, assumed control of the government in the name of Juana; but after he died suddenly in 1506, it was not clear whether Fernando alone or Cisneros alone should be regent for Charles (or for Juana). After Fernando managed to assert his authority in the kingdom and assume the regency in 1510, it was debated whether or not he had the power, as he claimed, to appoint his favorite, the duke of Alba, as his successor instead of Cisneros.

Historians have heaped opprobrium on everyone who had a part in the succession and regency disputes. But the legalities of both questions were so confused—especially by the codicil to Isabel's will—that the principal actors themselves were making decisions in conditions of chaos. True to the pattern of previous succession and regency disputes, the city councils split into factions. Municipal governments were paralyzed, and there were popular riots against Jews and conversos. Disaffected nobility took advantage of the chaos to seize long-coveted cities and fortresses. Ambitious nobility formed mutual assistance alliances in the hope of becoming kingmakers by swinging their support to the winning side at a crucial moment. Bureaucrats smuggled papers, extorted signatures, and buried documents in red tape. Prelates used their prestige and influence as confidants to sway the confused Juana, the impressionable Philip, or an indecisive Cortes. But even men of the greatest integrity—the most scrupulous legist or the most loyal vassal—found himself in the same position as Ayala more than a century earlier and Santillana sixty years earlier. It had once again become impossible to discern a correct course of action.

In this situation, the only men who were able to follow a consistent line of action were those who disregarded legal and political considerations and acted on the basis of personal loyalties alone. These men were very few: Bernardino de Velasco, the constable of Castile, remained loyal to Juana and her son throughout; don Juan Manuel remained loyal to the Hapsburgs, first Philip and then his father, Maximilian; Alba and Tendilla remained loyal to Fernando. When the Cortes recognized Fernando as the regent of Charles in 1510 and it appeared that the dispute was finally settled legally, no one was satisfied. Those who had supported Fernando were the most frustrated of all; for Fernando was so skilled at dissimulation, compromise, and opportunism that no one could read his true intentions; and an action that appeared to be in his service one day might turn out to be a disservice the next. Furthermore, Fernando became increasingly stingy about rewarding even the most devoted sacrifices—he was suspicious of over-mighty subjects, his finances were perilous most of the time, and when he did have money he poured it into his wars in Naples and Navarre. These men who had supported Fernando lived in the hope of reward and were repeatedly disappointed.

Tendilla had no delusions about Fernando's character. He was painfully aware of Fernando's stinginess, a serious political as well as personal defect; and he had learned early to guard himself against Fernando's duplicity. But Tendilla had great faith in Fernando's political skill and was convinced that no matter how bleak the king's prospects appeared at the moment in the end he would triumph over his enemies. Even in 1506 and 1507, when Fernando's political star was at its nadir, Tendilla repeatedly urged his friends and relatives to give their allegiance to Fernando so they would be favored and not punished when he reclaimed his control over the government.[22]

Tendilla's loyalty to the Catholic Monarchs had first and always been a loyalty to Fernando rather than to Isabel. Tendilla and the cardinal remained fond of Enrique IV's daughter, Juana; and the servants and clients of Juana's mother looked to Tendilla for protection and patronage. On his deathbed, Tendilla was still being attended by the physician,

Iñigo López, who had been physician to Juana's mother.[23] There was also a strong bond of friendship and respect between Tendilla and Fernando, based on their common expertise in military affairs. Tendilla claimed that it was easier to discuss military matters with the king than with Isabel, and in the two months before Isabel's death, Tendilla wrote to Fernando alone on matters of police and defense. Tendilla's letters to the two monarchs jointly were impersonal and formal. The letters to Fernando alone have the more intimate and informal character typical of Tendilla's letters to friends and family, and reflect devotion to Fernando personally.[24]

This devotion, which we will see carried to an extreme in Tendilla's politics, was also carried to extremes in Tendilla's personal life. His health and mood changed as Fernando's health and mood changed. In 1513, Fernando became seriously ill and his health remained perilous until late in 1514. Throughout this period, Tendilla was in bitter despair and often confined to his room by illness. When Fernando recovered and was again physically active, Tendilla's mood became sunny and playful, and he stopped complaining about his aches and pains. When he heard that Fernando had actually started hunting again, he joyously wrote to an old friend to arrange his first hunting trip in many months. Tendilla had no personal stake in Fernando's Italian venture, but he rejoiced over every victory as if it were his own. And he felt the greatest satisfaction when the newly elected Leo X acknowledged his debt to Fernando and praised his Italian policy.[25]

Tendilla's loyalty to Fernando during the confusion from 1504 to 1515 was also inspired by his assumptions about the nature of politics in the Castilian monarchy. Tendilla regarded the monarchy as a partnership of the king and his vassals—a partnership based on mutual aid in the expectation of mutual profit. Every stage of Tendilla's public career—his participation in the conquest of Granada, his governership of Alhama, his embassy to Rome, his governorship in the kingdom of Granada—was in the nature of an investment from which he hoped eventually to gain a profit of heritable income for himself and his sons. There is no suggestion in Tendilla's letters that service to the crown is an obligation of the nobility. On the contrary, it is a voluntary act and has no implicit merit. Its sole merit lies in the profit that will accrue to the noble family as a reward for service.[26]

Tendilla, of course, had many obligations to the crown as captain general of Granada, but he was careful not to confuse his official obligations and his politics. Every service he performed beyond his official duties he regarded as a service to Fernando personally, and he expected

Fernando to recognize this. It was because he regarded his support of Fernando and his position in Granada as investments that he was caught in an impossible choice. He had invested heavily and without reservation in Fernando's enterprises—probably more than any other nobleman except the duke of Alba—and he could not afford to throw away that investment. Tendilla had staked everything on Fernando; and no matter how clear it became that Charles and Cisneros should be cultivated for the sake of the family's future, Tendilla could not compromise himself in Fernando's eyes by establishing a good relationship with the king's enemies. Again and again he complains that he has never sent letters or messengers to Flanders, yet his loyalty is rewarded with losses instead of profits.[27] In politics, Tendilla maintained the same view of Castilian society as a free enterprise system that had been expressed by Guzmán fifty years earlier. In the early Trastámara period, the career of Tendilla's grandfather, Santillana, had been living proof that "as one's power and privilege mount, one takes for oneself as much as one can of honors, offices, and vassals." But Tendilla's career showed just as clearly that in the late Trastámara period Castile was no longer a free enterprise society and that his views were anachronistic.

Even on political matters in which Tendilla could exercise more emotional detachment, he never moved beyond the assumptions of his ancestors, Ayala, Guzmán, and Santillana. Tendilla assumed that the Castilian monarchy was made up of a delicately balanced cooperative effort between the king and powerful political groups. The king's ability to succeed in any venture was dependent upon his success in winning support from a substantial segment of the powerful groups and on his own abilities. Tendilla did not assume at any time that the king would have the support of all the nation; and even more significant, he never assumed that it would be the duty of every vassal to support the king just because he was king. Instead, he accepted without question a system in which the king was one of many political powers and had to negotiate with the other powers in the kingdom to carry out any venture successfully.

Once the king had acquired the support of a loyal group, Tendilla believed that he ought to do everything in his power to maintain this alliance—the king owed allegiance to his supporters as much as they owed allegiance to him. This mutual loyalty between the king and his adherents, to Tendilla, was the essence of political life. He suggested several ways in which the king and his vassals could fulfill this ideal. First, the king must be loyal to his supporters: "Princes cannot expect to succeed who, enjoying the support of only one party among their peoples, wish to make two, or indicate that they do not trust the party they already have by resuscitating an opposing party."[28] He also believed that it was a serious mistake for the king to compromise with his domestic enemies in a period of crisis, for the short-term advantages would be more than outweighed by the disadvantage of having empowered and enriched those who would betray the king once the crisis had passed. He complained that Isabel had made a serious error when she appointed Cisneros—a man who was not a *privado* and had never proved his loyalty—as archbishop of Toledo and that Fernando had compounded this error when in 1507 he had won a cardinalate for Cisneros after the archbishop had been openly disloyal.[29]

With his ideas of a permanent state of balanced but competing powers, Tendilla never conceived of a state in which all parties would agree. It was best to treat defeated parties with respect and dignity and leave the way open for them to cooperate with the king in the future. Tendilla repeatedly advised Fernando to exercise temperance in dealing with his enemies. He bitterly criticized Fernando for having excluded the marquis of Cenete from all the centers of power. And when Fernando stripped the marquis of Priego of his offices and some of his possessions in Córdoba, Tendilla was shocked and angry.[30] As much as he hated these two men and as much as he deplored their disloyal actions, he could not rejoice in their misfortune; for the king, by destroying his enemies, was also destroying that balance Tendilla believed to be the essence of a stable society. In this attitude, Tendilla was repeating the attitude of his uncle, the first duke of Infantado, who was willing to fight against and defeat the marquis of Villena in the Isabelline succession war but refused to cooperate in the queen's attempt to destroy Villena's power.

The vassals, in Tendilla's view of society, had the daily and fundamental duty of giving counsel to the king. Tendilla took this responsibility most seriously, and he kept up a steady flow of letters of advice, recommendation, warning, and criticism to the king. He reinforced these with similar letters to his friends and agents at the court in an effort to make sure that his ideas were clearly and accurately understood by Fernando. Among all those who were bombarding Fernando with advice, Tendilla often found himself a lone voice, the single dissenter, but he was convinced that he and Fernando were in agreement on the necessity for his advice, although it won him many enemies:

> That which the good servant has to do is to conform with the will of his lord and his highness does not expect that I will ever have to send

to say of anyone that he does not do as he should because I haven't won the enemies I have in any other manner except by saying the truth and giving his highness my letters and memorials to those who wish to destroy me because of it.[31]

Tendilla persisted in this attitude, even when he believed that the king was following the advice of those who were his enemies. When the lord was making a mistake, the loyal vassal must protect the lord's interests even if it meant fighting against the lord himself. Throughout the last two years of his life, Tendilla believed that this was his own situation and he complained repeatedly: "Here I am fighting for his highness against his highness himself."[32]

Tendilla believed that Fernando was acting against his own interests because he was taking the advice of men who were not qualified to counsel a king—the bureaucrats. Tendilla was convinced that giving counsel to the king was both the duty and the sole prerogative of the nobility. This attitude was based on two assumptions. First, he believed that only the nobility had the military expertise to advise the king in matters of defense and public order. Second, he believed that every policy—whether religious, military, or economic—should be judged by its consequences; and the nobles, as the men on the spot, were the only persons capable of assessing the consequences of a given policy in their area of jurisdiction. Tendilla was scornful of bureaucrats who presumed to give military advice to the king and of clerics who recommended religious policies without any realistic assessment of their political consequences. As usual, he could find a proverb to sum up his view: "Advice should come from where the action is."[33]

Tendilla's particularist view of politics and society was one of the attitudes that linked him most strongly with his ancestors—and caused the most conflict with the new, centralizing royal government. It must have been galling to men who had absorbed the hierarchical political theories of the letrados to see Granada, which the Catholic Monarchs had carefully kept in the royal jurisdiction, administered by this old-fashioned and arrogant man with his exalted view of the particularist, seigneurial regime. Once the first crack appeared in Tendilla's control over the Muslims (with the uprising in the Alpujarras), the royal officials lost no time in attacking the problem, and Tendilla spent much of his energy in the last ten years of his life in an effort to have his jurisdiction and discretionary powers in Granada guaranteed by a royal document, with a permanent title of viceroy or a royal cédula. As we have seen, Tendilla lost the most important round in his battle against the royal officials when the chancillería of Ciudad Real was moved to the city of Granada in 1505. His original wide-ranging discretionary powers in judicial matters were severely curtailed by the presence of this royal court, and the letrados looked back on this move as a great victory for their profession.[34]

Within the limitations imposed upon him by the presence of the chancillería, however, Tendilla continued to exercise his personal influence on the judiciary. He began to visit the chambers of the chancillería on the days when important cases were heard; and he must have been successful in exerting pressure on the proceedings, for in 1514 the royal *pesquisidor* threatened to bring charges against him of interfering with the royal justice. Tendilla's response to these charges is interesting because of its typical mixture of indignation and bravado and because it reveals his own assumptions about the origins of the law:

> If they are saying that I am absolute, let them say what I have done. If they are saying that I rob, let them say how or in what. Also they tell me that Peñaranda has repeated there [at court] many of the evils being said against me and has said many slanders and here they have written it down. I swear by God that I don't dare go to the house of the judges or of the president as often as I used to for fear that they will say I am dragging them by the ears. With all of this, don't you fail to say that if they should put me on a mountain with deer and wild boars I will have them doing whatever I wish, and there is no prudent man who would do otherwise.[35]

Echoing Valera's statements a generation earlier, he attributes the origins of his own power and status to a natural process, while he assumes that the powers of the chancillería and letrados are the imposition of an artificial law. If he were stripped of all his titles and offices and troops, he would still become the leader and judge of his community by virtue of his own qualities of leadership.

Because Tendilla could not conceive of government with a being and existence apart from the personalities of its leaders and administrators, he could not conceive of duty to a state. Instead, he continued to see the Castilian monarchy in terms of a network of deudos. He assumed that this network developed naturally out of a primitive state of anarchy because of the very nature of men and that since it was natural it was legitimate. On this basis alone, Tendilla was radically separated from the letrados who had taken up the idea of Hispania—the state as an abstract political, moral, and religious force to which everyone, including the monarchs, owed a duty and allegiance. While the letrados were speaking of the monarchy in terms of Hispania, Tendilla continued to speak of it in terms of family—the basic form of deudo. One of the most often repeated sentiments in his letters is that it is natural and proper that there should be loyalty and cooperation between parents and children, and he makes this observation in reference to national politics as well as the family affairs of his friends. When Fernando and Philip signed the agreement of Villafáfila, Tendilla remarked that they were in agreement as fathers and sons should be.[36] And he never believed that there could be real hostility between Fernando and Charles, for "the prince must serve his grandfather and his grandfather—since he will make the prince his heir—must work to leave him the greatest lord of the world."[37]

It was typical of Tendilla's Renaissance attitudes that he never attempted to explicate them in a systematic way. Yet it is only in view of his political ideas—his extraordinary loyalty to Fernando coupled with the traditional political attitudes of the Mendoza family—that Tendilla's actions in the succession crisis after 1504 make sense. And the contrast between Tendillas's actions and those of his Mendoza relatives strikingly illustrates the divisions in the family after the turn of the century.

Soon after Isabel's death, both Philip and Fernando began to solicit noble support.[38] Philip acquired the allegiance of the dukes of Nájera and Medina Sidonia, the marquis of Villena, and the count of Benavente, while Fernando received pledges of allegiance from the duke of Alba, the marquis of Denia, the count of Cifuentes, the adelantado of Murcia, and Tendilla. Fernando's son-in-law, the constable; Fernando's cousin, the admiral; and the duke of Infantado all remained neutral during this early period, allying with each other in the name of Juana but refusing to commit themselves to either Philip or Fernando. When Juana and Philip finally arrived in Castile (27 April 1506), the majority of the nobles and prelates of Castile rushed north to pay homage to them, including the party headed by Infantado, the constable, and the admiral. This party, which had remained neutral in the earlier dispute between Philip and Fernando, considered themselves to be paying homage to Juana, the legitimate heiress and, of course, sister-in-law and cousin of the constable and admiral, respectively. The two greatest prelates of Castile, who had previously remained loyal to Fernando, also gave their allegiance to Philip.

By mid-June 1505, Fernando had been abandoned by all the highest prelates and nobles of Castile except Alba, Denia, Cifuentes, Tendilla, and the adelantado of Murcia. Fernando was outmaneuvered; and in a series of moves subtly calculated to create the most sympathetic reaction, he abandoned the field to Philip. On 27 June 1506, at Villafáfila, Fernando agreed to abdicate the regency in favor of Philip alone and to leave Castile forever. On 13 July 1506, Fernando left Valladolid for Aragon, where he secretly renounced the treaty of Villafáfila, declared that Juana was incapable of ruling and that Philip was holding her prisoner, and embarked for Naples. Those who had been loyal to Fernando throughout and were not privy to his renunciation of the treaty of Villafáfila accepted Philip and Juana as joint rulers, believing that this was Fernando's wish. Tendilla gave the oath of homage to Philip and Juana on 29 August 1506,[39] and the city council of Granada, under his leadership, instructed the city's representatives in the Cortes to give the oath of homage to Philip on their behalf, as coruler with Juana.[40] There was widespread suspicion, especially in the remote regions of Castile and in Andalucía, that Juana was sane and that Philip was keeping her a prisoner. When Philip died on 25 September 1506, this suspicion was transferred to the provisional government formed under the leadership of the constable, Cisneros, and the duke of Nájera. Immediately, parties reformed, this time with Alba, Infantado, and the constable supporting the regency of Fernando in the name of Juana, while Nájera, Villena, and don Juan Manuel issued a Dictamen calling on Maximilian to assume the regency in the name of Charles.

With Philip dead, Fernando in Italy, and Juana either insane or being held prisoner, chaos was inevitable. In Valladolid and Toledo, the city councils broke up into warring factions. There were riots and violence in Medina del Campo, Ubeda, Avila, and Toledo. The Flamenco party—those who had issued the Dictamen—tried to kidnap the infante Fernando (then three years old) from the fortress in Simancas. The marquis of Cenete, always brash and opportunistic, kidnapped María de Fonseca from the convent of las Huelgas, where she had been sent until the courts could decide whether Cenete would be allowed to marry her or not, and married her without royal permission and without legal resolution of her status. The marquise of Moya attacked and took the alcázar of Segovia from the troops of don Juan Manuel. The count of Lemos laid siege to Ponferrada, and Medina Sidonia laid siege to Gibraltar. Nájera armed his household cavalry and defied the authority of the provisional government. Fernando could not have anticipated Philip's death, but he had counted on his inexperience and his foreignness to inspire a political crisis, and the chaos fitted into his plans perfectly. He wrote to the provisional government, promising that he would return to Castile to govern and that he would authorize

Cisneros to govern until his return. In the meantime, he appointed Tendilla as viceroy of Andalucía and the constable and Alba as his lieutenants in Castile and ordered them to pacify the kingdom. Satisfied with these arrangements, several of the most powerful nobles supporting Fernando left their positions in the provisional government in the hands of their lieutenants and returned to their estates. Infantado left Garcilaso in his place and the admiral left Alonso Téllez in his.

By the end of October 1506, the rebellions in Castile had been subdued by Alba and the constable without a single battle, and the military orders had organized their defenses to protect their own lands and lend support to the government's cavalry. The greatest number of disturbances and the greatest number of rebellious nobility were in Castile, but the most serious and persistent rebellions occurred in Andalucía; and they brought Tendilla into the midst of a political conflict that continued in open warfare or smoldering intrigue for the next ten years. As soon as the news of Philip's death reached Andalucía, in the first week of October, Medina Sidonia laid siege to Gibraltar, claiming that Philip had reinstated him in his family's position as alcaide of the fortress in Gibraltar, of which he had been dispossessed by Isabel in 1502.

The conflict over Gibraltar was made even more bitter by the circumstance that the crown's alcaide of the fortress was Garcilaso de la Vega, who was actively involved in the provisional government. As soon as the siege began, Garcilaso's lieutenant in the fortress asked the surrounding cities for help; and this request was met by Tendilla, who was anxious to assert his powers as viceroy over his rival, Medina Sidonia, and who organized an expedition to rescue the city. The marquis of Priego, one of the most powerful noblemen in Andalucía, openly refused to obey the orders of Tendilla without an order from the consejo real signed by Juana. Tendilla immediately wrote to the consejo real— presided over by Cisneros—requesting such an order and then he "anticipated" their response by persuading the chancillería of Granada to issue an order "signed by the queen." Priego did not send troops or any other help, but Gibraltar was able to hold out until Tendilla brought relief and raised the siege, again without a battle.

Medina Sidonia retaliated by forming an alliance with his relatives and friends in Andalucía: Priego, the counts of Ureña and Cabra, and the archbishop of Seville, Diego de Deza. By this time it was known in Andalucía that Cisneros had placed one hundred of his five hundred cavalry in Burgos as a guard on Juana, and it was widely assumed that he was holding her prisoner. The alliance formed by Medina Sidonia announced as its purpose the support and liberation of Juana, but it was clearly directed against the provisional government, especially Garcilaso. Then Juana, in one of her rare moments of political activity and in defiance of Cisneros, the consejo real, and the Cortes, issued a decree annulling all the decrees and mercedes of Philip. Thus, with one gesture, she removed the basis for the alliance's appeal to her as the upholder of Philip's wishes and their claim that she was being held prisoner. By the end of the year, all resistance to the provisional government and to Fernando's regency had been overcome, at least temporarily.

By mid-January 1507, the alliance of Alba, the constable, Infantado, and Garcilaso had solidly committed itself to Fernando and was dominating the consejo real. Juana had rejected Philip's policies and dashed the hopes of those nobility who expected her to support their claims to the mercedes granted by Philip, and she had foiled Cisneros's attempts to force her to assume the government and thus preclude Fernando's regency. Fernando had, without leaving Italy, subdued the rebellions, acquired the support of an important political bloc, and bribed or tricked into neutrality Cisneros and the Great Captain. When rebellions again erupted in the late winter and spring of 1507, it was the leaders of the Mendoza family who dealt with them. Infantado intervened in a dispute between two factions in Toledo and established a temporary peace in the city. Tendilla successfully retrieved the rebellious fortresses of Ubeda, Loja, Adra, Ronda, and Almería for the crown; and he secured the ports of Cádiz, Gibraltar, and Málaga.[41]

By the time Fernando returned to Spain in the summer of 1507, the political situation in the country had settled into the pattern it would maintain until his death. Fernando was accepted as the regent by everyone, and all parties now agreed that Juana would not or could not govern. In 1510, the Cortes of Castile recognized Fernando as regent, even if Juana were to die before Charles came of age. In effect, Fernando became regent for Charles, and Juana lost all effectiveness as a ruler. Royal documents continued to be issued in the name of "la reyna doña Juana," but they were written by the secretaries at the orders of Fernando, and Juana was confined to the castle at Tordesillas for the rest of her life. The issue was no longer whether Maximilian would rule as regent for Charles, or Fernando as regent for Juana: now the issue facing the political factions had become whether to cooperate fully with Fernando and consolidate political power during his lifetime, or to defy Fernando and ingratiate themselves with the Flemish court. In these few crucial years before Fernando's death, the Castilian nobles were forced to choose between the old, native Trastámara dynasty and the new, foreign Hapsburgs.

In this situation, the division in the Mendoza family became clearly and permanently fixed. The duke of Infantado's moves in the succession crisis have most commonly been described as vacillating, but this vacillation was based not on weakness or indecision but on hardheaded and carefully calculated efforts to make himself indispensable to whomever should emerge as the ruler, in the expectation that the new ruler would have to reward Infantado because no king could afford to have such a powerful enemy. The constable's first loyalties were to his sister-in-law, Juana, and his nephew, Charles. Even though Fernando was the constable's father-in-law, it was only after Fernando emerged as regent for Juana and Charles that the constable cooperated with the old king.

During the ten years from Fernando's reentry into Castile (21 August 1507) until Charles arrived in September 1517, Infantado and the constable maintained their cavalry at full strength, allied themselves with the powerful nobles in Spain, and cooperated with Fernando's enemies in the Castilian church and bureaucracy without engaging in any openly hostile actions against Fernando. The alliances they formed after Fernando's death (23 January 1516) indicate that their intention was to form a political bloc so powerful that the new dynasty would be forced to favor it just as the Catholic Monarchs had been forced to favor the Mendoza after their decisive role in the succession war from 1474 to 1480. Infantado and the constable seem to have been little affected by questions of legal rights, Castilian nationalism, loyalty to the monarchy, or even loyalty to Fernando. Infantado's loyalties were strongly oriented toward the family only, while the constable was loyal to the new generation of his royal in-laws; and they were successful in carrying most of the Mendoza with them to a position of strength which placed the Mendoza family in a favorable position under Charles V.[42]

But the Mendoza under the Hapsburgs were not nearly as powerful as they had been under the Trastámara, and this is in part due to the inability of Infantado and the constable to unite the family behind their policy of dealing from strength. Tendilla especially refused to cooperate. Throughout the succession dispute, Tendilla remained loyal to Fernando and invested much of his personal fortune in maintaining the military strength of the kingdom of Granada against those nobility in Andalucía who were trying to undermine Fernando's position. When Philip and Juana arrived in Castile in 1506, Tendilla offered to do homage to Fernando for the fortresses he commanded in Andalucía.

After rescuing Gibraltar from the duke of Medina Sidonia and manipulating the chancillería of Granada into assisting him, he sequestered the properties of the duchy of Medina Sidonia for Fernando. When several Andalucian nobles formed an alliance in support of Juana in 1507, Tendilla joined the alliance and persuaded a majority of the members to declare themselves a confederation in support of Fernando.[43]

Tendilla was also instrumental in separating his son-in-law, the count of Monteagudo, from an alliance Infantado had formed against Fernando. After Fernando was recognized as the regent of Charles in 1510, Tendilla never attempted to correspond with anyone at the Flemish court, and he refused to ally with those nobles who were withholding support from Fernando. He persistently tried to expose and discredit what he called "el bando de Toledo," a group of nobility in New Castile led by the marquis of Villena and cardinal Cisneros, whom Tendilla believed to be disloyal to Fernando. Most of the nobles who were Tendilla's neighbors in Andalucía formed a mutual assistance pact, "la liguilla," under the leadership of the Great Captain and the marquis of Priego; and in 1515, the liguilla allied with the bando de Toledo.

Surrounded by these powerful enemies, Tendilla remained aloof from all alliances and continued to serve Fernando loyally. Instead of trying to find a position of strength and then negotiate with the king, Tendilla gave his resources and his loyalty to Fernando without reservation. Since Fernando could always count on him, there was never any need to negotiate the terms under which Tendilla would serve Fernando. Once the service was performed, Tendilla was in a weak position to negotiate and had to depend on Fernando's sense of justice and gratitude for his reward.[44] Tendilla placed loyalty to Fernando above the family's welfare; and as a result, he placed his own immediate family in a weakened position and weakened the position of the Mendoza as a whole, by breaking up the family's ability to present a united front in times of crisis. As a result, the Mendoza received few rewards from either Fernando or the Hapsburgs.

The weaknesses that had developed within the family itself coincided with a major change in the government which made it difficult for the Mendoza (or the other nobles) to deal directly with the crown during the sixteenth century. The bureaucracy created by Enrique IV and nurtured by Fernando and Isabel became the single most effective political bloc during the years from 1504 to 1520. While the traditional political blocs of the nobility broke up into smaller, less effective units; while the Castilian monarchs were outside the country, or insane, or not recognized by the Cortes, or too ill to assume the responsibilities of government, the bureaucracy plodded on with the business of the country—collecting taxes, notarizing contracts, issuing licenses, dispensing justice, supervising municipal governments, and countersigning royal decrees. In the last three years of Fernando's life, from 1513 to 1516, when the king was too ill most of the time to do more than maintain a pretense of governing, the bureaucracy emerged decisively as the single most influential political group in the kingdom; and during the almost continuous absences of Charles, they solidified their position.

More than most nobles, Tendilla was adversely affected by the increasing powers of the bureaucracy. The strength of the great noble families in the fifteenth century, and especially of the Mendoza, was their independence of the royal government. But Tendilla could not detach himself from the royal government: he wanted to increase his fortune and therefore had to receive favors from the crown; and he was an officer of the crown and could not act independently, as the events of 1499–1500 had shown. As Fernando's health failed after 1513, his correspondence was taken over by the royal secretaries; and Tendilla lost that direct communication with the monarch which was the most important privilege of the nobility. He was in the worst possible position for a nobleman: he had to make his voice felt at court, but he could not do so in person. Instead, he had to influence these new centers of power at court—those who held the king's pen, he called them—and to do this he needed to use all the influence of his political powers in Granada and his connections among the nobility. Throughout the succession dispute, Tendilla had single-mindedly placed loyalty to Fernando before his own interests; and he had failed to build those alliances in Granada and Castile that would have protected his own interests. As all of Castile prepared to meet the new Hapsburg rulers of Spain, Tendilla found himself isolated and weak.

Tendilla's position became most clearly and dangerously evident in 1514–1515 when Fernando tried to collect enough political support in Castile to appoint his favorite, the duke of Alba, as regent for Charles, a violation of Isabel's will stipulating that cardinal Cisneros should act as regent after Fernando's death. Tendilla, of course, supported Fernando on this issue and pledged himself wholeheartedly to Alba. This time Tendilla had chosen the losing side. Cardinal Cisneros won the support of the nobles who had supported Philip in the succession dispute and of most of the bureaucracy. By mid-1515, even the constable and Infantado had pledged their support to Cisneros. Tendilla was left with only a handful of allies and a plethora of powerful enemies.

Tendilla's most dangerous enemy was the archbishop of Toledo, cardinal Cisneros, of whom he said: "I would rather remain in the power of the Muslims and devils than the cardinal because I see him ambitious and, as you know, he always wanted to put me down and humble me during the time when the king was absent."[45] Much of this antagonism between Tendilla and Cisneros was based on simple rivalry between two men who wanted to have power in appointments and in military affairs. After Tendilla failed to win the bishopric of Avila for his son, Francisco, in 1514, he could not help but compare the influence his family had held when cardinal Mendoza controlled appointments and his own lack of influence with Cisneros:

> I have been so disappointed and grouchy since the vacancy of Avila that I only felt like snapping like a dying horse at whoever comes near me. The truth is that where the cardinal [Cisneros] ventures forth there is nothing to say. The cardinal my uncle said to the marquise of Moya, "Tell the queen that if she gives the archbishopric of Seville to a favorite it doesn't bother me at all, but if she gives it to anyone except my nephew I will never again live at her court." Thus [the vacancy of Avila] was offered to a favorite.[46]

The antagonism between Tendilla and Cisneros was essentially a difference of attitudes toward the most pressing religious problem of Granada, the Arabic customs and clothing of the Moriscos. Tendilla, true to the traditions of his ancestors and aware of the political leverage this issue gave him, argued that these should not be forcibly changed, since they were irrelevant to the religious issues. Cisneros was equally convinced that these outer habits were symbolic of an inner apostasy, and he encouraged the crown and the local authorities to enforce the most rigid edicts against Muslim clothing and customs.[47] The hostility between Tendilla and Cisneros on this issue had existed since the up-rising of the Albaicín in 1499. By 1514, it had become a battle to see who could control the decisions of the consejo real, the city council of Granada, and the nobility of Andalucía.

Tendilla's other major enemy, the Great Captain, was also increasingly powerful in the last months of Fernando's reign, as his nephew, the marquis of Priego, and other dissident nobility attempted to reestablish control over local areas of Andalucía before a new regime could consolidate its position. Tendilla was hostile toward the Great Captain for several reasons, all arising from the incidents surrounding the Great Captain's return from Italy in 1507. Fernando had lured the Great Captain out of Italy by promising him the grand mastership of the

Order of Santiago and command of an expedition to Africa. Once back in Spain, the Great Captain plunged into the preparations for the African expedition, only to have Fernando cancel the whole undertaking after the men and supplies had already been collected. Instead of appointing him grand master of Santiago, Fernando made him alcaide of the fortress of Loja, just a few miles west of the city of Granada. Tendilla had hoped to receive this appointment himself, and he was angry with Fernando, not only for giving Loja to someone else but for giving it to an enemy in preference to an ally.[48]

Among the royal secretaries, Tendilla most frequently dealt with the powerful Lope Conchillos and the rising Francisco de los Cobos, but he never trusted Conchillos to be loyal to him or to the king's interests in Granada. For some time, Tendilla was successful in bribing both Conchillos and Cobos to gain their cooperation, but in 1514 both of them raised the price of their cooperation so drastically that Tendilla was unable to meet it. For most of 1514, Tendilla tried to ingratiate himself with Conchillos with flattery, even while he was complaining bitterly to his agent Ortiz about the secretary's avarice; but when Conchillos began to advise the king about military matters in Granada, Tendilla lost all control. The idea that a bureaucrat would presume to give advice on military matters, especially one who did not know the terrain, and the disrespect toward himself which this advice implied made Tendilla furious. His pride as a nobleman and his jurisdiction as an administrator could not have been more deeply intruded upon.[49]

When Fernando became seriously ill in the summer of 1515, Tendilla realized that in addition to the cardinal and the Great Captain all the royal secretaries had become his enemies and were trying to turn others against him. All of his favors and patronage for Cobos and all of his bribes and flattery for Conchillos had done nothing to win these men to his side when the king was at the point of death.[50]

In addition to acquiring all these enemies in high places and low, Tendilla was in constant conflict with his cousin, the third duke of Infantado. They had chosen opposing sides in the succession disputes, and Tendilla had the lowest opinion of Infantado's judgment in political affairs. But the real source of antagonism between them was litigation over the terms of the will of their grandfather, Santillana. Infantado had taken up the claims of Tendilla's sister-in-law, Catalina Laso de la Vega, and succeeded in 1515 in obtaining a court order which prevented Tendilla's tenants from harvesting the grapes on the disputed property. To Tendilla, the enmity of Infantado was just the final straw in a long series of conflicts which had left him without allies in the face of increasing dangers.

Tendilla's relations with the rest of the Mendoza family were not much better. His son-in-law, Antonio de Mendoza, count of Monteagudo, had allied himself with Infantado. His young cousin, the marquis of Cenete, had remained noncomittal throughout the succession dispute, pursuing personal interests rather than political affairs. Since Cenete was alcaide of Guadix, one of the strategic fortresses of the kingdom of Granada, Tendilla had to cooperate with him in the maintenance of public order, and especially in the policing of the highway between the cities of Guadix and Granada. But Tendilla was always suspicious of Cenete, and his spies in Guadix fed this suspicion by reporting on various occasions that Cenete was negotiating with the Great Captain, though he seems never to have committed himself to the Great Captain's party.

By late spring in 1515, Tendilla was isolated from the sources of power in Andalucía, and when he found that Cenete was again sending messengers to Loja to negotiate with the Great Captain, he complained to Ortiz in the most despairing (but typically pungent) terms:

> Now you will see what the marquis of Cenete intends in Guadix. I find myself well placed here on the cross, one hand nailed in Loja and the other in Guadix and my feet on the marquis of Priego and my head crowned by the corregidor of Granada and my side pierced by Zapata and Cobos.[51]

Even at this late date, with his enemies gaining allies every day, his authority in Granada usurped by "those who have the king's pen," and rumors flying that Fernando was dying or already dead, Tendilla would not give up his policy of loyalty to Fernando. He could depend on the constable, Infantado, and Cenete to guarantee that whatever else might happen he and his sons would not be completely ruined. The Mendoza in the past had worked to prevent the destruction of their enemies, let alone members of their own family. Despite their inability to work together and their political antagonisms, they were still concerned about the preservation of the family, and even such an irresponsible and defiant Mendoza as Cenete took the trouble to warn Tendilla of one of the Great Captain's plots and to pledge his support "to those of the Mendoza family, because the house was all one."[52]

But this was not enough; and in the end, Tendilla had to accept defeat. In his last report to Ortiz, two weeks before his own death, he instructed Ortiz to compromise with Fernando's enemies:

And they say that the duke of Infantado has allied secretly with the cardinal and they write to me from Guadalajara that they believe that the count of Coruña is secretly allied with the duke of Infantado. . . . On my behalf say to the comendador mayor of Castile [Hernando de Vega] and even to the duke [of Alba] when you speak to him that my enmity with the duke [of Infantado] is no more than that he does not want to give what is mine, which is a light thing and that whether I give in or he pays it can be agreed that it is not a thing which impedes. . . . Give him to understand that I am very much for the cardinal . . . for I am not able to do anything and they can do harm every hour.[53]

This is a pathetic reversal for a man who, eight months earlier, had pledged his support to Alba and the king in the strongest terms: "I will serve you for I am not dead yet nor do I intend to die until I bury a few more of those who wish me evil along with those whom I have already buried."[54]

By 1515, Tendilla had outlived most of his own generation of the conquest of Granada; he had tied his own fortune to the prosperity of the kingdom of Granada; he had isolated himself geographically and politically from the rest of the Mendoza and most of the nobility; he had lost his influence with Fernando; and he had acquired powerful enemies among the bureaucracy and church hierarchy. But Tendilla's most serious political weakness grew out of his own conservative and inflexible nature. The party to which he had committed himself had become the losing party and he knew it, but he refused to change his allegiance until it was too late to bring him any advantage. Instead of lending his strength to a party that would welcome and reward it, Tendilla, by his reversal in the summer of 1515, was simply accepting a *fait accompli*: cardinal Cisneros, Tendilla's most hated enemy, would be regent of Castile after Fernando's death. Even the duke of Alba, whom Tendilla had supported in the hope that he would become regent, had recognized this fact, but Tendilla, like Fernando himself, admitted defeat only on the point of death.

Perplexed, angry, and frustrated, Tendilla continued until the last month of his life to believe that Fernando could save him from all of his difficulties if he could only break through the circle of "those who have the king's pen." Blinded by his exaggerated confidence in Fernando, Tendilla could not see that the king had become apathetic and given up the active leadership of Alba's party. Thus isolated by geography, politics, and his own stubborn loyalty, Tendilla continued to act in a manner no longer relevant to the new realities of Castilian politics. By following this anachronistic policy of loyalty to the last of the Trastámara monarchs, Tendilla brought about his own failure. Through this same policy, he refused to cooperate with the rest of the Mendoza and so destroyed the family's ability to act as a single political bloc in periods of crisis. Throughout his career, Tendilla had followed the patterns established by his glorious ancestors; and even after he knew that it would result in political and economic disaster, he could not bring himself to abandon the Mendoza tradition. As he ruefully confessed to the royal secretary, Francisco de los Cobos, a week before he died, "I never was able to leave aside a course of action once I took it up."[55]

VIII

The Failure of the
Caballero Renaissance

During the reign of the Catholic Monarchs, the Mendoza family produced no poets or historians. Santillana's sons and grandsons continued to act as patrons of the arts, and some of their clients were among the most distinguished authors of the period. Santillana's descendants also collected impressive libraries, and some of these men are known to have been men of erudition; but not one of them produced a work of literature. By the beginning of the sixteenth century, the Mendoza looked on the family's Renaissance literary accomplishment as a thing of the past. These generations revered the literary talents of their ancestors, just as they revered their military exploits; but literary creativity was no longer a part of their active lives. Instead, they channeled their creative energies into architecture, building a series of palaces, churches, and schools in Guadalajara and Granada—the visible reminders of the Mendoza wealth and splendor. Throughout the Trastámara period, the most prestigious esthetic styles had been inspired by Avignon, Florence, and then Rome, as the Spanish traveled to and from the papal court and absorbed its taste. This had been true for both the Mendoza and the letrados.

During the reign of the Catholic Monarchs, however, the leaders of Castilian society turned to the courts of northern Europe and to their own medieval past for their artistic inspiration. Even in esthetics, an overtly safe issue that did not offend religious sensibilities or require the new expertise of the universities, most of the Mendoza followed the lead of the constable and the duke of Infantado and adapted to the new style. Only Tendilla and his sons would battle to maintain the Renaissance esthetic tradition. When the Tendilla extended their efforts into the emotionally charged issue of religion, the dimensions of the Mendoza failure became apparent: they did not have the political power, the intellectual prestige, or the personal influence to protect the family tradition, much less to impose it on the society of sixteenth-century Spain.

Many members of the Mendoza family were enthusiastic book collectors, regarding the libraries they had inherited as evidence of their ancestors' literary accomplishments. In order to perpetuate the family's intellectual reputation and remind future generations of this aspect of the family's history, they built some of the largest collections of their day and tried to attach them to more permanent institutions within the estate, such as the mayorazgo or a monastery. In his will, drawn up in 1475, the first duke of Infantado, ordered his eldest son to incorporate the books of the marquis of Santillana into the mayorazgo

> so that they may always go with and be attached to the other property in the mayorazgo . . . because I greatly desire that he and his descendants should give themselves to study, as the marquis my lord, may he rest in peace, and I and our ancestors did, firmly believing our persons and house to be greatly improved and elevated by it.[1]

Typically, the son did not follow his father's testamentary wishes; and in 1565, the fourth duke of Infantado, still adding to the collection, would write in his will:

> I have always heard it said that the library which is in this house was part of the mayorazgo and I leave it to the count of Saldaña my grandson and successor, including the books which the duke my lord and father inherited as well as those which I have accumulated and together with this I leave and bequeath to him the falcons, as many as there may be.[2]

Almost two hundred years after the king of Aragon wrote to Juan Fernández de Heredia in Avignon asking him to bring books and hunting dogs, the two were still lumped together in the minds of the military aristocracy. The nobles did not see letters in conflict with nobility, as some modern literary critics believe.

Given the intellectual atmosphere of a Castile dominated by letrados and the lack of intellectual leadership in the Mendoza family, it may have been inevitable that the Mendoza libraries became increasingly popular in their tastes. In 1455, the constable's grandfather, Pedro

Fernández de Velasco, first count of Haro, had commissioned many translations and transcriptions and donated them to the Hospital de la Veracruz, which he had founded on his estate of Medina de Pomar. Velasco's son and grandsons continued to donate books to this library throughout the fifteenth and sixteenth centuries, apparently at the expense of building up a library in their own household. Since the donations were selected for a monastery, the collection became overwhelmingly ecclesiastical and devotional in content. Cardinal Mendoza was also an active book collector and left a library of considerable value, although typically episcopal in its emphasis on canon and civil law. The Infantado library shunned these subjects in favor of literature, the patristics, and how-to-do-it books on subjects of interest to the nobility: law, letter writing, agriculture, hunting, architecture.[3]

The Mendoza libraries reveal the changing reading preferences of their owners in a generation otherwise singularly uncommunicative about its literary tastes: in all the library inventories there is an increased emphasis on devotional works; and in the case of the Infantado library, a new taste for the novel of chivalry. Novels of chivalry, inspired by Catalán adventures in the eastern Mediterranean and by the Breton chivalric cycles, had circulated in Spain as early as the fourteenth century, but they were not important in the intellectual life of Castile, and they do not appear in even the largest private libraries, such as that of Santillana.

Santillana was interested in "caballería"; and inspired by Bruni's treatment of the subject, exchanged letters on its nature with don Alfonso de Cartagena, citing historical examples from the Roman histories, etymological evidence, and the opinions of Cicero and other classical authorities.[4] To Santillana and his generation, *caballería* meant *nobility* rather than *chivalry*; but by the end of the century, this concept of caballería was replaced by the standards of the novel of chivalry, with its lovesick knights, courtly manners, and fantasies of war. These novels were the most widely read works of the end of the fifteenth century, and they became a craze after the publication of *Amadís de Gaula* in 1508, even among the Mendoza. It is curious that Infantado was indirectly responsible for the spread of this fad to France, for Francis I read the Amadís Cycle while he was lodged in Infantado's palace as a prisoner of war after Pavía and later ordered its translation into French.[5] This sort of romanticized knight errantry had long been popular at the Burgundian court,[6] but for the Mendoza the adoption of the novel of chivalry marked an important shift in their literary interests from classical antiquity to the medieval past.

While the dukes of Infantado—and the royal court—took up the literary tastes of northern Europe, Tendilla continued that interest in ancient history and the Latin classics typical of his ancestors. Without an inventory of Tendilla's library, it is impossible to be sure of what books he owned, but his letters give many indications of his reading habits.

During most of his tenure as captain general, Tendilla does not seem to have done much reading. His letters for 1504 through 1512 rarely mention books of any kind, and his few references to literary and historical matters are vague. In the summer of 1506, when he heard that Fernando and Philip had negotiated the agreement of Villafáfila while at a distance of four leagues from each other, he was reminded of the *romance* of the Cid and the Muslim.[7] These vague references to works Tendilla had read in his youth are largely replaced in the last two years of his life by specific references to works he was reading for the first time or works he was carefully rereading and annotating. This change in his reading habits was the result of his retirement and his increasing isolation from the local administration. As early as the spring of 1514, Tendilla claimed that he had "no other pastime but to read and write with my own hand in some books which I began a few days ago because I would like to finish them before I die."[8] By the time of his death in 1515, he had finished reading Augustine and Josephus and had reread and annotated Aeneus Sylvius' *Historia de Bohemia*.[9] There is no indication in his letters that he ever took up reading the popular chivalric novels; the books he wanted to finish before he died were classics from the Roman period and a history written by an Italian humanist pope whom he had seen and admired on his first visit to Italy in 1458. There is perhaps no greater evidence of Tendilla's conservatism than this Renaissance reading list, begun at the age of seventy-two, a full generation after the Renaissance had ceased to be fashionable in Castile.

As erudites themselves and patrons of erudition, the Mendoza developed their esthetic preferences in equally divergent directions. Those who remained loyal to Infantado and the constable associated themselves, peripherally, with universities and produced, or sponsored the production of, works that found favor at the court. Juan Hurtado de Mendoza, señor of Fresno de Torote and himself a poet of modest talents, often acted as a judge in poetry contests at the University of Alcalá.[10] Cardinal Cisneros asked the third duke of Infantado to be the patron of the University of Alcalá, although the relationship seems to have been distasteful to both. Cisneros wrote to the third Infantado: "If

I didn't esteem you, I would not have made you patron of my beloved university," and Infantado replied: "And if I didn't respect and want to serve you in such a great undertaking, I would not have taken the patronage of it."[11]

Cardinal Mendoza maintained a large household of clients, relatives, students, and employees. Of these, the most erudite was Diego de Muros, who was secretary to the cardinal for many years, became bishop of Mondoñedo and then of Oviedo, and founded the Colegio Mayor de San Salvador de Oviedo in Salamanca in 1517. His most important publication was an edition of the *Carmen Paschale* of Sedulius (Valladolid, 1497), a pale reflection of the Mendoza preference for Christian works in classical forms.[12]

The most famous of the cardinal's clients was Hernando del Pulgar, but he is also the most difficult to assess intellectually because his relationship with the cardinal created a conflict of interest with his duties as royal chronicler. Pulgar was not directly employed by the cardinal, but his royal pension was partly paid by cardinal Mendoza: in the mercedes reform carried out in 1480, Pulgar was reported to be receiving thirty-five thousand maravedís per annum from the royal revenues assigned to the cardinal.[13] Pulgar was proud of his close friendship with the cardinal and with the whole Mendoza family, and he imitated their works and used their styles as justification for his own.[14] His collection of biographical sketches, the *Claros varones*, was intended to be a more erudite continuation of Guzmán's *Generaciones*; and when someone criticized him for inserting humor into serious works, he used the Mendoza as an example of the validity of this technique:

> You accuse me likewise of being proud because I sometimes write jocular things and certainly, sir, underneath, you tell the truth; but I have seen those noble and magnificent men the marquis of Santillana, don Iñigo López de Mendoza; and don Diego Hurtado de Mendoza his son, duke of Infantado; and Fernán Pérez de Guzmán, señor of Batres, and other notable men write passages of great doctrine, sprinkling them with some funny things which give wit to the truth.[15]

When Pulgar wanted to object publicly to the operations of the Inquisition, it was to cardinal Mendoza that he addressed his letters.[16] As royal chronicler and propagandist, Pulgar had the duty of translating Palencia's account of the reign of Enrique IV and extending the letrados' version of Spanish history and politics to the reign of the Catholic Monarchs. Although he succeeded in achieving this goal, his sympathies for the people whom Palencia had most despised—the Mendoza and their clients—and the contradictions between the attitudes expressed in his royal chronicles and in his other writings make it difficult to find a consistent point of view in his work. He remains one of the most controversial chroniclers of the fifteenth century.[17]

The most notorious of the cardinal's secretaries was Alvar Gómez de Ciudad Real (d. 1491), a prime example of the deudo that bound patrons and clients together over generations. Alvar Gómez's father, Fernán Gómez de Ciudad Real (b. 1388), was a godson of Pedro López de Ayala, who had held him at the baptismal font; he became a bachelor in medicine by the age of twenty-four and later physician to Juan II and don Alvaro de Luna.[18] The son, Alvar Gómez (or Alvar García), became secretary to Enrique IV, and Palencia heaped abuse on him:

A certain Alvar García de Villarreal, an ignorant man, stupid, of obscure origin and low inclinations, and who, for these very reasons, Enrique IV named as his secretary when he had hardly ascended the throne, as if the profession and its exercise should correspond by right to a person inexpert, obscure, and of loose morals.[19]

Cardinal Mendoza lured Alvar Gómez away from the king's service into his own, an act he later regretted, and then had to cope with Alvar Gómez's errors. Alvar Gómez deserted Enrique IV, went over to the infante Alfonso, and was dispossessed by the king. In order to save Alvar Gómez, and for his own profit, the cardinal exchanged property with him; and throughout the sixteenth century, the secretary's descendants continued to reside in the Mendoza household in Guadalajara: Alvar Gómez's grandson and namesake (1488–1538) was one of the noted Latin poets of his day and married a daughter of the third duke of Infantado. In his neo-Latin works and in his use of the medieval poetic form of arte mayor for his religious meditations, this Alvar Gómez reflects the vogue for the idealized medieval forms that were also popular in northern Europe at the same time.[20]

The variety and diffuseness of the works produced by Mendoza clients in the late fifteenth and early sixteenth centuries is indicative of the lack of focus in the intellectual life of the Mendoza households in Guadalajara. Lacking strong commitment to any person, institution, or idea outside the family itself, the Mendoza would drift through the changing intellectual styles of the sixteenth century, taking up and enjoying whatever was current.

These amorphous attitudes are a striking contrast to the Tendilla stubbornness in clinging to the esthetics of the fifteenth-century Mendoza. We have seen that Tendilla provided support and encouragement to Hernán Núñez de Toledo, whose Renaissance humanism satisfied Tendilla's notions of the Mendoza family's intellectual tradition.[21] In his own writing, Tendilla displayed a strict adherence to the language and rhetoric fashionable in the caballero society of his youth which he had imbibed in the household of his grandfather, Santillana, with disastrous consequences. Tendilla's effectiveness in arguing with the letrados, with whom he already had serious substantive disagreements, was seriously weakened by his refusal to speak to them in a style they respected.

In theory, Tendilla admired the brevity his ancestors praised as the most effective vehicle for argument. When he wrote letters of recommendation, this was the characteristic he praised most highly: "This is a good man of few words."[22] He despised people who were verbose: Juan Hurtado de Mendoza "is a very forceful and daring man of few words who doesn't beat around the bush like Pero López" de Orozco.[23] When he wrote on professional matters in which he could maintain his detachment, his style was clear and to the point. When he wrote to someone he disliked or wanted to impress, he became cagily manipulative. On one of the rare occasions when he wrote to the Italian humanist, Pietro Martire d'Anghiera, whom Tendilla had brought to Spain although he habitually snubbed him, asking him to translate into Latin the inscription he wanted to put on the tomb of his brother, the archbishop of Seville, he employed the false modesty and flattery which were clichés of the time, claiming that he was sending him the inscription "so that you will put it in Latin because I lack that language when you are absent."[24] When he wrote to prelates whose erudition and Latin he respected, he could never resist inserting a few passages in Latin and making frequent allusions to the classics and the Bible. The intimate, humorous style, verging on the sacrilegious, he used in letters to his fellow nobles and the rambling, confessional intimacy of his letters to his agent, Francisco Ortiz, are a contrast to the sobriety and caution of his letters to letrados and royal secretaries. But when Tendilla wrote on religious issues, he became so carried away with the passion of his arguments that he lost sight of the audience and slipped into the rhetoric and colloquialisms most familiar and convincing to him, which must have been ineffective with the letrados.

This sort of impassioned argument, based on authorities no longer acceptable or convincing, became particularly frequent in Tendilla's letters during the spring of 1514, when the government refused to relax its edict against Morisco clothing. As the government hardened its position, Tendilla's arguments became more impassioned and less effective. By May, his arguments were based almost entirely on the sources that would have been familiar and convincing to his ancestors, Santillana and Guzmán:

> What, sir, is his highness doing, ordering that the Morisco clothing must be abandoned? Does he think that this is such a trivial thing? I swear by God that the kingdom will lose more than a million ducats in changing and buying clothes and doesn't the king realize that this way he is hardening those overseas [in Africa] to not become his subjects without resisting with their blood first? Doesn't he know that the clothing which the women in Rome wore when they were gentiles they still wear now? And so that you, sir, can speak about this with the authority of a doctor and even one such as Saint Augustine, read, your grace, in the nineteenth book of the *City of God* in the nineteenth chapter and you will see what he says. And what clothing, sir, did we here in Spain wear until the coming of king Enrique the Bastard and how did we wear our hair except in the Morisco style, and at what table did we eat? Did the kings stop being Christians and saints because of this? No, sir, by God.[25]

In this passage, Tendilla uses his best and his favorite arguments: the edict will have bad consequences economically, religiously, and politically; the Romans did not follow this policy; St. Augustine argues against it; and Castilian history provides no examples or precedents for it. Here Tendilla presents his models—Rome, Augustine, and Enrique de Trastámara—certainly the choice of his ancestors, Ayala, Guzmán, and Santillana, but no longer models for the royal court. Even his line of argument was shaped by the past: he assumed that the religious significance of fashion could best be judged by examining the history of clothing and manners, a historicism which would have little meaning for letrados trained to use law and logic in judging religious matters.

In the last few years of his life, Tendilla took up arguments from another historical source, the *Jewish Wars* of Josephus. He sometimes urges Ortiz to use examples from Josephus in his speeches to the court, and it is clear that Tendilla was well aware of the parallel between the Moriscos and the ancient Jews as rebellious religious minorities. In 1514, for example, he instructed Ortiz to warn the court against believing the local Morisco regidor, Miguel de León,—who had promised the Moriscos that he would be able to have the edict against Morisco clothing lifted—

by drawing a parallel with the promises of Jonathan the swindler who led a group of Jews to destruction in the same way.[26] In this case, Tendilla was arguing not only from a historical period (ancient Rome) that was no longer the model of the royal court but also from a source that must have been distasteful to the court because it was Jewish. We can imagine how the members of the royal council, who were becoming more and more suspicious of anything smacking of Judaism, might react to an argument that cited Josephus as its authority.

In the heightened atmosphere of religious extremism and suspicion prevalent in the royal council, Tendilla continued to use the historicist and eclectic arguments fashionable in his youth. He seems never to have realized how ineffectual this type of argument had become, nor did he ever recognize the irony of using a Jewish source to argue Christian religious issues. For Tendilla, the Roman model was still the best; and he was as incapable of adopting the new styles as he was of adopting the letrados' theories.

The most enduring example of Mendoza adaptation to the northern styles entering Castile was their taste for Flemish architecture. The structures built by the admiral and Santillana were typical of fifteenth-century Castilian architecture: they are built around a central open courtyard; the walls are plain and finished with ashlars; and the exterior walls are designed to functional, not esthetic, standards. The doors, windows, and other apertures are placed for functional convenience, and from the outside of the building appear haphazardly arranged; decoration is superficially applied to the wall surface immediately above the entrance but to no other portion of the wall; and all the apertures are designed with a strong, fortresslike simplicity. Neither the apertures nor the decoration give any indication of the number or levels of the interior floors. The beauty of these buildings is in their massive but pleasing proportions and their tasteful balance between rectangular walls and circular towers. Decoration is almost negligible as an esthetic factor in this style.

From 1475 to 1512, Santillana's children and grandchildren engaged in large-scale building projects; and the structures they put up have survived as the outstanding (and earliest) examples of a new Flemish style so closely associated with the reign of the Catholic Monarchs that it has popularly been called "Isabelline."[27] The first and second dukes of Infantado built a fortress-palace at Real de Manzanares which illustrates the changing architectural tastes of the Mendoza family.[28] The first Infantado constructed the building in two phases: in the first, the fortress itself was built, with the typical single entry, smooth walls, irregularly placed apertures, and harmoniously proportioned rectangular walls and circular towers; in the second, Infantado must have employed Italian stonemasons, for the smaller towers of this later phase are finished in a pattern of decorative half-spheres typical of Bolognese workmanship. Italian workmen were probably also responsible for the graceful cornice and parapet surmounting the walls and towers. The third and final phase of the construction was carried out after 1480 by the second Infantado, who added the large main tower and enclosed a portion of the parapet to form an airy covered gallery. The main tower is hexagonal, and the gallery has windows with stone frames carved in the shape of ogive arches. All the work of this final phase must have been the work of Flemish artists: it is delicate, graceful, flamboyant, and depends upon decoration for its esthetic impact.

The first building constructed entirely in the new Flemish style was the Palacio del Infantado in Guadalajara. The first Infantado razed the old family residences to build the present palace, a three-story structure built around a central square patio, which is circumscribed by a two-story gallery. The major innovation lies in the design of the patio's columns, arches, and balustrades and in the design and decoration of the façade. The arches of the patio are shaped like flamboyant trefoils and decorated, like the balustrades, with plaster and stone, carved and molded into intricate leaves, flowers, animals, and vines. The fifteenth-century columns are fluted in a spiral design, and both the fluting and the capitals are decorated with leafy vines, so that the impression is that the patio is encircled by trees whose leafy branches and trunks are entwined with vines. The Palacio del Infantado is the finest example of what has aptly been called "gothique délirant," combining the graceful curves of nature in its decorative elements with the severe simplicity of the ashlars and structural elements.[29]

Santillana's eldest daughter, Mencía de Mendoza, wife of the constable of Castile, built one of the most important religious structures in this flamboyant gothic style—the Capilla del Condestable in the cathedral of Burgos. The chapel differs from other gothic religious structures in the octagonal shape of its lantern—which became the model for the main lantern of the cathedral—and in the harmonious proportions and balancing of otherwise conventional gothic elements. The ashlars on the interior are decorated with stone and plaster carvings in lacelike detail, with the same motifs as the decoration on the façade of the Palacio del Infantado—hairy satyrs lifting their clubs and family shields entwined with vines, flowers, and leaves. These buildings, with their flamboyant forms and decorative themes from nature, mark an important shift to northern European artistic influences. They seem to translate into stone and plaster the graceful curves and loving attention to naturalistic detail of the international gothic painting style.

Architecture was one aspect of art in which Tendilla showed innovation; and even here he remained true to the Mendoza tradition—he followed the lead of the papal court. During his embassy to Innocent VIII in 1486–1487, Tendilla had been charged by his uncle, cardinal Mendoza, with the reconstruction of the Roman basilica of Santa Croce. It would have been natural for him to be impressed by the architectural projects of the papal chancellor, Rodrigo Borgia, whose friendship with the Mendoza was crucial to the success of Tendilla's embassy and whose preference for Renaissance architecture had been known to Tendilla since 1472, when cardinals Mendoza and Borgia met in Valencia and Guadalajara to negotiate the alliance between the Mendoza and the Catholic Monarchs in the Castilian succession dispute. Borgia was already engaged in building projects in Rome by 1472, and the cardinals spent their leisure time discussing "la obra del romano" while they were in Guadalajara.[30] Cardinal Mendoza and the members of his household, including his nephews, Tendilla and the duke of Medinaceli, had all been converted to the Renaissance style by these conversations, but it was not until Tendilla's embassy to Rome in 1486–1487 that they were able to put their architectural ideas into effect. Tendilla must have made himself knowledgeable about Roman styles and techniques before engaging an architect and workmen for the reconstruction of Santa Croce, and he brought back to Castile both his own newly acquired expertise and the Italian-trained architect, Lorenzo Vázquez.

The first building in Castile to be influenced by this Roman style was the colegio de Santa Cruz at the University of Valladolid.[31] In 1479, cardinal Mendoza received a papal license for the college, and construction was completed by 1491; but when the cardinal saw the building for the first time, he was so displeased with its awkward proportions and the mediocrity of its traditional style that he ordered a complete remodeling in the Roman style. For this he employed Lorenzo Vázquez who determined that only the superficial portions of the façade could be demolished without weakening the structure. He then put a Roman touch to the building by rebuilding the upper levels of the façade and adding half columns and a cornice in classical designs. Vázquez then moved to Guadalajara where he became master of works for the cardinal, supervising the final stages of the cardinal's new residence and designing an elegant classical gallery for the patio of the parochial church of Santa María, commissioned by the cardinal. After the cardinal's death in

1495, Vázquez continued to work in the Roman style for members of the Mendoza family who had been part of the cardinal's household. In the last years of the century, Vázquez designed and built the palace in Cogolludo for the duke of Medinaceli; before 1507, he had completed the house of Antonio de Mendoza in Guadalajara; and at the time of his death, he was building the monastery of San Antonio in Mondéjar for Tendilla.

The most important innovations introduced by Vázquez were his treatment of the façade as an esthetic object and his use of classical decorative elements. The palace in Cogolludo is built on the traditional plan with a central courtyard, but the arches of the gallery are Roman, supported by classical columns. The façade of the building is covered with rusticated stone, the entrance is placed in the center of the façade, and the windows are symmetrically spaced. A decorative line is sculpted across the entire width of the façade, serving as window sill and indicating the two interior floor levels. The entrance is flanked by classical half-columns, and a *tondo* directly above the door encloses the family coat of arms in a classical wreath. Throughout the palace in Cogolludo, Vázquez employed Renaissance principles of architecture. He integrated structural and decorative elements, emphasized the horizontal, and used classical orders and decoration. While Medinaceli could afford to use the best materials, Tendilla could supply Vázquez with only the poorest of local bricks and stone for the monastery of San Antonio de Mondéjar. Today it is in ruins, used as a corral by local farmers. Even the ruins have all the daring and beauty of Lorenzo Vázquez's work—soaring Roman arches and a floor plan proportioned to a single module.[32] Like the early Italian imitators of Roman architecture, most of the Mendoza and their architects considered the classical architectural orders and sumptuous decoration to be the essence of Roman architecture. Only Vázquez in his later years, while working for Tendilla, concerned himself with the problems of proportion and measurement that had become the preoccupation of late fifteenth-century Italian architects, a concern which is a constant theme of Tendilla's letters on architectural subjects.

In view of the Mendoza family's literary tradition, it is not surprising that some members of the family turned to ancient Rome and the papal court for inspiration when architecture became their major artistic interest. The Roman model, however, did not become popular during the reign of the Catholic Monarchs. Most of the Mendoza followed the leadership of the duke of Infantado and built in the gothic style; and even the monarchs adopted this style when they began building, late in the reign. The only Roman structures of the reign of the Catholic

Monarchs were built by a few members of the Mendoza family deeply influenced by cardinal Mendoza; and after 1504, only by the two mavericks of the family—Tendilla and Cenete. It has been noted that an enthusiasm for Roman architectural models was widespread among the "imperialists" under Charles V;[33] but during the reign of the Catholic Monarchs, it was limited to those Mendoza who clung most tenaciously to the old, particularist view of the Castilian monarchy and saw themselves as the cultural heirs of the ancient Romans.

By 1485, most of the Mendoza had abandoned the traditional Castilian architectural and literary standards for the standards of the north. Though they could no longer dominate the intellectual and religious life of Castile, they could sponsor the most lavish examples of the artistic fashions of the country. But by turning to the Middle Ages and the north instead of classical antiquity and the papal court for their esthetic standards, these generations were abandoning the Mendoza tradition just as they were abandoning it in political matters.

It is significant that those who adopted this new esthetic standard were the same Mendoza who followed the constable and the duke of Infantado in the political turmoil of the succession and regency conflicts after 1504. Tendilla, who refused to place family unity before family tradition and refused consequently to accept the political leadership of Infantado, did not adopt new esthetic standards. Furthermore, Tendilla never gave up his role as an erudite and as a patron of Renaissance art and letters. Thus the Mendoza family divided into two factions artistically and intellectually along the same lines it had divided politically. Infantado and most of the Mendoza followed a flexible political policy and an esthetic standard open to the new influences coming in from northern Europe. Tendilla followed an extremely traditional political policy and intellectual and religious standards conservative and resistant to new sources of influence. During his lifetime, the Mendoza tradition had become anachronistic and suspect, yet Tendilla clung to it as if it were still prestigious and influential. While the church, the monarchs, the councillors, and the secretaries were thinking and acting in terms of centralized monarchy, theology, and reform and the Mendoza of Guadalajara were enjoying the arts of the Burgundian court, Tendilla continued to advocate old policies and think in terms of particularism; and he continued to use the eclectic and historicist rhetoric of his ancestors and follow the artistic leadership of the papal court. Tendilla's failure to win favor at the royal court and his inability to influence royal policy were largely due to his continued adherence to the Mendoza tradition in a society which had rejected that tradition.

Tendilla was most separated from the letrados and the new policies of the monarchy by his adherence to the standards of religious toleration and eclecticism characteristic of his ancestors. These religious attitudes are notable because they had become a political liability, both because of his position as governor of the largest convert population in Spain and because of the changed attitudes toward religious heterogeneity at the royal court. Tendilla was personally sympathetic to the Moriscos, and he was acutely aware of the political leverage he could command as mediator between the Morisco community and the royal government. As the royal government became more intolerant of the Moriscos, Tendilla's ability to win concessions for them decreased, and he found himself regarded with suspicion by Cisneros and other zealous doctors. As his political effectiveness declined, Tendilla's statements about the Moriscos, the Inquisition, and religion in general became more strident. This in turn further decreased his effectiveness in arguing with the promoters of the new policies.

For Tendilla's own religious attitudes, the problem of the Moriscos created some confusion and tensions, especially over the question of the efficacy of works. Tendilla was himself a great practitioner of good works. The accounts of his works fill many pages: acts of charity; donations to religious causes; foundations of churches, monasteries, and hospitals; commissions for religious works of art and shrines; and the acquisition of many papal indulgences for himself, his family, and his tenants.[34] He continued to perform these works as long as he was financially able, but he was not sure that they were efficacious or even good Christian practice. At one point in 1514, for example, Tendilla wondered if God had not sent the archbishop of Granada to punish him for his pride in thinking that he was a good Christian just because he was doing good works, for Tendilla remembered reading in a vernacular source that "those who confess, take communion, and give alms and listen continuously to masses and sermons are poorer Christians than those who do neither one nor the other."[35] If he had not actually read Guzmán's statement on this subject, he must have read something very like it; and the distinction Guzmán had drawn between good works and the motives which prompted them Tendilla applied, in reverse, to the Moriscos. When the Inquisition in Córdoba began to persecute the Moriscos in 1506, Tendilla objected that whatever errors the converts had committed in practice they were not culpable because they had not sinned "with their hearts."[36]

Tendilla knew as well as anyone that the Moriscos were not sincere Christians, but he placed the blame for this on the zealots who had forced the conversions rather than on the Moriscos themselves. He had always agreed with archbishop Talavera that only education, persuasion, and good example should be used to bring about conversion and that these same methods should be used to bring those who had been forcibly converted to a sincere belief in Christ. To Tendilla, true conversion could occur only in freedom. To this end, he tried to set a good example himself, he treated the Moriscos' unorthodox customs with generosity and toleration, and he encouraged his subordinates to do likewise.[37]

In the ten years during which Tendilla coped with the problem of the Inquisition and the Moriscos (1506–1515), he developed a series of arguments based largely on St. Paul and St. Augustine. We do not know what the response of the letrados was to these arguments. We cannot even be sure that Tendilla's letters are a response to the letrados' arguments, for he often deliberately misunderstood or befuddled an issue out of stubbornness or obtuseness. But if the arguments about the Inquisition and the Moriscos were focused on the questions of faith and works, as Tendilla's letters indicate, then the church in Spain must already have developed arguments for the necessity of works before Luther attacked this position in 1517.

Tendilla's attitude toward faith and works was confused, but his attitude toward converts was clearly one of moderation and benevolence. While his tolerance of Morisco practices may be attributed in part to his political needs, his friendship with and protection of conversos had no political motivation and could only have been a manifestation of religious views. He employed conversos in important positions in his household throughout his life; and his agent at court, Francisco Ortiz, was a converso. One of the difficulties in dealing with this subject in relation to Tendilla is that we cannot be sure who was and who was not a converso, for Tendilla does not speak in these terms. He does describe specific men as "a good Christian" or "a bad Christian" but this description is based on his assessment of the man's character and not on racial or religious background. Captain Pedro López de Orozco was a "bad Christian." But Tendilla's physician, Iñigo López, whom we must assume to be a converso because of his name and profession, was "a good Christian."[38] His unawareness of the sensitivity of this issue, in fact, aroused the anger of Francisco Ortiz; and Tendilla, after protesting his innocence in typical terms of even-handed judgment, fought back with a biting satire of the letrados' arguments:

What you wrote me about the complaint I have about conversos gave me a good laugh because people complain about their father and their sons and no one holds it against them. Because of this I looked over what I wrote to you and what I wrote to my sister and even what I wrote to the *licenciado* [Vargas, his consuegro] and I don't find any threat in it for just because I say that I am dissatisfied does not seem to me to deserve such reprehension. The truth is, I tell you that I am—and with plenty of reason because although some of them may serve me well I have never received ill except from their hand and they don't have any regard for any good work which may have been done for them and if someone does ill to one of them they all take it personally and let this be said with great reverence, as those who dispute say.[39]

While the influential doctor Carvajal in the consejo real was urging Charles V to beware of conversos simply because they were conversos, Tendilla continued to practice the toleration practiced by his ancestors, and he continued to judge men by their merits rather than their lineage or credentials.

Tendilla's attitude toward other, broader religious issues was equally traditional. He persisted in judging the religious policies of the church in the same way he judged the political policies of the government—by their consequences. His most frequent argument against the Inquisition is that it leads to tragic consequences—riots, repression, and resentment. He urged the inquisitors to use prudence in their proceedings and to temper their rigor with good sense.[40] When an inquisitor arrived in the kingdom of Granada to begin proceedings in Guadix, Tendilla tried to smooth the way for him in order to avoid violence within royal jurisdiction.[41] Above all, Tendilla refused to allow the arguments of the inquisitors to distract him from what he considered the essential consideration in any religious policy—a moderation that would prevent violence. He once warned the inquisitors of Córdoba, "If you tell me that what is of God must precede everything, I say that to have temperance is of God and anything else is from I don't know whom."[42]

Tendilla also objected to the Inquisition because he thought it was being imposed on the kingdom of Granada by men who did not know the region and who underestimated the local reaction to it. He pointed out that religious considerations, no matter how correct, must not be allowed to blind the church to the peculiarities of the local situation and that "there never was anything in the world better ruled than Rome, but many errors have been made in this way of not believing those who have their hands in the dough."[43]

On every issue of religious significance, Tendilla was opposed to the most popular and prestigious attitudes in the Castile of the Catholic

Monarchs—he advocated toleration toward Muslims and Jews; he doubted the efficacy of works; he judged converts on the basis of their merits rather than their lineage; he opposed the Inquisition on religious, political, and jurisdictional grounds. With these attitudes and with his animosity toward the most powerful prelate in Castile—Cisneros—it is no wonder that Tendilla was regarded with suspicion by the royal court.[44]

Tendilla never succeeded in persuading the royal government to change its policies toward the Moriscos: the Inquisition continued to operate in the kingdom of Granada, and the edict against Morisco clothing was used as a continual threat to the Moriscos. He lost control over appointments to military offices in Granada, his influence in the city council declined steadily, and the royal government began to follow military policies in direct contradiction to his advice. Tendilla knew that all of these misfortunes were the result of his failure to make an impression on the royal officials with his letters and memorials, but he attributed this failure to the hostile interpretations of secretaries who were his enemies and of letrados who were hair-splitting and zealous. Tendilla's failure to convince the royal court of his point of view was his greatest failure of all, yet he never realized the degree to which this failure was due to his own rhetoric. Castilians, and many other Europeans at this time, were increasingly attuned to zealous and hair-splitting arguments in religious questions; and Tendilla's letters—old-fashioned with their pleas for tolerance, their use of Jewish and pagan as well as Christian sources, and their argument from historical example and natural consequences—fell on deaf ears.

Tendilla's tenacity in maintaining the traditions of the Mendoza family in the face of changing social and intellectual fashions would also characterize his descendants and lead to the same dismal results. Tendilla's eldest son, Luis, and Luis's eldest son, the second and third marquises of Mondéjar, inherited Tendilla's positions as captain general of the kingdom of Granada and alcaide of the Alhambra, and they also inherited his policies of toleration toward the Moriscos and antagonism toward the chancillería of Granada.[45]

Throughout the sixteenth century, and especially in the reign of Philip II, the Mondéjar's relations with the central government deteriorated steadily. The royal councils took an ever more rigid attitude toward the Moriscos' nonconformity, and the Mondéjars continued to defend Morisco customs. Like Tendilla, the Mondéjars were unable to protect either the Moriscos or themselves, and they found it necessary to take offices in the central government. Luis accepted the position of viceroy of Navarre in 1543—a sure sign of his need for greater financial resources. His eldest son assumed the responsibilities of the captaincy general of Granada. Neither Luis in Navarre nor his son in Granada could protect their interests at the royal court; and in 1546, Luis accepted the position of president of the Council of Castile. Luis thus accepted publicly a situation Tendilla had recognized privately: he could no longer influence royal policy from a distance and had to take up residence at the royal court in order to make his voice heard there.

Even this drastic move could not save the Mondéjars and the Moriscos from their enemies in the Council of Castile and in the chancillería of Granada. The great conflict of the sixteenth century between Morisco and Christian zealots, which culminated in the second rebellion of the Alpujarras in 1568, was simply an elaboration of the conflicts which had engulfed Tendilla at the beginning of the century. The lines between the captain general and the Moriscos, on the one hand, and the chancillería of Granada, the Inquisition, and the royal government, on the other, had been drawn during the succession crisis of 1504–1508; and Tendilla's policies during that crucial period would become the policies of his descendants in the reign of Philip II. Tendilla's policy of toleration toward the Moriscos had not been a manifestation of a new, open society in Castile but the continuation of a Mendoza family tradition which can be traced back to the works of Ayala, Guzmán, and Santillana. Much of the failure of Mondéjar policy, therefore, may simply be ascribed to its anachronism—it was old-fashioned and conservative to be tolerant in a society open to the dogmatism and intolerance of sixteenth-century Europe.

What saved Luis and the entire Granada branch of the Mendoza family was deudo with Charles V, a deudo Luis created through strenuous political and personal service to the emperor. During the Comunero revolt in 1520 and 1521, the duke of Infantado played a cautious waiting game to see which side would win. He did not take a strong stand in support of the monarchy until after his son, the count of Saldaña, had declared in favor of the rebels; and Infantado had publicly to repudiate the count and his party. In contrast, Luis had been the first nobleman in Andalucía to declare in the name of Charles as soon as the news of Fernando's death reached Granada, and he had been an early and staunch military opponent of the Comunero revolt. His sister, María Pacheco, and her husband, Juan de Padilla, had been leading the rebels in Toledo.

These political moves made it easier for Luis to gain the emperor's friendship during 1526, when the royal couple spent their honeymoon in the Alhambra. From the time of Charles's stay in the Alhambra through the rest of his reign, Luis poured his resources into the imperial ventures: the attack on the Muslim outpost of Peñón de los Vélez off the coast of Africa, the Tunis expedition in 1535, and Charles's military expeditions in France and Italy. Through these services, Luis was able to win from Charles the viceroyalties and posts in the royal councils that enabled him to balance to some degree the power of the chancillería of Granada in local politics.[46]

It was through Charles's honeymoon in Granada that the Mendoza's Renaissance style also came to enjoy a brief period of official support. By the time of his marriage, Charles had already assumed the title of Holy Roman Emperor and was assuming with it many of the trappings that his chancellor, Mercurino Gattinara (1465–1530), associated with the ancient Roman emperors. He signed himself "Carolus" instead of "Yo el Rey," grew a beard in imitation of ancient Roman busts, and added the word "Caesar" to the form in which he was to be addressed. This search for an ancient Roman style fitted neatly with the Tendilla preference for the "estilo romano," or Renaissance style in monuments and architecture. In Granada, Charles could see the rising walls of the new cathedral, which after a false start on a medieval plan, was being built on a Renaissance plan believed to be an imitation of the Church of the Holy Sepulchre in Jerusalem. Tendilla had been involved in the evolution of the cathedral's design, acting as arbitrator on behalf of the king in architects' disputes over proportions; and Luis now had the opportunity to oversee the construction of an even larger secular project on behalf of the emperor.

Charles had fallen in love with the Alhambra and decided to build a modern palace there which would more aptly serve his court.[47] As architect for this, his one great building project, he employed Pedro Machuca, who had designed the elaborate arches and tableaux that the city of Granada constructed for the emperor's entrance into the city. Machuca had been a disciple of Michelangelo in Rome, but it appears that there was not much work for a Renaissance architect in early sixteenth-century Spain, for when Charles met him, he was employed as one of Luis's escuderos—a position also held by his ancestor and namesake under the first count of Tendilla.

The palace Machuca designed for Charles was purely Renaissance; but after Charles left Spain, his royal councillors in Castile repeatedly overruled Luis, interfered with Machuca's plans, and prevented him from using the advanced Renaissance styles and construction techniques he had learned in Rome. Charles himself, having seen true Renaissance architecture for the first time in Italy, finally approved Machuca's plans when he returned to Spain in 1533. Thus Granada, under the influence of the Mendoza, came to have Europe's only Renaissance cathedral and one of her largest Renaissance palaces—architectural anachronisms in a Spain already evolving its own plateresque style by adding Renaissance and Isabelline decorative elements to the traditional Castilian style.

The persistence of such anachronisms among the sixteenth-century descendants of Tendilla was most pronounced in the life and works of Tendilla's youngest son, Diego Hurtado de Mendoza (1504–1575).[48] Diego was the most brilliant and cosmopolitan of all the Mendoza, and he is regarded by Spanish intellectual historians as "the last of the Spanish Renaissance men."[49] Although Diego was only twelve years old when Tendilla died, he seems to have been more deeply influenced by his father's ideas than the other sons, probably because Tendilla took over supervision of his young children's education and activities after Diego's mother died in 1510. Tendilla intended the boy for a position in the church, but because of the hostility of the archbishop of Granada he was not able to get the necessary episcopal permission for Diego to take holy orders. Diego entered the imperial diplomatic service about 1530 and quickly rose to the top of his profession. He served as imperial ambassador to Venice (1539–1547) and Rome (1547–1552), imperial legate to the first session of the Council of Trent, and governor of Siena. When his failure to prevent a revolt of the Sienese in 1552 ended his career as a diplomat, he returned to Spain where he filled a series of minor positions. After a scandalous incident in the royal palace, he was sent in exile to the frontier of Granada just in time to become a witness and chronicler of the second uprising of the Alpujarras.

It has been suggested that Diego's humanist skills and accomplishments were the product of his more than fifteen years' residence in Italy and his association with Agostino Nifo and Montes de Oca in Rome and Padua.[50] Certainly, there is ample evidence that Diego was at home with the humanists of sixteenth-century Italy. His methods in diplomacy have been described as Machiavellian, and he shared the imperialist enthusiasms of Erasmus and Gattinara. He was fluent in Latin, Greek, and Arabic; and he translated Aristotle's *Mechanics* from Greek into Spanish. He wrote poetry and history and maintained correspondence and friendships with several noted Italian humanists. He was an avid and knowledgeable collector of ancient coins, sculpture, and manuscripts, as well as modern paintings, manuscripts, and incunabula. He was appointed to the crucial post in Venice because Charles V's wars and diplomacy were as much dependent upon libel and propaganda as they were on military weapons, and Diego as a humanist had the necessary rhetorical skills to carry on such a propaganda war.[51]

Diego far exceeded his father and his ancestors in his professional mastery of linguistic, philological, and rhetorical skills; but instead of adopting the values of his own age of the Counter Reformation, he remained loyal to the esthetic and religious values of Tendilla. His esthetic values, with their emphasis on the Romans, were superficially compatible with the heady dreams of imperialism at the court of Charles V, but Diego's supposed imperialism was in fact based on traditions that had little connection with Charles's empire and none at all with the Spain of Philip II. These attitudes are displayed most fully in Diego's history of the second uprising of the Alpujarras, *De la guerra de Granada*. The tone of the work is calm, even-handed, controlled. Superficially it appears that everyone was at fault and that Diego is not taking sides. As many critics have noted, the work is an obvious imitation of Tacitus and Sallust; but there is hardly a passage which when closely examined does not emerge as an elegant and erudite expression of Tendilla's anachronistic attitudes. For example, Diego's introductory summation of the war he is about to describe is a skillful imitation of Tacitus:

> In short, to fight every day with the enemy, the cold, heat, hunger, lack of ammunition and equipment; everywhere new attacks, continuous deaths, until we closed with the enemy, a nation bellicose, vigorous, armed and confident in their position, favored by the Berbers and Turks, defeated, subdued, taken from their land and dispossessed of their houses and goods; prisoners bound man, woman, and child, captives sold at auction, or brought to inhabit lands far from theirs, captivity and transportation no less than that of other peoples which can be read in histories. A doubtful victory and with results so dangerous that sometimes one doubts if it was us or the enemy that God wanted to punish, until at the end, it was revealed that we were the threatened and they the punished.[52]

In its organization, irony, style, and even-handed assessment of one side and then the other, this passage is typical of the whole work. But it also subtly reminds us of another rebellion by a religious minority, another defeat at the hands of an empire, another dispersion of a whole nation. And it is clear, in the organization of the work, in its handling of military action, in its criticism of the zealots on both sides, and in its divided sympathies, that Diego's *De la guerra de Granada* is modeled on one of his father's favorite works, Josephus's *De Bello Judaico*. Throughout the work, Diego, by his judgments, draws a parallel between the two wars that is all the more significant because it operates on two levels—on the one hand, the parallel between the Moriscos and the ancient Jews; on the other, the parallel between the Spanish and the ancient Romans. He states this analogy explicitly only once, but it is placed in the crucial statement of his analysis of the causes of the uprising:

> It came to private causes and passions, even to asking judges of boundaries, not for divisions or lots of land like the Romans and our ancestors, but with the hope of restoring to the king or the public that which [the Moriscos] had occupied, and the intention of throwing some out of their inheritances. This was one of the sources of the destruction of Granada.[53]

Here the son of the "first praefect of the acropolis of Illíberis" concludes that the underlying cause of the disastrous war in Granada was the crown's abandonment of a system of justice common to both the Romans and their heirs—the Spaniards.

Another assumption Diego held in common with his father was that these pernicious changes in the system of justice were the result of the infusion of large numbers of letrados into the judicial system and the substitution of their justice through written law for the old seigneurial justice through arbitration. In Sallustian terms, Diego described the change from a Granada dominated by the captain general to a Granada dominated by the chancillería:

> The city and kingdom used to be governed as among settlers and companions; a form of justice by arbitration, sentiments united, resolutions implemented in common to the public good: this was ended with the life of the older generation. The zealots entered, division over trivial matters between the ministers of justice and of war, written agreements confirmed by cédulas, each one of the parties deriving an understanding of them according to his own opinion; the one desiring to be treated as an equal, the other to preserve his superiority, behaving with more dissimulation than modesty.[54]

This same antagonism toward formal written solutions also permeated Diego's attitudes toward religious problems. He believed that flexibility and a respect for the uniqueness of each individual case should govern religious policy; and like his father, he refused to judge a man's faith on the basis of his customs. In one of the few emotional passages of *De la guerra de Granada*, Diego places the following words in the mouth of the Morisco leader Abenjaguar: "Each nation, each profession, each estate uses its own manner of dress and all are Christians: we [are considered] Muslims because we dress in the Morisco manner, as if we wore the law in our clothing and not in our hearts."[55]

Such ideas were not easily tolerated in the Spain of Philip II; but even in the reign of Charles V, Diego's religious attitudes made him suspect. His intervention in the first session of the Council of Trent in particular brought Diego into conflict with the Spain of the Counter Reformation. As the faithful spokesman for the emperor, Diego used all of his considerable rhetorical talents to urge the council to make reform of the church hierarchy its first matter of business. On this issue, he had the full support of the Spanish prelates, led by his cousins the cardinals of Jaén, Pedro Pacheco, and Coria, Francisco de Mendoza. But this imperialist party within the Spanish delegation—made up of noble prelates without theological training—immediately came into conflict with the Spanish theologians, who wanted to make a definitive codification of the church's position on Justification the first order of business.[56] Even after the theologians and papal party had won this point, Diego continued to argue against the theologians and thereby made a bitter enemy of Domingo de Soto. Soto was a member of the theology faculty at Salamanca. He had received his theological education at Alcalá and Paris and was the principal architect of the council's decree on Justification.[57] We do not know exactly what Diego argued in his debates with Soto; but on the basis of his own statement a few years later—when Soto had become the imperial confessor—Diego must have been opposed to a theological settlement of this issue:

> You might tell Monseigneur [de Grenvelle] that the confessor does not like me because in Trent I defended a doctor Herrera whom he had slandered, calling him a heretic in the presence of many bishops. Besides, I refused to let him print at my expense a commentary about Aristotle's *Physics*; and furthermore, in our debates I always upheld against him and against Saint Thomas the part of Averroës, a thing I would not have done, had I known he would become the confessor. Also, [he dislikes me] because I know more philosophy than he.[58]

Apparently Diego had decided to fight fire with fire and tried to deny the validity of a theological approach by arguing from Averroës; but Diego, the most brilliant spokesman of the Mendoza tradition, could not overcome the influence of Soto, the spokesman for the brilliant new school of theological legalism at Salamanca. And the contrast between the old Spain and the new becomes even greater when Diego adds: "To tell the truth, wretched as my own conscience is, I would not trade it for his [Soto's] brains."[59] In the midst of a new, dogmatic, and theologically oriented Europe, Diego was still clinging to the fourteenth-century sentiment of Petrarch: "It is better to will the good than to know the truth."[60]

Diego was convinced that the decree on Justification would lead to the worst abuse of all—works without faith. This preoccupation with the dangers that might arise from an overemphasis on works was just the sort of attitude that Soto labeled heretical in several prelates at the Council of Trent, and it does verge on Luther's "faith without works." Yet it would be gratuitous to describe Diego as a secret Protestant or even as open to the religious ideas of northern Europe, for these same attitudes are fully developed in the letters and works of Tendilla and his fifteenth-century ancestors. Nor is it likely that Diego, when he argued from Averroës, advocated "the oneness of the passive intellect in all men; the denial of personal immortality to the individual, cogitative soul; the eternity of the world."[61] With that typical Renaissance and Mendoza suspicion of scholasticism and theology, it is more probable that Diego had used the Averroists' theory of the "double truth" to argue against a theological definition of Justification at Trent. Augustine himself had intimated the usefulness of this approach:

> And so, since we are too weak to discover the truth by reason alone and for this reason need the authority of sacred books . . . it seemed to me all the more right that the authority of Scripture should be respected and accepted with the purest faith, because while all can read it with ease, it also has a deeper meaning in which its great secrets are locked away. Its plain language and simple style make it accessible to everyone, and yet it absorbs the attention of the learned.[62]

At the Council of Trent, Diego argued against those who would attempt to place too much emphasis on the rational and the logical in religious matters. In De la guerra de Granada, he described the terrible consequences of a policy that emphasized works without regard to faith. He had little confidence in man's ability to discover religious truth through reason, and even less in the efficacy of a policy that sought to bring about true faith by legislating works. Diego's father, Tendilla, and his ancestor, Ayala, would have been in full agreement with this point of view.

Through all the intellectual and religious shifts of the sixteenth century, Diego, his brother Luis, and his nephew, the third marquis of Mondéjar, maintained the Mendoza tradition in religion and esthetics, to their own political and economic disadvantage. In the Counter Reformation Spain of Philip II, there was no room for statesmen with Renaissance values; and the Tendilla branch of the Mendoza continued the social decline begun by Tendilla.

Notes

Abbreviations

AHPM   Archivo Histórico de Protocolos. Madrid.

AGS   Archivo General de Simancas

ARCHG   Archivo de la Real Chancillería de Granada.

BAE   Biblioteca de Autores Españoles desde la Formación del Lenguaje hasta Nuestros Días. 273 vols. Madrid, 1850–1976.

BN   Biblioteca Nacional. Madrid.

Codoín   Colección de Documentos Inéditos para la Historia de España. 112 vols. Madrid, 1842–1895.

Copiador   López de Mendoza, Iñigo, [count of Tendilla and marquis of Mondéjar]. "Copiador de cartas por el marqués de Mondéjar." 2 vols. Osuna, 3406.

MHE   Memorial Histórico Español. Colección de Documentos, Opúsculos y Antigüedades que publica la Real Academia de la Historia. Madrid, 1851–1948.

Mondéjar   Mondéjar, marqués de [Gaspar Ibáñez de Segovia]. "Historia de la casa de Mondéjar; y sucesión de la baronía de Moncada." BN, MS 3315.

Osuna   Sección Osuna. Archivo Histórico Nacional. Madrid.

Registro   López de Mendoza, Iñigo, [count of Tendilla and marquis of Mondéjar]. "Registro de cartas referentes al gobierno de las Alpujarras, años 1508 a 1520." 2 vols. BN, MSS 10230–10231.

Salazar   Colección de don Luis de Salazar y Castro. Biblioteca de la Real Academia de la Historia. Madrid.

Notes

Preface

1. Francesco Branciforti, ed., *Las flores de los Morales de Job*, Florence, 1963.
2. Robert B. Tate, ed., *Colección Támesis*, Series B, vol. 2, London, 1965.
3. Archivo del Ayuntamiento, Granada.
4. Registro.
5. Copiador.
6. Mondéjar.
7. Salazar.
8. Francisco Layna Serrano, *Historia de Guadalajara y sus Mendozas en los siglos XV y XVI*, 4 vols., Madrid, 1942.
9. Spain, Consejo Superior de Investigaciones Científicas, Escuela de Estudios Medievales, *Normas de transcripción y edición de textos y documentos*, Madrid, 1944.
10. A few families who claimed royal lineage used the name of their royal ancestor as the family name—Manrique, Manuel, and Enríquez. This name system was systematically described by Liciniano Sáez, "Sobre el modo de tomar los apellidos o sobrenombres," in *Demostración histórica del verdadero valor de todas las monedas que corrían en Castilla durante el reynado del señor don Enrique III*, Madrid, 1796, pp. 315–320; and more recently Bonifacio del Carril, *Los Mendoza en España y en América en el siglo XV y en la primera mitad del siglo XVI*, Buenos Aires, 1954, pp. 35–36.
11. Cristina de Arteaga y Falguera, *La Casa del Infantado, cabeza de los Mendoza*, Madrid, 1940, I, 213; Osuna, Leg. 1.762.
12. See the problems this raises for Dámaso Alonso, *Dos españoles del siglo de oro*, Madrid, 1960, pp. 29–37.

Introduction

1. No tengo de hacer cosa que perjudique a my lealtad y a lo que soy obligado ny que sea ajena de lo que hizieron mys pasados." Copiador, Tendilla to the marquesa de Priego, [4 July 1506].

2. "General of the kingdom of Granada, captain and first praefect of the acropolis of Illíberis." His Castilian title was "capitán general del reyno de Granada y alcaide del Alhambra." The inscription is on the tomb of Tendilla's brother, Diego Hurtado de Mendoza, archbishop of Seville (d. 1502).

3. Elías Tormo, "El brote del renacimiento en los monumentos españoles y los Mendozas del siglo XV," *Boletín de la Sociedad Española de Excursiones*, 25 (1917), 51–65, 114–121; 26 (1918), 116–130.

4. W. H. Prescott, *History of the Reign of Ferdinand and Isabella the Catholic, of Spain*, 13th ed., Boston, 1857, II, 175–178.

5. José Cepeda Adán, "Andalucía en 1508: un aspecto de la correspondencia del virrey Tendilla," *Hispania*, Madrid, 22 (1962), 38–80; idem, "El Gran Tendilla, medieval y renacentista," *Cuadernos de Historia*, 1 (1967), 159–168.

6. William J. Entwistle, "Spanish Literature to 1681," in *Spain: A Companion to Spanish Studies*, ed. E. A. Peers, 5th ed., London, 1956, p. 113.

7. Benjamin Keen, Introduction to *The Spain of Ferdinand and Isabella*, by J. H. Mariéjol, New Brunswick, N.J. [1961], p. v.

8. J. H. Elliott, *Imperial Spain 1469–1715*, New York, 1967, pp. 126, 256–257.

9. On Pietro Martire in Spain, see J. H. Mariéjol, *Un Lettré italien à la cour d'Espagne, 1488–1526. Pierre Martyr d'Anghiera, sa vie et ses oeuvres*, Paris, 1887; Antonio Marín Ocete, "Pedro Mártir de Anglería y su Opus Epistolarum," *Boletín de la Universidad de Granada*, 73 (1943), 165–257. On the lack of evidence for his influence, see Angel González Palencia and Eugenio Mele, *Vida y obras de don Diego Hurtado de Mendoza*, Madrid, 1941–1943, I, 53.

10. On Lucio Marineo Sículo in Spain, see Caro Lynn, *A College Professor of the Renaissance; Lucio Marineo Sículo among the Spanish Humanists*, Chicago, 1937. For his use of a Spanish model and Spaniards' preference for the vernacular version, see Robert B. Tate, "A Humanistic Biography of John II of Aragon, a note," in *Homenaje a Jaime Vicens Vives*, Barcelona, 1965, I, 665–673.

11. Francesco Guicciardini, *La Legazione di Spagna*, in *Opere inedite*, Florence, 1857–1866, vol. 6.

12. Tarsicio de Azcona, *La elección y reforma del episcopado español en tiempo de los Reyes Católicos*, Madrid, 1960, p. 147.

13. Entwistle, "Spanish Literature," p. 118, in Peers, *Spain*, discussing works which he dates c. 1440 and 1463.

14. "En tal sentido debe considerarse como ejemplarísimo anticipo de esta acción cultural y religiosa el documento que fue impreso en 1472 y que ahora conmemoramos." Carlos Romero de Lecea, *El V centenario de la introducción de la imprenta en España, Segovia, 1472, antecedentes de la imprenta y circunstancias que favorecieron su introducción en España*, Madrid, 1972, p. 163.

15. "With the poets of Ferdinand and Isabel's reign, the Middle Ages may be said to come to an end as concerns lyric poetry. Juan Boscán and Garcilaso of the sixteenth century will usher in the Renaissance." Richard E. Chandler and Kessel Schwartz, *A New History of Spanish Literature*, Baton Rouge, 1961, p. 283.

16. A. D. Deyermond enhances the impression that the Renaissance did not start until after the reign of Fernando and Isabel by removing the playwright, Juan del Encina, from consideration in his survey of fifteenth-century literature: "At the end of the Middle Ages, an arbitrary line has to be drawn: the plays of Juan del

Encina and Lucas Fernández, the printed version of *Amadís de Gaula*, and the prose-works of the early humanists belong both to medieval and to Golden Age literature, and to avoid repetition they are treated not here but in the next volumes." *A Literary History of Spain: The Middle Ages*, New York, 1971, p. xv.

17. R. R. Bolgar, *The Classical Heritage*, New York, 1964, p. 316; Lewis W. Spitz, *The Renaissance and Reformation Movements*, Chicago, 1971, I, 288–289; Mariéjol, *Spain of Ferdinand and Isabella*, pp. 311–312. One student of Spanish literature has gone so far as to conclude that "in the sixteenth and seventeenth centuries Spain was too isolated from the rest of the world to feel the Renaissance deeply. Her history was therefore a continuation, in an expanded form, of the Middle Ages." Gerald Brenan, *The Spanish Labyrinth*, Cambridge, 1971, p. 225.

18. Hans Baron, *Crisis of the Early Italian Renaissance*, Princeton, 1966. See also idem, *From Petrarch to Leonardo Bruni*, Chicago, 1968; Charles Trinkaus, *In Our Image and Likeness, Humanity and Divinity in Italian Humanist Thought*, 2 vols., London, 1970; William J. Bouwsma, *Venice and the Defense of Republican Liberty*, Berkeley, 1968; Marvin Becker, "Individualism in the Early Italian Renaissance: Burden and Blessing," *Studies in the Renaissance*, 19 (1972), 273–297; Peter Burke, *The Renaissance Sense of the Past*, New York, 1970; Felix Gilbert, *Machiavelli and Guicciardini*, Princeton, 1965; Louis Green, *Chronicle into History*, Cambridge, 1972; Donald R. Kelley, *Foundations of Modern Historical Scholarship: Language, Law and History in the French Renaissance*, New York, 1970; Nancy Struever, *The Language of History in the Renaissance*, Princeton, 1970; B. L. Ullman, *The Humanism of Coluccio Salutati*, Padua, 1963.

19. The diversity of Catholic traditions in Spanish literature has recently been exhaustively described by Otis H. Green, *Spain and the Western Tradition*, 4 vols., Madison, Wis., 1963–1966. The pioneer work in describing the diversity of fifteenth-century Catholicism was Lucien Febvre, "Une question mal posée," *Au coeur religieux du 16e siècle*, Paris, 1957.

A modern account of the diversity of Catholic traditions in the fifteenth century by an official papal historian is Hubert Jedin, *A History of the Council of Trent*, trans. Ernest Graf, vol. 1, London, 1957. Ludwig von Pastor's views on this subject can best be seen in *History of the Popes*, vols. I–IV, trans. F. I. Antrobus, et al. 2nd ed., St. Louis Mo., 1901–1902.

20. H. A. R. Gibb, "The Influence of Islamic Culture on Medieval Europe," *Bulletin of the John Rylands Library*, 38 (1955–1956), p. 98. The diversity of fourteenth-century Judaism has been suggested by Joel H. Klausner, "Historic and Social Milieu of Santob's Proverbios Morales," *Hispania*, 48, New York, 1965; and, for the fifteenth century, Albert A. Sicroff, *Les controverses des statuts de "pureté de sang" en espagne du XVe au XVIIe siècle*, Paris, 1960. A similar diversity in fourteenth-century Islam and the crises which engendered it are described by Muhsin Mahdi, *Ibn Khaldun's Philosophy of History*, Chicago, 1964.

21. I know of only two works which treat Spanish literature of the period in this way: Anthony N. Zahareas, *The Art of Juan Ruiz, Archpriest of Hita*, Madrid, 1965; and Luis Beltrán, *Razones de buen amor: Oposiciones y convergencias en el libro del Arcipreste de Hita*, Madrid, 1977.

22. Nicholas G. Round, "Renaissance Culture and its Opponents in 15th Century Castile," *Modern Language Review*, 57 (1962), 204–215; Peter E. Russell, "Arms versus Letters," *Aspects of the Renaissance*, ed. Archibald R. Lewis, Austin, 1967; José Antonio Maravall, *El humanismo de las armas en Don Quijote*, [Madrid] 1948.

23. This combination of arms and letters is such a striking and important aspect of lyric poetry in fifteenth-century Castile that one of America's most eminent hispanists, Otis H. Green, has coined the term "warrior poet" to describe Garcilaso de la Vega and the long line of literary knights from whom he was descended, beginning with Fernán Pérez de Ayala and including Garcilaso's great-great-grandfather, Fernán Pérez de Guzmán. *Spain and the Western Tradition*, I, 128.

Chapter I

1. Fifteenth-century Castilian society has defied the analytic efforts of even the greatest historians. Although it is agreed that this is the formative period of Castilian politics, society, economy, religion, and arts, most historians have despairingly resorted to narrating events and then describing the whole period as "chaotic." Merriman's comment is typical: "Anarchy and disruption at home . . . are the most prominent features of the history of the time." Roger Bigelow Merriman, *The Rise of the Spanish Empire in the Old World and in the New*, New York, 1962, I, 95.

2. For a full description of the mayorazgo, see Chapter V.

3. Robert B. Tate, "The *Anacephaleosis* of Alfonso García de Santa María, Bishop of Burgos, 1435–1456," *Hispanic Studies in Honour of I. González Llubera*, Oxford, 1959, pp. 387–401; idem, "An Apology for Monarchy," *Romance Philology*, 15 (1961), 111–123; idem, "Italian Humanism and Spanish Historiography of the Fifteenth Century," *Bulletin of the John Rylands Library*, 34 (1951), 137–165; idem, "Mythology in Spanish Historiography," *Hispanic Review*, 22 (1954), 1–18; idem, "Nebrija the Historian," *Bulletin of the Hispanic Society*, 34 (1957), 125–146; "Rodrigo Sánchez de Arévalo (1404–1470), and his Compendiosa Historia Hispanica," *Nottingham Mediaeval Studies*, 4 (1960), 58–80. Most of this material has since been published in a single volume in Spanish translation, *Ensayos sobre la historiografía peninsular del siglo, XV*, Madrid, 1970. More recently, Tate has published fine critical editions of some of the works of Guzmán and Pulgar; and in the prefaces to these editions, he uses a more modern definition of humanism.

4. Aeneus Sylvius Piccolomini got to know don Alfonso at Basle and described him as the "delight of Spain." Pius II, *De Gestis Concilii Basiliensis Commentariorum Libri II*, ed. and trans. Denys Hay and W. K. Smith, Oxford, 1967, p. 10.

5. "Discurso sobre la precedencia del Rey Católico sobre el de Inglaterra en el Concilio de Basilea," in *Biblioteca de Autores Españoles*, vol. 116 (*Prosistas castellanos del siglo XV*), Madrid, 1959, pp. 205–233. See also "Carta dirigida al Rey por los embajadores de España en el Concilio de Basilea . . . dando cuenta de la acogida que tuvieron los enviados, primeras impresiones y de las manifestaciones sobre precedencia que impulsaron a don Alonso de Cartagena a pronunciar su discurso sobre la superioridad de España respecto a Inglaterra . . .

año 1434," transcription by Antonio Elías de Molins, *Revista de Archivos, Bibliotecas y Museos*, 3ª época, 1 (1897), 67–73.

6. R. H. Trame, R. *Sánchez de Arévalo, Spanish Diplomat and Champion of the Papacy*, Washington, D.C., 1958.

7. Tate, "Apology," p. 122.

8. Antonio Paz y Melia, *El cronista Alonso de Palencia: su vida y sus obras*, Madrid, 1914; Alfonso de Palencia, *Crónica de Enrique IV*, trans. Antonio Paz y Melia, 5 vols., Madrid, 1904.

9. Andrés Bernáldez, *Memorias del reinado de los Reyes Católicos*, ed. Manuel Gómez-Moreno and Juan de Mata Carriazo, Madrid, 1962.

10. Tate, "Apology," p. 122.

11. The study of the caballero chronicles is possible because of Juan de Mata Carriazo's editions of many previously unknown vernacular chronicles. See his "Estudio Preliminar" and edition of each of the following: Andrés Bernáldez, *Memorias del reinado de los Reyes Católicos*; *Crónica de don Alvaro de Luna, condestable de Castilla, maestre de Santiago*, Madrid, 1940; *Crónica del halconero de Juan II*, Pedro Carrillo de Huete, Madrid, 1946; Hernando del Pulgar, *Crónica de los Reyes Católicos*, Madrid, 1943; *Relación de los fechos del muy magnífico D. Miguel Lucas muy digno Condestable de Castilla*, Madrid, 1940; Diego de Valera, *Crónica de los Reyes Católicos*, Madrid, 1927; idem, *Memorial de diversas hazañas, crónica de Enrique IV, ordenada por mosén Diego de Valera*, Madrid, 1941.

12. Pedro López de Ayala, *Crónicas de los reyes de Castilla*. My citations of this work will be to the edition readily available in BAE, vols. 66 and 68, Madrid, reprint 1953, but my translations are based on the superior text in *Colección de las crónicas y memorias de los reyes de Castilla*, 2 vols., Madrid, 1779–1780.

13. Fernán Pérez de Guzmán, *Generaciones y Semblanzas*. Unless otherwise noted, citations of this work will be to the edition by Robert B. Tate, in *Colección Támesis*, Series B, vol. II, London, 1965.

14. For his life, see Lucas de Torre, "Mosén Diego de Valera. Su vida y sus obras," *Boletín de la Academia de Historia*, 75 (1914), 50–83, 133–168; Juan de Mata Carriazo, Estudio preliminar to Diego de Valera, *Memorial de diversas hazañas*. For his place in Spanish historiography see E. A. Peers, *Spain: A Companion to Spanish Studies*, 5th ed. London, 1929, p. 116; Jaime Vicens Vives, ed., *Historia social y económica de España y América*, Barcelona, 1957, II, 483; Julio Alonso Puyol, "Los cronistas de Enrique IV," *Boletín de la Real Academia de Historia*, 78 (1921), 399–415, 488–496; 79 (1922), 11–28, 118–144. For his works, see *La corónica de España*, Seville, 1538; *Crónica de los Reyes Católicos*, ed. Juan de Mata Carriazo; *Epístolas de mosén Diego de Valera, enbiadas en diversos tiempos e a diversas personas*, ed. José A. de Balenchana, Madrid, 1878; as well as the *Memorial de diversas hazañas*.

15. *Crónica*, p. 147; Torre, "Mosén Diego de Valera," pp. 134–135.

16. *Crónica*, p. 149.

17. Michel de Montaigne, *Essays*, trans. J. M. Cohen, Harmondsworth, (1958), 10, p. 169.

18. *Memorias*, p. 233.

19. *Ibid.*, pp. 129, 203, 209.

20. *Ibid.*, p. 22.

21. Ibid., p. 213.
22. Crónica, pp. 7, 136.
23. Ibid., pp. 161–165, 150, 193, 196.
24. Ibid., pp. 192–193; "Letter to don Fernando, 2 June 1485." Epístolas, p. 88.
25. Epístolas, p. 87.
26. Crónica, pp. 86, 119, 138, 141. This caballero attitude toward the Muslims had not changed since the composition of the Trailer to the Gran Crónica of 1344. The author of this work noted that "hay una ley de Dios por encima de las dos religiones y Dios 'administra justicia y milagro' sin atender al credo, sino a la verdad de cada uno." Diego Catalán, ed., Un cronista anónimo del siglo XIV, Canarias, n.d., p. 119.
27. Valera, Crónica, pp. 170–171; compare the similarity of this passage to his description of the battle of Toro, ibid., p. 60.
28. For the persistence of religious elements in Spanish chivalry and of secular elements in the Reconquest, see Juan de Mata Carriazo, "Cartas de la frontera de Granada, 1430–1509," Al-Andaluz, II (1946), 69–130; Catalán, Un cronista, pp. 66–67, 105, 114, 116–117, 118; don Juan Manuel, Libro de los estados, p. 294, cited by Américo Castro, The Structure of Spanish History, trans. Edmund L. King, Princeton, 1954, p. 221; José Goñi Gastambide, "La Santa Sede y la reconquista del reino de Granada," Hispania Sacra, 4 (1951), 49–63; P. G. Evans, "A Spanish Knight in Flesh and Blood. A Study of the Chivalric Spirit of Suero de Quiñones," Hispania, 15 (New York, 1932), 141–152.
29. "Ser siempre victorioso es don de la alta tribuna, mas pugnar contra fortuna exercicio es virtuoso," Generaciones, pp. 263–264.
30. José Luis Romero considers this confusion of Fortuna with Providence as a characteristic of the medieval mind, "Sobre la biografía española del siglo XV y los ideales de vida," Cuadernos de Historia de España, 1–2 (1944), 115–138, reprinted in Sobre la historiografía y la historia, Buenos Aires, 1945. José Cepeda Adán believes that it is an indication of Jewish ancestry, "El Providencialismo en las cronistas de los Reyes Católicos," Arbor, 17 (1950), 177–90.
31. Memorias, p. 661. Bernáldez's attitudes on these subjects are considered by many historians to be typical of the common people. See Castro, Structure, p. 215; A. Ballesteros y Beretta, Historia de España y su influencia en la historia universal, 2nd ed., 12 vols., Barcelona, 1943–1948, V, 32; F. Soldevila, Historia de España, Barcelona, 1952, II, 425–428, 416–418; J. H. Marièjol, L'Espagne sous Ferdinand et Isabelle, Paris, 1892, pp. 12–13.
32. Memorias, pp. 94–98, 225.
33. "Dos maneras son de derecho: una es natural, otra es legal . . . segunt el Philósofo lo nota en el quinto de las Héticas," Doctrinal de príncipes, in BAE, vol. 116 (Prosistas castellanos del siglo XV), p. 197.
34. Epístolas, pp. 62–69; Memorial, pp. xxxiii–xxxvi, 113; Crónica, pp. 32–34, 123–124; 149; La corónica de España, Parte IV, Chs., IX, XXXVII, XCIII, XCIV, XCVI, CXXV.
35. Crónica, p. 112.
36. See Pérez de Guzmán, Generaciones, pp. 9–97; Juan Torres Fontes, Estudio sobre la "Crónica de Enrique IV" del Dr. Galíndez de Carvajal, Murcia, 1946, pp. 19, 42; Luis Suárez Fernández and Juan de Mata Carriazo, La España de los

Reyes Católicos, 1474–1516, vol. XVII of *Historia de Espana*, directed by Ramón Menéndez Pidal, Madrid, 1969, I, 31.

37. Pulgar, *Crónica de los Reyes Católicos*, I: "Introducción," Ch. II.
38. Pulgar, *Crónica*, I, 71, 144–145, 237, 255, 277–281, 325, 333, 334–337, 415; Bernáldez, *Memorias*, pp. 3–9; Romero, "Sobre la biografía," pp. 161–166.
39. Torres Fontes, *Estudio*, pp. 11–33; B. Sánchez Alonso, *Historia de la historiografía española*, Madrid, 1941–1947, I, 302–306.
40. Puyol Alonso, "Los cronistas," p. 131.
41. Carriazo, Estudio preliminar to *Memorial* by Valera, p. xxxiii; Puyol Alonso, "Los cronistas," pp. 118–126; Torres Fontes, *Estudio*, pp. 31–32; Valera, *Memorial*, pp. 112, 293, 179; idem, *Epístolas*, pp. 17–20.
42. Puyol Alonso, "Los cronistas," p. 132.
43. Carriazo, Estudio preliminar to *Memorial* by Valera, p. xiii; Torre, "Mosén Diego de Valera," p. 160.

Chapter II

1. The pioneer and still unsurpassed work on the seigneurial regime and its relationship with the Castilian monarchy is Andreas Walther, *Die Anfänge Karls V*, Leipzig, 1911, pp. 39–65. A less reliable analysis can be found in J. R. L. Highfield, "The Catholic Kings and the Titled Nobility of Castile," in J. R. Hale et al., eds. *Europe in the Late Middle Ages*, Evanston, Ill., 1965. Both Walther and Highfield are based upon Antoine de Lalaing, *Relation du premier voyage de Philippe le Beau en Espagne, en 1501*, in *Collection des Voyages des Souverains des Pays-Bas*, Brussels, 1876, vol. I. The most important comprehensive histories of the Mendoza are those by Mondéjar in the seventeenth century and by Layna in the twentieth. The chapters of Mondéjar's work covering the period 1566–1571 are edited and published by Alfred Morel-Fatio, *L'Espagne au XVIᵉ e au XVIIᵉ siècle*, Heilbronn, 1878, pp. 66–96. A less successful seventeenth-century history of the family is Gabriel Rodríguez de Ardila y Esquivias, "Historia de los condes de Tendilla," ed. R. Foulché-Delbosc, *Revue Hispanique*, 31 (1914), 63–131. An eighteenth-century genealogical history based on documents now contained in Osuna is Diego Gutiérrez Coronel, *Historia genealógica de la Casa de Mendoza*, ed. Angel González Palencia, 2 vols., Madrid, 1946, See also Arteaga y Falguera, *La Casa del Infantado*; Carril, *Los Mendoza*; José Amador de los Ríos, *Vida del marqués de Santillana*, Buenos Aires, 1948; González Palencia, *Vida*, vol. 1.
2. *Siete Partidas*, Partida IV, 25, 1.
3. The territorial military governors had different titles according to the usage at the time each territory had been incorporated into the kingdom, i.e., *montero mayor de León*, *prestamero mayor de Vizcaya*, *adelantado de Murcia*, *capitán general de Granada*, *virrey de Nueva España*.
4. For the war and its aftermath, see Ayala, *Crónica del rey don Pedro*; Julio Valdeón Baruque, *Enrique II de Castilla: La guerra civil y la consolidación del régimen 1366–1371*, Valladolid, 1966.
5. Alfonso Andrés, "D. Pedro González de Mendoza él de Aljubarrota, 1340–1385," *Boletín de la Academia de la Historia*, 78 (1921), 255–273, 353–376, 415–436, 496–504; "Extracto del privilegio del rey Pedro de Castilla por el que hace

merced de la villa de Galve a Iñigo López de Orozco, Tordesillas, 28 October 1354," Salazar, M–158, ff. 67, 67v; "Extracto del privilegio del rey por el que concede cierta venta de trigo a Iñigo López de Orozco, Toledo, 7 January 1365," Salazar, M–158, f. 66v.

6. "Pedro González de Mendoza, Escribanías de Guadalajara y otras por Enrique II, 1366," Osuna, 1873/1; "Hita and Buitrago, escribanía a Pedro González de Mendoza, 1366," Osuna, 1873; "Duques del Infantado, Cédulas de algunos reyes a favor de Alvaro de Luna y los Duques del Infantado, 1361–1476," Osuna, 1724/3; "Extracto del privilegio del rey Enrique II por el que confirma a Iñigo López de Orozco y a doña Marina García de Meneses los privilegios de sus casas, Toledo, 10 May 1371," Salazar, M–158, f. 66v; Valdeón, Enrique II, pp. 125, 128–129.

7. English participation in the war in John Froissart, Chronicles of England, France and Spain, ed. H. P. Dunster, New York: Dutton, 1961, pp. 91–112; and P. E. Russell, English Intervention in Spain & Portugal in the Time of Edward III & Richard II, Oxford, 1955.

8. The mercedes of Enrique II were those gifts from the king that involved the alienation of a portion of the royal patrimony and were given in remuneration for services. "Merced de Buitrago e Hita a Pedro González de Mendoza, 1368," and "Confirmación, 1379," Osuna, 1652/6; Valdeón, Enrique II, pp. 121–123, 181–183, 214, 288–289; "Pedro González de Mendoza, Mayorazgo para su hijo Iñigo, 1373," Osuna, 1373/10; Amador de los Ríos, Vida, p. 22; Gutiérrez Coronel, Casa de Mendoza, I, 96–98; "Mayorazgo para su hijo Diego, 13 February 1380," Osuna, 1762, printed in Layna Serrano, Guadalajara, I, 282–284.

9. Burgos, 1 January 1366, "El rey don Enrique II hace merced de las villas de Buitrago y Hita a Pedro González de Mendoza," in Luis de Salazar y Castro, Historia genealógica de la Casa de Haro, ed. Dalmiro de la Válgoma y Díaz-Varela, Archivo Documental Español, 15 (1959), 316–322.

10. Emilio Mitre Fernández, Evolución de la nobleza en Castilla bajo Enrique III, 1396–1406, Valladolid, 1968; Luis Suárez Fernández, "Algunas consideraciones acerca de la crisis castellana de 1383," Anuario de Estudios Medievales, 2 (1965), 359–376; idem, "Problemas políticos en la minoridad de Enrique III," Hispania, 12 (1952), 163–231, 323–400. For the Mendoza connections with the Pecha and Ayala clans, see Luis María de Uriarte, ed., El fuero de Ayala by Fernán Pérez de Ayala, Madrid, 1912, pp. 37–49; Jerónimo de Sigüenza, Historia de la Orden de San Jerónimo, in Nueva Biblioteca de Autores Españoles, vols. 8, 12, Madrid, 1909; Juan Catalina García López, Biblioteca de escritores de la provincia de Guadalajara y bibliografía de la misma hasta el siglo XIX, Madrid, 1899.

11. "Testimonio de la entrega a don Diego Hurtado, el almirante, hecha por micer Ventura Venzón, del regimiento, alcaldía y alguacilazgo de Guadalajara, Segovia, 16 November 1401," Osuna, 1875, published in Layna Serrano, Guadalajara, I, 302.

12. Pérez de Guzmán, Generaciones, p. 17.

13. "Tendilla, Privilegio rodado escripto en papel que dió el señor rey don Enrique 3° al señor don Diego Hurtado de Mendoza señor de la Vega y Almirante de la Mar por la qual hace merced de la villa de Tendilla, Madrid, December 1395," Osuna, 2983/1.

14. Amador de los Ríos, Vida, pp. 22–23; "Santillana, Reconocimiento de vasallaje a

García Laso de la Vega, 1315," Osuna, 1798/6; "Santillana, Bienes de da. Leonor de la Vega, Poder sobre posesión de Potes y demás lugares de Liébana, 1408," Osuna, 4232/3; "Leonor de la Vega, Apuntes sobre sus tierras y vasallos," Osuna, 1788/3; "Leonor de la Vega, Carta de Per Alvarez sobre alcabalas de Castrillo, siglo XV," Osuna, 1864/6; "Santillana, Provision de Juan I a los alcaldes de Santander, S. Vicente de la Barquera y Santillana para la posesión de pozo de sal de Treceño, 1379," Osuna, 2266/1.

15. Hayward Keniston, Garcilaso de la Vega; A Critical Study of His Life and Works, New York, 1922.

16. "Otrosi mando que a mi fijo garcia que le muden el nonbre e le digan iohan furtado de mendoça." Osuna, 1762.

17. Santillana's property disputes with the Manrique and other relatives are described at length in Gutiérrez Coronel, Casa de Mendoza, I, 165–172; and Amador de los Ríos, Vida, pp. 23, 27, 45–56. See also "Mondéjar, Cesión por Sancho de Rojas Arzob. de Toledo a da. Leonor de Aragón que la habia dado Saldaña, 1415," Osuna, 1825/4; "Villa de Hita, Carta de Iñigo López de Mendoza para que sus vasallos de Buitrago e Hita le paguen lo que le orden, 1418," Osuna, 1648/6; "Merindad de Santillana, Sobre el secando de la sal de Cabezón en la Merindad de Santillana, 1423," Osuna, 2266/2; "Castillo de Saldaña, Sobre entrega por Diego Gómez de Sandoval, 1430," Osuna, 1965/5; "Santillana, Posesión, Gonzalvo Ruiz de la Vega, 1437," Osuna, 1826/2; "Tendilla, Carta de venta que otorgó fray Esteban de León religioso de monasterio San Jerónimo en San Bartolomé de Lupiana como albacea de la señora da. Aldonza de Mendoza . . . a favor de Juan de Contreras de la villa de Tendilla, 1441," Osuna, 2983; "Santillana y sus valles, 1444," Osuna, 1784–1797; "Capítulos entre Iñigo López de Mendoza y el Consejo para levantar con muralles de Hita, 1441," Osuna, 1670/1; "Saldaña, Derecho a nombrar teniente de alcalde y escribano, etc. por los Duques, 1797," Osuna, 1826/2.

18. For general information about the period 1407–1474, I have relied upon Luis Suárez Fernández, Angel Canellas López, and Jaime Vicens Vives, Los Trastámaras de Castilla y Aragón en el siglo XV, 1407–1474, (Vol. 15 of Historia de España directed by Ramón Menéndez Pidal). Madrid 1969; Luis Suárez Fernández, Castilla, el cisma, y el crisis conciliar, 1378–1440, Madrid, 1955; idem, Nobleza y monarquía, 2nd ed., Valladolid, 1974; and José María Font Ríus, Instituciones medievales españolas, Madrid, 1949. See also "Marqués de Santillana, Confederación con él de Villena y el conde de Plasencia, 1450," Osuna, 1860/7; "Priego, Lope de, Posesión en nombre de Juan de Luna de los lugares de Alcocer, etc. 1453," Osuna, 1727/4; "Confederación, 22 December 1456," Osuna, 1860/8; "Confederación, Segovia, 4 June 1457," Osuna, 1860/19. Suárez Fernández points out several times that both supporters and opponents of the crown switched sides many times and that there was no ideological or class conflict between the monarchy and the aristocracy, yet he continues to believe that the political conflict of the period can be explained as a conflict between the crown and the aristocracy, whom he inconsistently labels nobility.

19. The fifteenth-century admiration for Fernando de Antequera is repeated without criticism in I. MacDonald, Don Fernando de Antequera, Oxford, 1948.

20. Santillana was Guzmán's great nephew; Gutierre Gómez de Toledo, who led them in this action, was Guzmán's cousin and Alba's uncle; Santillana and Velasco be-

came *consuegros;* and Guzmán was a nephew of Velasco. Amador de los Ríos believes that Santillana and Alba were educated together in the household of Gutierre Gómez de Toledo while the latter was archdeacon of Guadalajara and that Alba's presence at Santillana's deathbed is evidence of a lifelong friendship. *Vida,* p. 77. J. H. Elliott suggests that the Mendoza and Alba were enemies in the fifteenth century: *Imperial Spain,* pp. 256–257. It is true that the Mendoza never had the close friendship with Alba that they had with some other great families, such as the Velasco and Guzmán, but they did have a consistent friendship based on common political interests, amply documented by the alliances between the Mendoza and Alba in Osuna, 1860.

21. "La acción de Tordesillas fué un pecado de juventud de don Iñigo." Carril, *Los Mendoza,* p. 30.

22. "Santillana, marqués de, Cédula para entrega de Juan de Puelles, 1455," Osuna, 1860/37; "Sevilla, 11 August 1455, Cédula original de Enrique IV," Osuna, 1860/37; "Cédulas para que los arrendadores del rey no cobren rentas en el condado del Real de Manzanares, Partido de Buitrago, Partido de Hita, marquesado de Santillana, 1456," Osuna, 1862/1; "Albalá del rey Juan II por el que hace merced del título de marqués de Santillana y de conde del Real de Manzanares a Iñigo López de Mendoza, Burgos, 8 August 1445," Salazar, M–92, ff. 295v.–297; "Testamento del primer marqués de Santillana, 8 May 1455, Guadalajara," Osuna, 1875, and "Codicilo al testamento del primer marqués de Santillana, Jaén, 5 June 1455," Osuna, 1762, both published in Layna Serrano, *Guadalajara,* I, 315–324; Amador de los Ríos, *Vida,* 45, 64; Gutiérrez Coronel, *Casa de Mendoza,* I, 173–178.

23. In 1436, Santillana's eldest son was married to Brianda de Luna, a cousin of don Alvaro—a marriage for which the king himself acted as *padrino* (godfather) in an attempt to establish peace between the two houses. Amador de los Ríos, *Vida,* pp. 52–55.

24. "Confederación, Guadalajara, 21 March 1459," Osuna, 1860/9; "Confederación, Logroño, 4 June 1461," Osuna, 1860/20, with a letter from the king in 1860/10.

25. For the following section, see Manuel Torres Fontes, "La conquista del marquesado de Villena en el reinado de los Reyes Católicos," *Hispania,* 13 (1953), 37–151; Tarsicio de Azcona, *Isabel la Católica: Estudio crítico de su vida y su reinado,* Madrid, 1964, pp. 3–205; "Confederación, Arévalo, 5 October 1465," Osuna, 1860/11; "Confederación, Arévalo, 8 October 1465," Osuna, 1860/12; "Confederación, 30 January 1466," Osuna, 1860, no number; "Confederación, March, 1466," Osuna, 1860/16; "Confederación, Atienza, 28 April 1466," Osuna, 1860/13; "Confederación, Valladolid, 29 August 1466," Osuna, 1860/14; "Confederación con doña Juana mujer de Enrique IV, 1467," Osuna, 1860/14; "Traslado autorizado del pleito omenaje que hiço el rey don Enrique IV a los . . . refrendado de Fernando del Pulgar en manos del Sr don Iñigo López de Mendoza, 28 June 1467," Osuna, 1860/38; "Confederación con Juan Alfon de Monjeca, 1468," Osuna, 1860/18; "Copia sin autorizar en papel de quartillo de la confederación . . . , Burgos, 29 July 1468," Osuna, 1860, no number; "Confederación, Trijueque, 30 July 1468," Osuna, 1860/18.

26. Fernando del Pulgar, *Crónica de los reyes católicos,* II, 9.

27. "Marqués de Santillana, Relación de la entrega de la Princesa Juana, 1468," Osuna, 1726/9; "Confederación, 11 March 1469," Osuna, 1860/6; "Confederación, 18 March 1469," Osuna, 1860/20; "Pedro González de Mendoza, Confederación para tener por reina a Isabel la Católica, 1474," Osuna, 417/20 bis; "Confederación, Carrión, 28 March 1474," Osuna, 1860/21; "Marqués de Santillana, Confederación para conquistar Carrión, 10 April 1474," Osuna, 1860/22.

28. The entire document from the private library of the present duke of Infantado is reproduced and transcribed in Arteaga, Casa del Infantado, I, 210–215. As Arteaga emphasizes, Isabel explicitly states that she is giving the title because the second Santillana was "el principal grande caballero de nuestros reinos, que conservan nuestro estado e sostienen nuestra corona."

29. Torres Fontes, "La conquista del marquesado de Villena."

30. Fernando's mother was Juana Enríquez, granddaughter of Juana de Mendoza and Alfonso Enríquez, the first Enríquez admiral.

31. Francisco de Medina y Mendoza, Vida del Cardenal D. Pedro González de Mendoza. Memorial Histórico Español, vol. VI, Madrid, 1853; Azcona, Isabel, p. 724.

Chapter III

1. "Fundación del mayorazgo de Ayala," in Marqués de Lozoya [Juan de Contreras y López de Ayala], Introducción a la biografía del Canciller Ayala, Prov. de Vizcaya, 1950, p. 61. Amada López de Meneses, "Nuevos datos sobre el canciller Ayala," Cuadernos de Historia de España, 10 (1948), 111–128; idem, "El canciller Pero López de Ayala y los reyes de Aragón," Estudios de Edad Media de la Corona de Aragón, 8 (1967), 189–264.

2. Uriarte, El fuero de Ayala, p. 39.

3. The genealogical history, with an appendix by Pedro López de Ayala, is printed in Lozoya, p. 147; the fuero in Uriarte, pp. 187–216. The fuero was revised and amplified in 1469 by García Lopez de Ayala. Uriarte, pp. 219–228.

4. Maurice Faucon, La Librairie des Papes d'Avignon, sa formation, sa composition, ses catalogues 1316–1420, Paris, 1886–1887, Bibliothèque des Ecoles Françaises d'Athènes et de Rome, fasc. 43, pp. 23–48; W. Braxton Ross, Jr., "Giovanni Colonna, Historian at Avignon," Speculum, 45 (1970), 533–563; Anthony Luttrell, "The Aragonese Crown and the Knights Hospitallers of Rhodes, 1291–1350," English Historical Review, 76 (1961), 1–19; idem, "Fourteenth-Century Hospitaller Lawyers," Traditio, 21 (1965), 449–456; Mario Schiff, La Bibliothèque du marquis de Santillane, Bibliothèque de l'Ecole des Hautes Etudes, fasc. 153, Paris, 1905, p. 87.

5. Josep Rius Serra, "Estudiants espanyols a Avinyò al segle XIV," Miscelánea Mons. José Rius Serra, I, 469–511 (first published in Analecta Sacra Terraconensis, 10 (1934), 87–112); Suárez Fernández, "Problemas políticos."

6. On Barroso, see Lozoya, Ayala, pp. 21, 27–30; Bernard Guillemain, La Cour Pontificale d'Avignon (1309–1376), Bibliothèque des Ecoles Françaises d'Athènes et de Rome, fasc, 201, Paris, 1962, pp. 190, 211, 229, 234, 256, 257, 269, 273, 275. On Alvaro Pelayo, see Faucon, Librairie, prol. pp. 22, 35, 36; Nicholas

lung, *Un Franciscain théologien du pouvoir pontifical au XIVᵉ siècle: Alvaro Pelayo*, Paris, 1931.

7.   Aquí estorvaron mucho algunos sabidores
        Por se mostrar letrados e muy disputadores,
        Fisieron sus questiones como grandes dotores
        E por esto la eglesia de sangre fas sudores
   Poesías, ed. E. A. Kuersteiner, New York, 1920, II, 37.

8. On the educational and intellectual activities of Albornoz, see Charles Faulhaber, *Latin Rhetorical Theory in Thirteenth and Fourteenth Century Castile*, Berkeley, 1972, p. 34; Berthe M. Martí, *The Spanish College at Bologna in the Fourteenth Century*, Philadelphia, 1966, pp. 31–32; Josep Rius Serra, "Bibliotecas medievales españolas," *Revista Eclesiástica*, II (1930), 318–326 (*Miscelánea, I*, 139–149); Emilio Sáez and José Trenchs, "Juan Ruiz de Cisneros (1295/1296–1351/1352) autor del Buen Amor," in *El Arcipreste de Hita: El libro, autor, la tierra, la época*, ed. Manuel Criado de Val, Actas del I Congreso International sobre el Arcipreste de Hita, Barcelona, 1973, pp. 365–368; Evelio Verdera y Tuells, ed., *El Cardenal Albornoz y el Colegio de España*, 2 vols., Saragosa, 1972.

9. López de Meneses, "Nuevos datos," pp. 112–116.

10. *Las flores de los Morales de Job*, ed. Francesco Branciforti. Ayala's translation of Livy was published anonymously in Salamanca, 1497, but was superseded by that of fr. Pedro de la Vega, Saragosa, 1520. Schiff, *La Bibliothèque*, p. 100.

11. For a different interpretation of Ayala's intentions in translation, see Robert B. Tate, "López de Ayala, Humanist Historian?" *Hispanic Review*, 25 (1957), 157–174.

12. Robert B. Tate, *Ensayos sobre la historiografía peninsular del siglo XV*, Madrid, 1970, pp. 46–47. In 1424, Alfonso V of Aragon, holding his younger brother, Juan of Navarre, responsible for a recent political incident, wrote to Juan reproaching him and advising him to read the *Crónica del rey don Pedro*. Cited by Suárez Fernández, *Nobleza y monarquía*, pp. 66–67.

13. The *Crónica del rey don Pedro* was published in Seville, 1495, 1542, 1549; and in Toledo, 1526. Francesco Branciforti, "Regesto delle opere di Pero López de Ayala," in *Saggi e ricerche in memoria di Ettore Li Gotti*, Palermo, 1961, pp. 289–319.

14. Gerónimo Zurita y Castro, *Emiendas y advertencias a la Crónica del rey don Pedro*, ed. Diego Josef Dormer, Saragosa, 1683, n.p.

15. Prosper Mérimée, *Histoire de don Pèdre Iᵉʳ Roi de Castille*, Paris, 1961; François Piétri, *Pierre le Cruel: Le vrai et le faux*, Paris, 1961; Gonzalo Pintos Reino, *El rey don Pedro de Castilla: Vindicación de su reinado*, Santiago, 1929; N. Sanz y Ruiz de la Peña, *Don Pedro I de Castilla: llamado el "Cruel,"* Madrid, 1943; Franco Meregalli, *Pietro di Castiglia nella letteratura*, Milan, [1951].

16. Claudio Sánchez-Albornoz, in Tate, "López de Ayala," pp. 158, 160.

17. "Ya aludimos a la sinuosidad de espíritu del Canciller," in Angel Valbuena Prat, *Historia de la literatura española*, Barcelona, 1937, I, 190–191.

18. Russell, *English Intervention*, p. 18.

19. The best critique of Ayala's chronicles is still José Amador de los Ríos, "Protexta del sentimiento nacional contra la innovación alegórica," *Historia crítica de la literatura española*, Madrid, 1862–1865, V, 99–159.

20. See Entwistle, "Spanish Literature," p. 115.

21. *Crónicas de los reyes de Castilla*, I, 31–35, 51–52 (the behetrías were lands whose tenants had the right to elect their seigneurial lords), 54–65.
22. Ibid., pp. 483–493.
23. Ibid., pp. 304–305; 329–330.
24. Ibid., pp. 239–242.
25. Ibid., pp. 554–557.
26. Ibid., pp. 140–144.
27. "Ca, señor, algunos Reyes vuestros antecesores en Castilla e en León ficieron algunas obras destas por las quales sus famas se dañaron e les vinieron grandes deservicios." Ibid., II, 207–208.
28. After Pedro's mother has murdered her rival, Leonor de Guzmán (the first murder in the chronicle), Ayala comments: "E desto pesó mucho a algunos del Regno; ca entendían que por tal fecho como este vernían grandes guerras e escándalos en el Regno, segund fueron despues, por quanto la dicha doña Leonor avía grandes fijos e muchos parientes. E en estos fechos tales, por poca venganza, recrescen despues muchos males e daños, que sería muy mejor escusarlos: ca mucho mal e mucha guerra nasció en Castilla por esta razón." Ibid., I, 36–37.
    In the last paragraph of the chronicle, describing Pedro, he says: "E mató muchos en su Regno, por lo qual le vino todo el daño que avedes oido. Por ende diremos aqui lo que dixo el Profeta David: Agora los Reyes aprended e sed castigados todos los que juzgades el mundo: ca grand juicio, e maravilloso fue este, e muy espantable." Ibid., p. 557.
29. Ibid., pp. 313–315, 317.
30. For the themes of soberbia and cobdicia in the *Libro de Alexandre*, see Deyermond, *Literary History*, p. 66; Ian Michael, *The Treatment of Classical Material in the Libro de Alexandre*, Manchester, 1970.
31. *Crónica del rey don Alfonso Onceno*, BAE, 66: 211.
32. *Crónicas de los reyes de Castilla*, I, 414–415.
33. Ibid., p. 483, n. 2.
34. Ibid., p. 143.
35. Ibid., p. 272.
36. Ibid., p. 293.
37. Ibid., p. 312.
38. Ibid., p. 321.
39. Ibid., p. 404.
40. Ibid., p. 144.
41. Ibid., pp. 38–43.
42. Ibid., p. 58.
43. "E por ende de aqui adelante yo Pero Lopez de Ayala con el ayuda de Dios, lo entiendo continuar asi lo mas verdaderamente que pudiere de lo que bí, en lo qual non entiendo decir si non verdad: otrosi de lo que acaesce en mi edad e en mi tiempo en algunas partidas donde yo non he estado, e lo supiere por verdadera relacion de señores e Caballeros, e otros dignos de fe e de creer, de quienes lo oí, e me dieron dende testimonio, tomandolo con la mayor diligencia que yo pude." Ibid., p. xx.
44. Guido delle Colonne, *Historia Troiana* [Strassburg, 1486]. This edition is not

paginated, but the reference is to a passage in the first column of the first page of text.

45. This reservation is stated in his addition to the genealogical history written by his father, Fernán Pérez de Ayala. Fernán Pérez traced the family and its position in Alava all the way back to the Visigothic period. Much of his material must be considered myth, but Fernán Pérez used it with no questions about its reliability. Pedro López de Ayala, treating the same period on his mother's side of the family, was extremely cautious about using this material and carried the genealogy back only seven generations to don Gonzalo Fernández, explaining that he could not find documents for earlier generations: "E todo esto fallé yo don Pero Lopez por escrituras del solar de Cevallos e de los demas solares. E non pude fallar el padre e la madre deste don Gonzalo Fernández mas de que venien de padre en padre del señor del solar de Cisneros desde mui luengo tiempos, e su divisa esta en la Iglesia de San Martín de Valdecayon." Lozoya, *Introducción*, p. 147.

46. *Crónicas de los reyes de Castilla*, I, xxx.
47. Ibid., pp. 31–35.
48. Ibid., pp. 51–65.
49. Ibid., II, 206–213.
50. Ibid., I, 449–453.
51. Ibid., II, 206–213.
52. *Amplificatio* is the device of dwelling on a minor detail in order to emphasize by implication the magnitude of the main object. Quintillian, *Inst.* 8.4.9 ff.

Chapter IV

1. Félix González Olmedo, *Diego Ramírez de Villaescusa (1459–1537), fundador del Colegio de Cuenca y autor de los Cuatro diálogos sobre la muerte del príncipe Don Juan*, Madrid, 1944, pp. 9–10; Adolfo Bonilla y San Martín, *Luis Vives y la filosofía del Renacimiento*, Madrid, 1903, pp. 376–379, 674–675; Schiff, *La Bibliothèque*, pp. 143–144, 194–195.
2. Rafael Lapesa, *La obra literaria del marqués de Santillana*, Madrid, 1957, p. 1.
3. Martinus Cordubensis, "Breve Compendium Artis Rethorice," Madrid, Biblioteca Nacional, MS. 9309. For an overview of rhetorical texts in Spain, see Faulhaber, *Latin Rhetorical Theory*.
4. "Demás de lo [el oficio de armas] aver mamado en la leche y desde mi mocedad en la escuela de uno de los mas famosos maestros que como vuestra merced bien sabe ovo en nuestros tiempos que fue mi señor e mi hermano don Rodrigo Manrique maestre de Santiago digno de loable memoria. Alli aprendi a sofrer peligros e trabajos e nescesidades juntamente. . . . Y esto no podre decir que aya fecho en el estudio de las sciencias ni del arte de la poesia, porque yo estas nunca aprendi nin tove maestro que me las mostrase de lo qual las obras mias dan verdadero testimonio y aun no valgo mas por ello." Gómez Manrique, *Cancionero*, ed. Antonio Paz y Melia, Madrid, 1885, I, 1–2.
5. Werner Bahner, *La lingüística española del siglo de oro*, Madrid, 1966, p. 29.
6. On Castilian diplomatic relations with Avignon, see Suárez Fernández, *Castilla, el cisma, y el crisis conciliar, 1378–1440*. Other famous Spaniards in Avignon during this period were the Dominican, Nicholas Eymeric (c. 1320–1399), who

wrote the *Directorium Inquisitorum* in Avignon in 1376, and don Pedro Tenorio, who studied under Pietro Baldo in Bologna, became archbishop of Toledo in 1375, and was one of the regents whom Ayala and his allies would outmaneuver during the minority of Enrique III.

7. On Heredia, see Juan Fernández de Heredia, *La grant cronica de Espanya, libros I–III,* ed. Regina af Geijerstam, Uppsala, 1964; M. Serrano y Sanz, *Vida y escritos de d. Juan Fernández de Heredia, gran maestre de la Orden de San Juan de Jerusalén,* Saragosa, 1913; José Vives, *Juan Fernández de Heredia, gran maestre de Rodas,* Barcelona, 1928; Anthony Luttrell, "Juan Fernández de Heredia at Avignon: 1351–1367," in *El Cardenal Albornoz y el Colegio de España,* ed. Evelio Verdera y Tuells, I, 287–316.

8. "El Rey. Castella: pues en cara no sodes con nuestro primogenito el duch, al qual deviades ir segunt sabedes, rogamos vos affectuosament que, todos otros afferes dexados, vengades encontinent a nos, e aquesto por res, si a nos deseades fazer servicio e plazer, no tardedes ne mudedes como nos por grandes e cuytados afferes vos hayamos menester. Dada en Tortosa, dius nuestro siello secreto, a V dias de janero del anyo mccclxx. Otrossi vos rogamos que trayades los libros de Paulus Europius e de Isidorus maior e menor e la suma de las istorias en ffrances, e no res menos los sihuesos e otros canes que hayades por caza de puerco e de ciervo e los munteros vuestros, en manera que vengan convos, porque nos queremos fazer la dita caza en estes partes don ha grant avinenteza." Cited by Serrano, *Vida,* p. 48.

9. B. L. Ullman, *The Humanism of Coluccio Salutati,* p. 121. In one letter, Salutati wrote to Heredia, "Inter alia quibus delectaris, est copia cumulatioque librorum, in qua re tanto studio, tantaque cura vacasti, ut iam sit omnibus persuasum frustra librum quaeri quem apud te non contigerit reperiri. Sed inter alios te praecipue dilexisse semper historicos." Cited by Serrano, *Vida,* p. 48.

10. Ibid., pp. 3–6.

11. "Et otrosí así como el ocio, segund dicho avemos, traye estos dapnos et males al alma, así trae grand dapno al cuerpo, que quando el ome esté ocioso sin fazer exercicio et trabajar con el cuerpo et mudar el ayre, fatíganse los humores et al cuerpo dende le recrecen dolencias et enfermedades . . . et por esto acordé de trabajar por non estar ocioso de poner en este pequeño libro todo aquello que más cierto fallé." *El libro de las aves de caça . . . ,* Madrid, 1869, pp. 3–5.

12.   Entre labradores vivo . . .
       pues, entre rústica gente
       me fizo vivir fortuna
       donde no se trata alguna
       obra clara y excelente

Cited by J. Domínguez Bordona in the introduction to his edition of *Generaciones y semblanzas,* by Fernán Pérez de Guzmán, Madrid, 1924, p. xvi.

13. "A ruego e instancia mia, primero que de otro alguno, se han vulgarizado en este reyno algunos poemas, asy como la *Eneyda* de Virgilio, el libro mayor de las *Transformaciones* de Ovidio, las *Tragedias* de Lucio Aneo Seneca, e muchas otras cosas, en que yo me he deleytado fasta este tiempo e me deleyto, e son asy como un singular reposo a las vexaciones e trabajos que el mundo continuamente trahe, mayormente en esto nuestros reynos." *Obras,* p. 481.

14. Francisco López Estrada, "La retórica en las 'Generaciones y semblanzas' de Fernán Pérez de Guzmán," *Revista de Filología Española*, 30 (1946), 310–352; Tate, Prólogo to *Generaciones*, pp. xiii–xxiii. All page references are to the Tate edition, unless otherwise noted.

15. Ibid., p. 4.

16. Ibid., pp. 10, 18, 38.

17. Ibid., pp. 3–4.

18. Ross, "Giovanni Colonna," p. 553.

19. *Generaciones*, pp. 4, 9, 14, 16, 17, 21, 45.

20. Alfonso X el Sabio, *Primera crónica general*, Nueva Biblioteca de Autores Españoles, Madrid, 1906, V, 3–4.

21. *Generaciones*, p. 2.

22. "The order of knowing or preaching is not the same as the order of writing down. Two were of the followers of the Lord in the flesh, they saw and heard him. But in the order of writing down these two became the first, i.e. Matthew, and the last, i.e. John. The other two were not of their number, yet are nevertheless followers of the Christ who spoke through them and they are embraced as sons by the first two." Augustine, *De Consensu Evangelistarum*, I. 2, 11, 11–23. I owe this reference and paraphrase to Professor G. Caspary.

23. *Generaciones*, pp. 2–3.

24. Guido delle Colonne, *Historia Troiana*. This edition is not paginated, but the reference is to a passage in the first column of the first page of text.

25. Ibid., pp. 12, 45.

26. Ibid., pp. 43–44.

27. Ibid., pp. 12, 13.

28. Ibid., pp. 41–53.

29. Tate, Prólogo to *Generaciones*, pp. ix–x.

30. *Generaciones*, p. 15.

31. Ibid., pp. 1–2.

32. Ibid., pp. 10, 18; Tate, Prólogo to *Generaciones*, p. xvi.

33. "No Spanish poet of his own or of earlier times could compete with him in the vast sweep of his interests; none had given himself over so avidly to the Latin classics (in compendiums or translations) or to the great writers of Italy." Green, *Spain and the Western Tradition*, III, 9. For Santillana's literary career, see Rafael Lapesa, "La cultura literaria activa en la poesía juvenil de Santillana," *Atlante*, 2 (1954): 119–125; idem, *La obra literaria del marqués de Santillana*, Madrid, 1957.

34. Villena's mother, Juana de Castilla, was the sister of Santillana's stepmother, María de Castilla; so by the canonical standards of the time, they were stepbrothers. Villena had an enormous influence on both Aragonese and Castilian writers of the early fifteenth century, both as a translator of the classics and as an author and poet. Enrique de Villena, *Arte de Trovar*, ed. F. J. Sánchez Cantón, Madrid, 1923; Bahner, *La linguistica española*, pp. 31–35.

35. In a letter requesting a clarification of a passage in Bruni's work on chivalry, Santillana described Alfonso de Cartagena as the greatest historiographer and researcher in Spain. Marqués de Santillana [Iñigo López de Mendoza], *Obras*, ed. José Amador de los Ríos, Madrid, 1852, p. 487.

36. Cited by Amador de los Ríos, in ibid., p. iii.

37. "Prohemio e carta quel marqués de Santillana envió al condestable de Portugal con las obras suyas," *Obras*, pp. 1–28.

38. "E asy faciendo la via de los stoycos, los quales con grand diligencia enquirieron el origine e cabsas de las cosas." Ibid., p. 4.

39. The retablo is reproduced in Suárez et al., *Los Trastámaras de Castilla y Aragón en el siglo XV*, p. 256. Details of the portraits of Santillana and his wife are facing pp. 176, 224.

40. Guzmán's library at Batres was inherited by his great-grandson, Garcilaso de la Vega, father of the poet. An inventory made at the time of Garcilaso's death in 1512 is printed in Tate's edition of the *Generaciones*, pp. 99–101.

41. See Schiff, *La Bibliothèque*.

42. See the biographical sketch of Nuño de Guzmán (Nugno Gusmano) in Vespasiano da Bisticci, *Renaissance Princes, Popes and Prelates*, New York, 1963, pp. 431–434; and Schiff, *La Bibliothèque*, pp. 449–459.

43. For the contents of several letrado libraries, see the following articles by Josep Rius Serra, reprinted in *Miscelánea Mons. José Rius Serra*, vol. I: "Bibliotecas medievales españolas," pp. 139–149; idem, "Subsidios para la historia de nuestra cultura," pp. 294–297; idem, "Inventaris episcopals," pp. 375–389; idem, "La llibreria d'un rector de Sovelles," pp. 105–117.

44. The inventory of the Benavente library was published in the eighteenth century by Liciniano Sáez, "Coste de los Libros," in *Demostración histórica*, pp. 368–379.

45. Juan Alfonso de Baena, *Cancionero*, ed. José María Azáceta, Madrid, 1966, pp. 1018–1048. See also Joaquín Gimeno Casalduero, "Pero López de Ayala y el cambio poético de Castilla a comienzos del XV," *Hispanic Review*, 33 (1965), 1–14; Charles F. Fraker, Jr., "Gonçalo Martínez de Medina, the Jerónimos and the Devotio Moderna," *Hispanic Review*, 34 (1966), 197–217.

46. Trinkaus, *In Our Image and Likeness*, I, 60. The following generalizations about the religion of the Florentine humanists are based upon recent scholarship in the Italian Renaissance, of which Trinkaus' work is the most cohesive treatment.

47. It is significant that Guzmán took his argument here from Diego de Campos, one of the few medieval scholastics of Spain, but he chose to use Campos' work for a pietist argument rather than a theological one. *Generaciones*, ed. Domínguez Bordona, pp. 198–220.

48. Ibid., p. 220.

49. Green, citing Santillana's use of Boccaccio's definition of poetry, considers this electicism to be a form of Neoplatonism common to both Spain and Italy. *Spain and the Western Tradition*, I, 87–91; III, 8–11. See also Melquíades Andrés Martín, "Evangelismo, humanismo, reforma y observancias en España (1450–1525)," *Missionalis Hispania*, 67 (1966), 5–25. For a description of this eclecticism in Renaissance Florence, see Trinkaus, *In Our Image and Likeness*, II, 683–688.

50. *Crónica del rey don Pedro*, I, 195–197, 323, 557; Santillana, *Obras*, p. 14.

51. *Generaciones*, pp. 29–31.

Chapter V

1. The analyses of noble titles, family structure, and estate building which follow are my own, based on the documents in Osuna, Mondéjar, and Salazar. They

differ in several important respects from the usual interpretations which, I believe, are anachronistic because they are based on juridical and theoretical works that date, for the most part, from the sixteenth and seventeenth centuries. This is especially the case in Bartolomé Clavero, *Mayorazgo: Propiedad feudal en Castilla, 1369–1836*, Madrid, 1974.

2. "El fijo o fija casado e velado, sea avido por hemancipado en todas las cosas para siempre," and "Mandamos que de aqui adelante el fijo o fija, casandose o velandose, ayan para sy el usofruto de todos sus bienes adventicios, puesto que sea bivo su padre, el qual sea obligado a gelo restituyr, syn le quedar parte alguna del usofruto dellos." *Cortes de Toro de 1505*, Nos. 47 and 48, *Cortes de los antiguos reinos de León y de Castilla*. Real Academia de la Historia, Madrid, 1882, Vol. IV (1476–1537), 194–219.

3. Osuna, 1860/5.

4. Mondéjar, ff. 316v, 317.

5. "El signo de la guerra civil es una constante negociación." Suárez, *Nobleza y monarquía*, p. 148.

6. Osuna, 1860/30. This attitude also extended to foreign relations: "Ante que partiesen los embaxadores de los Reyes de Aragon e Navarra del Burgo, hablaron secretamente con algunos de los del Consejo del Rey, diciendoles que les parescia ser gran cargo de no suplicar al Rey que se diesen algunos medios para haber paz entre estos Reyes, entre quien tan gran debdo habia." *Cronica de Juan II*, BAE 68:485b.

7. Osuna, 1860/42.

8. Arteaga, *Casa del Infantado*, I, 212–213.

9. For some recent work based solidly on fourteenth and fifteenth century sources, see Mitre, *Evolución de la nobleza*; Salvador de Moxó, "De la nobleza vieja a la nobleza nueva. La transformación nobiliaria castellana en la Baja Edad Media," *Cuadernos de Historia* 3 (1969), 1–120.

10. Osuna, 1762, printed in Layna, *Guadalajara*.

11. Osuna, 291–2/11.

12. For example, the town of Saldaña, which Santillana received as a royal merced in December 1445, changed hands four times before he reacquired it permanently in exchange for the town of Coca in December 1451. Osuna, 1825/5.

13. See, for example, Santillana's manipulations of the estates of Alcovendas and Torija in 1453. Osuna, 1873/26, 27.

14. All of these wills are in Osuna, 1762.

15. Eduardo Ibarra y Rodríquez, *El problema cerealista en España durante el reinado de los Reyes Católicos, 1475–1516*, Madrid, 1944, especially the tables on pp. 159–165; Miguel Angel Ladero Quesada, "Los cereales en Andalucía del siglo XV," *Revista de la Universidad de Madrid*, 18 (1969).

16. See the duke's investigation of his stewards' accounts for Saldaña in 1501 and Castrillo in 1488, in Osuna, 1825/8; 1825/38¹⁻².

17. Based on a 1501 estimate of income and household cavalry by Lalaing, *Relation*, pp. 231–237.

18. *Generaciones*, p. 17.

19. For the Mendoza architectural projects, see Francisco Layna Serrano, *Castillos de Guadalajara*, Madrid, 1962; Vicente Lampérez y Romea, *Los Mendoza del*

siglo XV y el castillo del Real de Manzanares, Madrid, 1916. These projects are also discussed in greater detail in Chapter VIII.

20. Osuna, 1875, printed as appendixes in Layna, *Guadalajara*, III.
21. Ibid., I, 286–288.
22. *Generaciones*, ed. Domínguez Bordona, p. xvi.
23. "Aunque todos afirman que estays en arenas yo no creo a todas gentes porque dize un sabio que las aldeas son para ver y no para morar." Copiador, Tendilla to Gutierre Gómez de Fuensalida, 11 June 1515.
24. "Deje la mia y deshize mi casa alla de criados de mis abuelos y de mi padre y niños." Copiador, Tendilla to Francisco Ortiz, 10 March 1514.
25. Francisco de Medina y Mendoza, *Vida del Cardenal D. Pedro González de Mendoza*, in Memorial Histórico Español, vol. VI, Madrid, 1853; Francisco Layna Serrano, "El Cardenal Mendoza como político y consejero de los Reyes Católicos," Madrid, 1935, Biblioteca Nacional, Varios, Q 1509–10.
26. "Carta de Iñigo López de Mendoza, marqués de Santillana, a su hijo Pedro González de Mendoza cuando estaba estudiando en Salamanca, encargándole que tradujera del latin al castellano la Iliada de Homero, Buitrago, n.d., Salazar, N–44, f. 567v (323v moderna).
27. See especially Osuna 1860/15, 16, 17, 20, 38.
28. Osuna 2028.
29. For continued relations between Borgia, the Catholic Monarchs, and cardinal Mendoza, Osuna 844; Caja 7/15; 616/68.
30. Osuna 762/9; 750/22; 1873/29; 1703/3,4; 1706/1,2; 1707/7; 1730/1; 1760/4–11; 1883/1; 1887/1,2; 1891; 1914/2,3; 2021; 2048; 1893/2; 1953/6; 2020; 2045/3; 1833; 1932; 1934. Many of the documents for these estates are copied in Salazar, D–13. See also Layna Serrano, "El Cardenal," p. 21; Lalaing, *Relation*, pp. 252–56.
31. Osuna 417/20; bis 1827/4; 1840/10. For a sample of Mendoza mercedes in the city of Guadalajara alone, Osuna 1842; 1862/3; 1876/1,2; 1878; 1879.
32. "Dixo el cardenal mi tio a la marquesa de Moya, 'Dezi[d] a la reyna que sy da el arzobispado de Sevilla a privado no me da nada, mas sy lo da a otro syno a my sobrino nunca mas viviera en su corte.' " Copiador, Tendilla to the Bishop of Málaga, 9 August 1514; Osuna 1873/8; 1970/4,6; Medina y Mendoza, *Vida*, pp. 292–293.
33. Pulgar, *Crónica*, Ch. 95.
34. Ibid., Ch. 78, Bernáldez, *Memorias*, pp. 99–103; Azcona, *Isabel*, pp. 385–408.
35. The traditional view is especially noticeable in Arteaga (sister of the present duke of Infantado), *La Casa del Infantado*; Layna Serrano (provincial archivist of Guadalajara), *Guadalajara*; and Medina y Mendoza (a "poor relation" of the family), *Vida*. In 1501, Lalaing reported that the constable was the head of the Mendoza, *Relation*, p. 250; members of the Mendoza family made formal alliances with the constable, rather than Infantado, in times of need. Osuna, 1860/34; 1873. Tendilla believed that Infantado was stupid: "A lo que decis que os hablo Juan Herrera que tiene ay cargo de los negocios del duque del Infantado, plugiese a Dios que su amo tuviese el seso que el tiene. Mas parece me que podemos decir que el que avia de guardar el baño es rey." Copiador, Tendilla to Francisco Ortiz, 5 December 1514. He repeatedly refers to the constable rather than Infantado as the head of the Mendoza in Guadalajara.

Copiador, Tendilla to Iñigo de Velasco, 3 May 1509; 20 August 1509; 29 September 1509; Tendilla to Diego López de Mendoza, [November, 1509]. Both Walther, *Die Anfänge*, p. 46, and Suárez, *Nobleza*, p. 239, include the constable in the Mendoza family but fail to recognize him as its head.

36. Osuna 1765/9; 1878/1,2; 2023.

37. Particularly interesting in revealing Cenete's wild career and the problems posed by the continued Muslim customs of his tenants in Granada and Valencia are Osuna 750/1; 1717/1⁻¹; 1897/4; 1899/20; 1906; 1908; 1909; 1933; 1934; 1942/16; 1968; 1969; 1973. The best account of his life is in Vicente Lampérez y Romea, *El castillo de la Calahorra* (Granada), Madrid, 1914.

38. Elliott, *Imperial Spain*, pp. 247–249.

Chapter VI

1. Elliott, *Imperial Spain*, p. 90.

2. These are the conclusions drawn by William D. Phillips, Jr., *Enrique IV and the Crisis of Fifteenth-Century Castile, 1425–1480*, Cambridge, Mass., 1978.

3. Antonio Matilla Tascón, ed., *Declaratorias de los Reyes Católicos sobre reducción de juros y otras mercedes*. Madrid, 1952, pp. 1–60. The same point is made by Stephen Haliczer, "The Castilian Aristocracy and the Mercedes Reform of 1478–1482," *Hispanic American Historical Review*, 55 (1975) 449–467.

4. Lorenzo Galíndez de Carvajal, "Informe que dió al emperador Carlos V sobre los que componían el Consejo Real de S.M., Codoin, I, 122–127.

5. Hayward Keniston, *Francisco de los Cobos, Secretary of the Emperor Charles V*, Pittsburgh, 1958.

6. The medieval chronicle that served as the principal model was Rodrigo Jiménez de Rada, *De Rebus Hispaniae in Opera*, ed. Francisco Lorenzana, Madrid, 1793, reprint, Valencia, 1968, especially Lib. I, Capit. VII, VIII.

7. Albert A. Sicroff, *Les Controverses des statuts de "Pureté de sang" en Espagne du XVᵉ siècle*, Paris, 1960, pp. 31–62; Alfonso de Cartagena, *Defensorium unitatis christianae. Tratados en favor de los judíos conversos*, ed. Manuel Alonso, Madrid, 1943.

8. In addition to Tate, see don Alfonso's covering letter to Fernán Pérez de Guzmán, *Generaciones*, ed. Domínguez Bordona, pp. 217–219.

9. Vicente Beltrán de Heredia, "Los comienzos de la reforma dominicana en Castilla particularmente en el convento de San Esteban de Salamanca y su irradiación a la provincia de Portugal," *Archivum Fratrum Praedicatorum*, 28 (1958), 221–237.

10. See a summary and extension of this interpretation in Ottavio di Camillo, "Spanish Humanism in the Fifteenth Century," Ph.D. diss., Yale University, 1972.

11. See A. Birkenmaier, "Der Streit des Alonso von Cartagena mit L. B. Aretino," *Beiträge zur Geschichte der Philosophie des Mittelalters* 20, Heft 5 (1922), 129–236; Jerrold E. Seigel, *Rhetoric and Philosophy in Renaissance Humanism*, Princeton, 1967, pp. 123–133; George Holmes, *The Florentine Enlightenment, 1400–1450*, New York, 1969, p. 114, where don Alfonso's argument is described

as "the only serious attack on humanist philosophy from the scholastic camp which has come down to us."

12. Richard Kagan, *Students and Society in Early Modern Spain*, Baltimore, 1974.

13. Henry Kamen, *The Spanish Inquisition*, New York, 1965; proposes the thesis that it was the nobility who initiated the Inquisition and profited from it at the expense of the bourgeoisie.

14. Cited by Melquíades Andrés Martín, *Historia de la Teología en España, 1470–1570*, Rome, 1962, pp. 102–103. On the Franciscan reforms in general, see *Archivo Ibero-Americano. Las reformas en los siglos XIV–XV, introducción a los orígines de la observancia en España*, Madrid, 1958; and Fidel de Lejarza and Angel Uribe, "¿Cuándo y dónde comenzó Villacreces su Reforma?" *Archivo Ibero-Americano*, ser. 2, 20 (1960), 79–94.

15. Andrés Martín, "Evangelismo," p. 7.

16. For a summary of recent work on fifteenth-century reform in Castile, see L. Sala Balust, "Espiritualidad española en la primera mitad del siglo XVI," *Cuadernos de Historia*, 1 (1967), 169–187. The Dominican reform in the late fifteenth century has been extensively studied by Vicente Beltrán de Heredia, "Los comienzos de la reforma dominicana en Castilla particularmente en el convento de San Estéban de Salamanca y su irradiación a la provincia de Portugal," *Archivum Fratrum Praedicatorum*, 28 (1958), 221–237; idem, *Los corrientes de espiritualidad entre los Domínicos de Castilla durante la primera mitad del siglo XVI*, Salamanca, 1941; idem, *Historia de la reforma de la Provincia de España, 1450–1550*, Rome, 1939.

17. Recent work on the reforms tends to reduce the significance of individual reformers, such as Cisneros, in contrast to earlier works which are summarized in R. Aubenas and Robert Ricard, *L'Eglise et la Renaissance, 1449–1517*, Histoire de l'Eglise, vol. XV, ed. Augustin Fliche and Victor Martin, Paris, n. p., 1951.

18. Azcona, *La elección*; Hubert Jedin, *Council of Trent*, I, 154; Cotarelo, *Fray Diego de Deza*, p. 131; Valdéon, *Enrique II*, p. 315; Azcona, "El tipo ideal," pp. 21–64.

19. On Santillana's use of Latin models, see Fernando Rubio, "*De Regimine Principum* de Egidio Romano en la literatura Castellana de la Edad Media, siglo XV," *Ciudad de Dios* [Real Monasterio de el Escorial], 174 (1961), pp. 658–662; Lapesa, "La cultura literaria," pp. 121–124. On translations commissioned by Guzmán, see Domínguez Bordona, Prólogo to *Generaciones* by Fernán Pérez de Guzmán, pp. xxiii–xxvi. On Dr. Pedro Díaz de Toledo's translations, see Adolfo Bonilla y San Martín, *Ion, diálogo platónico, traducido del griego por Afanto Ucalego*, Madrid, 1901, pp. ix-xxv; Marcel Bataillon, *Erasmo y España*, Mexico, 1950, I, 50–51.

20. "Con singular elegancia, la poca e pobre substancia con verbosidad ornando," *Loores*, p. 209, cited by Romero, *Sobre la biografía*, p. 113. Alfonso X el Sabio had said, "Non convenie a rey de ser muy fablador . . . porque el uso de las muchas palabras envilece al que las dice," and "El home debe fablar en pocas palabras," *Siete Partidas*, II, 21–22. His nephew, don Juan Manuel, advised, "Et poniendo declaradamente cumplida la razon que quiere decir, ponelo con las menos palabras que pueden seer." *Libro de los estados*, cited by Faulhaber,

Latin Rhetorical Theory, p. 74. For Spanish use of Seneca, see Karl Alfred Blüher, *Seneca in Spanien: Untersuchungen zur Geschichte der Seneca-Rezeption in Spanien vom 13. bis 17. Jahrhundert*, Munich, 1969.

21. Letter of 7 December 1435, in BN, MS 10.214, cited by Adolfo Bonilla y San Martín, *Fernando de Córdoba* (¿1425–1486?) *orígenes del Renacimiento filosófico en España: Episodio de la historia de la lógica*, Madrid, 1911, p. 29. Don Alfonso also took the opportunity, while he was in Basle, to have his father's work, *Scrutinium Scripturarum*, "published." The library of the University of Basle possesses a manuscript of this, copied by Albert Löffler von Rheinfelden, Dominican, who included the following note: "Allata autem est materia huius libri per Hyspanos ad sacrum concilium Basiliense, quod viguit etiam tempore iam dicto." Cited by Romero de Lecea, *El V centenario*, p. 32.

22. Théodore, le conte de Puymaigre, *La Cour littéraire de Don Juan II, roi de Castille*, 2 vols., Paris, 1873; Marcelino Menéndez y Pelayo, *Poetas de la corte de don Juan II*, Madrid, 1943.

23. See, for example, Suárez, "Problemas," p. 210.

24. Alvaro de Luna, *Libro de las virtuosas e claras mujeres*, ed. Marcelino Menéndez y Pelayo, in Colección de libros publicados por la Sociedad de Bibliófilos Españoles, Madrid, 1892, vol. 28; Green, *Spain*, I, 90–91.

25. Unless otherwise noted, the following section on secretarial education at the royal court is my own interpretation, based on the following: Nicholas G. Round, "Politics, Style and Group Attitudes in the *Instrucción del Relator*," *Bulletin of Hispanic Studies*, 46 (1969), 289–319; *Crónica de Juan II*; Juan Batista Avalle-Arce, "Los herejes de Durango," *Homenaje a Rodríguez-Moñino*, Madrid, 1966, I, 44–55; AGS, Registro General del Sello, Leg. 97, Segovia, 23 January 1475; Leg. 116, Seville, 20 January 1478; Leg. 379, Valladolid, 2 April 1475; Leg. 3339, Seville, 28 December 1477/1478/; Fermín Caballero, *Elogio del doctor Alonso de Montalvo*, Madrid, 1950; Hernando del Pulgar, *Letras, Glosa a las coplas de Mingo Revulgo*, ed. J. Domínguez Bordona, Madrid, 1929.

26. Keniston, *Francisco de los Cobos*, p. 7.

27. On the history of Spanish universities and colleges, see Alfonso X, *Siete Partidas*, Partida II; George M. Addy, *The Enlightenment in the University of Salamanca*, Durham, N. C., 1966; C. M. Ajo González y Sáinz de Zúñiga, *Historia de las universidades hispánicas: orígenes y desarrollo desde su aparición hasta nuestros días*, vol. I, *Medioevo y renacimiento universitario*, Madrid, 1957; Mariano Alcocer y Martínez, *Historia de la Universidad de Valladolid*, Valladolid, 1918–1922; Gonzalo de Arriaga, *Historia del Colegio de San Gregorio de Valladolid*, Valladolid, 1926; E. Esperabé Arteaga, *Historia de la Universidad de Salamanca*, vol. I, Salamanca, 1914; María Febrero Lorenzo, *La pedagogía de los colegios mayores a través de su legislación en el siglo de oro*, Madrid, 1960; Vicente de la Fuente, *Historia de las universidades, colegios y demas establecimientos de enseñanza en España*, vol. I, *Edad Media*, Madrid, 1885; idem, *La enseñanza tomística en España; Noticia de las universidades, colegios y academias tomísticos con las fundaciones de ellas y sus cátedras principales . . . .*, Madrid, 1874; Albert Jiménez, *Historia de la universidad española*, Madrid, 1971; Kagan, *Students and Society*; Josef Kohler, "Die spanische Schule von Salamanca im Siglo de Oro," *Archiv für Rechts-und Wirtschaftsphilosophie*, 10 (1916), 236 ff.; C. Lascaris Comneno, *Colegios mayores*, Madrid, 1952; Diego López de

Ayala, "Constitutciones del Colegio de Sta. Catalina de Toledo," BN, MS 933; José López Navio, "Don Juan de Fonseca, Canónigo Maestrescuela de Sevilla," *Archivo Hispalense*, 126–127 (1964), 83–128; José López Rueda, *Helenistas españoles del siglo XVI*, Madrid, 1973; Francisco Martín Hernández, *La formación clerical en los colegios universitarios españoles*, 1371–1563, Vitoria, 1961; idem, *Los seminarios españoles: Historia y pedagogía*, vol. I, 1563–1700, Salamanca, 1964; J. Puyols, *El Colegio Mayor de Santa Cruz y los Colegios Mayores*, Madrid, 1929; Gustave Reynier, *La Vie universitaire dans l'ancienne Espagne*, Paris, 1902; José de Rújula y de Ochoterna, *Indice de los colegiales del mayor de San Ildefonso y menores de Alcalá*, Madrid, 1946; Antonio de la Torre y del Cerro, *La Universidad de Alcalá*, Madrid, 1910; Félix González Olmedo, *Diego Ramírez Villaescusa*, (1459–1537), fundador del Colegio de Cuenca y autor de "Los cuatro diálogos sobre la muerte del príncipe don Juan," Madrid, 1944.

28. Cited in Marti, *The Spanish College*, pp. 31–32. See also Verdera, *El Cardenal Albornoz y el Colegio de España*.

29. Rius Serra, "Estudiants."

30. Vicente Beltrán de Heredia, "Nebrija y los teólogos de San Esteban de principio del siglo XVI," *La Ciencia Tomista*, 61 (1941), 37–65.

31. On Nebrija as a historian and professor, see B. Sánchez Alonso, "Nebrija historiador," *Revista de Filología Española*, 29 (1945), 129–152; I. G. González Llubera, *Nebrija, Gramática de la lengua española*, Oxford, 1926; Félix González Olmedo, *Humanistas y pedagogos españoles: Nebrija (1441–1522), debelador de la barbarie, comentador eclesiástico, pedagogo, poeta*, Madrid, 1942; idem, *Nebrija en Salamanca (1475–1513)*, Madrid, 1944; P. Lemus y Rubio, "El maestro Elio Antonio de Lebrixa," *Revue Hispanique*, 22 (1910), 459–508; 29 (1913), 13–120.

32. Andrés Martín, "Evangelismo," p. 25.

33. For the life of Hernán Núñez see Helen Nader, "The Greek Commander Hernán Núñez de Toledo, Spanish Humanist and Civic Leader," *Renaissance Quarterly*, winter 1979; for his works see María Dolores de Asís, *Hernán Núñez en la historia de los estudios clásicos*, Madrid, 1977.

34. Bahner, *La lingüística española*, pp. 36–63.

35. A. H. de Oliveira Marques. *Daily Life in Portugal in the Late Middle Ages*, trans. S. S. Wyatt, Madison, Wis., 1971, p. 233; Friedrich Stegmüller, *Filosofia e teologia nas Universidades de Coimbra e Evora no Sécolo XVI*, Coimbra, 1959.

36. Bataillon, *Erasmo y España*, pp. 24–47.

37. Vicente Beltrán de Heredia, "La Teología en la Universidad de Alcalá," *Revista Española de Teología*, 5 (1945), 406–417; Andrés Martín, *Historia de la teología*, pp. 109–120.

38. Beltrán de Heredia, *Corrientes*, pp. 17–20; Aubenas, *L'Eglise et la Renaissance*, pp. 309–310.

39. See Chapter VIII, note 56.

Chapter VII

1. Unless otherwise noted, the following biographical information on Tendilla is from Mondéjar. This material is summarized in González Palencia, *Vida*, I,

3–44. The recent biographical sketches of Tendilla by Cepeda, "El Gran Tendilla," and Emilio Meneses García, appearing in Iñigo López de Mendoza, *Correspondencia del conde de Tendilla, I (1508–1509): Biografía, estudio y transcripción*, in *Archivo Documental Español*, vol. XXXI, Madrid, 1974; confuse Tendilla with several of his homonyms.

2. AGS, Registro General del Sello, VII–1478, f. 108, 17 July 1478.

3. Joaquín Durán y Lerchundi, *La toma de Granada y caballeros que concurrieron a ella*, Madrid, 1893, II, 329–347.

4. Mondéjar does not explain how Tendilla knew about the siege of Faenza. The defense of Alhama is described in Mondéjar, ff. 179–180v.

5. Salazar, M–131, fols. 232v–233; Mondéjar, ff. 184–186v; Azcona, *La elección*, pp. 295–296; Goñi Gastambide, "La santa sede," pp. 46–57; "Carta de los RRCC a conde de Tendilla su embaxador en Roma, ordenándole que no entendiese en los pleitos que en la corte Romana seguían Pero Carrillo, vuestro cuñado e Alvaro Carrillo su hermano," Córdoba, 13 May 1486, Salazar, M–1, f. 13.

6. But the papal secretary Johannis Burchardi noted: "et quia comes nesciebat expedite loqui latinum, protonotarii responderunt alternatis vicibus." Cited by González Palencia, *Vida*, I, 6.

7. "El Conde de Tendilla fué enbaxador en Roma, y estando en Florencia tomó amistad con Lorenço Médicis, el qual desseava casar una hija con un sobrino del Papa Inocencio, y el Conde lo effectuó, y de allí vino a tener el capello el que después fué Papa León," *Floreto de anécdotas y noticias diversas que recopiló un fraile domínico residente en Sevilla a mediados del siglo XVI*, ed. F. J. Sánchez Cantón, in *Memorial Histórico Español*, vol. XLVIII, pp. 32–33.

8. Eugene F. Rice, Jr., *The Foundations of Early Modern Europe, 1460–1559*, New York, 1970, p. 85. Mondéjar admits that other ambassadors are reported to have done these same things, but believes that they were all imitating Tendilla, f. 186v.

9. The polychrome is reproduced in Tormo, "El brote," facing p. 61.

10. "El dia Martes a Dos de Henero año 1492 vino esta ciudad de Granada a poder del Rey Don Gernando y de la Reyna doña Isabel despues de largo sitio que la tenian puesto. El mismo dia hizieron sus Altezas Alcayde, y capitan de la dicha ciudad, y fortaleza del Alhambra a Iñigo Lopez de Mendoza conde de Tendilla, y señor de Mondejar a cuyo adbitrio cometieron toda su guarda, y presidio con no despreciable numero de cavallos, e infantes, y pasados pocos dias despues se partieron sus Magestades a Cataluña, dexando al sobredicho Conde en el Alcaçar y ciudad, habitando en ella mas de veynte mil Moros." This is a note written in Tendilla's hand in Latin in the margin of a copy of Aeneus Sylvius' *Historia de Bohemia*, which Tendilla had brought with him from Rome. Mondéjar gives only this Spanish translation, ff. 217–217v.

11. "Quando el rey n. s. y la reina n. s. que aya gloria me mandaron dar este cargo asentaron me aqui como en nueva naturaleza y dexe la mia y deshize mi casa alla de criados de mis avuelos y de mi padre y mios y he la hecho aca con esperanza que como el rey n. s. lo ha concertado a hacer duraran estos cargos en mi y en mis subcesores para sienpre." Copiador, Tendilla to Francisco Ortiz, 10 March 1514.

12. Osuna 293/1; Salazar, M–121, f. 222v. For an example of his actions as

arbitrator, see his decision in a dispute over the boundaries of the *términos* of the cities of Vélez Málaga and Alhama, given at Ventas del Alcaycería, Copiador, 28 January 1506. For the powers and responsibilities of the captaincy-general, see J. I. Rubio Mañé, "El concepto histórico de capitanía general," reprint from *Diario de Yucatán*, 19–20 March 1938; idem, *Introducción al estudio de los virreyes de Nueva España, 1535 a 1746*, vol. I, *Orígenes y jurisdicciones y dinámica social de los virreyes*, Mexico, 1955, pp. 1–16.

13. I have relied on the Actas del Cabildo and the following published works for the general history of Granada in the sixteenth century: Julio Caro Baroja, *Los Moriscos del reino de Granada*, Madrid, 1957; Durán y Lerchundi, *La toma de Granada*; Francisco Bejarano, "El almirantazgo de Granada y la rebelión de Málaga en 1516," *Hispania* 15 (1955), 73–109; Francisco Bermúdez de Pedraza, *Antigüedad y excelencias de Granada*, Madrid, 1608; J. L. Cano de Gardoquí and A. de Bethencourt, "Incorporación de Gibraltar a la Corona de Castilla, 1435–1508," *Hispania* 26 (1966), 325–381; Juan de Mata Carriazo, "Cartas de la frontera de Granada, 1430–1509," *Al-Andaluz*, 11 (1946), 69–130; Alfonso Gámir Sandoval, "Organización de la defensa de la costa del Reino de Granada desde su reconquista hasta finales del siglo XVI," *Boletín de la Universidad de Granada*, 73 (1943), 259–337; Kenneth Garrad, "La industria sedera granadina en el siglo XVI y su conexión con el levantamiento de las Alpujarras, 1568–1571," *Miscelánea de Estudios Arabes y Hebraicos*, 5 (1956), 73–104; idem, "La inquisición y los moriscos granadinos, 1526–1580," *Bulletin Hispanique*, 67 (1965), 67–78; idem, "The Original Memorial of Don Francisco Núñez Muley," *Atlante*, 2 (1954), 199–226; idem, "La renta de los habices 'de los mezquinos' de las Alpujarras y Valle de Lecrín: Algunos datos sobre su administración a mediados del siglo XVI," *Miscelánea de Estudios Arabes y Hebraicos*, 2 (1953), 41–48. Francisco Henríquez de Jorquera, *Anales de Granada, parayso español*, ed. Antonio Marín Ocete, Granada, 1934; Diego Hurtado de Mendoza, *De la guerra de Granada*, ed. Manuel Gómez Moreno, Memorial Histórico Español, vol. 49, Madrid, 1948; T. D. Kendrick, *St. James in Spain*, London, 1960; Miguel Angel Ladero Quesada, *Granada: Historia de un país islámico, 1232–1571*, Madrid, 1969; "La repoblación del reino de Granada anterior al año 1500," *Hispania*, 28 (1968), 489–563; Lafuente y Alcántara, *Historia de Granada*; Henri Lapeyre, *La Géographie de l'Espagne morisque*, Paris, 1959; José Francisco de Luque, *Granada y sus contornos* . . . , Granada, 1858; Francisco Martín Hernández, *Un seminario español pretridentino, el Real Colegio Eclesiástico de San Cecilio de Granada, 1492–1842*, Valladolid, 1960; Erika Spivakovsky, "Some Notes on the Relations between Diego Hurtado de Mendoza and D. Alonso de Granada Venegas," *Archivum*, 14 (1964), 212–232; idem, *Son of the Alhambra: Diego Hurtado de Mendoza, 1504–1575*, Austin Texas, 1970.

14. Many of Zafra's reports to the monarchs are published in Codoín, vols. VIII and XI. On Talavera, see Tarsicio de Azcona, "El tipo ideal de obispo en la iglesia española antes de la rebelión luterana," *Hispania Sacra*, 11 (1958), 21–64.

15. "Vivir como 'mudéjares,' dentro de la tradición establecida en los siglos xii, xiii, y xiv sobre todo, no hubiera parecido intolerable a los granadinos. Y las dos personalidades cristianas más destacadas a las que se encargó en un principio del goviemo del reino y la ciudad, don Iñigo López de Mendoza, conde de

Tendilla, primer alcaide y capitán general de Granada y Fray Hernando de Talavera, su arzobispo, parecían estar dispuestas a esta clase de convivencia, de 'mudejarismo' clásico, aparte de que eran tolerantes y de carácter apacible." Caro Baroja, Los Moriscos, pp. 13–14.

16. "Del arzobispo de Toledo que nunca vió Moro, ni los conoció, no me maravillo, pero de vos, y del corregidor que tanto tiempo ha que los conoceis de no haberlo dicho." Seville, 22 December 1499, transcribed in Mondéjar, ff. 223v–224. This account of the uprising in the Albaicín is taken from the history written by Tendilla's youngest son, Diego Hurtado de Mendoza, De la guerra de Granada, and has been repeated almost verbatim by all later historians. The earliest published account of the uprising, by Hernán Núñez de Toledo, lacks some of the dramatic embellishments of Mendoza's version, Prólogo to La historia de Bohemia en romance, Seville, 1509, ff. ii–iii. See also the anonymous "Relación del caso de Granada . . . principio de la rebelión de los moros después de la conquista (1499)," Codoin, XXXVI, 441–449; and "Minuta de carta de los RRCC a Enrique Enriquez encargándole que fuera a Granada y tratara de conformar a los arzobispos de Toledo y de Granada para que con conde de Tendilla, con el Gran Capitán, con el corregidor y con el pesquisidor, entendieran en la conversion de los moros." Seville, 3 January 1500, BN, MS 226/137.

17. "Yo nunca estuve mal con corregidor ninguno de los pasados antes muy bien con todos ellos hasta que vino el pesquisidor y este corregidor." Copiador, Tendilla to Ortiz, 12 June 1515.

18. "E non fagades apuntamiento diciendo que la Inquisition es otro jurisdiccion porque todo es nuestro." Cited by A. Cotarelo y Valledor, Fray Diego de Deza. Ensayo biográfico, Madrid, 1902, p. 149.

19. "Suplico a v. m. me haga saber que hizo el termino que esperavedes, y si Dios ordenare otra cosa de lo que queriamos, hazed vos señor y la señora doña Isabel a cuyas manos beso la que haciamos la condesa y yo que perdimos dos hijos en una semana y tres hijas y otro hijo en pocos dias y despues a los señores dos cardenales y a mi hermano don Pedro y a hermanos de la condesa y consolavamonos el uno con el otro que no hay ninguna otra consolacion." Copiador, Tendilla to don Iñigo Manrique, 22 April 1514. Tendilla often used his own losses and his own stoic conduct as an example in consoling friends. When the royal secretary Miguel Pérez de Almazán died, he wrote to Conchillos: "No se que os diga sino que mires a mi que perdi a mi tio y mi hermano cardenales y despues a my muger y trabajo por vivir." Copiador, Tendilla to Conchillos, 5 May 1514.

20. The only historian to treat this internal history in detail is Azcona, Isabel, pp. 709–742.

21. The constable, Pedro Fernández de Velasco, and the adelantado of Andalucía, Pedro Enríquez, in January; Enrique de Guzmán, duke of Medina Sidonia, and his rival, Rodrigo Ponce de León, marquis of Cádiz, in August; Pedro de Stúñiga, count of Miranda, in September; and Beltrán de la Cueva, duke of Alburquerque, in October. Miguel Lafuente y Alcántara, Historia de Granada, comprendiendo la de sus cuatro provincias Almería, Jaén, Granada, y Málaga, desde remotos tiempos hasta nuestros días, Paris, 1852, II, 344n.

22. Many of these arguments are summed up by Zurita and repeated by Mondéjar, ff. 231v–232v.

23. "Yñigo Lopez fue fisico de la señora reyna doña Juana tia de v. al. y sirvio la con mucha lealtad y mucho tienpo." Copiador, Tendilla to the king of Portugal, 30 April 1514; "Yñigo Lopez mi fisico ya sabes señor como es loco y si no lo sabes sabeldo. Es muy cobdicioso y fantaseo se le que agora puede cobrar 100,000 que le deve la hija de la reyna de quando fue su fisico. Dijo me que quiere ir alla a cobrarlos di le una carta para el rey de Portugal." Copiador, Tendilla to Vargas, 12 May 1514.

24. "Y tambien le dezid que en esto de las galeras no osa onbre hablar a su al. como a la reyna nuestra señora que aya gloria." Copiador, Tendilla to Ortiz, 6 April 1514.

25. At one point during Fernando's illness, he instructed Ortiz to tell the court that he (Tendilla) "ni va a cabildo ni entiende en negocio chico ni grande ni habla a nuevamente convertido ninguno ni los consiente que saban a el manera que acaesce estar xv dias que no abaxa abaxo e tres y quatro que no sale de un estudio y de su camara." Copiador, Tendilla to Ortiz, 23 March 1514; "Pesado me ha porque v.m. no esta sano porque quisiera ir a comer los pollos y anades de Cazalla y si estais para ello todo es tres dias de tardanza en que podamos ir daca y v.m. venir de alla sino que creo que es como el azor quando sopesa a la perdiz que no quiere esperar a quien le quiere cojer y por esta no querra v.m. volver. . . . De la corte no se nada sino que el rey n.s. andava a monte en Ventosilla y en la torre del monte que es cabo Aranda. Otros decian que habia poca caza y que se tornaran presente." Copiador, Tendilla to Rodrigo Mexia, 13 October 1514; Tendilla to the comendador mayor de Castilla, 14 June 1515; Tendilla to Juan Hurtado de Mendoza, 1 September 1514; Tendilla to Rodrigo Mexia, 16 June 1515; Tendilla to the comendador mayor de Castilla, 14 June 1515; Tendilla to Fernando, 13 June 1515.

26. This attitude is the basis of his complaints about not receiving favors. For example: "Digo asi que yo tengo la necesidad que Dios y el mundo sabe y cada dia vendo mi hacienda para comer y por esto es me necesario y forzado que no puedo hacer otra cosa. Suplico a su al. que me mande dar de tomar como lo da a otros que tienen cargos." Copiador, Tendilla to Ortiz, 6 September 1514.

27. "Yo en todo el mundo no tengo en este reyno arrimo ny ayuda ninguna sino la vida del rey ny esperanza en onbre de Flandes ny de Alemaña porque nunca vieron carta mia y unas recomiendos y que solo al duque d'Alba me he ofrecido de servir y seguir y el segundo es el a quien tengo de mirar como a señor verdadero y que por esto me parece que puedo y devo seguramente pedille por merced." Copiador, Tendilla to Ortiz, 7 July 1515.

28. "Que no espera poder mucho los principes que no aviendo mas de una parcialidad en sus pueblos quieren hacer dos o señal que no se fian de la parte que tienen por suya quando le resucitan otra contraria." Copiador, Tendilla to the comendador mayor de Castilla, 14 May 1515.

29. Copiador, Tendilla to the bishop of Málaga, 15 August 1514; Tendilla to Francisco Ortiz, 6 October 1514.

30. "He tenydo pena y congoxa y a me pesado mucho del enojo que en vuestra casa a avido." Tendilla to Hernando de Córdoba, 29 June 1508, printed in Cepeda, "Un aspecto de la correspondencia," p. 74; Copiador, Tendilla to Ortiz, 7 July 1515.

31. "Porque lo quel buen servidor ha de hacer es conformarse en la voluntad de su

señor y no espere su alteza que jamas yo le tengo de enbiar a decir de nadie que no haze lo que deve porque no he ganado yo los enemigos que tengo de otra manera syno diziendo verdad y dando su alteza mis cartas y memoriales a los que por ello me querrian destruir." Copiador, Tendilla to Ortiz, 5 December 1514.

32. "Que yo estoy aqui peleando por su al. con su al. mismo." Copiador, Tendilla to Ortiz, 7 July 1515.

33. "De donde vienen los hechos han de venir los consejos." Copiador, Tendilla to the alcaide de los donceles, 10 June 1506.

34. Bermúdez de Pedraza, Antigüedad, pp. 16, 132–141. Bermúdez was a judge of the chancillería of Granada in the seventeenth century.

35. "Si dicen que soy absoluto digan que he hecho. Si dicen que robo digan como o en que. Tanbien me dicen que Peñaranda ha confirmado alla quantos males se dicen de mi y a dicho diabluras y aca lo han escrito. Juro por Dios que no oso ir a la casa de los oidores como solia ni al president tantas veces porque no digan que los traigo por el oreja. Con todo eso no dexes de decir que si me ponen en el monte con venados y puercos jabalies les hare hacer algo de lo que quisiere y no hay ningund onbre cuerdo que no haga otro tanto." Copiador, Tendilla to Ortiz, 6 October 1514.

36. "Costunbre es que los amigos quando saben alguna buena nueva la digan a sus amigos porque ayan placer. El rey don Fernando y el rey don Felipe y la reyna doña Juana n.s. estan juntos y amigos como Dios y la razon requiere que esten padres y hijos." From a speech Tendilla made to the Muslims of the Albaicín, reported in his letter to don Luis, Copiador, [3 July] 1506.

37. "A buen seso a de servir el principe a su avuelo y su avuelo pues le ha de heredar a de trabajar por dexar le el el mayor señor del mundo." Copiador, Tendilla to Ortiz, 7 July 1515.

38. This account of the succession crisis is based on Geronimo Zurita y Castro, Anales de la corona de Aragón [Zaragoza, 1578–1585], vol. VI; Fernández Alvarez, La España de los Reyes Católicos, vol. 17: 2; Konrad Häbler, Der Streit Ferdinand's des Katholischen und Philipp's I um die Regierung von Castilien, 1504–1506, Dresden, 1882; Cano de Gardoquí, "Incorporación de Gibraltar." Tendilla's activity during the succession crisis is described in Mondéjar, ff. 225v–239. My interpretation of the attitudes of the nobility in this crisis is based on the following documents from Osuna and Salazar, and differs in many important points from that of Elliott, Imperial Spain, pp. 133–142. "Confederación y alianza original . . . que hicieron don Diego Hurtado de Mendoza hijo mayor de don Iñigo López de Mendoza duque del Infantado . . . de una parte y de la otra don Alonso Pimentel conde de Benavente." Benavente, 12 December 1499, Osuna, 1860/23; "Confederación original que hicieron don Bernardino de Velasco, condestable de Castilla . . . y doña Mencia de la Vega, su prima." n.p., [1500], Osuna, 1860/24; "Confederación y amistad original que hicieron don Francisco de la Cueva, duque de Alburquerque . . . y don Diego Hurtado de Mendoza y Luna, duque del Infantado." Cuellar, 26 September 1501, Osuna 1860/25; "Carta de Diego Pérez a Fernando el Católico comunicándole diversas noticias relacionadas con el conde de Tendilla; el adelantado de Murcia, y el marqués de Villena," Jumilla, 24 July 1505, BN, MS 20.214 (11); Copiador, Tendilla to Francisco Ortiz, 7 July 1515.

39. "Escritura otorgada por Iñigo López de Mendoza, conde de Tendilla, por la que hace pleito homenaje por la fortaleza de la Alhambra de Granada a los reyes Felipe I y doña Juana," Granada, 29 August 1506, Salazar, M–23, f. 106.

40. "Instrucción que se envió a los procuradores de cortes de Granada y su reyno, Copiador, [September] 1506.

41. Duque de Baena y de San Lúcar la Mayor, "El Gran Capitán y el maestrazgo de Santiago," *Hispania*, 13 (1953), 189–194; "Escritura original que hicieron y otorgaron los condes de Cifuentes y Fuensalida . . . porque el señor duque del Infantado movido con buen celo de dar paz entre ellos y la dicha ciudad se lo enbió arrogar con don Antonio de Mendoza tío del dicho duque y con Pero Gómez, señor de la villa de Pros, dijeron que davan su fe al dicho duque y hacían pleito omenaje en manos del dicho don Antonio de Mendoza, de que guardaran la dicha paz." Toledo, 28 February 1507, Osuna, 1860/26. "Provisión del consejo de Castilla, en nombre de la reina doña Juana, para que el conde de Tendilla prenda a Antonio Manrique," Palencia, 5 May 1507, Salazar, M–131, ff. 238v–239.

42. "Escritura de reclamación original que hizo y otorgó don Diego Hurtado de Mendoza, duque del Infantado," Burgos, 29 October 1507, Osuna 1860/27. Here Infantado reveals his hard-headed and materialistic motives for having supported Fernando. It is only in these rare statements of renunciation that the nobility stated their material motives: the treaties of alliance and allegiance continue to claim the most exalted and patriotic motives in their wording, just as Infantado here claims that he is going to serve and follow Charles as his prince and natural lord because he is the legitimate heir to the throne. During Fernando's final illness, Infantado and his eldest son (Iñigo López de Mendoza, conde de Saldaña) signed a treaty of friendship with Juan de Aragón, duque de Luna (Aragon), and Alonso de Aragón, conde de Rivagorza, "to better serve the king," who is not named but is clearly Charles. Luna, 3 December 1515, Osuna, 1860/28. Note that Infantado is here allying with Fernando's Aragonese relatives, who would hardly have felt the sentiments of "many Castilian nobles, who hated Ferdinand as a strong ruler and also as a Catalan." Elliott, *Imperial Spain*, p. 135. See also "Confederación . . . entre [el] duque del Infantado y D. Diego de Cárdenas, adelantado de Granada," Guadalajara, 3 February 1516, Osuna 1860, no number; "Confederación entre . . . Infantado y Iñigo de Velasco, condestable de Castilla," Berlanga, 12 August 1516, Osuna, 1860/29; "Confederación entre . . . Infantado y don Alvaro de Zuñiga, duque de Béjar," Guadalajara, 18 September 1516, Osuna, 1860, no number.

43. Copiador, Tendilla to Ortiz, 7 July 1515. "Carta del rey dirigida a todas las ciudades de Andalucía para que asistan en lo que necesitase marqués de Mondéjar que se disponía por su orden a dar posesión de sus estados al duque de Medina Sidonia," Salazar, M–131, ff. 205v–206; "Doña Juana . . . manda al marqués Iñigo López de Mendoza . . . que vaia a poner en la posesión de la casa y estado de Medina Sidonia a don Alonso Pérez de Guzmán . . . y para ello llebe todas las gentes de pie, y de caballo que fuere menester según que mas largamente se contiene en las cartas y poderes que sobre ello le mande dar," Medina del Campo, 9 March 1513, Salazar, M–131, f. 205v; "Carta del rey Fernando V al corregidor de Jerez de la Frontera (Cádiz) ordenándole que

ayude a marqués de Mondéjar dar posesión de los estados de su casa a[l] duque de Medina Sidonia por fallecimiento de su hermano." Medina del Campo, 22 February 1513, Salazar, M–1, f. 13v.

44. Tendilla was aware of this pattern and complained about it in 1508: "Como se sabe cierto que he de servir asy, asy y asy ponenme en la baraja." Tendilla to Gonzalo del Campo, 30 June 1508, printed in Cepeda, "Andalucía en 1508," p. 77.

45. "Yo querria mas quedar en poder de los moros y de los diablos que del cardenal porque yo le veo ambicioso y como vos sabes sienpre deseo abatir me y abaxar me en el tiempo quel rey estuvo ausente." Copiador, Tendilla to Francisco Ortiz, 7 July 1515.

46. "Esto tan desesperado y regañado despues de la vacante de Avila que no querria syno morder a quantos llegan a mi como haca matada. Verdad es que donde el cardenal se atraviesa no hay que decir. Dixo el cardenal mi tio a la marquesa de Moya, 'Dezi a la reyna que si da el arzobispado de Sevilla a privado no me da nada. Mas si lo da a otro sino a mi sobrino [Tendilla's brother], nunca mas viviera en su corte.' Asi que a privado se dio en ofrecimientos. Ni para v.s. ni para mi no tengo cauza ninguna ni fago otra cuenta sino que v.s. medrara para quien es y my hijo para quien fuere." Copiador, Tendilla to the bishop of Málaga, 9 August 1514.

47. When Ortiz, on Tendilla's orders, tried to speak to the cardinal about easing the financial burdens of the Moriscos, the cardinal replied that "era muy malo dexarllos ser moros." Tendilla denied the implication that he, by supporting the Moriscos' request to wear Arabic clothing without financial penalties, was giving the Moriscos license to remain Muslims. Copiador, Tendilla to Francisco Ortiz, 23 March 1514.

48. The twenty-five letters published by Cepeda in "Andalucía en 1508," were written immediately after Loja was given to the Great Captain. On the basis of these letters, Cepeda has concluded that Tendilla was simply supporting the protests of the citizens of Loja that they were being cut off from the royal power and being turned over to the whims of a nobleman (p. 58), and that Tendilla's gracious letters of congratulation to the Great Captain indicate a sincere desire to establish friendly relations with this powerful neighbor (p. 57). But these letters to the Great Captain and other officials in Andalucía must be taken with a grain of salt, since Tendilla's letters to Ortiz, where he expresses his true feelings, show that he hated the Great Captain and was envious of his royal favors.

49. "Escrevi[d]me si tomo el secretario [Conchillos] el vasillo que yo os juro a Dios tomandole o no sea la postre mas porque no diga que le tengo por cobdicioso." Copiador, Tendilla to Francisco Ortiz, [April 1514]; "Seria bien que su alteza no la diese [Tendilla's letter] a Conchillos porque es descubierta la celada que me quexo en ella de ese rapaz de Cobos aunque no le nonbro." 10 May 1515; "Se que don Miguel [de León] del conde de Ureña es y dineros le da y a mi hace Conchillos desservidor del rey y aun enemigo." 10 March 1514; "Nunca vi cosa mas donoso que ver el esgremir que hace el [Conchillos] que dio el memorial y decir que ha de guardar fuentes y rios y veredas y aguas que aquello es tan imposible hacerse con ninguna gente de guerra como bolar un buey quanto mas con docientos onbres. Maravillo me quien oso dar tal memorial a su al. y para que lo viesen esos señores que entienden en las cosas de guerra." Tendilla to Francisco de los

Cobos, 12 August 1514; "Nunca vi cosa tan vana ni tal trastras, diciendo cosas imposibles de hacer por Dios que no se guarde todo el reyno con quadrillas de mill y quinientos onbres y que ellos roben y destruian mas que los Moros y alli andara la cosa a saber si lo avian hecho los contrarios o los amigos. Yo maravillado estoy porque donde hay capitan general no se les dice, 'Tomad tanta gente,' y 'Tened esta orden y esa,' y 'Buscad quien lo haga,' sino que de alla enbien el capitan y le den la orden como si yo fuese bestia o onbre que acostunbrase estarme hilando." Tendilla to Francisco Ortiz, 12 August 1514.

50. "Basta que Conchillos y Cobos acuerdan sy el rey muriese o le acaesciese algo semejante a lo de la otra vez de dexarme condenado con los vecinos y con los de la cibdad y enemigo no yendo les otro ynterese en ello syno el que todo el mundo vee. Aviendo yo hecho por Cobos mas que ningun del reyno porque yo le hize dar la contaduría de Granada y yo le di lo del campo de Dalias a pesar de todos yo le di agora la procuracion y le he hecho otras buenas obras que no cuento aqui. . . . Al señor comendador mayor de Calatrava dezi leeys con quanto estudio trabajan Conchillos y Cobos y Zapata por su parte por enemistarme con estos en quien tengo parte." Copiador, Tendilla to Francisco Ortiz, 7 July 1515.

51. "Ay veres en que entiende el marques del Zenete en Guadix. Yo estoy bien que esto[y] en la cruz la una mano enclavada en Loja y la otra en Guadix y los pies en el marques de Pliego y la cabeza coronada del corregidor de Granada y el costado abierto por Zapata y Cobos." Copiador, Tendilla to Francisco Ortiz, 12 May 1515.

52. "En tal caso el no podia fallecer a los de Mendoza porque la casa era toda una que me lo hazia saber." Copiador, Tendilla to Francisco Ortiz, 7 July 1515. Tendilla himself was not devoid of such family feeling. He voted for his cousin Bernardino Suárez de Mendoza, count of Coruña, in an election to fill the trezenazgo of the Order of Santiago vacated by the death of the royal secretary, Miguel Pérez de Almazán. Copiador, Tendilla to Fernando, 15 May 1514.

53. "Aves de saber que se an juntado el Gran Capitan y el marques de Villena y el almirante y no se sy el condestable y tanbien dizen que de secreto el duque del Infantado con el cardenal y escriven me de Guadalajara que creen quel conde de Coruña esta de secreto concertado con el duque del Infantado y porque porventura al duque Dalva por algund concierto que terna con el duque del Infantado se le hara algo grave el mostrase muy claro por mi dires al comendador mayor de Castilla aun al duque cuando le hablardes que mi enemistad con el duque no es syno sobre que no me quieren dar lo mio ques cosa liviana y que o callando yo o pagando el lijeramente se puede concertar que aquello no es cosa que enpacha y all almirante que como veres en su carta del conde de Coruña ha escrito al conde y es mucho del cardenal dalde a entender que yo soy mucho del cardenal y al comendador mayor dezilde la verdad tanbien al de Calatrava como al de Castilla y aun sy os paresciere aunque no ayays de dar la carta larga a Conchillos mostralda al comendador mayor y dezi que no la quieres dar por no enemistar me pues yo no puedo hacer nada y ellos pueden dañar cada ora." Copiador, Tendilla to Francisco Ortiz, 7 July 1515, postscript.

54. "Ellos [his sons] y yo le serviremos que aun no soy muerto ni esto de intencion de morir me hasta que entierre otros pocos de los que me quieren mal con los que he enterrado." Copiador, Tendilla to Alba, 2 December 1514.

55. "Nunca supe dexar el camino que una vez comence a andar." Copiador, Tendilla to Francisco de los Cobos, 7 July 1515.

Chapter VIII

1. "Porque yo desseo mucho quel et sus descendientes se den al estudio como el marques mi señor que sancta gloria aya e yo e nuestros antecesores lo fecimos creyendo mucho por ello ser crescidas e alzadas nuestras personas e casas." Cited by Amador de los Ríos, Vida, p. 131.

2. "Declaro que la libreria que en esta casa esta, siempre oi decir que era del mayorazgo expreso la dejo al conde de Saldaña mi nieto y subcesor asi los libros que del duque mi señor y padre herede como los que yo he acrecentado y juntamente con esto le dejo y mando los halcones pocos o muchos que quedaron." Osuna, 1763/11.

3. Antonio Paz y Melia, "Biblioteca fundada por el conde de Haro (Pedro Fernández de Velasco) en 1455," Revista de Archivos, Bibliotecas, y Museos, 3ª época, 1 (1897), 18–24.

4. Santillana, Obras, pp. 487–490. For don Alfonso's ideas on this subject, see G. L. Boarino, "Alonso de Cartagena's 'Doctrinal de los Cavalleros,' Text, Tradition and Sources," Ph.D. diss., University of California, Berkeley, 1965.

5. Chandler and Schwartz, A New History of Spanish Literature, pp. 168–169; Amada López de Meneses, "Francisco I de Francia y otros ilustres extranjeros en Guadalajara en 1525," Cuadernos de Historia de España, 39–40 (1965), 309–364.

6. For an extensive discussion of the chivalric novel at the Burgundian court during the fourteenth and fifteenth centuries, see Johan Huizinga, The Waning of the Middle Ages, New York, 1949.

7. "Se va el uno cuatro leguas uno de otro que parece al romance del Cid y del moro." Copiador, Tendilla to the marquesa del Priego, [4 July 1506].

8. "No tengo otro pasatiempo sino leer y escribir de mi mano en unos libros que a dias que comiença hacer porque querria acabar los antes que me muriese." Copiador, Tendilla to Ortiz, 10 March 1514.

9. Tendilla's citations of Josephus and Augustine are specifically to chapter and verse, and his progress through these works can be traced by the progress of the citations. He finished Josephus in the spring of 1514 and Augustine in early 1515. Mondéjar, in the seventeenth century, utilized Tendilla's marginalia in the Historia de Bohemia, Mondéjar, ff. 217–217v.

10. Alonso, Dos españoles, pp. 63–75.

11. "Si no os estimase no os hubiera hecho patrono de mi querida universidad complutense," and "Y si yo no os respetase y quisiese servir en tan grande empresa no hubiera tomado el patronazgo della." Cited in Layna, Guadalajara, III, 29–30.

12. Azcona, La elección, p. 226; Andrés Martín, "Evangelismo," p. 13.

13. Matilla Tascón, Las declaratorias, pp. 190–191.

14. Letras, XII.

15. Ibid., XXI.

16. Ibid., XXXI; Francisco Cantera Burgos, "Fernando del Pulgar y los conversos," Sefarad, 4 (1944), 295–348.

17. Carriazo, Nota preliminar to *Crónica* by Pulgar.
18. See his 105 letters in *Centón epistolario del bachiller Hernán Gómez de Cibdadreal, físico del muy poderoso e sublimado rey d. Juan el segundo de este nombre*, in BAE, 13: 1–36.
19. Palencia, *Crónica de Enrique IV*, I, 167.
20. Osuna, 1873/29; García López, *Biblioteca*, p. 157; Otis H. Green, "On the 'coplas castellanas' in the 'Siglo de Oro,' " *Homenaje a Rodríguez-Moñino*, Madrid, 1966, I, 214.
21. See pp. 145–146.
22. "Este es un onbre de bien y de pocas palabras." Copiador, Tendilla to the duke of Alba, 10 April 1514.
23. "ques un onbre muy esforzado y muy atrevido y de pocas palabras que no acuchilla el aire como Pero Lopez." Copiador, Tendilla to Francisco Ortiz, 6 October 1514.
24. "Para que me lo hagais en latin porque yo carezco de aquel lenguaje vos absente." Registro, Tendilla to Pietro Martire, 17 July 1509.
25. "Que cosa es señor mandar su al. quitar los vestidos moriscos. Piensa que es asi cosa liviana. Juro por Dios con los que han de tornar a comprar mas cuesta al reyno de un milion de ducados y no se acuerda el rey n.s. que con esto se hace un tallo a los de allende para no ser suyos sino derremada la sangre primero. Ni sabe como en Roma el habito que trayan las mugeres siendo gentiles traen ahora y porque mejor podais señor hablar en esto con autoridad de dotor y tal como San Agostino lea v. m. en el libro diez y nueve del Civitate Dei en el diez e nueve capitulo y veres que dize. Pues nosotros señor en España hasta la venida del rey don Enrique el bastardo que habito que cabello trayamos sino el morisco y en que mesa comiamos. Dejaban los reyes de ser Christianos y santos por eso. No por Dios señor." Copiador, Tendilla to the comendador mayor de Castilla, 12 May 1514.
26. "El otro es como uno que llamaban Junatas de quien hace mencion Josefo De Belo Judaico en el capitulo cinquenta y uno del libro setimo." Copiador, Tendilla to the marquesa del Priego, [4 July 1506].
27. The term "gothic" is ill-defined in current Spanish usage and can mean anything from "Visigothic" to "pre-Renaissance." I am using it as Bayon does, for a style introduced into Castile after 1480 having many parallels to international gothic painting. We now know that all the royal structures in this style were built by Fernando after Isabel's death in 1504, but the Spanish still call the style "Isabelline." The following observations on architecture are my own, based on the plates and information in Vicente Lampérez y Romea, *Arquitectura civil española de los siglos I al XVIII*, Madrid, 1922, vol. I; *El castillo de la Calahorra; Los Mendoza del siglo XV y el castillo del Real de Manzanares*; Damien Bayon, *L'Architecture en Castille au XVe siècle*, Paris, 1967.
28. The chronology of the building phases of this fortress has been studied by Lampérez, *Los Mendoza*. Infantado must also have employed Italian stonemasons for the construction of the principal wall of the Palacio del Infantado, whose façade is finished with stone carved in a diamond-point pattern. Infantado imitated only those Italian features which were contemporary rather than antique. These Italian stone finishes were popular in Castile for a few

years after 1480. The most famous examples are the Casa de los Picos in Segovia and the Casa de las Conchas in Salamanca.

29. Bayon, *Architecture*, p. 228.

30. Medina y Mendoza, *Vida del cardenal*, pp. 191-192. On Borgia's architectural projects, see Michael Mallett, *The Borgias, The Rise and Fall of a Renaissance Dynasty*, London, 1969.

31. In the fifteenth and sixteenth centuries, this style was referred to as "estilo romano," or "estilo antiguo." In modern times it is sometimes also called "estilo Mendoza."

32. M. Gómez Moreno, "Hacía Lorenzo Vázquez," *Archivo Español de Arte*, 1 (1925), 1-40.

33. Earl Rosenthal, "The Image of Roman Architecture in Renaissance Spain," *Gazette des Beaux-Arts*, 52 (1958), 336.

34. Mondéjar, ff. 189v-196v.

35. "Por ventura me dio Dios aquel angel de estañas para que me quite la soberbia de buen Christiano que tengo. No se en que me lo vido ni en que libro de romance leyo que los que confiesan, comulgan, y dan limosna, y oyen continuo misas y sermones sean peores Christianos que los que ni en uno ni en otro no lo son." Copiador, Tendilla to Carvajal, [1 September 1514].

36. Copiador, Tendilla to conde de Cabra and marqués de Priego, 18 June 1506.

37. "Tanbien recibi merced en lo que dezis que hazes y hares por los nuevamente convertidos. Obligacion tenemos todos a ellos pues no se conbidaron ellos syno que los hezimos entrar por fuerza y mayor que la tuvieramos sy se conbidaran pero obligados somos a acordarnos de como se hizo." Copiador, Tendilla to the alcaide of Almería, 20 May 1515.

38. "[Orozco] no es hombre para fiarle cargo ninguno porque es loco y mal Christiano." Copiador, Tendilla to Francisco Ortiz, 12 August 1514. "Juro por Dios que le [Iñigo López] tengo por tan bueno Christiano como al mejor que hay en Granada." Copiador, Tendilla to Vargas, 12 May 1514.

39. "Lo que me escrevis sobre la quexa que tengo de conversos me ha hecho reir un rato porque de su padre y de su hijo se suelen los onbres quexar y no les hazen mal. Por eso yo mire lo que os escrevi a vos y lo que escrevi a mi hermana y aun lo que escrevi al licenciado y no fallo amenaza ninguna en ella pues porque diga que esto quexoso no me parece digno de tanta reprehension. En verdad os digo que lo estoy y con mucha razon porque aunque algunos dellos me sirvan bien nunca recivi mal sino por su mano y ningund acatamiento tienen a buena obra que se les aya hecho y sy haze onbre mal a uno toman lo todos por si y esto sea dicho con mucha reverencia como dizen los que disputan." Copiador, Tendilla to Francisco Ortiz, 12 May 1514.

40. Copiador, Tendilla to lic. Concha, 27 May 1515.

41. "Lo que me parece es que vos señor sy fuerdes a lugar de señorio temples el rigor quanto pudieredes porque hablando con vos claramente yo recelo que sy en alguna parte an de osar hacer algun atrevimiento a de ser antes en señorio que en realengo y por esto querria y me parece que deves de ay yr derecho a Almuñecar y pasar a la parte de Velez Malaga." Copiador, Tendilla to lic. Concha, 1 June 1515.

42. "Y sy me decis que lo de Dios a de preceder a todo digo que tener esta templanza

es lo de Dios y es otro no se de quien." Copiador, Tendilla to the inquisitors of Córdoba, 18 June 1506.

43. "No habia en el mundo cosa mejor regada que Roma mas muchos yerros se hazian de esta manera por no creer a los que tenian las manos en la masa." Copiador, Tendilla to comendador mayor de Calatrava, 9 October 1514.

44. "Señor, lo que sea de haber por errado es que digan tal dia, 'Por vuestra negligencia se perdio esto,' y 'Porque vos les decis esto y esto contra la fe o conforme a los ritos de su sete no son Christianos.' Quando fuere ahorquen me mas que digan al rey, 'Perdido esta el reyno y el marques hace que no sean Christianos,' y que por palabras generales sin prueba de cosa particular se encarezcan mis servicios que los he hecho muy grandes y muy señalados en el ausencia de su al. y en su presencia y que su al. me quite el favor y credito con la gente para darlo a sus enemigos que asi lo digo claro no creo que es bien." Copiador, Tendilla to comendador mayor de Castilla, 12 May 1514.

45. On the policies of the marquises of Mondéjar, see Elliott, *Imperial Spain*, pp. 232–237. My interpretation differs only slightly from Elliott's.

46. "El marqués de Mondéjar con los alcaldes del crimen de la Chancillería de Granada, sobre competencia de jurisdicción: El real consejo acuerda amonestar a los alcaldes por haberse excedido en sus atribuciones," ARCHG, 321, 4319/10; "Auto del real consejo para que el presidente y oidores de la Chancillería de Granada no den a nadie licencia para llevar armas," ARCHG, 321, 4430/107.

47. For Renaissance architecture in Spain, see Earl E. Rosenthal, *The Cathedral of Granada: A Study in the Spanish Renaissance*, Princeton, 1961; idem, *Diego Siloe arquitecto de la catedral de Granada*, Granada, 1966; idem, "The Image of Roman Architecture in Renaissance Spain," *Gazette des Beaux–Arts*, 52 (1958), 329–346; idem, "The Invention of the Columnar Device of Emperor Charles V at the Court of Burgundy in Flanders in 1516," *Journal of the Warburg and Courtauld Institutes*, 36 (1973), 198–230; idem, "The Lombard Sculptor Niccolò da Corte in Granada from 1537 to 1552," *Art Quarterly*, 29 (1966), 209–244; idem, "The Lost 'Quarto de las Helias' in the Arabic Palace on the Alhambra," in *Miscelánea de estudios dedicados al profesor Antonio Marín Ocete*, Granada, 1974, pp. 933–943. For the architectural projects which Tendilla must have observed during his embassy to Rome in 1486–1487, see Torgill Magnuson, *Studies in Roman Quattrocento Architecture*, Rome, 1958.

48. On Diego's life and works, see González Palencia, *Vida*, and Spivakovsky, *Son of the Alhambra*. Spivakovsky brings to light a great deal of new material.

49. José Antonio Maravall, *Carlos V y el pensamiento político del Renacimiento*, Madrid, 1960, pp. 314–315.

50. Spivakovsky, *Son of the Alhambra*, pp. 38–43.

51. Maravall, *Carlos V*, p. 64.

52. "En fin, pelearse cada día con enemigos, frío, calor, hambre, falta de munición y aparejos, en todas partes daños nuevos, muertes a la continua hasta que vimos a los enemigos, nación belicosa, entera, armada y confiada en el sitio, en el favor de los bárbaros y turcos, vencida y rendida, sacada de su tierra y desposeída de sus casas y bienes; presos atados hombres y mugeres, niños, captivos vendidos en almoneda o llevados a habitar tierras lexos de la suya: captiverio y trans-migración no menor que la que de otras gentes se lee por las historias; vitoria dudosa y de sucesos tan peligrosa que alguna vez se tuvo duda si éramos nosotros

o los enemigos a quien Dios quiera castigar, hasta que el fin descubrió que nosotros éramos los amenaçados y ellos los castigados." *De la guerra de Granada*, pp. 2–3. Helen Nader, "Josephus and Diego Hurtado de Mendoza," *Romance Philology*, 26 (1973), 554–555.

53. "Vínose a causas y pasiones particulares, hasta pedir jueces de términos, no para divisiones o suertes de tierra, como los romanos y nuestros pasados, sino con voz de restituirse a el rey o al público lo que tenían ocupado, e intento de echar algunos de sus heredamientos. Este fué uno de los principios en la destruición de Granada." *De la guerra de Granada*, p. 11.

54. "Governávase la ciudad y el reino como entre pobladores y compañeros; una forma de justicia arbitraria, unidos los pensamientos, las resoluciones encaminadas en común al bien público: esto se acabó con la vida de los viejos. Entraron los celos, la división sobre cosas livianas entre los ministros de justicia y de guerra, las concordias en escripto confirmadas por cédulas, trayendo el entendimiento dellas por cada una de las partes a su opinión; el querer la una no sufrir igual, y la otra conservar la superioridad, tratada con más disimulación que modestia." Ibid.

55. "Cada nación, cada profesión, cada estado usa su manera de hábito y todos son cristianos; nosotros moros, porque vestimos a la morisca, como si tragésemos la ley en el vestido y no en el coraçon." Ibid., p. 21.

56. Throughout the first session, the Spanish theologians at Trent sided with the papal party and the theologians from the University of Paris, a fact that can be attributed to their educational backgrounds. Of the twenty-five Spanish theologians at Trent, fourteen can be identified. Of these, eight received their theological training at Paris, one at Valladolid, three at Alcalá, and two at Salamanca where they were taught by Paris graduates. Compiled from Constancio Gutiérrez, *Españoles en Trento*, Valladolid, 1951.

57. This, at least, is what don Diego believed, according to a letter to Charles V, 28 October 1546, cited by Spivakovsky, *Son of the Alhambra*, p. 143.

58. English translation by Spivakovsky, ibid., pp. 139–140.

59. Ibid., p. 145.

60. Francesco Petrarch, "On His Own Ignorance and That of Many Others," in *The Renaissance Philosophy of Man*, ed. Ernst Cassirer et al. Chicago: Phoenix Books, 1956, p. 105.

61. Spivakovsky, *Son of the Alhambra*, p. 145.

62. *Confessions*, Baltimore: Penguin Books, 1961, p. 117.

List of Works Cited

Primary Sources

Alfonso X el Sabio. *Primera crónica general*. Nueva Biblioteca de Autores Españoles, vol. 5. Madrid, 1906.

——. *Las Siete Partidas*. *Los Códigos Españoles*, vols. 2–5. Ed. Antonio de San Martín. Madrid, 1872–1873.

Augustine [Aurelius Augustinus]. *Confessions*. Trans. R. S. Pine-Coffin. Middlesex, 1961.

——. *De Consensu Evangelistarum*. *Opera Omnia*, vol. 3:2. Ed. J. P. Migne. Paris, 1837.

Baena, Juan Alfonso de. *Cancionero*. Ed. José María Azáceta. Madrid, 1966.

Bernáldez, Andrés. *Memorias del reinado de los Reyes Católicos*. Ed. Manuel Gómez-Moreno and Juan de Mata Carriazo. Madrid, 1962.

Bisticci, Vespasiano da. *Renaissance Princes, Popes and Prelates*. Trans. William George and Emily Waters. New York, 1963.

Carrillo de Huete, Pedro. *Crónica del halconero de Juan II*. Ed. Juan de Mata Carriazo. Madrid, 1946.

Cartagena, Alfonso de. "Carta dirigida al Rey por los Embajadores de España en el Concilio de Basilea dando cuenta de la acogida que tuvieron los enviados, primeras impresiones y de las manifestaciones sobre precedencia que impulsaron a don Alonso de Cartagena a pronunciar su discurso sobre la superioridad de España respecto a Inglaterra," Transcription Antonio Elías de Molins. *Revista de Archivos, Bibliotecas y Museos*, 3ª época, 1 (1897), 67–73.

——. *Discurso sobre la precedencia del Rey Católico sobre el de Inglaterra en el Concilio de Basilea*. Biblioteca de Autores Españoles, vol. 116. Madrid, 1959.

——. *Defensorium Unitatis Christianae. Tratados en favor de los judíos conversos*. Ed. Manuel Alonso. Madrid, 1943.

Colonne, Guido delle. *Historia Troiana*. [Strassburg, 1486].

"Cortes de Toro de 1505," *Cortes de los antiguos reinos de León y de Castilla*, vol. 4 (1476–1537). Real Academia de la Historia. Madrid, 1882.

Crónica de don Alvaro de Luna, condestable de Castilla, maestre de Santiago. Ed. Juan de Mata Carriazo. Madrid, 1940.

Crónica de Juan II. Biblioteca de Autores Españoles, vol. 68. Madrid, 1953.

Crónica del rey don Alfonso el onceno. Biblioteca de Autores Españoles, vol. 66. Madrid, 1953.

Fernández de Heredia, Juan. *La grant cronica de Espanya, libros I–III*. Ed. Regina af Geijerstam. Uppsala, 1964.

Floreto de anécdotas y noticias diversas que recopiló un fraile domínico residente en Sevilla a mediados del siglo XVI. Ed. F. J. Sánchez Cantón. Memorial Histórico Español, vol. 48. Madrid, 1947.

Froissart, John. *Chronicles of England, France and Spain*. Ed. H. P. Dunster. New York, 1961.

Galíndez de Carvajal, Lorenzo. "Informe que dió al emperador Carlos V sobre los que componían el consejo real de S. M." Codoín, I, 122–127.

Gómez de Ciudad Real, Fernán. *Centon epistolario del bachiller Hernan Gomez de Cibdadreal, fisico del muy poderoso e sublimado rey d. Juan el segundo de este nombre*. Biblioteca de Autores Españoles, vol. 13. Madrid, 1872.

Guicciardini, Francesco. *La legazione di Spagna. Opere inedite*, vol. 6. Florence, 1857–1866.

Hurtado de Mendoza, Diego. *De la guerra de Granada*. Ed. Manuel Gómez Moreno. Memorial Histórico Español, vol. 49. Madrid, 1948.

Jiménez de Rada, Rodrigo [el Toledano]. *De Rebus Hispaniae*. In *Opera*. Ed. Francisco Lorenzana. Madrid, 1793; rpt. Valencia, 1968.

Lalaing, Antoine. *Relation du premier voyage de Philippe le Beau en Espagne, en 1501*. Collection des voyages des souverains des Pays-Bas, vol. I. Brussels, 1876.

López de Ayala, Diego. "Constituciones del Colegio de Sta. Catalina de Toledo." Biblioteca Nacional, MS 933.

López de Ayala, Pedro. *Colección de las crónicas y memorias de los reyes de Castilla*. 2 vols. Madrid, 1779–1780.

———. *Crónica del rey don Pedro*. Biblioteca de Autores Españoles. vol. 66. Madrid, 1953.

———. *Las flores de los Morales de Job*. Ed. Francesco Branciforti. Biblioteca Letteraria, vol. 7. Florence, 1963.

———. *El libro de las aves de caça del canciller Pero López de Ayala con las glosas del duque de Alburquerque*. Madrid, 1869.

———. *Poesías*. Ed. A. F. Kuersteiner. 2 vols. New York, 1920.

López de Mendoza, Iñigo, count of Tendilla and marquis of Mondéjar. "Copiador de cartas por el marqués de Mondéjar." 2 vols. Osuna, 3406.

———. *Correspondencia del conde de Tendilla, I (1508–1509): Biografía, estudio y transcripción*. Ed. Emilio Meneses García. Archivo Documental Español, vol. 31. Madrid, 1974.

———. "Registro de cartas referentes al gobierno de las Alpujarras, años 1508 a 1520." 2 vols. Biblioteca Nacional, MSS 10230–10231.

Luna, Alvaro de. *Libro de las virtuosas e claras mujeres*. Ed. Marcelino Menéndez y Pelayo. Colección de libros publicados por la Sociedad de Bibliófilos Españoles, vol. 28. Madrid, 1892.

Manrique, Gómez. *Cancionero*. Ed. Antonio Paz y Melia. 2 vols. Madrid, 1885.

Martinus Cordubensis. "Breve Compendium Artis Rhetorice." Biblioteca Nacional, MS 9309.

Mondéjar, Marqués de [Gaspar Ibáñez de Segovia]. "Historia de la Casa de Mondéjar; y sucesión de la Baronía de Moncada." Biblioteca Nacional, MS 3315.

Núñez de Toledo, Hernán. *La historia de Bohemia en romance*. Seville, 1509.

Palencia, Alfonso de. *Crónica de Enrique IV*. Trans. Antonio Paz y Melia. 5 vols. Madrid, 1904.

Pérez de Ayala, Fernán. *El fuero de Ayala*. Ed. Luis María de Uriarte Lebario. Madrid, 1912.

Pérez de Guzmán, Fernán. *Generaciones y semblanzas*. Ed. Robert B. Tate. Colección Tamesis, series B, vol. 2. London, 1965.

———.*Generaciones y semblanzas*. Ed. José Domínguez Bordona. Clásicos Castellanos, 61. Madrid, 1924.

Petrarch, Francesco. "On His Own Ignorance and That of Many Others." In *The Renaissance Philosophy of Man*. Ed. Ernst Cassirer et al. Chicago, 1956.

Pius II [Aeneas Sylvius Piccolominus]. *De Gestis Concilii Basiliensis Commentariorum Libri II*. Ed. and trans. Denys Hay and W. K. Smith. Oxford, 1967.

Pulgar, Hernando del. *Crónica de los Reyes Católicos*. Ed. Juan de Mata Carriazo. 2 vols. Madrid, 1943.

———. *Letras, Glosa a las coplas de Mingo Revulgo*. Ed. José Domínguez Bordona. Madrid, 1929.

Quintillian [Marcus Fabius Quintilianus]. *Instituto Oratoria*. With English trans. by H. E. Butler. (Loeb Classical Library.) New York, 1921–1922.

Relación de los fechos del muy magnífico D. Miguel Lucas muy digno condestable de Castilla. Ed. Juan de Mata Carriazo. Madrid, 1940.

"Relación del caso de Granada . . . principio de la rebelión de los Moros después de la conquista (1499)." Codoín, XXXVI, 441–449.

Santillana, marqués de [Iñigo López de Mendoza]. *Obras*. Ed. José Amador de los Ríos. Madrid, 1852.

Valera, Diego de. *La corónica de España*. Seville, 1538.

———. *Crónica de los Reyes Católicos.* Ed. Juan de Mata Carriazo. Madrid, 1927.

———. *Doctrinal de príncipes.* Biblioteca de Autores Españoles, vol. 116. Madrid, 1959.

———. *Epístolas de Mosén Diego de Valera, enbiadas en diversos tiempos e a diversas personas.* Ed. José A. de Balenchana. Madrid, 1878.

———. *Memorial de diversas hazañas: Crónica de Enrique IV.* Ed. Juan de Mata Carriazo. Madrid, 1941.

Villena, Enrique de. *Arte de trovar.* Ed. F. J. Sánchez Cantón. Biblioteca Española de Divulgación Científica, vol. 3. Madrid, 1923.

Secondary Works

Addy, George M. *The Enlightenment in the University of Salamanca.* Durham, N. C., 1966.

Ajo González y Sáinz de Zúñiga, C. M. *Historia de las universidades hispánicas: orígenes y desarrollo desde su aparición hasta nuestros días.* Vol. I: *Medioevo y renacimiento universitario.* Madrid, 1957.

Alcocer y Martínez, Mariano. *Historia de la Universidad de Valladolid.* Valladolid, 1918–1922.

Alonso, Dámaso. *Dos españoles del siglo de oro.* Madrid, 1960.

Amador de los Ríos, José. "Protexta del sentimiento nacional contra la innovación alegórica." *Historia crítica de la literatura española.* Madrid, 1862–1865. V, 99–159.

———. *Vida del marqués de Santillana.* Buenos Aires, 1948.

Andrés, Alfonso. "D. Pedro González de Mendoza él de Aljubarrota (1340–1385)." *Boletín de la Real Academia de Historia,* 78 (1921), 255–273, 353–376, 415–436, 496–504.

Andrés Martín, Melquíades. "Evangelismo, humanismo, reforma y observancias en España (1450–1525)." *Missionalis Hispania,* 67 (1966), 5–25.

———. *Historia de la Teología en España (1470–1520).* Rome, 1962.

Archivo Ibero-Americano. *Las reformas en los siglos XIV–XV, introducción a los orígines de la observancia en España.* Madrid, 1958.

Arriaga, Gonzalo de. *Historia del Colegio de San Gregorio de Valladolid.* Valladolid, 1926. Vol. I.

Arteaga y Falguera, Cristina de. *La Casa del Infantado, cabeza de los Mendoza.* 2 vols. Madrid, 1940.

Asís, María Dolores de, *Hernán Núñez en la historia de los estudios clásicos.* Madrid, 1977.

Aubenas, Roger, and Robert Ricard. *L'Eglise et la Renaissance.* Histoire de l'Eglise, vol. 15. Ed. Augustin Fliche and Victor Martin. Paris, 1951.

Avalle-Arce, Juan B. *El cronista Pedro de Escavias. Una vida del siglo XV.*

Studies in Romance Languages and Literatures, vol. 127. Chapel Hill, 1972.

——. "Los herejes de Durango." *Homenaje a Rodríguez-Moñino: Estudios de erudición que le ofrecen sus amigos o discípulos hispanistas norteamericanos.* Madrid, 1966. I, 44–55.

Azcona, Tarsicio de. *La elección y reforma del episcopado español en tiempo de los Reyes Católicos.* Madrid, 1960.

——. *Isabel la Católica: Estudio crítico de su vida y su reinado.* Madrid, 1964.

——. "El tipo ideal de obispo en la iglesia española antes de la rebelión luterana." *Hispania Sacra,* 11 (1958), 21–64.

Baena y San Lúcar la Mayor, duque de. "El Gran Capitán y el maestrazgo de Santiago." *Hispania,* 13 (1953), 189–194.

Bahner, Werner. *La lingüística española del siglo de oro.* Madrid, 1966.

Ballesteros y Beretta, A. *Historia de España y su influencia en la historia universal.* 12 vols. 2nd ed., Barcelona, 1943–1948.

Baron, Hans. *The Crisis of the Early Italian Renaissance.* Princeton, 1966.

——. *From Petrarch to Leonardo Bruni.* Chicago, 1968.

Bataillon, Marcel. "L'Arabe à Salamanque aux temps de la Renaissance." *Hespéris,* 21 (1935), 1–17.

——. *Erasmo y España.* 2 vols. Mexico, 1950.

Bayon, Damien. *L'architecture en Castille au XVe siècle.* Paris, 1967.

Becker, Marvin. "Individualism in the Early Italian Renaissance: Burden and Blessing." *Studies in the Renaissance,* 19 (1972), 273–297.

Bejarano, Francisco. "El almirantazgo de Granada y la rebelión de Málaga en 1516." *Hispania,* 15 (1955), 73–109.

Beltrán, Luis, *Razones de buen amor: Oposiciones y convergencias en el libro del Arcipreste de Hita.* Madrid, 1977.

Beltrán de Heredia, Vicente. "Los comienzos de la reforma dominicana en Castilla particularmente en el convento de San Esteban de Salamanca y su irradiación a la provincia de Portugal." *Archivum Fratrum Praedicatorum,* 28 (1958), 221–237.

——. *Los corrientes de espiritualidad entre los Dominicos de Castilla durante la primera mitad del siglo XVI.* Salamanca, 1941.

——. *Historia de la reforma de la Provincia de España (1450–1550).* Rome, 1939.

——. "Nebrija y los teólogos de San Esteban de principios del siglo XVI," *La Ciencia Tomista,* 61 (1941), 37–65.

——. "La Teología en la Universidad de Alcalá." *Revista Española de Teología,* 5 (1945), 406–417.

Bermúdez de Pedraza, Francisco. *Antigüedad y excelencias de Granada.* Madrid, 1608.

Birkenmaier, A. "Der Streit des Alonso von Cartagena mit L. B. Aretino."

Beiträge zur Geschichte der Philosophie des Mittelalters, 20, Heft 5 (1922), 129–236.

Blüher, Karl Alfred. *Seneca in Spanien: Untersuchungen zur Geschichte der Seneca-Rezeption in Spanien vom 13. bis 17. Jahrhundert.* Munich, 1969.

Boarino, G. L. "Alonso de Cartagena's 'Doctrinal de los Cavalleros,' Text, Tradition and Sources." Ph.D. diss., University of California, Berkeley, 1965.

Bolgar, R. R. *The Classical Heritage and its Beneficiaries from the Carolingian Age to the End of the Renaissance.* New York, 1964.

Bonilla y San Martín, Adolfo. *Fernando de Córdoba (¿1425–1486?): Orígenes del Renacimiento filosófico en España: Episodio de la historia de la lógica.* Madrid, 1911.

————. *Ion, diálogo platónico, traducido del griego por Afanto Ucalego.* Madrid, 1901.

————. *Luis Vives y la filosofía del Renacimiento.* Madrid, 1903.

Bouwsma, William J. *Venice and the Defense of Republican Liberty.* Berkeley, 1968.

Branciforti, Francesco. "Regesto delle opere di Pero López de Ayala." In *Saggi e ricerche in memoria di Ettore Li Gotti.* Palermo, 1961.

Brenan, Gerald. *The Spanish Labyrinth.* Cambridge, 1971.

Burke, Peter. *The Renaissance Sense of the Past.* New York, 1970.

Caballero, Fermín. *Elogio del doctor Alonso de Montalvo.* Madrid, 1950.

Cano de Gardoquí, J. L., and A. de Bethencourt. "Incorporación de Gibraltar a la corona de Castilla, 1435–1508." *Hispania*, 26 (1966), 325–381.

Cantera Burgos, Francisco. "Fernando del Pulgar y los conversos." *Sefarad*, 4 (1944), 295–348.

Caro Baroja, Julio. *Los Moriscos del reino de Granada.* Madrid, 1957.

Carriazo, Juan de Mata. "Cartas de la frontera de Granada, 1430–1509." *Al-Andalus*, 11 (1946), 69–130.

Carril, Bonifacio del. *Los Mendoza; Los Mendoza en España y en América en el siglo XV y en la primera mitad del siglo XVI, comprobaciones sobre la genealogía de don Pedro de Mendoza, fundador de Buenos Aires.* Buenos Aires [1954].

Casalduero, Joaquín Gimeno. "Pero López de Ayala y el cambio poético de Castilla a comienzos del XV." *Hispanic Review*, 33 (1965), 1–14.

Castro, Américo. *The Structure of Spanish History.* Trans. Edmund L. King. Princeton, 1954.

Catalán, Diego. *Un cronista anónimo del siglo XIV.* Canarias, n.d.

Cepeda Adán, José. "Andalucía en 1508: Un aspecto de la correspondencia del virrey Tendilla." *Hispania*, 22 (1962), 38–80.

————. "El Gran Tendilla, medieval y renacentista." *Cuadernos de Historia*, 1 (1967), 159–168.

————. "El providencialismo en los cronistas de los Reyes Católicos." *Arbor*, 17 (1950), 177–190.

Chandler, Richard E., and Kessel Schwartz. *A New History of Spanish Literature*. Baton Rouge, 1961.

Cirot, Georges. *Histoires générales d'Espagne*. Bordeaux, 1904.

Clavero, Bartolomé. *Mayorazgo: Propiedad feudal en Castilla 1369–1836*. Madrid, 1974.

Cotarelo y Valledor, A. *Fray Diego de Deza. Ensayo biográfico*. Madrid, 1902.

Deyermond, A. D. *A Literary History of Spain: The Middle Ages*. New York, 1971.

di Camillo, Ottavio. "Spanish Humanism in the Fifteenth Century." Ph.D. diss., Yale, 1972.

Díaz-Plaja, Guillermo. *Historia general de las literaturas hispánicas*. 5 vols. in 6. Barcelona, [1949–1958].

Durán y Lerchundi, Joaquín. *La toma de Granada y caballeros que concurrieron a ella*. 2 vols. Madrid, 1893.

Elliott, J. H. *Imperial Spain, 1469–1716*. New York, 1967.

Entwistle, William J. "Spanish Literature to 1681." In *Spain, A Companion to Spanish Studies*. Ed. E. A. Peers. 5th ed., London, 1956. pp. 88–154.

Esperabé Arteaga, E. *Historia de la Universidad de Salamanca*. vol. I. Salamanca, 1914.

Evans, P. G. "A Spanish Knight in Flesh and Blood. A Study of the Chivalric Spirit of Suero de Quiñones." *Hispania* (New York), 15 (1932), 141–152.

Faucon, Maurice. *La Librairie des Papes d'Avignon, sa formation, sa composition, ses catalogues, 1316–1420*. Bibliothèque des Ecoles Françaises d'Athènes et de Rome, Fascicules 43, 50. Paris, 1886–1887.

Faulhaber, Charles. *Latin Rhetorical Theory in Thirteenth and Fourteenth Century Castile*. Berkeley, 1972.

Febrero Lorenzo, María. *La pedagogía de los colegios mayores a través de su legislación en el Siglo de Oro*. Madrid, 1960.

Febvre, Lucien. "Une Question mal posée: les origines de la Réforme française et le problème générale des causes de la Réforme." *Au Coeur religieux du XVI siècle*. Paris, 1957.

Fernández Alvarez, Manuel, and Luis Suárez Fernández. *La España de los Reyes Católicos 1474–1516*. Historia de España, vol. 17:2. Ed. Ramón Menéndez Pidal. Madrid, 1969.

Font Rius, José María. *Instituciones medievales españolas*. Madrid, 1949.

Fraker, Charles F., Jr. "Gonçalo Martínez de Medina, the Jerónimos and the Devotio Moderna." *Hispanic Review*, 34 (1966), 197–217.

Fuente, Vicente de la. *Historia de las universidades, colegios y demás establecimientos de enseñanza en España*. Vol. I, Edad Media. Madrid, 1885.

————. *La ensenañza tomística en España. Noticia de las universidades, colegios y academias tomistas con las fundaciones de ellas y sus cátedras principales* . . . . Madrid, 1874.

Gámir Sandoval, Alfonso. "Organización de la defensa de la costa del Reino de Granada desde su reconquista hasta finales del siglo XVI." *Boletín de la Universidad de Granada*, 73 (1943), 259–337.

García López, Juan Catalina. *Biblioteca de escritores de la Provincia, de Guadalajara y bibliografía de la misma hasta el siglo XIX*. Madrid, 1899.

Garrad, Kenneth. "La industria sedera granadina en el siglo XVI y su conexión con el levantamiento de las Alpujarras (1568–1571)." *Miscelánea de Estudios Arabes y Hebraicos*, 5 (1956), 73–104.

————. "La inquisición y los moriscos granadinos, 1526–1580." *Bulletin Hispanique*, 67 (1965), 67–78.

————. "The Original Memorial of Don Francisco Núñez Muley." *Atlante*, 2 (1954), 199–226.

————. "La renta de los habices 'de los mezquinos' de las Alpujarras y Valle de Lecrín: Algunos datos sobre su administración a mediados del siglo XVI." *Miscelánea de Estudios Arabes y Hebraicos*, 2 (1953), 41–48.

Gibb, H. A. R. "The Influence of Islamic Culture on Medieval Europe." *Bulletin of the John Rylands Library*, 38 (1955–1956), 82–98.

Gilbert, Felix. *Machiavelli and Guicciardini*. Princeton, 1965.

Gómez-Moreno, Manuel. "Hacía Lorenzo Vázquez." *Archivo Español de Arte*, 1 (1925), 1–40.

Goñí Gastambide, José. "La Santa Sede y la reconquista del reino de Granada." *Hispania Sacra*, 4 (1951), 43–80.

González Llubera, I. G. *Nebrija, Gramática de la lengua española*. Oxford, 1926.

González Olmedo, Félix. *Diego Ramírez Villaescusa (1459–1537), fundador del Colegio de Cuenca y autor de "Los cuatro diálogos sobre la muerte del príncipe Don Juan."* Madrid, 1944.

————. *Humanistas y pedagogos españoles: Nebrija (1441–1522), debelador de la barbarie, comentador eclesiástico, pedagogo, poeta*. Madrid, 1942.

————. *Nebrija en Salamanca (1475–1513)*. Madrid, 1944.

González Palencia, Angel, and Eugenio Mele. *Vida y obras de Don Diego Hurtado de Mendoza*. 3 vols. Madrid, 1941–1943.

Green, Louis. *Chronicle into History*. Cambridge, 1972.

Green, Otis, H. "On the 'coplas castellanas' in the 'Siglo de Oro.'" *Homenaje a Rodríguez-Moñino*. Madrid, 1966, I, 205–219.

————. *Spain and the Western Tradition: The Castilian Mind in Literature from El Cid to Calderón*. 4 vols. Madison, 1963–1966.

Guillemain, Bernard. *La Cour Pontificale d'Avignon (1309–1376)*. Bibliothèque des Ecoles Françaises d'Athènes et de Rome, fasc. 201. Paris, 1962.

Gutiérrez, Constancio. *Españoles en Trento*. Valladolid, 1951.

Gutiérrez Coronel, Diego. *Historia genealógica de la Casa de Mendoza.* Ed. Angel González Palencia. 2 vols. Madrid, 1946.

Häbler, Konrad. *Der Streit Ferdinand's des Katholischen und Philipp's I um die Regierung von Castilien, 1504–1506.* Dresden, 1882.

Haliczer, Stephen. "The Castilian Aristocracy and the Mercedes Reform of 1478–1482." *Hispanic American Historical Review,* 55 (1975), 449–467.

Henríquez de Jorquera, Francisco. *Anales de Granada. Parayso español.* Ed. Antonio Marín Ocete. 2 vols. Granada, 1934.

Highfield, J. R. L. "The Catholic Kings and the Titled Nobility of Castile." In *Europe in the Late Middle Ages.* Ed. J. R. Hale et al. Evanston, Ill., 1965.

Holmes, George. *The Florentine Enlightenment, 1400–1450.* New York, 1969.

Huizinga, Johan. *The Waning of the Middle Ages.* New York, 1949.

Ibarra y Rodríguez, Eduardo. *El problema cerealista en España durante el reinado de los Reyes Católicos (1475–1516).* Madrid, 1944.

Iung, Nicholas. *Un Franciscain théologien du pouvoir pontifical au XIVe siècle: Alvaro Pelayo.* Paris, 1931.

Jedin, Hubert. *A History of the Council of Trent.* Trans. Ernest Graf. 3 vols. London, 1957–1961.

Jiménez, Albert. *Historia de la universidad española.* Madrid, 1971.

Kagan, Richard. *Students and Society in Early Modern Spain.* Baltimore, 1974.

Kamen, Henry. *The Spanish Inquisition.* New York, 1965.

Kelley, Donald R. *Foundations of Modern Historical Scholarship: Language, Law and History in the French Renaissance.* New York, 1970.

Kendrick, T. D. *St. James in Spain.* London, 1960.

Keniston, Hayward. *Francisco de los Cobos, Secretary of the Emperor Charles V.* Pittsburgh, 1958.

——. *Garcilaso de la Vega; A Critical Study of His Life and Works.* New York, 1922.

Klausner, Joel H. "The Historic and Social Milieu of Santob's Proverbios Morales." *Hispania* (New York), 48 (1965), 783–789.

Kohler, Josef. "Die spanische Schule von Salamanca im Siglo de Oro." *Archiv für Rechts- und Wirtschaftsphilosophie,* 10 (1916), 236 ff.

Ladero Quesada, Miguel Angel. "Los cereales en Andalucía del siglo XV." *Revista de la Universidad de Madrid,* 18 (1969).

——. *Granada: Historia de un país islámico (1232–1571).* Madrid, 1969.

——. "La repoblación del reino de Granada anterior al año 1500." *Hispania,* 28 (1968), 489–563.

Lafuente y Alcántara, Miguel. *Historia de Granada, comprendiendo la de sus cuatro provincias Almería, Jaén, Granada, y Málaga, desde remotos tiempos hasta nuestros días.* 2 vols. Paris, 1852.

Lampérez y Romea, Vicente. *Arquitectura civil española de los siglos I al XVIII.* Madrid, 1922. Vol. I.

──────. *El castillo de La Calahorra (Granada).* Madrid, 1914.

──────. *Los Mendoza del siglo XV y el castillo del Real de Manzanares.* Madrid, 1916.

Lapesa, Rafael. "La cultura literaria activa en la poesía juvenil de Santillana." *Atlante,* 2 (1954), 119–125.

──────. *La obra literaria del marqués de Santillana.* Madrid, 1957.

Lapeyre, Henri. *La Géographie de l'Espagne morisque.* Paris, 1959.

Lascaris Comneno, C. *Colegios mayores.* Madrid, 1952.

Layna Serrano, Francisco. "El Cardenal Mendoza como político y consejero de los Reyes Católicos." Madrid, 1935. Biblioteca Nacional, Varios, Q 1509–10.

──────. *Castillos de Guadalajara.* Madrid, 1962.

──────. *Historia de Guadalajara y sus Mendozas en los siglos XV y XVI.* 4 vols. Madrid, 1942.

Lejarza, Fidel de, and Angel Uribe. "¿Cuándo y dónde comenzó Villacreces su reforma?" *Archivo Ibero-Americano,* series 2, 20 (1960), 79–94.

Lemus y Rubio, P. "El maestro Elio Antonio de Lebrixa." *Revue Hispanique,* 22 (1910), 459–508; 29 (1913), 13–120.

López Estrada, Francisco. "La retórica en las 'Generaciones y semblanzas' de Fernán Pérez de Guzmán." *Revista de Filología Española,* 30 (1946), 310–352.

López de Meneses, Amada. "El canciller Pero López de Ayala y los reyes de Aragón." *Estudios de Edad Media de la Corona de Aragón* 8 (1967) 189–264.

──────. "Francisco I de Francia y otros ilustres extranjeros en Guadalajara en 1525." *Cuadernos de Historia de España,* 39–40 (1964), 309–364.

──────. "Nuevos datos sobre el canciller Ayala." *Cuadernos de Historia de España,* 10 (1948), 111–128.

López Navio, José. "Don Juan de Fonseca, canónigo, maestrescuela de Sevilla." *Archivo Hispalense,* 126–127 (1964), 83–128.

Lopez Rueda, José. *Helenistas españoles del siglo XVI.* Madrid, 1973.

Lozoya, Juan de Contreras y López de Ayala, marquis of. *Introducción a la biografía del canciller Ayala.* Vizcaya, 1950.

Luque, José Francisco de. *Granada y sus contornos: Historia de esta célebre ciudad desde los tiempos mas remotos hasta nuestros días, su arqueología y descripción circunstanciada de cuanto digno de admiración se encuentra en ella.* Granada, 1858.

Luttrell, Anthony. "The Aragonese Crown and the Knights Hospitallers of Rhodes, 1291–1340." *English Historical Review,* 76 (1961), 1–19.

──────. "Fourteenth-Century Hospitaller Lawyers." *Traditio,* 21 (1965), 449–456.

──────. "Juan Fernández de Heredia at Avignon: 1351–1367." In *El*

Cardenal Albornoz y el Colegio de España. Ed. Evelio Verdera y Tuells. Zaragoza, 1972. I, 287–316.

Lynn, Caro. A College Professor of the Renaissance: Lucio Marineo Sículo among the Spanish Humanists. Chicago, [1937].

MacDonald, I. Don Fernando de Antequera. Oxford, 1948.

Magnuson, Torgil. Studies in Roman Quattrocento Architecture. Rome, 1958.

Mahdi, Muhsin. Ibn Khaldun's Philosophy of History. Chicago, 1964.

Mallett, Michael. The Borgias: The Rise and Fall of a Renaissance Dynasty. London, 1969.

Maravall, José Antonio. Carlos V y el pensamiento político del Renacimiento. Madrid, 1960.

——. El humanismo de las armas en Don Quijote. [Madrid], 1948.

Mariéjol, J. H. L'Espagne sous Ferdinand et Isabelle. Paris, 1892.

——. Un Lettré italien à la cour d'Espagne (1488–1526). Pierre Martyr d'Anghierra, sa vie et ses oeuvres. Paris, 1887.

——. The Spain of Ferdinand and Isabella. Trans. Benjamin Keen. New Brunswick, N. J., [1961].

Marín Ocete, Antonio. "Pedro Mártir de Anglería y su Opus Epistolarum." Boletín de la Universidad de Granada, 73 (1943), 165–257.

Marti, Berthe M. The Spanish College at Bologna in the Fourteenth Century. Philadelphia, 1966.

Martín Hernández Francisco. La formación clerical en los colegios universitarios españoles (1371–1563). Vitoria, 1961.

——. Un seminario español pretridentino: El Real Colegio Eclesiástico de San Cecilio de Granada, 1492–1842. Valladolid, 1960.

——. Los seminarios españoles: Historia y pedagogía, I, 1563–1700. Salamanca, 1964.

Matilla Tascón, Antonio, ed. Declaratorias de los Reyes Católicos sobre reducción de juros y otras mercedes. Madrid, 1952.

Medina y Mendoza, Francisco de. Vida del Cardenal d. Pedro González de Mendoza. Memorial Histórico Español, vol. 6. Madrid, 1853.

Menéndez y Pelayo, Marcelino. Poetas de la corte de don Juan II. Madrid, 1943.

Meregalli, Franco. Pietro di Castiglia nella letteratura. Milan, [1951].

Mérimée, Prosper. Histoire de don Pèdre Ier Roi de Castille. Paris, 1961.

Merriman, Roger Bigelow. The Rise of the Spanish Empire in the Old World and in the New. 4 vols. New York, 1925.

Michael, Ian. The Treatment of Classical Material in the Libro de Alexandre. Manchester, 1970.

Mitre Fernández, Emilio. Evolución de la nobleza en Castilla bajo Enrique III (1396–1406). Valladolid, 1963.

Montaigne, Michel de. Essays. Trans. J. M. Cohen. Harmondsworth, Middlesex, [1961].

Morel-Fatio, Alfred. *L'Espagne au XVIe e au XVIIe siècle.* Heilbronn, 1878.

Moxó Salvador de. "De la nobleza vieja a la nobleza nueva. La transformación nobiliaria castellana en la Baja Edad Media." *Cuadernos de Historia,* 3 (1969), 1–120.

Nader, Helen. "The Greek Commander Hernán Núñez de Toledo, Spanish Humanist and Civic Leader." *Renaissance Quarterly,* winter 1979.

———. "Josephus and Diego Hurtado de Mendoza," *Romance Philology,* 26 (1973), 554–555.

———. "Noble Income in Sixteenth Century Castile: The Case of the Marquises of Mondéjar, 1480–1580." *Economic History Review,* 2nd ser., 30 (1977), 412–428.

Oliveira Marques, A. H. de. *Daily Life in Portugal in the Late Middle Ages.* Trans. S. S. Wyatt. Madison, 1971.

Pastor, Ludwig von. *History of the Popes.* Trans. F. I. Antrobus et al. 2nd ed. St. Louis, 1901–1902. Vols. I–V.

Paz y Melia, Antonio. "Biblioteca fundada por el conde de Haro (Pedro Fernández de Velasco) en 1455." *Revista de Archivos, Bibliotecas y Museos,* 3ª época, 1 (1897), 18–24.

———. *El cronista Alonso de Palencia. Su vida y sus obras.* Madrid, 1914.

Peers, E. A. *Spain: A Companion to Spanish Studies.* London, 1929.

Phillips, William D., Jr. *Enrique IV and the Crisis of Fifteenth-Century Castile, 1425–1480.* Cambridge, Mass., 1978.

Piétri, François. *Pierre le Cruel: Le vraie et le faux.* Paris, 1961.

Pintos Reino, Gonzalo. *El rey don Pedro de Castilla: Vindicación de su reinado.* Santiago, 1929.

Prescott, W. H. *History of the Reign of Ferdinand and Isabella, the Catholic, of Spain.* 3 vols. 13th ed. Boston, 1857.

Puymaigre, Théodore, le conte de. *La Cour littéraire de Don Juan II, Roi de Castille.* 2 vols. Paris, 1873.

Puyol Alonso, Julio. "Los cronistas de Enrique IV." *Boletín de la Real Academia de Historia,* 78 (1921), 399–415, 488–496; 79 (1922), 11–28, 118–144.

Puyols, J. *El Colegio Mayor de Santa Cruz y los colegios mayores.* Madrid, 1929.

Reynier, Gustave. *La Vie universitaire dans l'ancienne Espagne.* Paris, 1902.

Rice, Eugene F., Jr. *The Foundations of Early Modern Europe, 1460–1559.* New York, 1970.

Rius Serra, Josep. "Bibliotecas medievales españolas." *Revista eclesiástica,* 2 (1930), 318–326.

———. "Estudiants espanyols a Avinyò al segle XIV." *Analecta Sacra Terraconensis,* 10 (1934), 87–112.

———. "Inventaris episcopals." *Estudis Universitaris Catalans.* 17 (1932).

———. "La llibreria d'un rector de Sovelles." *Miscelánea,* vol. I, pp. 105–117.

—————. *Miscelánea Mons. José Rius Serra*. 2 vols. Biblioteca filológica-histórica, 14–15. [Barcelona] Abadía de San Cugat del Valle, 1964.

—————. "Subsidios para la historia de nuestra cultura." *Miscelánea*, vol. I, pp. 294–297.

Rodríguez de Ardila y Esquivias, Gabriel. "Historia de los Condes de Tendilla." Ed. R. Foulché-Delbosc. *Revue Hispanique*, 31 (1914), 63–131.

Romero, José Luis. "Sobre la biografía española del siglo XV y los ideales de vida." *Cuadernos de Historia de España*, 1–2 (1944), 115–138.

—————. *Sobre la historiografía y la historia*. Buenos Aires, 1945.

Romero de Lecea, Carlos. *EI V centenario de la introducción de la imprenta en España, Segovia, 1472, antecedentes de la imprenta y circunstancias que favorecieron su introducción en España*. Madrid, 1972.

Rosenthal, Earl E. *The Cathedral of Granada: A Study in the Spanish Renaissance*. Princeton, 1961.

—————. *Diego Siloe arquitecto de la catedral de Granada*. Granada, 1966.

—————. "The Image of Roman Architecture in Renaissance Spain." *Gazette des Beaux-Arts*, 52 (1958), 329–346.

—————. "The Invention of the Columnar Device of Emperor Charles V at the Court of Burgundy in Flanders in 1516." *Journal of the Warburg and Courtauld Institutes*, 36 (1973), 198–230.

—————. "The Lombard Sculptor Niccolò da Corte in Granada from 1537 to 1552." *Art Quarterly*, 29 (1966), 209–244.

—————. "The Lost 'Quarto de las Helias' in the Arabic Palace on the Alhambra." In *Miscelánea de estudios dedicados al Profesor Antonio Marín Ocete*, pp. 933–943. Granada, 1974.

Ross, W. Braxton, Jr. "Giovanni Colonna, Historian at Avignon." *Speculum*, 45 (1970), 533–563.

Round, Nicholas G. "Politics, Style and Group Attitudes in the *Instrucción del Relator*." *Bulletin of Hispanic Studies*, 46 (1969), 289–319.

—————. "Renaissance Culture and its Opponents in 15th Century Castile." *Modern Language Review*, 57 (1962), 204–215.

Rubio, Fernando. "*De Regimine Principum* de Egidio Romano en la literatura castellana de la Edad Media, siglo XV." *Ciudad de Dios* [Real Monasterio de el Escorial], 174 (1961), 645–667.

Rubio Mañé, J. I. "El concepto histórico de Capitanía General." Reprint from *Diario de Yucatán*, 19–20 March 1938.

—————. *Introducción al estudio de los virreyes de Nueva España, 1535 a 1746: Vol. I, Orígenes y jurisdicciones y dinámica social de los virreyes*. Mexico, 1955.

Rújula y de Ochoterna, José de. *Indice de los colegiales del mayor de San Ildefonso y menores de Alcalá*. Madrid, 1946.

Russell, Peter E. "Arms versus Letters: Towards a Definition of Spanish Fifteenth-Century Humanism." In *Aspects of the Renaissance: A Symposium*. Ed. Archibald R. Lewis. Austin, 1967. pp. 47–58.

————. *The English Intervention in Spain & Portugal in the Time of Edward III & Richard II.* Oxford, 1955.

————. "Fifteenth Century Lay Humanism." In *Spain: A Companion to Spanish Studies.* Ed. P. E. Russell. London, 1973. pp. 237–242.

Sáez, Emilio, and José Trenchs. "Juan Ruiz de Cisneros (1295/1296–1351/ 1352) autor del *Buen amor.*" In *El Arcipreste de Hita: El libro, autor, la tierra, la época.* Ed. Manuel Criado de Val. Actas del I Congreso Internacional sobre el Arcipreste de Hita. Barcelona, 1973. pp. 365–368.

Sáez, Liciniano. *Demostración histórica del verdadero valor de todas las monedas que corrían en Castilla durante el reynado del señor Don Enrique III.* Madrid, 1796.

Sala Balust, L. "Espiritualidad española en la primera mitad del siglo XVI." *Cuadernos de Historia,* Anexos de la revista *Hispania,* 1 (1967), 169–187.

Salazar y Castro, Luis. *Historia genealógica de la Casa de Haro.* Ed. Dalmiro de la Válgoma y Díaz-Varela. Archivo Documental Español, vol. XV. Madrid, 1959.

Sánchez Alonso, B. *Historia de la historiografía española.* 3 vols. Madrid, 1941–1947.

————. "Nebrija historiador." *Revista de Filología Española,* 29 (1945), 129–152.

Sánchez Cantón, F. J. *La biblioteca del marqués del Cenete, iniciada por el Cardenal Mendoza.* Madrid, 1942.

Sanz y Ruiz de la Peña, N. *Don Pedro I de Castilla: llamado el "Cruel."* Madrid, 1943.

Schiff, Mario. *La Bibliothèque du marquis de Santillane.* Bibliothèque de l'Ecole des Hautes Etudes, fasc. 153. Paris, 1905.

Seigel, Jerrold E. *Rhetoric and Philosophy in Renaissance Humanism.* Princeton, 1968.

Serrano y Sanz, M. *Vida y escritos de D. Juan Fernández de Heredia, Gran Maestre de la Orden de San Juan de Jerusalén.* Zaragoza, 1913.

Sicroff, Albert A. *Les Controverses des statuts de "pureté de sang" en Espagne du XVe au XVIIe siècle.* Paris, 1960.

Sigüenza, Jerónimo de. *Historia de la Orden de San Jerónimo.* Nueva Biblioteca de Autores Españoles, vols. 8, 12. Madrid, 1909.

Soldevila, F. *Historia de España.* Vol. II. Barcelona, 1952.

Spain. Consejo Superior de Investigaciones Científicas, Escuela de Estudios Medievales. *Normas de transcripción y edición de textos y documentos.* Madrid, 1944.

Spitz, Lewis W. *The Renaissance and Reformation Movements.* Chicago, 1971.

Spivakovsky, Erika. "Some Notes on the Relations between Diego Hurtado de Mendoza and D. Alonzo de Granada Venegas." *Archivum,* 14 (1964), 212–232.

―――. Son of the Alhambra: Diego Hurtado de Mendoza, 1504–1575. Austin, Texas, 1970.

Stegmüller, Friedrich. Filosofia e teologia nas Universidades de Coimbra e Évora no século XVI. Coimbra, 1959.

Struever, Nancy. The Language of History in the Renaissance. Princeton, 1970.

Suárez Fernández, Luis. "Algunas consideraciones acerca de la crisis castellana de 1383." Anuario de Estudios Medievales, 2 (1965), 359–376.

―――. Castilla, el cisma, y el crisis conciliar, 1378–1440. Madrid, 1955.

―――. Nobleza y monarquía. 2nd ed. Valladolid, 1974.

―――. "Problemas políticos en la minoridad de Enrique III." Hispania, 12 (1952), 163–231; 323–400.

Suárez Fernández, Luis, and Juan de Mata Carriazo. La España de los Reyes Católicos (1474–1516). Historia de España. vol. 17:1. Ed. Ramón Menéndez Pidal. Madrid, 1969.

Suárez Fernández, Luis; Angel Canellas López; and Jaime Vicens Vives. Los Trastámaras de Castilla y Aragón en el siglo XV (1407–1474). Historia de España, vol. 15. Ed. Ramón Menéndez Pidal. Madrid, 1969.

Tate, Robert B. "The Anacephaleosis of Alfonso García de Santa María, Bishop of Burgos, 1435–1456." Hispanic Studies in Honour of I. González Llubera. Oxford, 1959. pp. 387–401.

―――. "An Apology for Monarchy." Romance Philology, 15 (1961), 111–123.

―――. Ensayos sobre la historiografía peninsular del siglo XV. Madrid, 1970.

―――. "A Humanistic Biography of John II of Aragon, a note." In Homenaje a Jaime Vicens Vives. Barcelona, 1965, I, 665–673.

―――. "Italian Humanism and Spanish Historiography of the Fifteenth Century." Bulletin of the John Rylands Library, 34 (1951), 137–165.

―――. "López de Ayala, Humanist Historian?" Hispanic Review, 25 (1957), 157–174.

―――. "Mythology in Spanish Historiography." Hispanic Review, 22 (1954), 1–18.

―――. "Nebrija the Historian." Bulletin of Hispanic Studies, 34 (1957), 125–146.

―――. "Rodrigo Sánchez de Arévalo (1404–1470) and his Compendiosa Historia Hispanica." Nottingham Mediaeval Studies, 4 (1960), 58–80.

Tormo, Elías. "El brote del Renacimiento en los monumentos españoles y los Mendoza del siglo XV." Boletín de la Sociedad Española de Excursiones, 25 (1917), 51–65, 114–121, 26 (1918), 116–130.

Torre, Lucas de. "Mosén Diego de Valera. Su vida y sus obras." Boletín de la Real Academia de Historia, 64 (1914), 50–83, 133–168, 249–276, 365–412.

Torre y del Cerro, Antonio de la. La Universidad de Alcalá. Madrid, 1910.

Torres Fontes, Juan. *Estudio sobre la "Crónica de Enrique IV" del Dr. Galíndez de Carvajal*. Murcia, 1946.

Torres Fontes, Manuel. "La conquista del marquesado de Villena en el reinado de los Reyes Católicos." *Hispania*, 13 (1953), 37–151.

Trame, R. H. *R. Sánchez de Arévalo, Spanish Diplomat and Champion of the Papacy*. Washington, D.C., 1958.

Trinkaus, Charles. *In Our Image and Likeness: Humanity and Divinity in Italian Humanist Thought*. 2 vols. London, 1970.

Ullman, B. L. *The Humanism of Coluccio Salutati*. Padua, 1963.

Valbuena Prat, Angel. *Historia de la literature española*. Barcelona, 1937. Vol. I.

Valdeón Baruque, Julio. *Enrique II de Castilla: La guerra civil y la consolidación del régimen (1366–1371)*. Valladolid, 1966.

Verdera y Tuells, Evelio, ed. *El Cardenal Albornoz y el Colegio de España*. 2 vols. Studia Albornotiana, vol. XII. Zaragoza, 1972.

Vicens Vives, Jaime, ed. *Historia social y económica de España y América*. 4 vols. in 5. Barcelona, 1957.

Vives, José. *Juan Fernández de Heredia, gran maestre de Rodas*. Barcelona, 1928.

Walther, Andreas. *Die Anfänge Karls V*. Leipzig, 1911.

Zahareas, Anthony N. *The Art of Juan Ruiz, Archpriest of Hita*. Madrid, 1965.

Zurita y Castro, Gerónimo. . . . *Anales de la corona de Aragón*. [Zaragoza, 1578–1585]. Vol. VI.

———. *Emiendas y advertencias a la Crónica del Rey don Pedro*. Ed. Diego Josef Dormer. Zaragoza, 1683.

Index

Modern Spanish names are alphabetized according to modern cataloging practice. Spanish names from the Renaissance are alphabetized by last name, according to the usage of that period. For a description of the name system in the Spanish Renaissance, see p. xi.

A

Adelantado, 37, 42, 57, 108. *See also* Manrique, Diego Gómez; Vega, Garcilaso de la

Admiral, 37, 42–43. *See also* Enríquez, Alfonso; Enríquez, Fadrique; Mendoza, Diego Hurtado de (d. 1404)

Aeneid, 93, 119, 138

Aesop's *Fables*, 78

Aguilar, Alonso de, 157

Ajarquía, ambush at (1483), 29

Alaejos, battle of (1467), 53

Alava, 36, 39

Alavese in Castile, 36–39, 41–42, 57, 108–109

Alba, first count of, Fernán Alvarez de Toledo, 48–49, 84, 110

Alba, second duke of, Fadrique de Toledo (d. 1531), 161–162, 164, 168–171, 174, 178–179

Alba, third duke of, Fernán Alvarez de Toledo (1507–1582), court faction of, 5, 125

Albaicín uprising (1499), 157, 175

Albornoz, Gil Alvarez de (1310–1367), archbishop of Toledo (1337–1350) and cardinal (1350–1367), 60, 142–143, 147

Albornoz family, 39

Alburquerque, Juan Alfonso de, 38

Alburquerque, duke of, Beltrán de la Cueva (d. 1492), 32, 51–52, 107

Alburquerque, estate of, 45, 47

Alcaide, 37, 116, 125–126, 154, 156, 176–177

Alcalá de Henares, University of (Complutense), 4, 145–149, 183, 202

Alcalde entregador, 38

Alcalde mayor, 60, 117

Alexander VI (1492–1503). See Borgia, Rodrigo

Alexander the Great, 68, 83, 154

Alférez mayor de la banda, 39

Alfonso X el Sabio (1252–1284), 36–37, 46, 74, 80, 94, 133, 139, 142, 146

Alfonso XI (1312–1350), 36, 38, 46, 57, 64, 67